CANVAS AND UPHOLSTERY PROJECTS
for Boats and RVs

Other TAB books by the Author

No. 1297	*The Fiberglass Repair & Construction Handbook*
No. 1639	*Wood Carving, with Projects*
No. 1669	*The Kite Building & Kite Flying Handbook with 42 Kite Plans*
No. 1779	*Make Your Own Exercise Equipment*
No. 1839	*Designing and Constructing Mobiles*
No. 1949	*The Computer Furniture Plan and Project Book*
No. 1959	*Working with Acrylic Plastics, including 77 Projects*

CANVAS AND UPHOLSTERY PROJECTS
for Boats and RVs

JACK WILEY

 TAB BOOKS Inc.
Blue Ridge Summit, PA 17214

FIRST EDITION

FIRST PRINTING

Copyright © 1986 by TAB BOOKS Inc.

Printed in the United States of America

Reproduction or publication of the content in any manner, without express permission of the publisher, is prohibited. No liability is assumed with respect to the use of the information herein.

Library of Congress Cataloging in Publication Data

Wiley, Jack.
   Canvas and upholstery projects for boats and RVs.

   Includes index.
   1. Upholstery—Amateurs' manuals. 2. Marine canvas work. 3. Boats and boating—Maintenance and repair. 4. Recreational vehicles—Maintenance and repair. I. Title.
TT198.W55   1986   684.1'8   85-27674
ISBN 0-8306-0119-8
ISBN 0-8306-2719-7 (pbk.)

Camper photograph courtesy of Beckley's Camping Center, Thurmont, MD 21788

Contents

Introduction vii

1 Why Do It Yourself? 1
Basic Considerations—The Scope of Canvas and Upholstery Work—Kits—Reasons for Doing Your Own Canvas and Upholstery Work—Tools and Equipment—A Place to Work—Classes in Canvas and Upholstery Work—How to Learn Canvas and Upholstery Work—Canvas and Upholstery Jobs That You Can Do

2 Materials and Supplies 12
Fabrics—Twine and Wax for Hand Sewing—Sewing Machine Thread—Transparent Flexible Vinyl—Foam—Nylon Mosquito Netting—Zippers—Velcro® —Cord—Binding Tape—Paper—Canvas Fasteners—Top Frames and Fittings—Adhesives and Sealers—Curtain Fabrics and Hardware—Carpeting—Where to Purchase Materials and Supplies

3 Tools, Equipment, and Work Areas 23
Tools and Equipment—Work Areas

4 Hand Sewing 36
Basic Hand Sewing Stitches—Hand Sewing Heavy Fabrics—Using a Sewing Awl

5 Machine Sewing 57
How Sewing Machines Work—Preparation for Sewing—Sewing—Troubleshooting, Adjustments, and Simple Repairs—Sewing Basic Seams—Sewability of Fabric

6 Patterns and Cutting 106
Making and Transferring Pattern Markings—Laying Out Patterns—Cutting—Organizing Patterning and Cutting Work—Fitting—Kits

7 Fasteners and Adhesives   120
Permanent Fastenings—Take-Apart and Opening Fasteners—Frame Support Systems

8 Overall Planning   141
Selecting a Project—Organizing a Project—Quality of Work—Introduction to the Projects

9 Bags and Carrying Cases   147
Open Top Bags With Handles—Bags With Drawstring Closures—Zipper Closed Bags With Handles

10 Covers   168
Recreational Vehicle Covers—Boat Covers

11 Awnings, Enclosures and Weather Cloths   211
Recreational Vehicle Awnings and Enclosures—Boat Awnings, Enclosures, and Weather Cloths

12 Canvas Tops, Side and Stern Curtains   221
Canvas Recreational Vehicle Tops and Side Curtains—Canvas Boat Tops and Side and Stern Curtains

13 Fabric Mosquito Screens   264
Materials—Velcro® Attachments—Tie Down and Snap Attachments

14 Cushions and Seat Covers   271
Materials—Foam Padding—Fabric Covers for Cushions With Wood Bases—Independent Cushions With Foam Padding and Fabric Covers—Making Covers—Seat Covers

15 Upholstered Panels and Headliners   304
Replacing Fabric on Upholstered Panels and Headliners—Adding Upholstered Panels and Headliners—Frame-Suspended Headliners in Recreational Vehicles

16 Curtains   308
Curtain Suspension Systems—Curtain Fabrics—Patterning Curtains—Sewing Curtains—Curtain Tie-Backs—Partition Curtains

17 Carpets   317
Recreational Vehicle Carpeting—Boat Carpeting

Suppliers   321

Index   323

Introduction

There are many good reasons for doing your own boat and recreational vehicle canvas and upholstery work. First, you can save money. By doing it yourself, you avoid the expensive labor charges of having it done for you. Second, you can do the job when and how you want it done. Third, you have the satisfaction of doing it yourself.

This book is primarily intended for the do-it-yourselfer who wants to learn the skills and techniques necessary for doing quality canvas and upholstery work. No prior knowledge or skill is assumed.

Compared to many shop and hobby activities, canvas and upholstery work is relatively clean. Only one major power machine—a sewing machine—is required. For some jobs, a standard home sewing machine (or even hand-sewing) will suffice. For most work, however, a heavy-duty commercial-type upholstery machine is recommended. Suitable used models can often be purchased for a few hundred dollars, and considering the expensive labor costs charged by commercial shops, this expense can be amortized by a few canvas and upholstery projects. I more than paid for a used upholstery sewing machine by doing the canvas and upholstery work on a single small boat. I saved the several hundred dollars in labor it would have cost to have the job done at a commercial shop.

The money saved is largely a result of your supplying the labor.

At first, you will probably take a long time to get the job done, much longer than it would take an experienced professional. With practice and experience, however, your speed will increase. Regardless, an important advantage that the do-it-yourselfer has over the professional at a commercial shop is that of not having to consider time as money . . . at least not to the same degree.

The primary purpose of this book is to show how to do upholstering yourself and obtain professional results. The material covered in this book will form a sound basis for those who want to do work for others or to set up a canvas and upholstery shop or business. The fundamental skills and techniques are essentially the same, with the exception that the time it takes to do the work must be carefully taken into consideration in order to make a profit from the work.

This book covers not only materials, tools, supplies, work areas, and basic techniques, but also gives detailed how-to instructions for a wide variety of canvas and upholstery projects for boats and recreational vehicles, including canvas tops, covers, awnings, cushions, mattresses, curtains, carpets, and even tote bags.

Once you have learned the basic skills and techniques, you will be able not only to repair and replace existing canvas and upholstery work, but also to make modifications to existing items and design and construct original projects. Canvas and upholstery work can form the basis for a creative hobby and pastime.

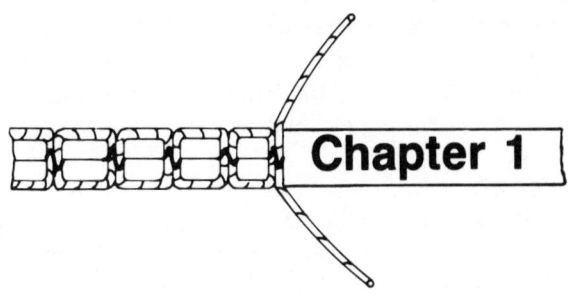

Chapter 1

Why Do It Yourself?

Modern boats and recreational vehicles make use of a variety of canvas and upholstery items, including covers, awnings, tops, panels and liners, cushions, and curtains. In many cases, these items are subject to considerable abuse both from use and from natural elements such as sunlight and moisture, resulting in a considerable need for repair and replacement.

Many boat and recreational vehicle owners want to add canvas and upholstery items or improve existing ones. For example, a canvas cover can be constructed to give weather protection and cushions can be made thicker for more comfort.

There are two basic choices: you can have the work done for you at a commercial shop, or you can do it yourself. The first method has the advantage of, hopefully, having an experienced professional do the work. The main disadvantage is that this service is generally very expensive. In most cases, you pay not only expensive labor rates but also top prices for the materials used.

The do-it-yourself method allows you to reap a substantial saving in the cost of the projects. First, you avoid paying someone else by providing your own labor. Second, you can save by carefully shopping for materials and taking advantage of sale and discount prices. In addition, you will have the advantage of doing the work when and how you want it done and the satisfaction of doing it yourself.

You must learn the necessary skills and techniques, which is what this book is all about, before you can achieve professional or even satisfactory results. These skills and techniques are generally easier to master than is typically imagined.

Compared to most shop repair and construction activities, canvas and upholstery work is relatively clean and safe. Toxic chemicals are not generally required, and the main piece of machinery required, a sewing machine, is generally quite safe when properly used.

Some people do canvas and upholstery work solely to save money. Their main satisfaction seems to be not having to fork over the money to pay someone else to do the work. This alone often justifies the time and effort that it takes to learn to do satisfactory work.

For many people, canvas and upholstery work also becomes a rewarding hobby and pastime. Although this book deals specifically with boat and recreational vehicle work, the skills and techniques are easily transferred to related areas, such as furniture upholstery and camping and sports gear fabrication.

Some people like the creative aspect of boat and recreational vehicle canvas and upholstery work. They can try out new designs and methods and do custom work. For others, boat and recreational vehicle canvas and upholstery work becomes a means of earning money, perhaps on a part-time basis. I know of several people who have earned their way on world cruises in small sailboats by taking sewing machines along and earning money doing canvas and upholstery work for others in exotic ports around the world.

Although this book is intended primarily for the do-it-yourselfer who wants to do his or her own canvas and upholstery work, the same basic skills and techniques are also used for doing work for others, with the exception that the do-it-yourselfer seldom has to consider time spent on the job as money.

BASIC CONSIDERATIONS

Boat and recreational vehicle canvas and upholstery work should be functional, durable and long lasting, easy to clean and maintain, and pleasing to the eye. The materials used must be affordable.

Functional Aspects

Although some boat and recreational vehicle canvas and upholstery work is strictly for "looks," most have a functional aspect. Canvas tops, awnings, and covers give protection from sun and rain. Headliners add insulation and deaden sound. Cushions and mattresses provide padding for comfortable sitting and sleeping. Curtains give privacy and allow the adjustment of light passing through windows.

Canvas and upholstery must be designed to be as functional as possible. Rain covers must keep rain out. Headliners must give effective insulation. Seating and sleeping arrangements must be comfortable. This may seem obvious, but it is surprising how many manufactured boats and recreational vehicles come with canvas and upholstery work that is poorly designed or constructed. Frequently, modifications are needed to correct these functional defects. For example, when recovering cushions, better and/or thicker foam or other padding is frequently used to improve them.

When constructing and designing canvas and upholstery items, the functional aspects must be kept in mind. In canvas and upholstery work, the functional aspects are a primary consideration. If a boat cover does not keep rain water out, it fails in its functional purpose, regardless of how long it will last or how good it looks.

Durability

Boat and recreational vehicle canvas and upholstery work must endure our pleasure and recreational use, which generally translates to rough treatment. In addition, the canvas and upholstery must often face a harsh environment, including sunlight, dampness, rain, and varying temperature conditions. This is especially true of items such as the protective covers used on the exteriors of boats and recreational vehicles.

A large selection of synthetic canvas and upholstery materials is now available. Some of these are especially designed to give long life under harsh environmental conditions. Natural cotton canvas, even when treated, often rots and is useless in a year or less of outdoor exposure in tropical conditions. Modern acrylic canvas will often stand up to years of such exposure.

When selecting canvas and upholstery materials, durability for the particular use should be kept in mind. Materials available and their durability for particular uses are covered in Chapter 2.

Some materials are easier to work with than others, and this must be taken into consideration when making a selection. The ease of working may or may not be related to the durability of a particular material.

It is generally a waste of time to use materials that will not stand up to the intended hard use of the canvas and upholstery work. Use quality materials.

Appearance

Appearance is another important aspect of canvas and upholstery work. The type of materials used and color schemes and patterns play an important role in the appearance of both boats and recreational vehicles, especially of interiors. Although how it looks is perhaps secondary to how it functions and how long it lasts, it is still extremely important. A neat, clean job with pleasing colors and combinations can add greatly to the pleasure of using a boat or recreational vehicle. Thus, careful consideration should be given to this aspect, too.

Ease of Cleaning and Maintaining

Canvas and upholstery items should be easy to clean and maintain, and materials should be selected accordingly. Cushions can be constructed with removable covers for easy laundering or dry cleaning.

Cost of Materials

In most cases, quality canvas and upholstery materials carry a higher price tag than those of lower grades. In the long run, though, quality materials are usually the best buy. Some brands of quality materials are sold at various prices depending on where you buy them and other factors. I can purchase one top brand of acrylic canvas at a local store for $8.50 a linear yard. Or, I can mail-order the same brand of fabric in the same width for $5.95 a yard. Even with the cost of shipping figured in, the savings by mail order are considerable. Because the mail order firm must be making a profit to stay in business, the local store, assuming the same wholesale prices, has a much larger markup. In addition, the mail-order firm offers a discount for quantity purchases, something that the local store won't do.

In Chapter 2, considerable emphasis is placed on the proper selection of materials for particular jobs. The basic idea is to keep costs down without sacrificing on the quality and durability, or making the best compromises possible when these factors are not compatible.

THE SCOPE OF CANVAS AND UPHOLSTERY WORK

The terms *canvas* and *upholstery* are used here to mean the fabric parts of boats (not including sails) and recreational vehicles. Included are woven fabrics that are uncoated and coated, usually with a plastic such as vinyl. The term canvas will be used to mean not only traditional cotton canvas, which may or may not be chemically treated, but also modern synthetics, which often have more than the necessary strength and similar physical properties of traditional canvas.

It is frequently difficult to draw a line between what constitutes canvas and what constitutes upholstery. In some cases, the same materials that are used to make canvas covers are used for upholstery coverings for cushions.

In this book, many related projects, including tote bags, curtains, and carpets, are also considered to be canvas and upholstery work.

Our concern will be with two main aspects of canvas and upholstery work: the repair, replacement, and modification of existing items and the design and construction of new items.

Repair, Replacement, and Modification

Canvas and upholstery work is subject to wear, damage, and deterioration. In some cases, simple repairs are all that are needed. Minor tears and rips can often be satisfactorily repaired. On woven fabrics, this is often done by sewing. For vinyl, special repair kits are available. Instructions for making a variety of repairs are included in Chapter 4.

When the replacement of some or all of the fabric is necessary, the material used originally can often serve as patterns for shaping new fabric. In the case of cushions, it may also be necessary to replace foam and other types of padding.

It may be desirable to modify existing canvas and upholstery work. Under use, various faults and deficiencies in existing design and construction often become apparent. Canvas covers leak. Cushions bottom out because the padding is not thick or firm enough. Curtains don't completely cover the windows and need to be made larger. Modifications in existing canvas and upholstery work will often take care of these and similar problems. Most often, a simple modification is all that is required, such as adding snaps or other fasteners to a cushion back to hold it in place in a moving recreational vehicle or a boat that is underway. In other cases, the modifications will be more difficult, such as adding thicker foam padding to cushions and constructing complete new covers for them.

Design and Construction

Sometimes, you may want to design and construct canvas and upholstery items. For this, you will need to take measurements and make your own patterns, which is generally somewhat more difficult than when you have old items to use as patterns. Once you learn the basic techniques, however, you will be able to design and construct items that are functional, durable, and neat in appearance. The basic idea is to custom make the items so that they fit.

For many projects detailed in the later chapters of this book, basic design patterns are given, but you can adapt these to a particular boat or recreational vehicle. For example, a canvas top is constructed to fit a particular set of frames or bows and a sail cover must fit a particular boat. Sound, workable designs are given; you must fit these to your particular needs. Measurements, patterns, and fitting are important aspects of canvas and upholstery work.

KITS

A variety of canvas and upholstery products are now offered in kit form, including canvas tops, tote bags, sail covers and boat covers. These generally cost more than if you purchase the materials separately, but you get everything you need in one package. Sources for kits are given in the Suppliers section. Once you learn the basic skills and techniques of canvas and upholstery work, however, kits will be unnecessary.

REASONS FOR DOING YOUR OWN CANVAS AND UPHOLSTERY WORK

Canvas and upholstery work is used extensively in modern boats and recreational vehicles as both standard and optional equipment for comfort, protection, convenience, appearance, and a variety of other reasons. The vast majority of people who want canvas and upholstery work done on boats and recreational vehicles have the work done for them at commercial shops. Why do some people do the work themselves? Here are some reasons.

Save Money

Perhaps the most important reason is to save money. Having

canvas and upholstery work done for you generally ranges from expensive to very expensive. By doing your own work, you save money not only by providing your own labor, but also by being able to purchase materials and supplies from discount supply firms. Most canvas and upholstery shops charge $10 or more an hour for labor and, to add to their profits, they buy the materials wholesale or at dealer discount prices and charge the customers retail prices—usually with a healthy markup to boot.

Get the Work Done the Way You Want It

By doing your own canvas and upholstery work, you have the opportunity to do it the way you want it. The commercial-shop is likely to look at the job you need done only in terms of how much profit can be made for the job. Once an estimate is given, the worker is likely to attempt to do the job in the shortest amount of time possible, with the minimum expense for materials used. This often means cutting corners. If you have only a small job, it's often difficult to find a commercial shop that wants to bother with it.

Although many canvas and upholstery shops have competent workers who do quality work, others don't. Because there are no set qualifications or standards for "professional" canvas and upholstery workers, it's often difficult to judge competency.

By doing your own work, you can get around these problems. You can take the time to do the job the way you want it done. But, you must first take the time to learn the necessary basic skills and techniques detailed in this book.

Get the Work Done When You Want It Done

Getting work done for you when you want it done can be a problem, especially if it is a relatively small job. This generally also applies to TV repair, auto repair, home repairs, and practically every other type of work that you have done for you, but seems to be a special problem in the case of boat and recreational vehicle canvas and upholstery work, where commercial shops seem to always have a backlog of work.

Avoid Getting Ripped Off

There are probably less rip-offs and rackets in canvas and upholstery work than in auto repair, but they do exist. Most people have little idea of how much a particular canvas or upholstery job should cost, so they are open to price gouging. You can avoid this by doing your own work.

The Challenge and Satisfaction of Doing It Yourself

Some people only do canvas and upholstery work to save money, but other people relish the challenge and derive satisfaction from doing this work themselves.

TOOLS AND EQUIPMENT

Compared to many shop and hobby activities, relatively little in the way of tools and equipment is required. Perhaps the most important piece of equipment is a heavy duty commercial type upholstery sewing machine. While a standard home sewing machine or even hand sewing will suffice for some jobs, the heavy duty commercial machine is recommended if you plan to do more extensive work. Hand sewing is slow and most standard home sewing machines will not stand up to sewing heavy fabrics.

Heavy duty upholstery machines can be purchased new or used or even rented, depending on how much canvas and upholstery work you intend to do and how much you can afford to spend. Selecting suitable sewing machines is also detailed in Chapter 2.

In addition, a variety of other hand tools are needed, including scissors, measuring rules and marking sticks, hand sewing needles, and marking chalk or pen. Special tools are available for installing fasteners. A portable electric drill and common wood- and metalworking hand tools will find many uses in typical canvas and upholstery work. A portable electric knife is useful for cutting foam rubber. These and other tools and equipment are further detailed in Chapter 2.

You won't need all of the tools to start. You can begin with a few essentials and add to these as a need develops. A professional canvas and upholstery worker generally has more and better tools and equipment than the typical do-it-yourselfer. The emphasis in this book is on doing quality work with a limited amount of tools and equipment, because the do-it-yourselfer usually has to absorb the cost of the tools and equipment with relatively few canvas and upholstery jobs. The professional can spread this cost over hundreds of jobs.

A PLACE TO WORK

Because canvas and upholstery work is relatively clean, a

special workshop isn't essential. Many people do upholstery and canvas work inside their houses. Fabrics can be spread out on a floor for pattern marking and cutting, but a large cutting table (see Chapter 3) makes this work easier and more convenient.

You can set up a special work area in a spare room or garage. Three basic items are the sewing machine, the cutting table, and a workbench. There should also be an arrangement for storage of tools, equipment, materials, and supplies. A number of possibilities are detailed in Chapter 3.

It should be pointed out that while a good work area is desirable, some people are able to turn out quality work in very limited work areas. I've known people who were able to do this aboard small boats and inside small travel trailers.

CLASSES IN CANVAS AND UPHOLSTERY WORK

While classes in canvas and upholstery work geared toward boats and recreational vehicles are rare, many adult education programs and community colleges offer courses in standard upholstery. This can be an ideal way to get started. In most cases, you will gain valuable experience using a variety of heavy duty upholstery sewing machines. You will be able to use their tools and equipment, and after you have learned basic skills and techniques, they will often let you work on your own projects, including the canvas and upholstery work detailed in this book. This generally seems to be the case even though the instructors may not be familiar with boat and recreational vehicle canvas and upholstery work, per se.

HOW TO LEARN CANVAS AND UPHOLSTERY WORK

This book is intended as a complete how-to guide for learning the basic skills and techniques of boat and recreational vehicle canvas and upholstery work. Reading and studying this book alone will not make you competent at actually doing canvas and upholstery work, however. At the same time, you must also actually practice the basic skills and techniques and do canvas and upholstery work.

The book details the skills and techniques and shows how to go about learning them. You will gain knowledge about doing canvas and upholstery work, as well as practice exercises and short cuts, but to actually learn the skills and techniques, you must practice them.

You can learn about swimming by reading about it, but you

must get wet to learn to swim. The same principles apply to boat and recreational vehicle canvas and upholstery work.

At first, it may appear that there are an endless number of skills and techniques that must be learned. Actually, once you learn a few key skills, the rest is relatively easy. For example, if you have never operated an upholstery sewing machine before, it will be necessary to learn to install the bobbin and pull the thread through, to thread the machine, to work the variable speed foot control (which usually seems like anything but control at first), and so on. At first, you may find that the thread breaks for no apparent reason or that you have the bobbin in wrong or that any one of a number of other problems develop, or worse, a number of them at once. Of course, if you know how to sew on a standard home sewing machine, the transfer to a heavy duty commercial machine will probably be somewhat easier. In any case, with a few hours of practice, most people find that they can actually sew with some control over the machine, instead of the other way around. Any problems that develop, such as the bobbin running out of thread or the needle coming unthreaded, can be quickly corrected.

Before long, operating the sewing machine will be automatic and you won't even have to think consciously about it. You will then be able to concentrate on holding the fabric in the right position and putting the stitches where you want them.

The manual that comes with the sewing machine (hopefully) generally gives diagrams of the proper way to thread the machine, but this probably won't mean much until you actually thread the machine.

Before doing actual canvas and upholstery work on your boat or recreational vehicle, I feel that it is important to do practice projects first. This way, you make mistakes on practice materials, rather than on the real thing. A number of practice projects are detailed in this book to aid you in learning the skills and techniques necessary for doing professional quality work.

Right from the beginning, I suggest that you take the time necessary to do each job right. Small errors and mistakes can accumulate. Even if you are only doing a practice project, try to do it as well as possible.

CANVAS AND UPHOLSTERY JOBS THAT YOU CAN DO

The range of possible jobs you can do varies from minor repairs on existing canvas and upholstery to doing all of the canvas and upholstery work on a boat or recreational vehicle. Typical work includes making new covers for cushions and replacing worn or deteriorated canvas tops, covers, or awnings. When converting vans to campers, you can do all of the canvas and upholstery work as part of the conversion. When building boats and recreational vehicles from kits, you can generally save a considerable amount of money by doing your own canvas and upholstery work rather than purchasing the items from the manufacturers of the kits.

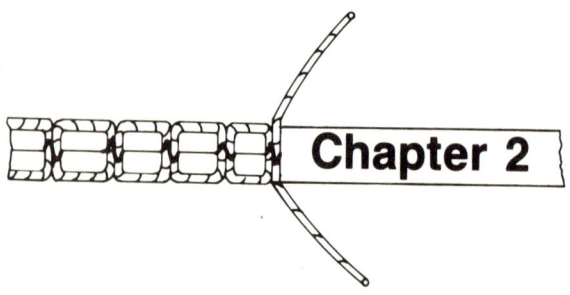

Chapter 2

Materials and Supplies

Many fabrics, threads, cords, zippers, fasteners, glues, sealers, flexible window materials, foam paddings, metal tubing and fittings, and other materials and supplies are used for boat and recreational vehicle canvas and upholstery work. With experience and practice, you will be able to tell at a glance just which materials you need for a particular job.

FABRICS

The term *fabric* is used here to mean the flexible materials used for canvas and upholstery work. The term canvas traditionally meant a heavy-duty material tightly woven from cotton or other natural fibers. The term *cloth* generally referred to lighter fabrics woven from natural fibers. Then along came nylon, polyester, acrylic, and other synthetic fabrics, which could in turn be coated with vinyl and other plastics, and the line between canvas and cloth became less clear. Fabrics could now have the strength of, and even greater durability than, traditional canvas in a much lighter weight that looked more like what had previously been referred to as cloth than canvas.

A similar situation exists for upholstery fabrics. These used to be heavy materials woven from natural fibers. Now, they are also available in a variety of synthetics and combinations of natural and synthetic fibers, with or without vinyl and other plastic coatings.

For our purposes here, we will refer to all of the fabrics, whether natural or synthetic fibers, chemically treated or not, coated or uncoated, used for boat and recreational vehicle canvas and upholstery work as fabrics, even though the materials have varying degrees of strength, flexibility, weight, durability, waterproofness, and other properties. More important concerns are selecting the best fabric for a particular job while still keeping cost in mind.

It is also interesting to note that fabrics commonly considered to be canvas are often used for covers for cushions and other upholstery functions. Again, no attempt will be made to define what is canvas and what is upholstery. Instead, the emphasis will be on selecting the best fabric, keeping economy in mind, for the particular job at hand.

Natural Fiber Cotton Canvas

Natural fiber cotton canvas is still available for boat and recreational vehicle use. The material is available in various weights (10 ounces per square yard, 12 ounces per square yard, and so on) woven from single filled duct and double filled (the yard from which the canvas is made is twisted with a second yarn to give added strength).

Cotton canvas is subject to rot and mildew. Special treatments, such as Vivatex, are used to reduce susceptibility to these factors. In general, only canvas with dry treatments, such as Vivatex, are suitable for boat and recreational vehicle canvas work. Those that are waxed or oil-tempered should be avoided, as they feel oily to the touch and are a lot heavier than dry-finished canvas.

A breathing-type waterproof canvas is frequently used for a variety of covers. This keeps water from passing through, yet allows air to pass through so that the cloth can "breath," thus helping to prevent condensation underneath. The fact that cotton fibers swell when wet tightens the weave, adding to their waterproofness.

The main advantages of cotton canvas over newer synthetic types are lower cost (generally) and that they are generally more pleasant to work with and sew. Main disadvantages are shorter life due to the rot and mildew of natural fibers even when they are treated. Also, cotton canvas will shrink.

In my opinion, the disadvantages far outweigh the advantages. I have made sail covers from both dry-treated cotton canvas and acrylic fabric. The cotton material deteriorated to the point where it was useless in a couple of years; some of the acrylic covers are still serviceable after ten years. The cotton canvas is generally cheaper (one company charges $3.50 a yard for dry-treated cotton canvas and $6 a yard for the same width of acrylic canvas), but the synthetic fabric can work out to be a much better way in the long run.

Cotton canvas can also be coated with vinyl and other plastics. These materials are covered later in this chapter.

Synthetic Canvas

The three main types of synthetic canvases used for boat and recreational vehicle work are nylon, polyester, and acrylic. *Nylon* is strong, lightweight, and resistant to abrasion, but does not stand up well to sun exposure. It also has considerable stretch, which can be an advantage or disadvantage depending on the particular use. It makes good utility bags, but poor covers when a snug fit is desired.

Nylon fabric is available with a waterproof resin finish and a water resistant breathing finish. The breathing type is recommended for utility bags. This is generally listed as uncoated nylon, water repellent, or breathing-type in catalogs and is available in various weights from about 1 ounce per square yard to 7 ounces or more per square yard. It's recommended for tents, tarps, canopies, boat covers, and other similar uses, but keep in mind that long term sun exposure will cause the material to become brittle and useless.

Nylon fabric is easily vat dyed, making the more expensive yarn dyed method unnecessary. It is available in a choice of colors. For the projects detailed in this book, 4-ounce-per-square-yard, water repellent, breathing-type nylon is recommended for sail, utility, and ditty bags.

A second main type of fibers used for boat and recreational vehicles is *polyester*. It should be noted that *Dacron* is a registered trademark of the DuPont Company for its polyester fibers and fabrics.

Polyester fibers are strong and stretch resistant. They are highly resistant to sunlight; much more resistant than nylon and almost as resistant as acrylic (described later in this section). Polyester is difficult to dye and is not as colorfast as acrylic.

Although many polyester fabrics have a resin finish, such as sailcloth, a spun polyester fabric that has a canvas look is now available. This can be used for covers, awnings, tops, and so on.

The strength of this material allows the use of light weight fabrics. It's presently available in 5-ounce-per-square-yard and 8.2-ounce-per-square-yard weights.

A claimed advantage is that polyester fabric is less expensive than acrylic. This requires using a lighter weight polyester fabric than acrylic, however. For the same weight fabrics, acrylic is less expensive, at least from my sources (Defender Industries, Inc., 255 Main Street, New Rochelle, NY 10801).

The third main type of synthetic fibers used for boat and recreational vehicle canvas is *acrylic*. Acrylic is generally considered to be superior to both nylon and polyester for use in sunlight. Popular brands are *Yachtcrillic* and *Acrylan®* (a registered trademark of Monsanto Company).

Acrylic fabrics are usually of a water resistant breathing type. Acrylic fibers can be yarn-dyed before they are woven or vat-dyed after they have been woven. Yarn-dyed is superior but more expensive.

Acrylic fabrics are available in a variety of colors, with perhaps blue, white, yellow, and red being the most popular. Color patterns are also available, but this is somewhat limited if they are woven from yarn-dyed fibers, because all color changes must be made by changing colors of warp or fill threadlines. Patterns of stripes running across the fabric are a popular design for awnings.

For covers used in sunlight and salt air that must be of the breathing type, acrylic fabric is highly recommended. It is also a fairly easy material to work with and sew.

I recommend that you use name brands intended for marine use. Some low cost imported acrylic fabrics are of lower quality and do not hold their colors well, because they are vat-dyed.

Vinyl and Other Coatings

Cotton, nylon, and polyester fabrics are available with vinyl and other plastic coatings. These change the fabrics into waterproof nonbreathing materials. These materials can be used for covers when ventilation underneath is good and condensation will not be a problem. Boat and recreational vehicle tops are often made from these materials. They are also popular for covering cushions, although some people prefer plain woven fabrics for this purpose.

The coating can be on one or both sides of the woven fabric. The latter is called *two-plied* or *core material*. It's also called *laminated convertible top material*. It's available with either cotton or synthetic cores. More typical is to have the coating on one side of the woven fabric only.

Naugahyde is a popular brand of vinyl-coated knitted cotton material that is popular for boat and recreational vehicle upholstery. It's waterproof and has slight stretch.

Vinyl-coated nylon is available in a variety of weights and is popular for boat covers and canopies. Vinyl-coated polyester is another popular fabric. *Weblon*, a popular brand, is a vinyl-coated Dacron. *Hypalon*-coated Dacron material is also available.

Upholstery Fabrics

In many cases, upholstery fabrics used for boats and recreational vehicles need not be waterproof or even water resistant. Although many of the above described fabrics, both coated with vinyl and uncoated, are used to make covers for cushions and to serve other upholstery functions, a variety of other fabrics is also popular. Upholstery stores generally have a large selection. These fabrics are woven from natural or synthetic fibers, or some combination of the two. Although fabrics containing natural fibers can be used for boat and recreational vehicle upholstery, synthetic fabrics are generally recommended.

The cost of fabrics depends on a number of factors, including the type of fibers, backing, weave, dye, and color pattern used, who manufactures it, and where you buy it. Usually, you will want a fabric that is resistant to mildew and staining, yet will clean easily. It should not stretch out of shape or burn easily. It should be durable and not show wear. It should be of an attractive color or color pattern. The fabric should be easy to work with and sew.

TWINE AND WAX FOR HAND SEWING

A *twine* is a strong string or cord formed of two or more threads twisted together. Although standard machine thread will suffice for many hand sewing jobs, twine is generally recommended when greater strength is required.

Twine is made from cotton, nylon, polyester, and other materials. Polyester is generally recommended for canvas and upholstery work.

Three-strand or *ply-twisted* twine doubled through the needle is generally recommended for canvas and upholstery seaming work that joins two or three layers or panels of fabric together. Five- and seven-strand or ply-twisted twine can be used when greater strength is required.

Beeswax is applied to the twine before use so the twine will not chafe in the sewing process. The wax is sold in cake form. Twine is also available with wax already applied.

SEWING MACHINE THREAD

Although cotton thread can be used, this generally isn't recommended. Cotton thread tends to rot, and thread tends to fail long before most fabrics anyway. Synthetic thread is now used for most canvas and upholstery work used for boats and recreational vehicles.

Two types of synthetic thread are in popular use for canvas and upholstery work: *nylon monofilament* and *polyester*. Nylon monofilament is strong and very rot-resistant. It is similar to monofilament fishing line.

Some people favor nylon monofilament thread for machine sewing, but I much prefer polyester thread. I recommend a pure polyester thread rather than cotton-wrapped polyester. Use a good quality thread. Thread size can vary depending on the particular fabrics being sewn; I have found #16 Z-twist polyester to be about right for most canvas and upholstery work.

Large rolls of polyester thread for commercial sewing machines are often sold by the pound rather than by length. Polyester thread is also available in tubes. The thread is pulled out of the top of the tube as it is used. Nylon monofilament thread is sold in similar tubes.

Polyester thread is available in white and a variety of colors. In order not to have to switch colors, and because the dyeing process tends to weaken the polyester thread somewhat, some canvas and upholstery workers use only white thread. I have had satisfactory results with the dyed threads when quality brands were used, though.

TRANSPARENT FLEXIBLE VINYL

There is frequently a need for a clear, transparent, flexible material for use as windows on canvas tops, side curtains, and other locations. While a number of plastic materials have been used for this purpose, highly polished clear transparent vinyl seems to be most popular. The material is available in various thicknesses, with

.012-gauge and .016-gauge being about right for most boat and recreational vehicle use. The material is easy to sew and has a slight give when stretched, which tends to prevent tearing.

FOAM

A variety of foam suitable for cushions is on the market. Firm, high density foam is recommended for both boats and recreational vehicles. Various numbering systems are used by manufacturers to grade density or firmness of foam. A foam that requires about 30 to 36 pounds for 75 percent compression per square foot is about right for seating and sleeping cushions. This foam weighs about 1.5 to 1.65 pounds per cubic foot.

Standard *latex foam* and *polyester foam* are both commonly used for boats and recreational vehicles, even though they will absorb moisture to a certain extent. Inexpensive low density *poly foam* is available at discount stores, but it tends to deteriorate quickly when used for cushions.

Ideal, if you can afford it, is *closed cell foam*. This type will not absorb water even if torn or punctured. This is ideal for use on boats, because the foam has positive flotation. In fact, it's the same material that is used in a variety of flotation devices. The main disadvantage is that it costs approximately three times as much as standard foam of the same dimensions.

Foam is usually sold in sheets of various thicknesses from 1 inch or less to 6 inches or more. For berth and seating cushions, I recommend at least 4-inch thickness, and 6 inches is generally even better. Although 2- or 3-inch thicknesses will sometimes suffice if firm foam is used, greater thickness, within limits, generally gives greater comfort.

Standard foam is also available in various cavity forms and in blocks of various sizes. The closed cell foam is presently only available in 1-, 1 1/2-, and 2-inch thicknesses. A special adhesive is available for attaching sheets together for greater thicknesses.

Foam distributors are listed in the yellow pages of phone books. Both standard and closed cell foam can be mail ordered from Defender Industries, Inc. (see Suppliers section for address).

Special *foam adhesives* for joining pieces of foam are available in liquid and spray-can form. Make certain that you purchase the kind that is made especially for foam.

NYLON MOSQUITO NETTING

Nylon mosquito netting is available in a variety of colors. This material can be sewn to fabrics to form hatch screens and so on. It's sold by the yard in various widths.

ZIPPERS

Zippers are frequently used in canvas and upholstery work. Zippers made of metal tend to corrode and break quickly, especially when used on boats. Plastic zippers, such as those made from *lexan*, generally give much better service, as these will not rust or corrode. They are commonly available in #5 and #10 sizes. They are easy to sew to standard canvas and upholstery fabrics.

VELCRO®

Velcro® is a registered trademark for woven tape fasteners that consist of two mating strips. The hook or male section is covered with stiff little hooks. The loop or female section is covered with tiny, soft loops. When pressed together, the hooks and loops engage, creating an adjustable, highly versatile and secure closure. To open, it is simply peeled apart. They can be opened and closed many thousands of times. They are constructed of nylon and can be easily sewn to canvas and upholstery fabrics. Velcro® is also available with a pressure sensitive backing for attachment to solid surfaces. The tape is available in widths from 5/8 inch to 2 inches in a selection of colors. There are many uses for Velcro® tape in boat and recreational vehicle canvas and upholstery work. It is usually sold by the foot.

CORD

Nylon and polyester cord finds a number of uses in canvas and upholstery work. Braided cord in small diameters is easily sewn to canvas fabrics for tie-downs and other purposes. It can also be sewn in fabric or binding to form *piping*, as shown in Fig. 2-1. Usually, cord about 1/8 inch or so in diameter is used for this.

BINDING TAPE

Binding tape is basically long strips of fabric that have edges that will not fray. These can be sewn to raw edges of canvas and upholstery fabric (Fig. 2-2) to protect the edge and keep the fabric from unravelling. Binding tape is available in a variety of widths in a number of materials, including vinyl, polyester, nylon, and

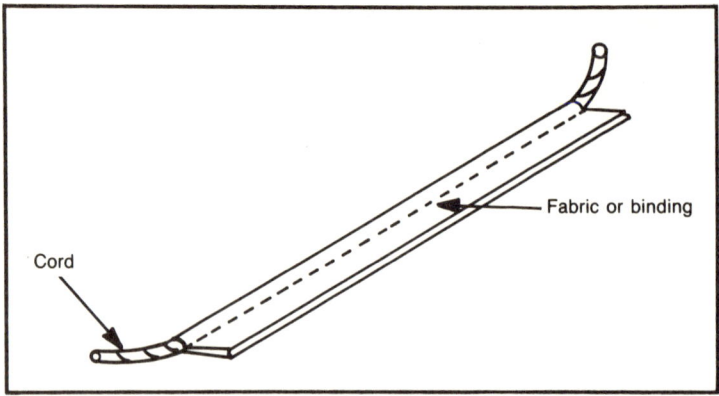

Fig. 2-1. Braided nylon or polyester cord is used to form piping.

acrylic. A large selection of colors is available. Binding tape about 5/8-inch or so in width is about right for binding the edges of most canvas fabrics used in boat and recreational vehicle work.

PAPER

A number of paper items are useful for canvas and upholstery work, including a paper pad for marking down dimensions, and shelf or tracing paper for making patterns.

CANVAS FASTENERS

A variety of fasteners is available for use with canvas and other fabrics, including snaps, grommets, *Lift the Dot* and *Common Sense*,

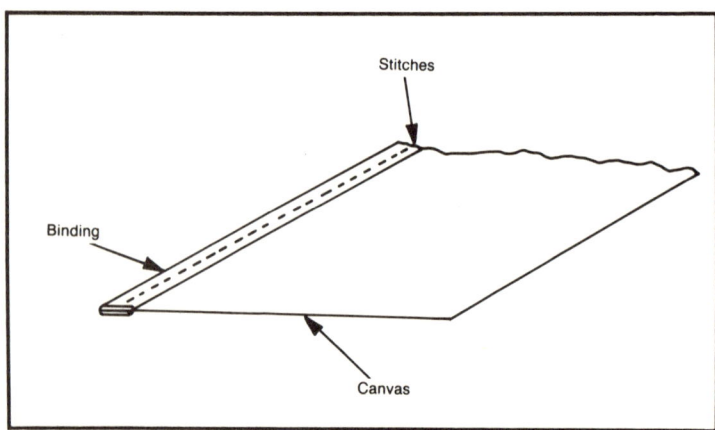

Fig. 2-2. Binding tape sewn to edge of canvas.

and hook-and-eye. Staples, tacks, and other similar fasteners are also useful for canvas and upholstery work. Canvas fasteners are detailed along with installation methods in Chapter 7.

TOP FRAMES AND FITTINGS

Frames and fittings for canvas boat and recreational vehicle tops are sold individually or in kit form. You can also purchase stock aluminum or stainless steel tubing and make your own frames. Canvas top fittings are available in plastic, aluminum, brass, bronze, and stainless steel. These are detailed in Chapter 7.

ADHESIVES AND SEALERS

Many adhesives and sealers are available for canvas and upholstery work. *Fabric cement* is available for basting panels of materials together. Regular *silicone adhesive* can also be used for this purpose.

A variety of sealers are available for sealing small holes in canvas, such as those left by needles around thread. Fabric proofing chemicals are available for restoring water repellant finishes to fabrics. These are available for brush application or in spray cans.

CURTAIN FABRICS AND HARDWARE

A wide selection of fabrics can be used for boat and recreational vehicle curtains and drapes, as detailed in Chapter 16. Hardware and tracking systems are also available at most department stores.

CARPETING

Carpet, especially the indoor-outdoor type, is widely used for floor covering and upholstery purposes in boats and recreational vehicles. A wide selection of types, designs, and colors are available at any good flooring store.

WHERE TO PURCHASE MATERIALS AND SUPPLIES

The above items are by no means everything that you might need. As you go along, you will probably discover a need for additional materials and supplies.

It is generally most convenient, though not necessarily least expensive, to purchase materials and supplies in the area where you live, provided that the stores have what you want.

Upholstery supply stores often stock materials and supplies suitable for boat and recreational vehicle canvas and upholstery work. Another possibility is commercial canvas and upholstery shops, especially those that do boat and recreational work. You can generally expect to pay top prices here, however.

Marine, auto, recreational vehicle, hardware, and discount stores may have some of the materials and supplies that you will need. Another possibility is mail order. My favorite source is Defender Industries, Inc., 255 Main Street, New Rochelle, NY 10801. They stock most of the materials and supplies detailed above, including many hard to find fabrics. Their materials and supplies are name brands, yet are sold at discount prices. I've found that even with the cost of shipping figured in, the cost is generally much less than I can get them for locally, assuming that I can even find what I need. The savings often offset the inconvenience of having to order the materials and wait for delivery. I've found that materials shipped by U.P.S. generally arrive very quickly.

Defender Industries, Inc., has a 168-page catalog that sells for $1. In addition to canvas and upholstery materials and supplies, they offer a complete line of marine products.

There are also a number of other mail-order sources for canvas and upholstery materials and supplies (see Suppliers section).

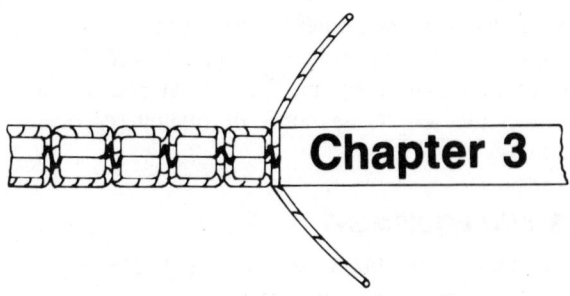

Chapter 3

Tools, Equipment, and Work Areas

Compared to many types of shop and hobby work, the tools, equipment, and work areas required for boat and recreational vehicle canvas and upholstery work are generally less costly and extensive than most. Additional tools and better work areas will enable you to do the work faster with less effort on your part, but most people start with a few essentials, often things that they already have on hand, and add to these gradually over a period of time as a need develops. At first, the work can be done in any convenient place in your house, garage, or elsewhere. Later, an improved work area may be called for.

You will probably want to keep the amount of money invested in tools, equipment, and work areas to a minimum, especially until you are certain that canvas and upholstery work is something that you want to pursue further. One way to do this is to take an adult education course in upholstery, and use their tools, equipment, and work areas until interest develops to the point where you want to purchase tools and equipment of your own and set up your own work area in your house, garage, or elsewhere. This gives you an opportunity to use a variety of tools and equipment, especially various brands of sewing machines, which in turn will give you a better idea of what tools and equipment you need and want to purchase.

The tools required for specific canvas and upholstery jobs vary greatly, and not all of them are required for an individual job. Thus, selection of tools will depend not only on how much you can afford to spend, but also on the particular type of canvas and upholstery work you intend to do.

Renting tools and equipment is another possibility. For example, it may be more economical to rent a heavy duty upholstery sewing machine than to buy one. Explore all possible alternatives before investing any large sums of money, especially at the beginning.

TOOLS AND EQUIPMENT

Although it is possible to do canvas and upholstery sewing by hand, for our purposes here a power sewing machine will be considered an essential piece of equipment. Because this is generally the main piece of machinery required, we will consider it first.

Sewing Machines

The basic machine stitch used for most canvas and upholstery work is the *lock stitch* (Fig. 3-1). Both a needle thread and a bobbin thread are required to form this. The upper portion of the lock stitch is the needle thread and the lower portion is the bobbin thread. When the needle thread passes through the layers of fabric being sewn together and the throat plate, a loop is formed by the needle thread. This is taken around over the bobbin and released. When the machine is properly adjusted, the tension of the needle and bob-

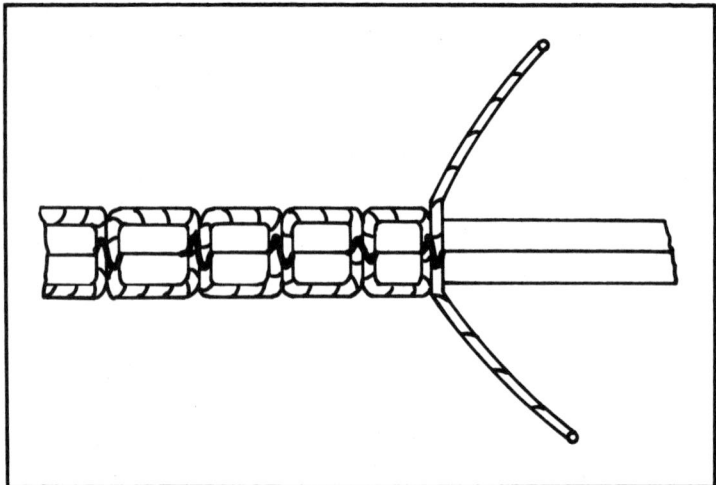

Fig. 3-1. Lock stitch.

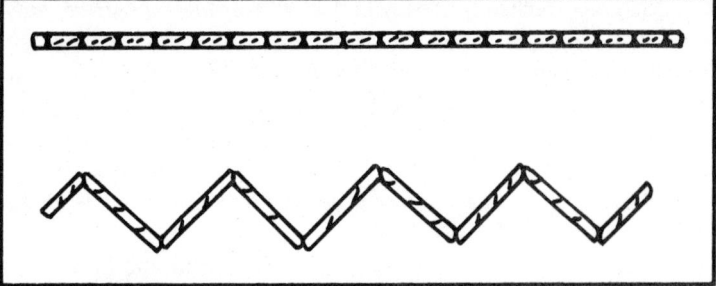

Fig. 3-2. Straight stitch (top), and zigzag stitch (bottom).

bin threads controls the intersection of the joining threads so that they meet in the middle of the fabric being sewn.

The machine method of forming lock stitches is covered in Chapter 5. An understanding of this is basic to selecting and operating sewing machines, yet it is surprising how many people operate sewing machines for years without having this basic understanding of how the machine works. On an actual sewing machine, the action can be observed by removing the bobbin inspection plate and turning the machine slowly by hand while sewing fabric.

The type of machine most commonly used for canvas and upholstery work has a *straight stitch*. Some sewing machines will also make *zigzag stitches* (Fig. 3-2) and a variety of other special stitches. Usually only the straight stitch is generally required for canvas and upholstery work, although a zigzag stitch can be used for some work if desired.

Virtually all zigzag stitch machines can be adjusted for straight stitching, but many straight stitch machines (and almost all of the ones with walking feet) only make this one type of stitch. *Feed mechanisms* feed the fabric through the machine so that the stitches are of a consistent length. The main problem is that there are very few zigzag machines with a walking foot feed, which is preferred by most canvas and upholstery workers.

One case where you might want to go with a machine with zigzag capabilities is if you intend to also do sailmaking. A zigzag stitch is usually used for machine sewing of sails.

Although portable sewing machines are available for canvas and upholstery work, a machine with a power stand and 1/3- or 1/2-horsepower clutch drive motor is generally preferred if space will permit. A belt usually connects the drive to the power head of the sewing machine.

Not all powerheads used with this type of stand and drive, however, are designed for heavy-duty canvas and upholstery work. Machines designed for standard sewing and tailoring sometimes use this same arrangement, especially if they are intended for industrial use. A heavy-duty commercial-type upholstery sewing machine is recommended for the canvas and upholstery work detailed in this book, but a standard home sewing machine may suffice for some work.

Even in the case of heavy-duty commercial-type upholstery machines, there are subtle and not so subtle differences between brands and even models of the same brand. The machine must be able to sew the fabrics in the number of layers used without damaging the machine or losing power. Most heavy-duty machines with power stands and 1/3 or 1/2 horsepower motors with clutch drives will accomplish this, but standard home machines and other machines with less power are frequently damaged by sewing through layers of heavy fabrics or do not have enough power to do this. Most industrial machines give a maximum of 6,000 to 9,000 stitches a minute; standard home machines go up to only about a thousand stitches per minute. The slower speed is generally not all that critical for the do-it-yourselfer; it simply will take longer to do the sewing. But lack of power is. The heavy-duty machine generally has not only a larger horsepower motor but also a heavier flywheel, which adds greatly to the penetrating power of the machine.

The sewing machine should not only make straight stitches, but also have a mechanism for adjusting the length of the stitches. A stitch length of around 3/16 inch is about right for most canvas and upholstery work, but this should be adjustable from about 1/16 inch up to 1/4 inch or more for special jobs. After the stitch length regulator has been adjusted to the desired stitch length, there should be a means for locking this adjustment firmly in place.

Several mechanisms are available to feed fabric through the machines. This must be done in a consistent manner if a constant stitch length is to be achieved. The most common mechanism is the *drop feed*. Most home sewing machines use this method, as do machines that sew zigzag and other special stitches. Most drop feed mechanisms do not work well when sewing heavy canvas and upholstery fabrics, however. A common problem is inconsistent stitch length. In spite of this problem, quality canvas and upholstery sewing can be, and has been, done on sewing machines with this type of feed.

The *walking foot feed* is generally a much better arrangement for canvas and upholstery sewing. This arrangement allows more consistent feeding of heavy fabrics. If you have a choice, a machine with a walking foot feed is recommended.

Top-driven pullers are also available. This consists of rollers in back of the needle that turn at the correct rate for pulling the fabric through the machine. These are generally only used for industrial applications where high speed sewing is required.

The sewing machine should have two tension adjustments: one for the needle thread, and one for the bobbin thread. The adjustment for the needle thread should be convenient and easy to operate, as frequent changes are required. The bobbin generally requires less frequent adjustments. This is usually accomplished by turning a small screw. Tighten the screw to increase the tension, loosen it to decrease the tension.

Reverse stitching capability is a handy feature that is found on some machines, especially newer models. This saves having to pull the fabric around to sew in reverse at the end of a stitch.

Bobbins should be easily accessible and easy to wind. To avoid having to wind your own bobbins, prewound bobbins on paper or plastic spools are available to fit most upholstery machines.

The machine should be easy to thread. Most of the new machines are, but some older machines require inserting the thread through small closed eyelets, which can be tedious and time-consuming.

Good lighting is important. Most machines with a power stand have an adjustable light mounted on the table behind the power head. Make certain that the light can be adjusted to the position that you want it. Good lighting is especially important around the needle area.

Before purchasing a sewing machine for canvas or upholstery work, try out as many brands and models of machines as possible. Standard portable and cabinet model home sewing machines will sometimes suffice for limited canvas and upholstery work, but sewing heavy fabrics with these may damage the machine. You may want to purchase an inexpensive used model for this purpose and take a chance with it.

My opinion is that home sewing machines are generally unsatisfactory for doing quality canvas and upholstery work. I've seen too many do-it-yourselfers turn out shoddy work simply because they were unable to sew properly with the machine they were attempting to use. These machines are fine for light fabrics, but many canvas and upholstery fabrics are beyond their capacity.

The next step upward is a heavy-duty portable sewing machine. One popular model is the Reads Sail Maker. It sews straight or zigzag, operates on 110 V or 12 V or by hand crank and will sew up to eight layers of 8-ounce polyester fabric. It's available from Cook Marine Products, P.O. Box 1133, Stamford, CT 06904. This machine is frequently used aboard cruising boats.

Another popular machine is the Sailrite Sailmaker. It sews straight or zigzag, operates on 110 V or by hand crank. It's available from Sailrite Enterprises, Route 1, Columbia City, Indiana 46725.

Most recommended is a heavy-duty upholstery machine with power stand and 1/3 or 1/2 horsepower clutch drive motor. A straight stitch model with a walking foot feed mechanism is generally preferred.

These machines can be purchased new or used or even rented. A used machine may be a good buy provided that you know what to look for in a machine. If possible, first learn to sew using a variety of machines. This is often possible by taking an upholstery class in an adult education program or elsewhere. They often have a number of machines of various brands and models that you can use. Try as many as possible and learn the advantages and disadvantages of each.

In many cases, the best bargains are found listed in classified ads in local newspapers, but it takes considerable experience and knowledge about sewing machines to select a good buy in this manner. Be careful. Many machines listed in these ads are damaged or worn out.

Another possibility is to purchase a used machine from a reputable dealer of a name brand machine. The used machines have often been traded in on new ones. Sometimes these have been reconditioned, although this can mean anything from simple application of oil and minor adjustments to a major overhaul. Get a one year repair guarantee in writing. Dealers will be reluctant to back machines in poor condition in this manner.

Make certain that the instruction manual for the particular machine comes with the machine. Check model number of machine to make certain that you are getting the correct manual. Dealers may tell you that you don't need the manual or that you can write to the factory and get one. Don't listen to this. Have the dealer get the manual for you before you buy.

Test the machine on the most difficult to sew materials that you will be using in the greatest number of thicknesses. Dealers usually have easy-to-sew fabrics for trying out machines. Bring your own fabrics along.

Make certain that needles and bobbins for the particular machine are commonly available. This can be a problem with some older model machines.

When sewing, the machine should not have any unusual rubbing or grating sounds. Listen for good rhythm. Excess oil may indicate an attempt to silence a machine that is badly worn.

On a straight-stitch machine, the needle should enter hole in throat plate in the exact center. If it doesn't, the needle or needle bar may be bent. Try a new needle. If this doesn't correct the problem, needle bar is probably bent. Replacement can be expensive. Don't buy unless replacement is made first.

Used machines should generally cost half as much or less than a similar new machine. Naturally, you will want to pay as little as possible for a particular machine. A completely rebuilt (major overhaul) machine is generally priced one third to one half lower than the price of a similar new machine.

In the case of heavy-duty commercial machines, there are two basic units that can be easily separated: the power stand, table, motor and clutch drive assembly and the power head. If you have one of these units in good condition, you can often purchase just the other unit to go with it. In many cases, rebuilt sewing machines mean the power head only.

If you can afford it, a new machine is usually the best way to go. New upholstery machines, complete with power stands and 1/3 or 1/2 horsepower motors, and currently priced from about $700 up to about $1,300 and more.

Most dealers will allow you to try out the machines. Take along pieces of fabric of the type that you intend to use.

The best bet is generally an established, reputable dealer who handles one or more name brand machines. Go to a dealer who handles heavy-duty commercial machines on a regular basis. While dealers who sell standard home machines can usually order heavy-duty machines for you, you won't get to try it out first, and the dealer may or may not be equipped to service and repair the machine.

Make certain that you get a written guarantee with the machine and that the dealer will take care of any problems that develop. In any case, make certain that you will not have to ship the machine back to the factory should it prove defective.

Make certain that you get lessons on operating and maintaining the machine with the purchase. Take the lessons even if you already know how to sew on a similar machine. You can learn about the particular machine, how to make tension and other adjustments, and basic troubleshooting for when problems develop. If possible, take the lessons on the same machine that you buy. If this is not possible, make certain that it is the same brand and model.

Make certain that a good user's manual comes with the machine. This should contain complete instructions for operating, maintaining, and adjusting the machine. You may also want to get a copy of the factory service manual for the machine. If the dealer doesn't have this in stock, he can usually order this for you.

Make certain that all special attachments that you will need either come with the machine or can be purchased separately. For example, you will need both a regular and zipper foot for canvas and upholstery work. These are interchangeable.

While opinions vary on exactly what is the best machine for the do-it-yourselfer, I favor a simple, sturdy machine that has the features that I need (ample power, straight-stitch, walking foot, a responsive controller that allows variable speeds, yet stops instantly when foot pressure is released, and so on).

Most upholstery sewing machines are heavy. Make certain that you have a means for delivering it. Most dealers provide free delivery.

Some companies offer service and maintenance agreements for reasonable prices. Although these are purchased mainly by those who use the machines for commercial use, these may also be worth the cost for the do-it-yourselfer, especially if extensive work is planned.

Sewing Machine Needles

The size of needles used depends on the type and weight of fabric being sewn. See Table 5-1.

Needles are available with various types of points (wedge-shaped points for leather, etc.). Standard points will suffice for most canvas and upholstery work. In general, you will want to use the smallest size needle possible that will work with the thread and fabrics being sewn. This will result in smaller holes being made in the fabric. This is important when sewing rain covers, vinyl and other materials where large holes could cause problems.

For starting out and general practice work, a #18 (110) size needle is about right. It's best to have spare needles on hand, though, and an assortment of sizes. Make certain that you get needles that fit your particular machine.

Hand Sewing Needles

Needles for hand sewing come in an assortment of sizes and shapes. Straight stitching needles (Fig 3-3) are used for general sewing, such as for stitching edges. Circular or *slipping needles* (Fig. 3-3) are useful for slip stitching, such as for sewing the openings in cushion covers after padding has been installed. *Bayonet* or *triangular* shank needles (Fig. 3-3) are triangular down about one third their length. These points open a rather large hole, but make sewing through heavy canvas and leather easier.

All three types of needles, in an assortment of sizes from about #14 to #18, are recommended. Always purchase quality brand needles.

Seaming Palm

A *seaming palm,* also called *sailmaker's palm*, is shown in Fig. 3-4. These are useful for handsewing heavy fabrics and leather. Make certain that you get one that fits your hand. Some have an adjustable strap, others don't. Some palms also have a shield over the thumb for "roping." This allows twine to be wrapped over the thumb and pulled very hard. Seaming palms are available in right- and left-hand models.

Seaming palms are often included in sewing kits that also in-

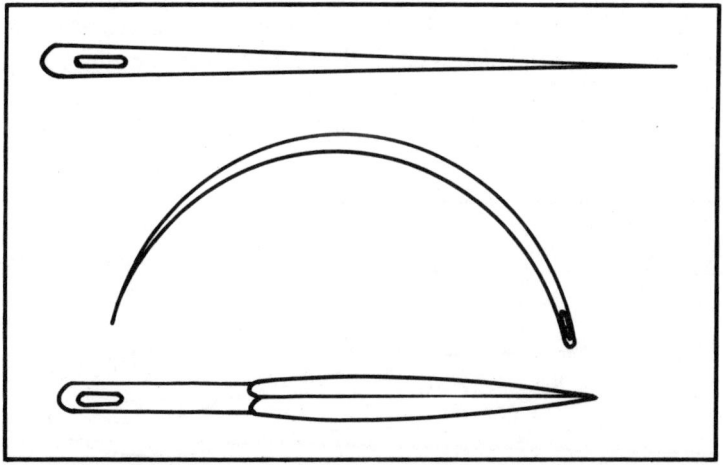

Fig. 3-3. Straight stitching needle (top), circular or slipping needle (center), and bayonet or triangular shank needle (bottom).

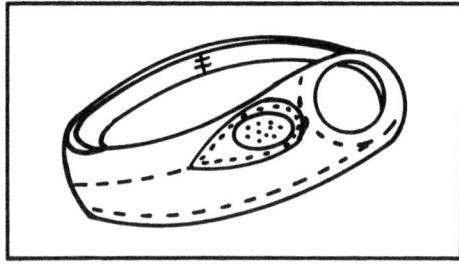

Fig. 3-4. Seaming palm.

clude needles, twine, and wax. These kits are often priced lower than if the items are purchased separately.

Sewing Awl

A *sewing awl* (Fig. 3-5) is another useful device for sewing heavy fabrics and leather with a lock stitch. Methods for using a sewing awl are detailed in Chapter 4. Sewing awls are sold separately or in kits with waxed thread and needles.

Scissors

You will need a small pair of scissors for cutting or snipping thread at the machine and when hand sewing, and at least one larger pair of scissors or shears for cutting fabrics. For the cutting work, 10-inch shears are about right. Special shears with one knife edge blade and one serrated blade are available and are designed especially for cutting polyester and other synthetic fabrics. These make a clean cut even on slippery fabrics. Cutting scissors or shears generally have the blades offset (Fig. 3-6) so that one edge of the scissors will slide along the cutting table.

It is extremely important to purchase quality brand scissors. Cheap ones quickly dull.

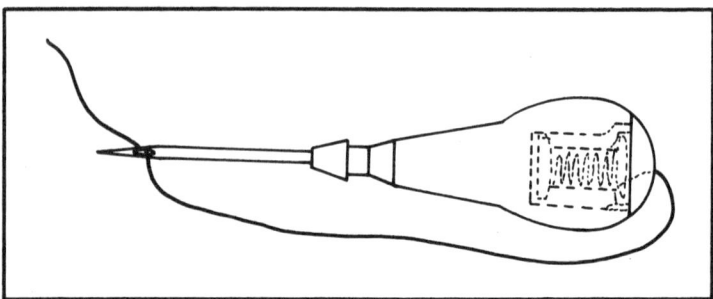

Fig. 3-5. Sewing awl.

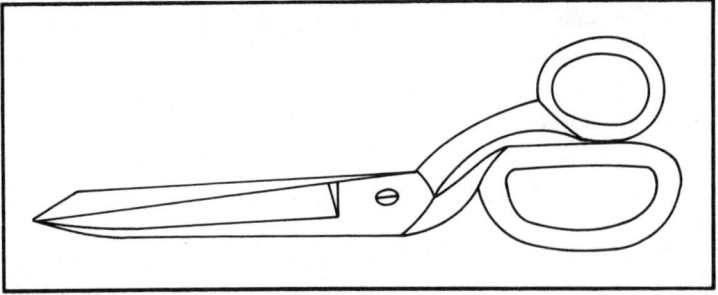

Fig. 3-6. Cutting scissors with offset blades.

Hot Knife

Special *hot knives* are available for cutting polyester, acrylic and other synthetic fabrics. This method also melts the fabric along the cut and keeps the edge from unravelling. These tools are fairly expensive, however, and not really needed for most canvas and upholstery work. The cutting can generally be done faster with scissors or shears and edges can be sewn under, as is customary even when hot knife cuts are used. *Do not* attempt to use a hot knife to cut cotton or other natural fiber canvas.

Seam Ripper

A *seam ripper* (Fig. 3-7) is a useful tool for opening stitching. Select one with a narrow beak and a protective ball on the hook to help prevent accidentally cutting fabric.

Measuring Tools

A tape or expanding steel rule at least 6 feet or 2 meters long is required for measuring long lengths. With the present trend toward the metric system, a tape or expanding steel rule that is marked in both imperial and metric units is useful.

A wood or steel rule in one piece is needed for measuring shorter lengths and as a straightedge for drawing lines. Also, a long straight rule or board with a straightedge is useful for drawing long straight lines.

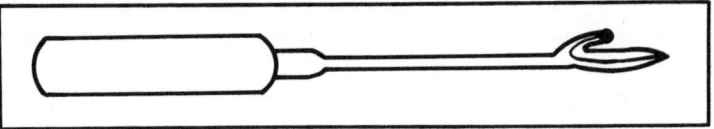

Fig. 3-7. Seam ripper.

A carpenter's square is useful for marking square corners. Squares are available at most hardware stores.

Marking Tools

Chalk is useful for marking patterns. It can easily be dusted away from most fabrics. The chalk should be sharpened to a chisel edge.

Pencils can also be used for marking, but they leave a hard-to-remove line on some fabrics. A felt pen can be used to mark foam padding and fabrics in places that will not show in finished work.

Die Sets and Cutters for Grommets and Canvas Fasteners

A variety of *die sets* and *cutters* is available for grommets and canvas fasteners. These are detailed in Chapter 7, along with their use.

Electric Knife

An electric knife is handy for cutting foam. Limited cutting can also be done with a fine-tooth hacksaw blade. Although special foam cutters are available, I've noticed that many commercial shops use the less expensive electric knives instead.

Tube Benders and Cutters

Tube benders are useful for bending aluminum tubing for top frames. The need for these will depend on the type of work you intend to do. Heavy-duty tube benders can also be used for bending stainless steel tubing.

A *tube cutter* is useful for making straight cuts on aluminum tubing. These cuts can also be made with a hacksaw, but care must be taken to get straight cuts.

Portable Electric Drill

A portable electric drill is useful for drilling holes to install canvas fasteners to wood, fiberglass, metal, and other materials and to perform a variety of other jobs related to canvas and upholstery work.

Other Tools

Many standard wood and metalworking tools will find uses in

canvas and upholstery work. These include hammers, punches, awls, pliers, screwdrivers, saws, and so on. The particular tools required depend on the type of work you intend to do.

Many minor sewing items will also be found useful, such as pins, thimbles, and so on. A broom, dustpan, and vacuum cleaner are useful for clean up work.

These are the main tools and equipment that you will need, but the list is by no means complete. Other tools and equipment can be added as a need develops.

WORK AREAS

Compared to many shop activities, canvas and upholstery work is relatively clean. It can usually be done inside your house. Basements, garages, and shop areas are other possibilities.

If extensive canvas and upholstery work is planned, you may want to set up a work area especially for this, if space permits. You will need a cutting area. A large table is ideal. This should be at a convenient working height. A kitchen, ping-pong, or other large table can be used, or you can construct a special table using 4- x -8-foot piece of plywood (or larger) for the top. Make the base sturdy so that the table will not rock.

You will need an area for the sewing machine, and a work bench with typical shop tools and a vise is also useful. You will also need storage areas for tools, materials and supplies.

Good overhead lighting is extremely important, especially over the cutting table. Because many fabrics have defects in them, good lighting is needed so that these can be located and taken into account so that they will not appear in the finished work.

A large block of wood is useful for backing fabric when punching and doing other similar tasks. A short section of a large log is useful for this.

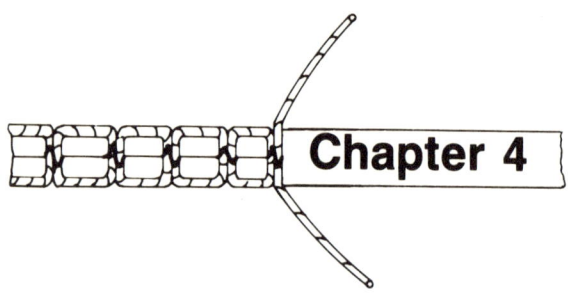

Chapter 4

Hand Sewing

Even if you intend to do most of your canvas and upholstery sewing with a machine, it's still important to learn hand sewing. Hand sewing is a good way to learn the principles of sewing. Even when machine sewing is used, there are certain jobs, such as closing a cushion, that are commonly done by hand. Hand sewing is also useful for canvas and upholstery repair work.

It's also possible to do even large canvas and upholstery jobs entirely by hand. This can be slow monotonous work, however, so unless you don't have a sewing machine available to use or you have an extreme case of antitechnology, you will probably want to do the bulk of the sewing with a sewing machine.

If you are unfamiliar with the basic hand stitches, I suggest that you begin with lightweight fabric, a #12 or 14 needle size, and machine-type thread. The fabric should be such that you can easily push the needle through it. The purpose is to learn the basic stitches without having to worry about forcing the needle through heavy fabric.

After the basic hand stitches become automatic, then you can advance to heavier fabric, a bayonet or triangular shank needle, twine, wax and a seaming palm. It should be pointed out that many of the fabrics used in modern canvas and upholstery work are lightweight and are easily sewn without the use of a seaming palm.

After basic hand sewing has been mastered on heavier fabrics, you will probably want to learn to sew with a sewing awl. The instructions that follow use the above learning progression.

BASIC HAND SEWING STITCHES

A traditional sailmaker's bench has a post in one corner to which a lanyard with a sailhook was attached. When sewing heavy canvas, the sailhook is passed through the canvas as shown in Fig. 4-1. The hand sewing is then done outward away from the hook or inward toward the hook, depending on the stitching used. This allows you to stretch the fabric with the left hand while sewing with the right.

Although you probably won't need a traditional sailmaker's bench, a cord with a hook on one end and attached to a post or other convenient place is useful. Without this, the material will tend to draw up into a bunch when you try to make the stitches.

You will need scrap pieces of fabric that allow the needle to be passed through by hand. The fabric pieces should be at least a couple of feet long and a foot wide. These should be woven fabric without vinyl or other plastic coating. You will also need a #12 or 14 hand sewing needle and machine-type thread.

Begin by threading the needle. To do this, cut the end of the

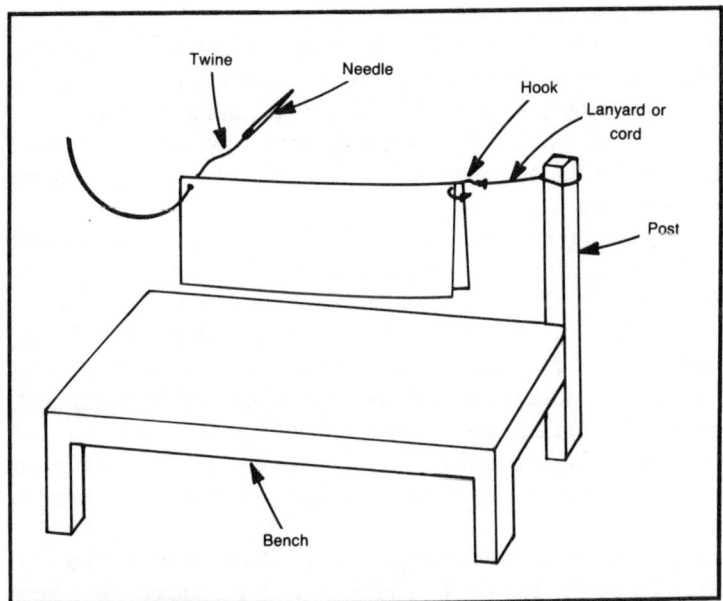

Fig. 4-1. Traditional sailmaker's bench. Post and lanyard with hook holds canvas while hand sewing.

37

thread using sharp scissors. Never break thread, as this frays the end and makes it difficult to thread through the eye of the needle. Hold the needle in your left hand. Hold thread near end in right hand between thumb and index finger. If you are left-handed, you will probably want to reverse the hands from the above directions. Thread the end of the thread through the eye of the needle and grasp needle with thumb and index finger of right hand. Release left hand from needle and draw thread end out from eye. Although hand sewing can be done with a single thread, a double thread is used for most canvas and upholstery work.

Pull thread through the needle eye until you have a double thread two or three feet long. Cut off the thread from the spool, assuming that this wasn't done before you threaded the needle. Knot the ends of the thread.

A knot on the end of the thread or threads is the usual method for anchoring a stitch at the start of a seam, but an alternate method is to leave the ends of the threads free. Begin the seam by passing the needle through the fabric. Pull all of the thread through except for an inch or so on the end. This end is then pushed ahead under the seam and the stitches are made over it, alternating from one side to the other.

When *basting* (loosely sewing two pieces of fabric together), the knot can be visible, because the thread is usually removed after final sewing is completed. When making permanent stitching, the knot is usually placed out of sight against an inside layer.

The end of a row of stitches is often secured with a *backstitch*. The beginning of a row of stitches can also be secured by backstitching.

At the beginning of hand stitching, pass needle and thread from underside of fabric through all layers of fabric, as shown in Fig. 4-2, A through D. Then pass needle and thread back through fabric a short distance from original pass. Pull all thread through except for about an inch on the end. Next, make a backstitch and bring it out close to start of stitch. Pull the thread through leaving a small loop. Take another short backstitch, but this time pass needle and thread through loop. Pull thread to secure stitches. Original thread end can then be cut off close to the fabric. You are now ready to make seam.

The procedure is similar at the end of hand stitching. Starting with the needle and thread pulled through the underside, take a short backstitch at point just behind where thread emerges. Pull thread through but leave a thread loop. Make a second small

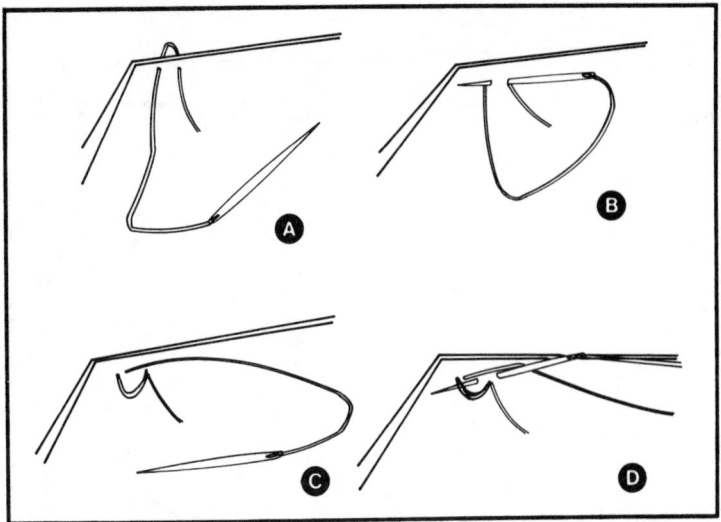

Fig. 4-2. Running backstitch. Pass needle and thread through all layers of fabric and pull all thread through except for about an inch on the end (A). Make backstitch and bring it out close to start of stitch (B). Pull thread through, leaving a small loop (C). Make another short backstitch and pass needle and thread through loop (D).

backstitch on top of the first one. Pass needle and thread through loop and pull both stitches taut. Cut off thread. Practice all of the above methods using pieces of scrap fabric.

Flat Seam

The *flat seam* is a very simple method of hand sewing. Figure 4-3 shows a straight flat seam. Even when the stitches are spaced close together, this does not provide a very strong seam, and for this reason the straight flat seam is generally used only for basting or holding the fabrics in temporary position until permanent sewing can be done. The stitches can be short, long, or uneven, as desired.

In canvas and upholstery work, flat seams are usually done in a diagonal pattern. This provides a strong seam and it can be done in the middle of large pieces of fabric, where it is usually impractical to get to both sides of the fabric. Figure 4-4 shows typical *diagonal flat seaming* stitch. Notice that the stitches form a diagonal pattern on one side and a side to side pattern on the other side. This pattern is normally used, although a zigzag pattern is also possible.

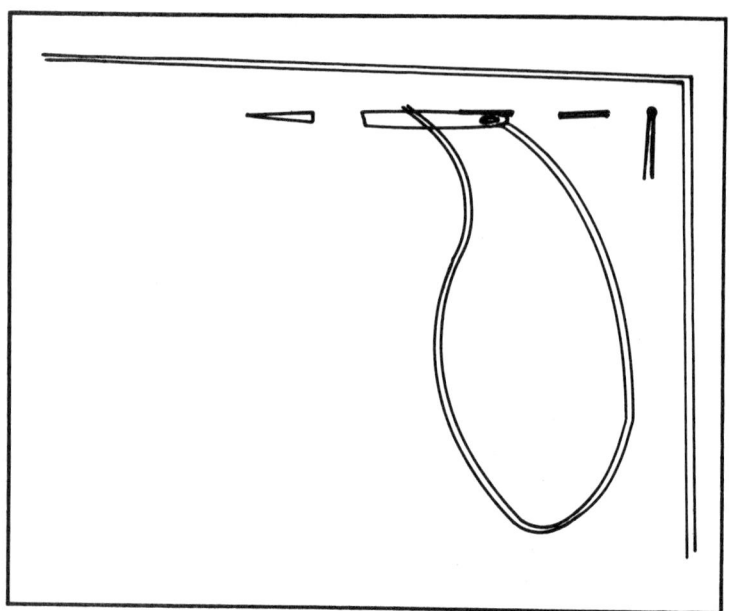

Fig. 4-3. Straight flat seam.

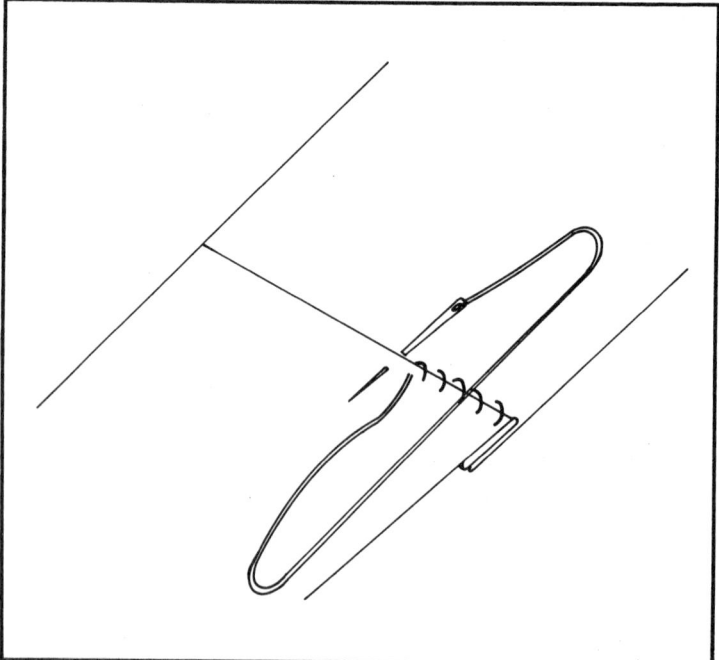

Fig. 4-4. Flat seaming stitch.

To practice this stitch, arrange two pieces of scrap fabric as shown in Fig. 4-5. Use a hook device as shown to steady the fabric and pull it taut so that it will not bunch up while the seam is being made. Notice that the edge of the fabric is turned under. This is standard practice. It hides the edge of the canvas and keeps it from unravelling. This is especially important when sewing unselvedged edges.

Right-handed people generally work from right to left, starting at the hook. The needle is passed from the far side toward you. This is done with the right hand, while the fabric is held taut with the left hand. The needle should enter the lower fabric close to the upper, turned-under fabric. The needle is then brought up through the turned-under fabric in an even pattern.

After completing the first seam and securing the end of the thread, turn the fabric over. Turn the edge under as shown in Fig. 4-6. Then sew the second seam in the same manner. It is generally best to sew with the upper, turned-under fabric on the side of the seam toward you. Although this method is generally used, some people prefer to push the needle away from them, in which case the fabric should be turned around.

At the end of the seam, secure the end of the thread. You should now have two pieces of fabric securely joined together with the edges turned under.

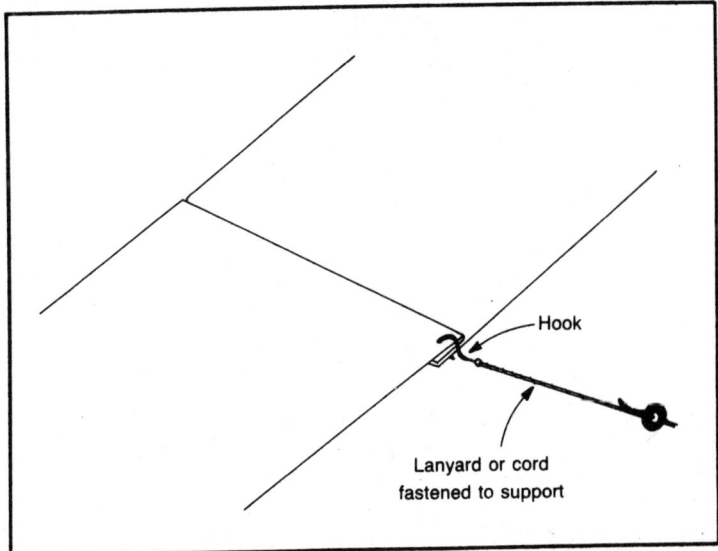

Fig. 4-5. Fabrics arranged for flat stitching with hook to steady fabric.

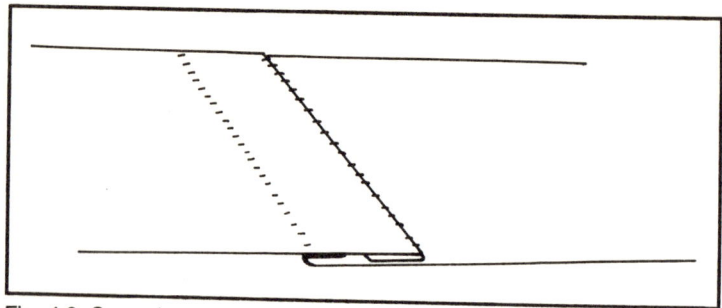

Fig. 4-6. Second seam is stitched to form flat-felled seam.

Round Seam

A *round stitch* is shown in Fig. 4-7. This is used when you can conveniently get to both sides of the fabric. In most cases, the edges of the fabric are turned under, as shown in Fig. 4-8.

The round stitch is usually made from your left to your right, starting at the end away from the hook. This is opposite the method used for the flat seam. The needle is generally pushed through the

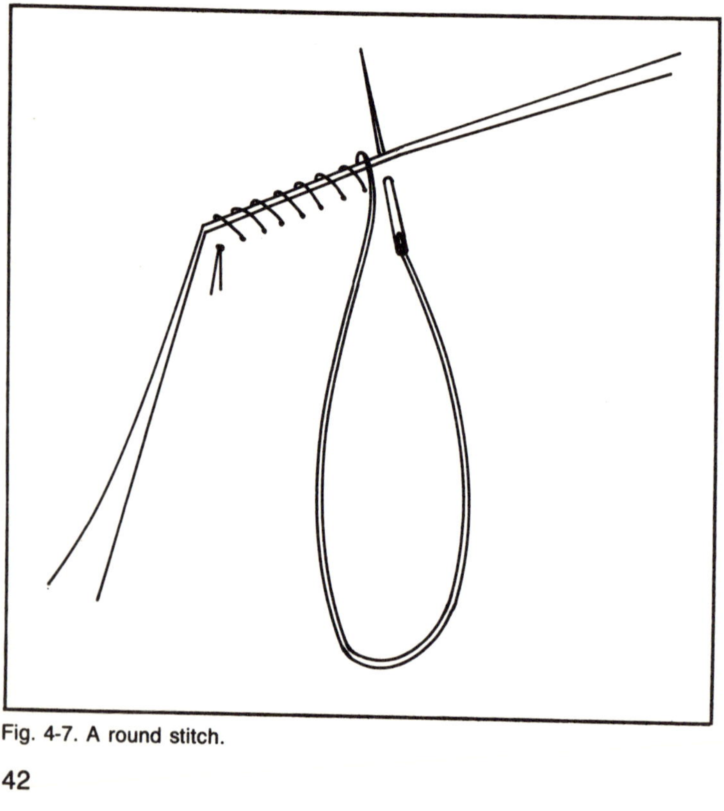

Fig. 4-7. A round stitch.

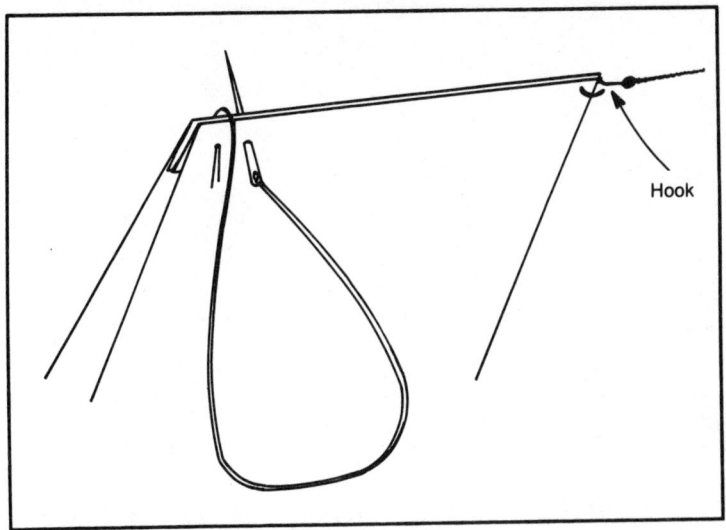

Fig. 4-8. Round stitching with edges turned under. Fabric is held by hook for sewing round stitch.

four layers of fabric from the side closest to you to the side away from you. The needle is then brought out the opposite side and carried back around towards you. It is then pushed through the fabric the desired distance from the first pass. The sewing is generally done with the right hand, while the fabric is pulled taut with the left hand.

Practice by arranging two scrap pieces of fabric as shown in Fig. 4-8. Use a hook device, as shown. Complete the seam and secure the end of the seam.

A *flat-felled seam* similar to that created with the flat seaming stitch can be made with round stitching. Trim one edge of the fabric, as shown in Fig. 4-9. Then turn the untrimmed edge under, as shown in Fig. 4-9. Position the fabric as shown in Fig. 4-10. Then use a round stitch to sew the second seam, as was done for the first seam. When the seam is completed, secure the end and cut off excess thread.

Compare this with the previous flat-felled seam that was flat stitched. The stitches are very similar, with the main difference being that the flat stitch tends to form a zigzag pattern, while round stitching is more perpendicular to the work. Because the round stitch is usually faster and easier to make, it is generally used when it is convenient to get to both sides of the work. Also, to make the round stitch, it is necessary to fold the fabrics together, something

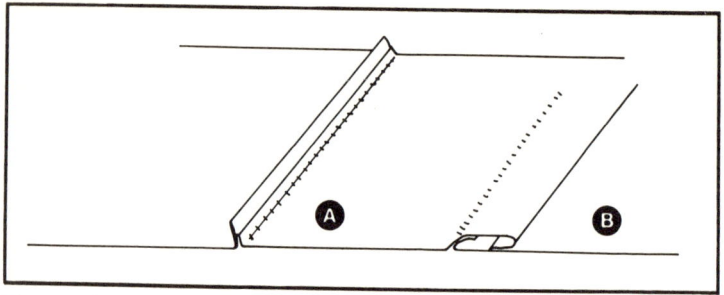

Fig. 4-9. One edge of fabric is trimmed (A), then untrimmed edge is turned under (B).

that is not always possible when repairing existing canvas items.

Darning

Darning is a stitch used for repairing small rips and tears in canvas. Figure 4-11 shows the stitch. At the start of the stitch, the thread is usually knotted. The stitching is usually done from left to right. Start by passing the needle upward through the fabric on the far side of the tear, as shown in Fig. 4-12A. Pull thread up.

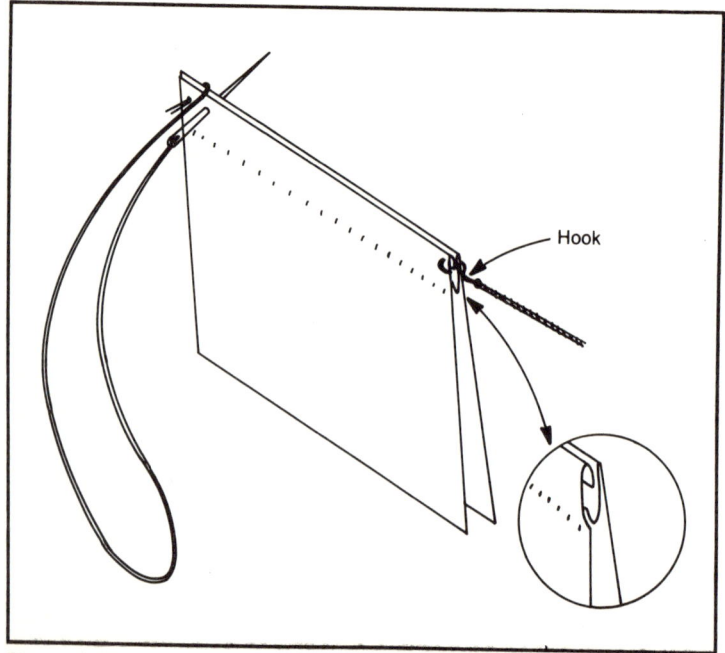

Fig. 4-10. Fabric positioned for round stitching.

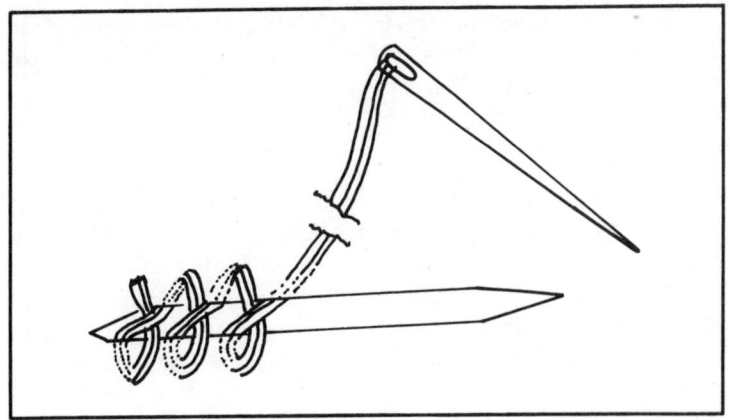

Fig. 4-11. Darning or herringbone stitch.

Bring the needle back over the tear and pass it down through the near side of the tear. Bring it up through the tear on the left side of the stitch, as shown in Fig. 4-12B. Pull thread up.

Pass the needle and thread over the stitch and through the tear. Pass the needle upward through the far side of the tear (Fig. 4-12C). Then repeat the darning stitch, as was done on the first stitch. Do not pull the stitch any tighter than is necessary to hold the two sides of the tear together. A common mistake is to pull the stitch too tight. Continue the stitch to the end of the tear. The end of the thread is usually secured with a half hitch and tucked under.

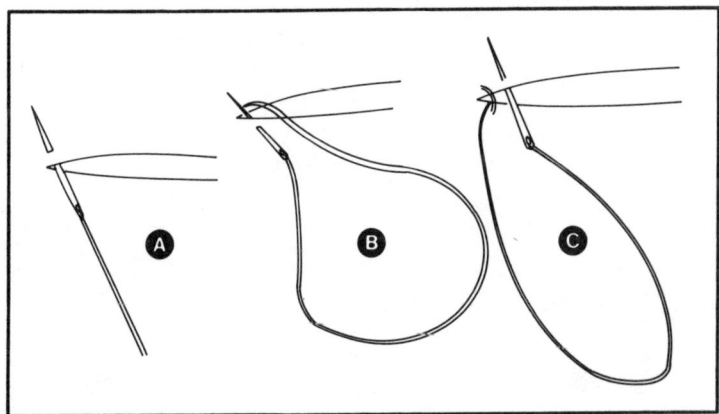

Fig. 4-12. Darning. Needle is passed upward through fabric on far side of tear (A); needle passes downward through near side and is brought up in tear left of thread (B); needle and thread pass over stitch, through tear, and upward through far side of fabric (C).

Because of its appearance, this stitch is also called a *herringbone stitch*. Because it is frequently used to repair tears in sails, it is also called the *sailmaker's darn*.

Slip Stitch

Slip stitching is used to join fabrics without the stitching showing from the outside (or right side) of the fabrics. Because the stitch is largely invisible, it is sometimes called a *blind stitch*.

Although the stitch can be made with a regular needle, a curved slipping needle is frequently used. A frequent use of this type of stitching is for closing cushion covers after the foam padding has been installed.

Practice the stitch using scrap fabrics and either a regular straight stitching needle or a curved slipping needle and machine thread. Position the two pieces of fabric with the edges folded inward, as shown in Fig. 4-13. Start the stitching by passing the needle through from underneath, as shown in Fig. 4-13A. The end of the thread is usually secured by a knot. Bring the needle and thread back and pass it downward through the near layer of fabric and then back out again a short distance further along, as shown in Fig. 4-13B.

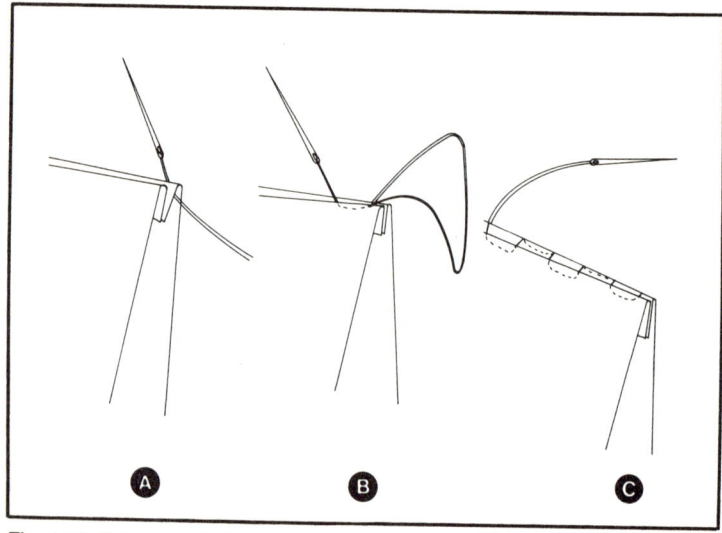

Fig. 4-13. Edges are folded inward and stitching is started by passing needle through from underneath (A); needle is passed downward through near layer of fabric and brought back out a short distance further along (B). Same pattern is continued. Thread is pulled tight to close seam.

Continue with the same pattern. Pull the thread tight so that the seam closes. Secure thread at end of stitching.

HAND SEWING HEAVY FABRICS

The basic stitches are best learned on lightweight, easy to sew fabrics. This allows you to pass the needle easily through the fabric.

After the basic stitches have been learned to the point where they are more or less automatic (that is, you don't have to consciously think about the sewing pattern), you are ready to go on to heavier fabrics. A seaming palm is usually used for this. You will need a seaming palm that fits your hand comfortably (see Chapter 3). Straight-stitch needles with standard rounded shanks can be used, but bayonet or triangular shank needles penetrate heavy fabrics more easily. You will also need twine and beeswax (see Chapter 2).

The sewing is usually done with the twine doubled back. Usually about 4 to 6 feet of twine is used, giving 2 to 3 feet of doubled sewing thread. Any longer than this and it becomes awkward to pull through; any shorter will require frequent joins. If the twine isn't already waxed, draw the doubled over twine through beeswax several times.

Figure 4-14 shows the correct position for steadying the butt of the threaded needle in the raised "iron" section of the palm. The point of the needle can then be pushed through the fabric, the thumb and forefinger transferred to the needle tip on the other side of the fabric, and the needle pushed on through, all with one hand. With practice, this will become one continuous motion, and sewing can then be done quite rapidly.

Flat Seam

Begin practice by making a flat seam as was done previously with lightweight fabric, only this time use a heavier weight fabric. Arrange two pieces of fabric with a hook arrangement to your right (Fig. 4-5). The canvas should pass over your legs. In order to avoid sticking the needle into your legs, it's a good idea to place a heavy piece of canvas over your legs.

Steady the fabric and pull it taut with your left hand, while you make the stitches with your right hand, using the seaming palm to push the needle through the fabric. Most right-handed people prefer to work from right to left, starting at the hook and working away from it. The needle is pushed through the lower fabric that

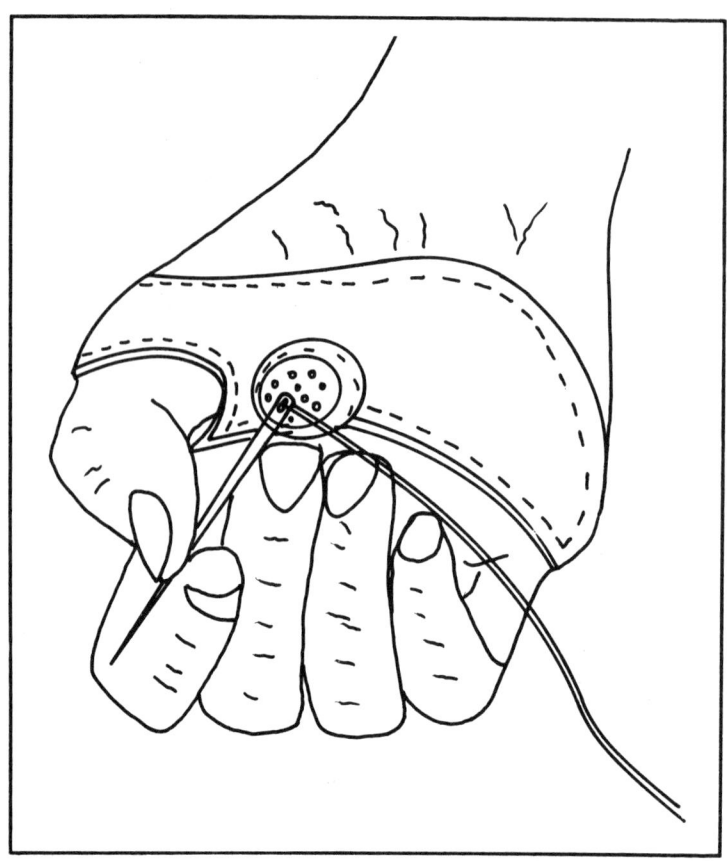

Fig. 4-14. Position for steadying the butt of the threaded needle in raised "iron" section of palm.

is away from you first. The needle is pushed towards you. The needle is then brought up through the turned-under fabric in an even pattern. This should be done with the right hand, pushing the needle through with the raised iron section of the palm and transferring the thumb and forefinger as the needle passes through the fabric layers. At the same time, the fabric should be pulled taut with the left hand. It will take some practice, of course, before a straight seam can be made with evenly spaced stitches.

The twine is then pulled up and the action is repeated for the second stitch. And so on.

The spacing of the stitches depends on the particular fabric and the size of the needle and twine being used, with typical stitches being about 1/8 inch to 1/4 inch apart. If the fabric tears easily, even wider spacing is sometimes used.

After completing the first seam on the practice project and securing the end of the thread, turn the fabric over. The edge is turned under (Fig. 4-6). Then sew the second seam in the same manner as the first seam. At the end of the seam, secure the end of the twine.

When sewing canvas, securing the end of the twine at the start and finish of a stitch with a knot is sometimes undesirable because of the lump that the knot makes. For this reason the twine is often secured by passing it under the stitch. This can be done at the start and end of a flat seaming stitch.

You should now have two pieces of heavy fabric securely joined together with turned-under edges. If the seam is a little uneven or the stitches are not all the same distance apart, don't worry. It takes hours of practice to do this consistently.

Round Seam

Begin practice by making a round seam as before with lightweight fabric, only this time use a heavier weight fabric that does not allow the needle to pass through the fabric by finger pressure alone. Arrange two pieces of fabric as before with a hook arrangement to your right (Fig. 4-8). The canvas should pass over your legs. In order to avoid sticking the needle into your legs, it's a good idea to place a heavy piece of canvas over your legs.

Steady the fabric, and pull it taut with your left hand while you make the stitches with your right hand, using the seaming palm for pushing the needle through the fabric. Most people who are right-handed prefer to do the round stitch from left to right, opposite the direction used for the flat stitch. The seam is started at the end of the fabric away from the hook. The needle is generally pushed through the four layers of fabric from the side closest to you to the side away from you. This should be done with the right hand, pushing the needle through with the raised iron section of the palm and transferring the thumb and forefinger as the tip of the needle passes through the fabric layers. At the same time, the fabric should be held in position and pulled taut with the left hand.

The end of the twine can be secured by pulling all but about an inch or so of twine through the fabric and then making the next several stitches over the end of the twine. This makes a knot unnecessary.

After pushing the needle through the fabrics toward you, pull the twine through until it is taut. Then take the needle back over and push it through the fabric for the next stitch.

Continue this sewing pattern until the desired length of seam has been completed. The end of the seam can be secured by passing the needle back under one or more stitches making a knot unnecessary.

Next, make a flat-felled seam. Trim one edge of the fabric, then turn the untrimmed edge under. Then position the fabric, hooking one end of the seam, for sewing, as was done for the first seam on the opposite side of the fabrics (Fig. 4-10). Use a round stitch to sew second seam in same manner as the first seam.

When the seam has been completed, compare it with the seam with flat stitches done in the previous practice exercise. The stitches should be similar, with the main difference being that the flat stitches tend to form a zigzag pattern, while the round stitching is more perpendicular to the work. Because round stitching is usually easier and faster, it is generally used when it is convenient to get to both sides of the work. Also, to make the round stitches, it is necessary to fold the fabrics together, something that is not always possible when repairing existing canvas items. When making a typical hem as shown in Fig. 4-15, a flat seam is normally

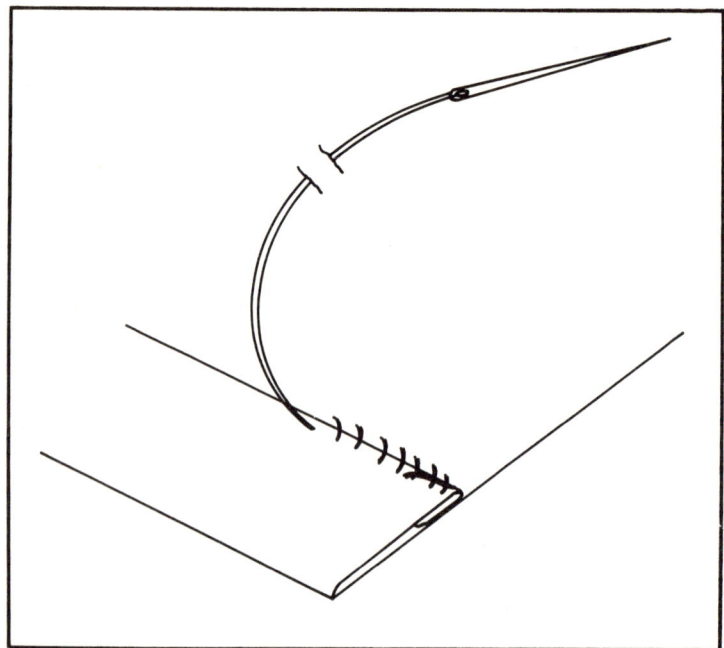

Fig. 4-15. Typical hem made with flat seam.

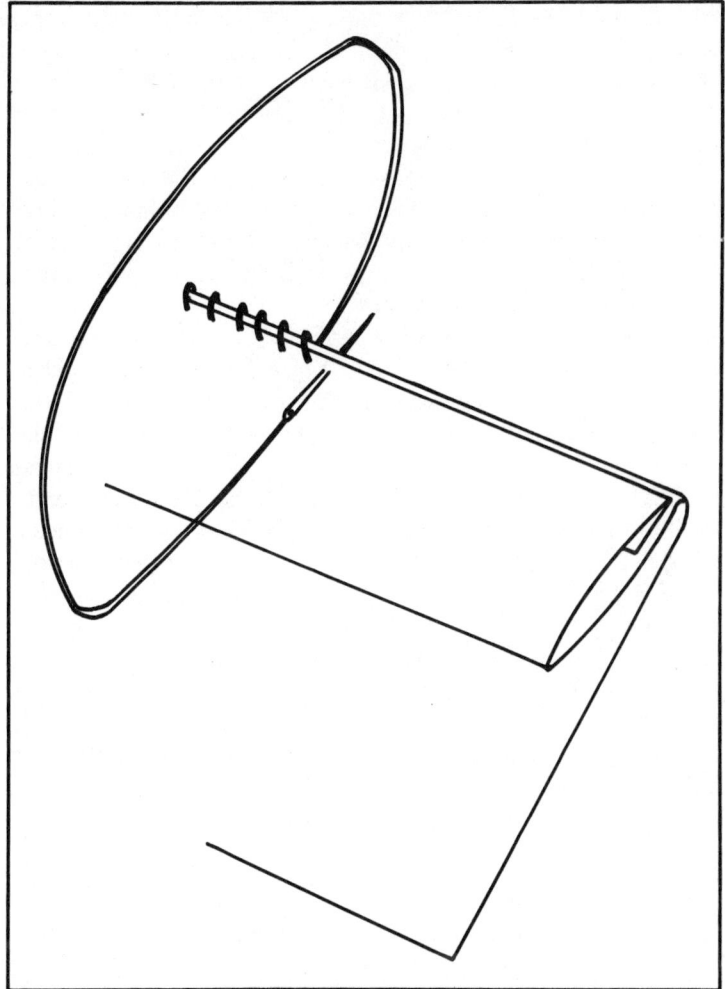

Fig. 4-16. Using round seam for hem.

used instead of a round seam. Although the canvas could be folded on back as shown in Fig. 4-16 and a round seam made, this normally isn't done, because it is difficult to get a straight seam.

Herringbone Stitch

The *herringbone stitch* is useful for repairing small tears in canvas fabrics. This practice exercise is similar to the previous exercise using this stitch on lightweight fabric, except that this time heavier canvas that does not allow you to push the needle through with finger pressure alone. Make a small tear in the fabric with a knife.

The stitching is usually done from left to right. Start by passing the needle upward through the fabric on the far side of the tear, using the raised iron section of the palm to push the needle through. Transfer the thumb and forefinger to the tip of the needle on the other side of the fabric as the needle passes through. In most cases, the start of stitch is secured by two half hitches around first stitch and then stitching over ends of twine. A knot is sometimes used to secure the end of the twine.

Continue with the stitching pattern shown in Fig. 4-11. That is, bring the needle back over the tear and pass it down through the near side of the tear, pushing the needle through with aid of sewing palm. Bring the needle up through the tear on the left side of the stitch. Pass needle and twine over the stitch and through the tear. Push needle upward through the far side of the tear.

Stitch pattern is then repeated for the length of the tear. Do not pull the stitches any tighter than is necessary to hold the two sides of the tear together. A common mistake is to pull the stitch too tight.

There is a danger of the herringbone stitching coming undone if the end of the twine is merely passed back under several stitches. It is generally better to make two half hitches around the last stitch, and then pass the end of the twine back under several stitches before cutting it off.

Slip Stitching

Next, practice slip stitching as was done previously with lightweight fabrics, only this time use heavier canvas that requires you to use sewing palm.

A curved slipping needle can be used, but this does not work very well with a sewing palm. For this reason, I suggest that a straight needle be used.

Position the two pieces of scrap canvas fabric as was done previously (Fig. 4-13). The edges are tucked inward. Start the stitching by passing the needle through from underneath, as shown in Fig. 4-13A. The end of the twine is usually secured by tying a knot in the end of the doubled back twine and pulling the knot up tight against the fabric of the first pass of the needle and twine.

Next, bring the needle and twine back and pass it downward

through the near layer of fabric and then back out again a short distance further along, as shown in Fig. 4-13B. Use the sewing palm to push the needle through.

Continue the same pattern. Pull the twine tight so that the seam closes. At the end of the seam, secure the end of the twine and cut the end off.

When done properly, the twine should not show from the right side of the fabric, making it useful for closing cushion covers after the padding has been added.

Adding a Patch

A hole or tear in canvas fabric is often repaired by hand sewing a patch in place. A square or rectangular shaped patch is usually used. The patch is usually cut so that it overlaps the damaged area by a couple of inches on all sides. The edges of the patch are turned under about a half inch all the way around. The patch can be held in position for sewing with pins or several pieces of adhesive tape. The twine is usually doubled back after it is threaded through the eye of the needle. Run the two pieces of twine through beeswax several times so that they join together.

The patch is then sewn in place using a flat seam, as shown in Fig. 4-17A. The beginning and end of the stitching is usually secured by passing the ends of the twine under several stitches. Use a seaming palm for pushing the needle through the layers of fabric.

After the patch has been stitched all the way around and the ends of the twine secured and cut off, the fabric being patched is turned over. Cut the damaged area of the fabric with a pair of scissors as shown in Fig. 4-17B. Be careful not to cut the patch.

Next, turn the edges under, as shown in Fig. 4-17C. These can be held in position for sewing with pins or several pieces of adhesive tape.

Then sew the folds to the patch, as shown in Fig. 4-17D. Use a seaming palm to push the needle through the layers of fabric. Again, use a flat stitch, pushing the needle through towards you with the aid of the seaming palm. Secure the ends of the twine by passing them under several stitches.

This type of patch generally makes a strong repair and is frequently used, especially when machine sewing is not possible. Sails are frequently patched in a similar manner.

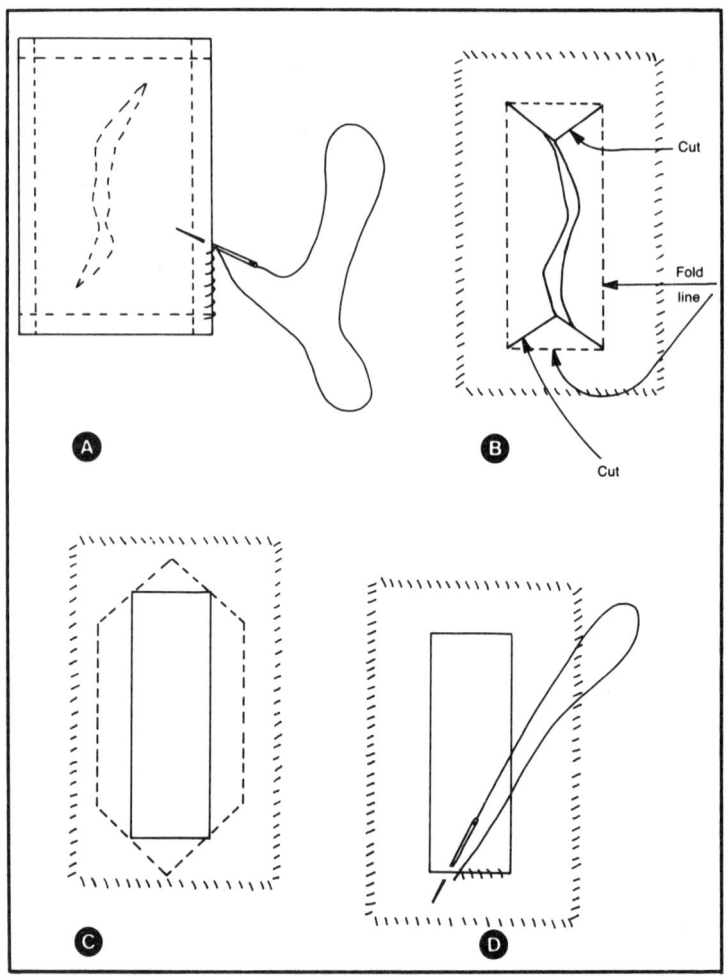

Fig. 4-17. Patch is sewn in place with a flat seam (A); fabric is cut (B); edges of fabric are turned under (C); the folds are sewn to the patch (D).

USING A SEWING AWL

A *sewing awl* is a hand tool that makes a lock stitch similar to that made by a sewing machine. Waxed nylon or polyester thread is used. The thread is held on a small spool in the handle of the awl and fed out through a small hole to the eye of the needle, as shown.

Practice making a seam in two pieces of heavy fabric with the edges turned under so that you will be making the stitches through four layers, as shown in Fig. 4-18A.

Begin by pushing the awl point through the layers of fabric at the desired start of stitching, as shown. Then pull thread through the needle eye to go the length of desired seam, plus a little extra. It's better to have too much than too little.

Next, pull needle back out and push it through fabric again in location of next desired stitch, usually from about 1/8 inch to 1/4 inch from the first needle pass. Five or six stitches to the inch is typical.

Insert end of thread through loop (Fig. 4-18B) and pull it tight. This thread can be considered as the bobbin thread. If desired, it can be threaded to a needle to make passing the thread through the loops easier.

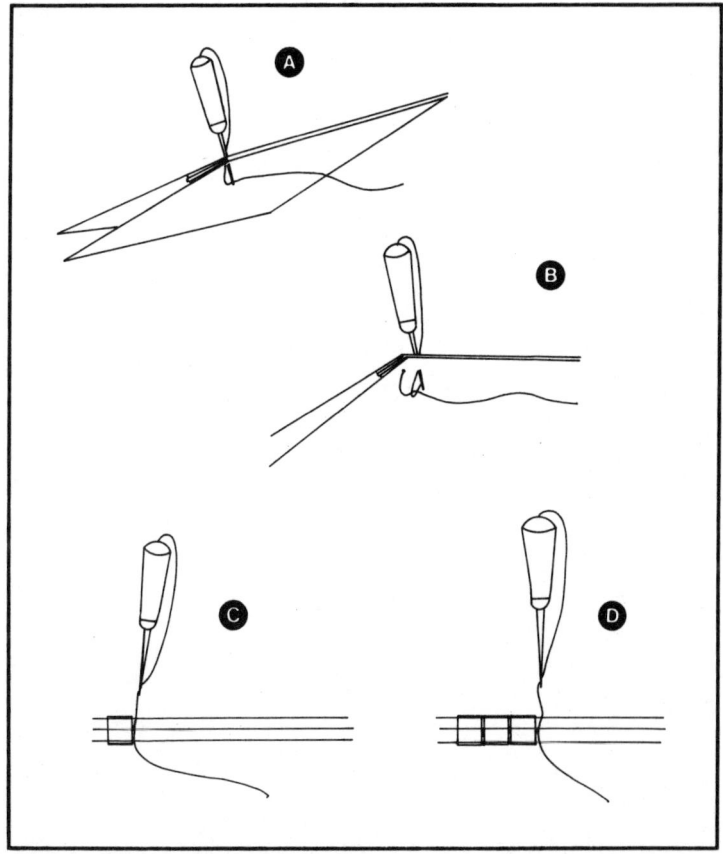

Fig. 4-18. Fabric positioned for sewing with awl (A); end of thread is inserted in loop (B); lock is formed midway between layers of fabric (C); stitching is continued (D).

Pull awl needle back out, making a lock stitch. When done correctly, the lock should form midway between the layers of fabric, as shown in Fig. 4-18C.

Continue this stitching pattern (Fig. 4-18D) the length of the desired seam. It is important to regulate the tension of the thread so that the threads loop together at the center of the layers of fabric throughout the stitching and that the stitches be spaced evenly and in a straight line.

To secure the end of the seam, the awl thread can be passed through the layers of fabric and tied to the bobbin thread. Hand sewing with an awl is a useful method for the limited sewing of heavy fabrics.

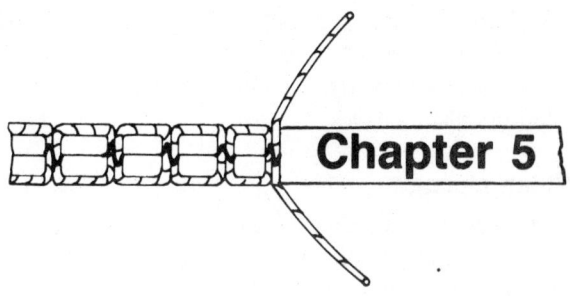

Chapter 5

Machine Sewing

Machine sewing is an extremely important part of canvas and upholstery work. You need not only a suitable sewing machine, but also the knowledge and skill necessary to operate, maintain, adjust, and repair it. You may want to leave all but simple repairs to a sewing machine mechanic, but you should be able to do your own maintenance, make adjustments, and perform simple repair tasks.

Most people who take up canvas and upholstery work do not take the time and trouble to learn how to properly operate a sewing machine and, as a result, their work appears amateurish. On the other hand, by mastering the skills and techniques of machine sewing, professional looking canvas and upholstery work becomes possible.

To learn machine sewing, a basic understanding of how a sewing machine works is extremely important. Yet, it's surprising how many people attempt machine sewing without bothering to "see how it works."

HOW SEWING MACHINES WORK

There are two basic types of sewing machines: the chain-stitch and lock-stitch machines.

Chain-Stitch Machine

These machines have only one thread that goes through the

needle and the fabric being sewn. A hook called a *looper* pulls one looped stitch into the next, forming a chain stitch. The needle is withdrawn from the fabric, the fabric advanced forward, and the process repeated for the next stitch. These machines are used mainly for sewing sacks and other items where an easily ripped seam is required. Chain-stitch machines are not ordinarily used for canvas and upholstery work.

Lock-Stitch Machine

A lock-stitch machine has both a needle and bobbin thread supply. Two or more pieces of fabric are sewn together with a lock stitch, which consists of two threads that interlock in the center of the layers of fabric being sewn together.

We will first consider a *straight-stitch* machine; that is, a machine that makes the stitch in a straight line. Figure 5-1 shows the parts of a typical sewing machine.

To form a lock stitch, precisely timed movements of the needle and shuttle hook are required to manipulate the top or needle thread and the bottom or bobbin thread. Tension devices and guides help to control the flow of the threads.

The threaded sewing machine needle penetrates through the layers of fabric being sewn together to bring the needle or top thread into the bobbin area, as shown in Fig. 5-2A. The needle is going downward, and the shuttle hook around the bobbin is rotating counterclockwise. The stitch is being made from the left side of the fabric to the right side.

A loop is formed in the needle or top thread as the needle starts to rise. The rotating shuttle hook catches this and brings the loop around the bobbin case, as shown in Fig. 5-2B. Needled is headed upward, and shuttle hook is rotating counterclockwise.

The shuttle hook carries the thread loop on around under the bobbin case, as shown in Fig. 5-2C. Notice that one side of the loop of needle or top thread is on each side of the bobbin. Although a special mechanism is required to allow this and yet hold the bobbin in place, it's best not to concern yourself with this when trying to understand the basic formation of the lock stitch.

As the shuttle hook continues to rotate, the needle or top thread loop slides off the hook with the loop now on the opposite side of the bobbin case, as shown in Fig. 5-2D. The loop is now around the bobbin thread.

The loop is then pulled up by the needle. There is also tension

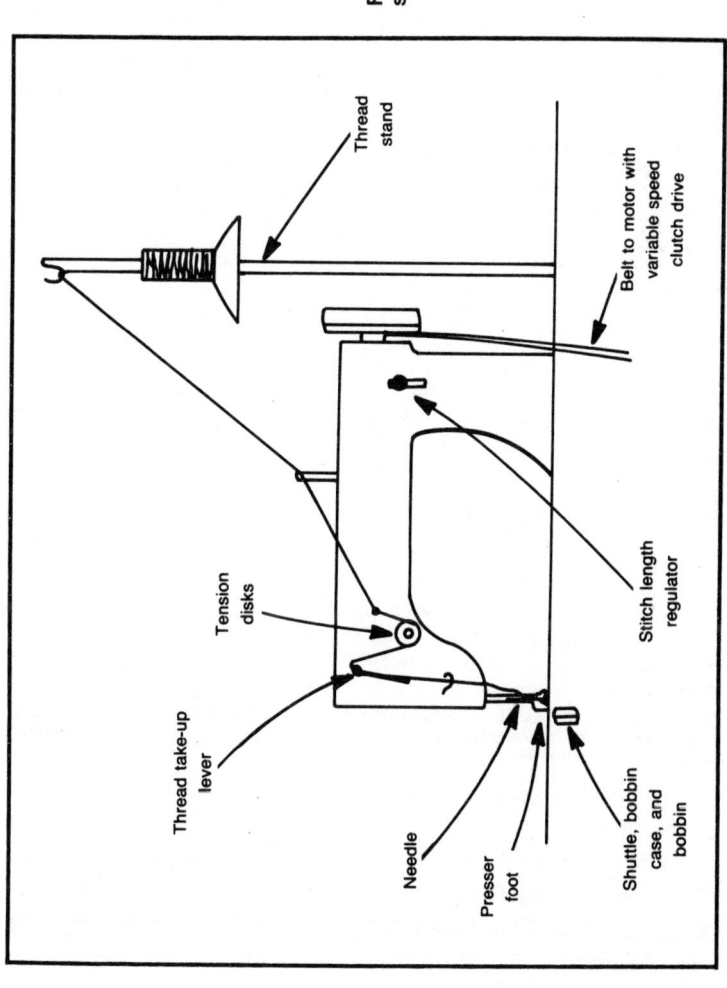

Fig. 5-1. Parts of typical upholstery sewing machine.

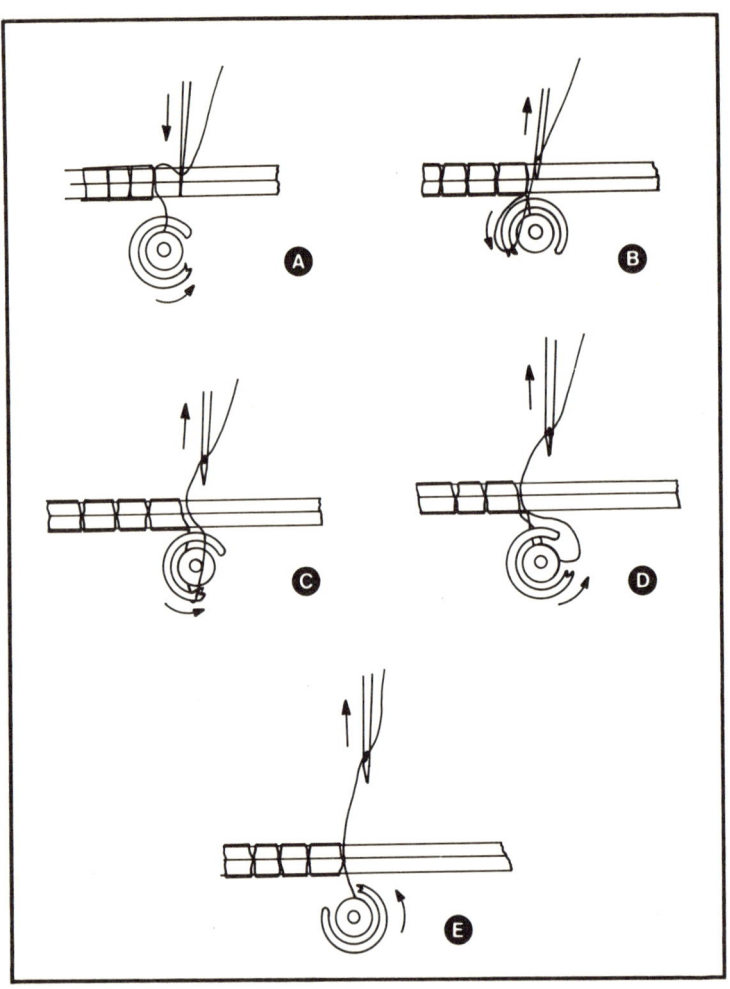

Fig. 5-2. How a sewing machine works. Needle penetrates fabric to bring upper thread into bobbin area (A); the rotating shuttle hook picks up loop in needle thread (B); the shuttle hook carries the thread loop on around under the bobbin case (C); loop of thread slides off hook on opposite side of bobbin (D); and the lockstitch is set in fabric by tension on needle and bobbin threads (E).

on the bobbin thread. The lock stitch is set into the fabric, as shown in Fig. 5-2E.

The shuttle hook then goes all the way around again as the needle passes through the layers of fabric, forming a loop in the needle or top thread that is again caught by the shuttle hook. The cycle is repeated for each lock stitch formed. Notice that the shuttle hook only picks up the loop on every other rotation. On the rotations in between, it drops the loop off on the other side of the bobbin.

The above description applies to sewing machines with rotary hook shuttle systems. The shuttle rotates in one direction only. Not all rotary hook shuttle systems are mounted sideways. There are also angled and horizontal arrangements.

A second type of shuttle system in common use is the *oscillating shuttle*. The lock stitch is formed in a manner similar to the rotary hook shuttle, with the main difference being that the oscillating shuttle oscillates back and forth. It picks up the loop from the needle or top thread on its forward motion and takes the loop completely around the bobbin, then releases the loop before starting back the opposite direction of rotation to return to position to pick up the next loop of thread. With both the rotary hook and oscillating shuttle systems, it's important to note that the bobbin and bobbin case remain stationary, only the shuttles rotate or move back and forth.

Although there are many differences in the design and construction of shuttle systems, the basic purpose is to take the loop of needle or top thread around over the bobbin so that it can loop the bobbin thread and form the lock stitch.

During each sewing cycle, various thread-control devices guide the needle or top thread and the bobbin or bottom thread. As the needle or top thread is unwound from a spool, it passes through various guides and then into disks that are specially designed to control the thread tension. Next, the thread passes through a *check spring*, which is behind the tension disks. This takes up the slack in the needle or top thread until the needle enters the fabric. The thread then passes through the *take-up lever*, an up and down moving lever that allows the loop of needle thread to form so that the shuttle hook can pick it up. The needle thread is kept in a loop by the shuttle until thread has encircled the bobbin thread, which is also under tension.

Another important part of a lock stitch machine is the *feed system*, which moves in time with the sewing cycles. This is what moves the fabric forward as the stitches are being formed.

The most common feed mechanism is the *drop feed*. When the needle is descending, the fabric is fed forward away from the operator by a toothed *feed dog* (Fig. 5-3). When the needle enters the fabric, the feed dog drops to a position below the needle plate surface, allowing the fabric to remain motionless while the stitch is being formed. As the needle starts upward, the feed dog moves backward toward the operator to its starting position. As the nee-

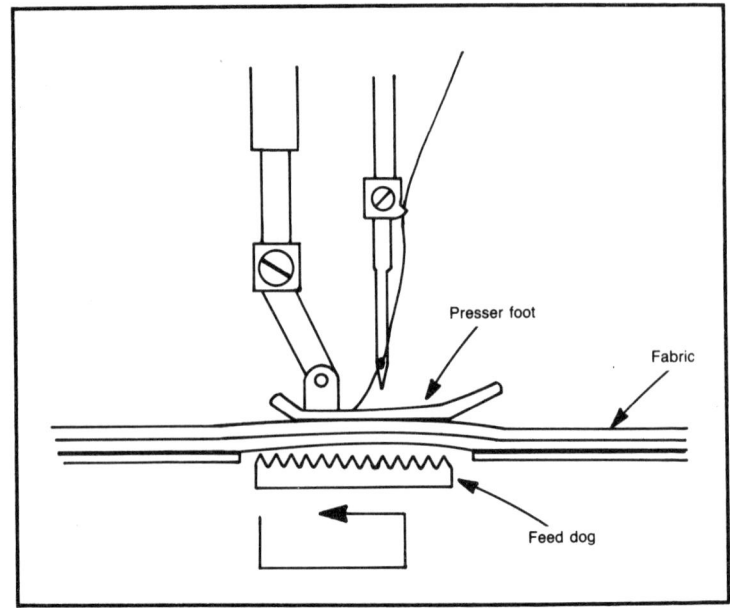

Fig. 5-3. Drop feed mechanism.

dle leaves the fabric, the feed dog rises again, gripping the fabric and moving it forward again, starting a new cycle.

A *walking foot feed* is a useful variation for canvas and upholstery work. In addition to the lower toothed feed dog, described above, there is an upper feed dog that comes down on the fabric when the needle rises out of the fabric. Both the upper and lower feed dogs draw the fabric through the machine at the same time, as shown in Fig. 5-4. This is generally a considerable advantage when sewing heavy canvas and upholstery fabrics, especially large pieces. The walking foot allows the fabric to feed through the machine in a consistent manner.

Thus, if you have a choice, the walking foot machine is usually best, but the regular drop feed mechanism will usually give satisfactory results. Slight inconsistency in stitch lengths generally isn't critical.

It should be noted that the fabric stops moving forward as the needle enters the fabric, and the fabric remains stationary until the needle leaves the fabric. The fabric actually moves forward in a stop, start, stop, start pattern, although this is difficult to see when the machine is operated at high speed. To observe the action, operate the machine slowly by hand.

There are also other feed mechanisms in use, including the *top-*

driven puller, which is basically a set of rollers mounted just in back of the needle, which turn in time with the feed dog to draw the fabric through the machine; and the *compound feed*, which is similar to the walking foot, except that the needle pivots from front to back while it is in the fabric. These feeds are not normally found on upholstery machines used by do-it-yourselfers, however.

All sewing mechanisms are activated by a *main shaft* that runs through the upper machine arm. This main drive shaft connects the *balance wheel* to the *needle bar*. The balance wheel, also called *hand wheel*, is attached to the right-hand end of the shaft and is usually driven by a belt.

The needle bar movement in the upper part of the machine and the shuttle and bobbin assembly and feed system in the lower part of the machine are controlled by a series of eccentric cams.

Some machines feature a *feed reverse*. This is basically an offset cam attached to the feed linking bar. The cam moves the feed bar in the direction opposite to that of forward direction when the reverse is activated. This is a handy feature, because it allows fixing the start and finish of a stitch without turning the material in the machine or tying square knots in the thread by hand.

The *bed* of the machine head is the flat portion that rests in

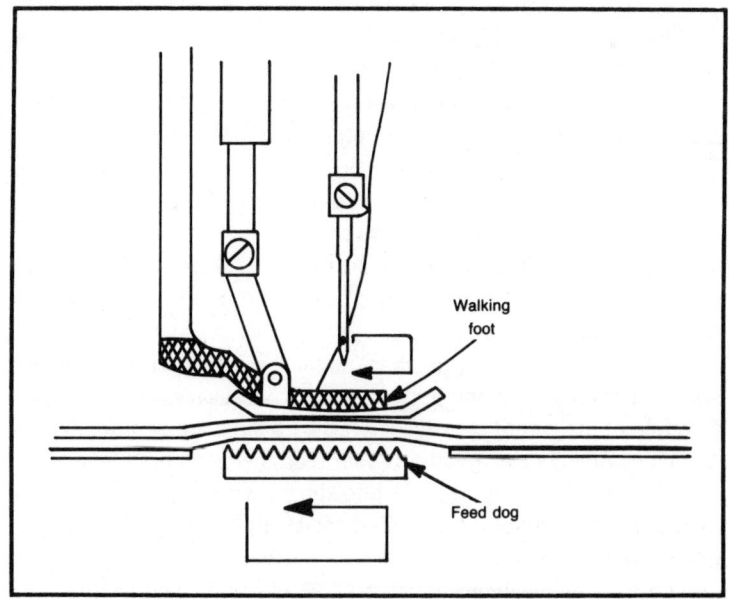

Fig. 5-4. A walking foot works in unison with lower feed dog to draw fabric through.

the cutout section of the sewing table. Its purpose is to support the *arm* and provide mountings for the parts upon which the fabric moves and the moving parts underneath, including the *bed shaft*, which extends horizontally and is supported by bearings. It is connected to the main drive shaft by a connecting rod, eccentric belts, or gears. The bed shaft drives the shuttle either directly or indirectly by connection to an auxiliary shaft.

The complete upper portion of the machine, including the arm and bed, is called the *head* or *power head* of the sewing machine.

Portable sewing machines usually come in cases, which allow the machines to be carried from place to place. These machines are usually placed on a table for use.

Other machines are mounted to a sewing or *power stand*. Most canvas and upholstery machines are of this type. Commercial machines usually have industrial tables and 1/3-horsepower or 1/2-horsepower clutch drive motors with variable speed foot controls. These machines usually also have a *thread stand*, which consists of a rod and base that is attached to the top of the right rear corner of the sewing table. In most cases, a light mounted on an adjustable flexible stand is mounted on the table behind the center portion of the power head. Some machines also feature a knee activated control raising up the presser bar. The *presser bar* is a vertical bar in the needle portion of the arm to which the presser foot is attached to the lower end.

Our concern to this point has been with straight-stitch sewing machines, but there are also machines that make zigzag and a variety of other stitches. A zigzag operates in a manner similar to a straight-stitch machine, except that the needle bar is mounted on a hinged bracket, which allows the needle bar to move not only up and down, but also from side to side. These machines are generally adjustable from a straight stitch to a certain maximum width of zigzag stitch.

Most canvas and upholstery sewing is done with a straight stitch. A zigzag machine generally isn't necessary, and there are a couple of disadvantages associated with such a machine. Zigzag machines rarely have a walking foot feed mechanism, which is extremely useful for canvas and upholstery sewing. Although zigzag machines can usually be adjusted for straight stitching, they are generally more complicated and expensive.

Lock-stitch machines have a number of supplemental parts. The needle bar is the vertical bar that carries the needle up and down. On the lower end is the *needle clamp*, with a clamping screw for holding the needle firmly in place to the needle bar.

A *throat* or *needle plate* is attached to the bed directly underneath the needle. There is a small hole for the passage of the needle and openings for movement of the feed dog.

The *presser bar* is a vertical bar that holds the presser foot at its lower end. The presser foot holds the fabric down to the bed during sewing. For canvas and upholstery work, you will need both a regular (Fig. 5-5) and zipper or *piping* foot. The zipper or piping presser foot allows sewing close to a zipper or piping cord.

The presser foot can be raised or lowered by means of a lever located in the rear of the arm called a *presser bar lifter*. Some machines also have a knee activated control for the presser bar. This is handy, as the presser foot can be raised or lowered without use of hands.

A bobbin is a small spool around which the bottom or lower thread is wound. The metal type can be rewound. Disposable paper and plastic types with bobbin thread prewound are also available.

Most machines have a *bobbin winder*, which is used for winding bobbins. A regulator adjusts the thread tension. Many bobbin winders have an automatic shutoff when the bobbin has the proper amount of thread wound on it.

For sewing, the bobbin is inserted in a bobbin case. Access is usually by means of a sliding plate on the bed of the machine.

PREPARATION FOR SEWING

A number of steps are required for getting ready for sewing. The machine must be properly threaded and adjusted. The fabric

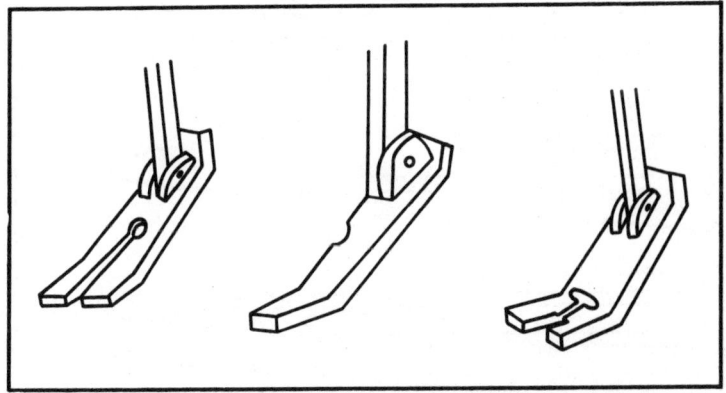

Fig. 5-5. Regular straight-stitch presser foot (left); zipper or piping foot (center); and zigzag foot (right).

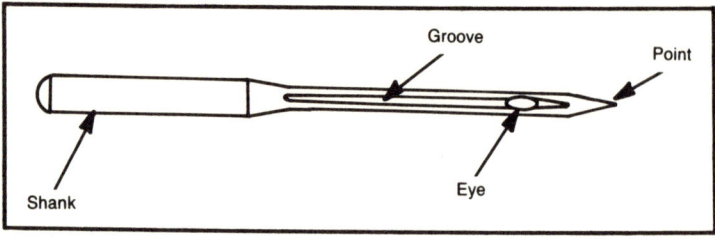

Fig. 5-6. Parts of a machine needle.

must be placed in position under the presser foot, the machine must be turned on, and so on.

Machine Needles

The needle must be of the correct length and shape to fit the particular machine. The instruction manual that comes with the machine gives information on the correct needle to fit the machine.

Figure 5-6 shows the parts of a machine needle. There are three basic types of points: *regular sharp, ball-point,* and *wedge-point* (Fig. 5-7). The regular sharp needle is ideal for all woven fabrics, including synthetic canvas fabrics. It produces an even stitching pattern with a minimum of fabric puckering or bunching up. The slightly rounded ball-point is used for knit and elastic fabrics so that the needle can push through the fabric yarns rather than piercing them. The wedge-point needle is designed for use on leather and vinyl coated fabrics. This point easily pierces these

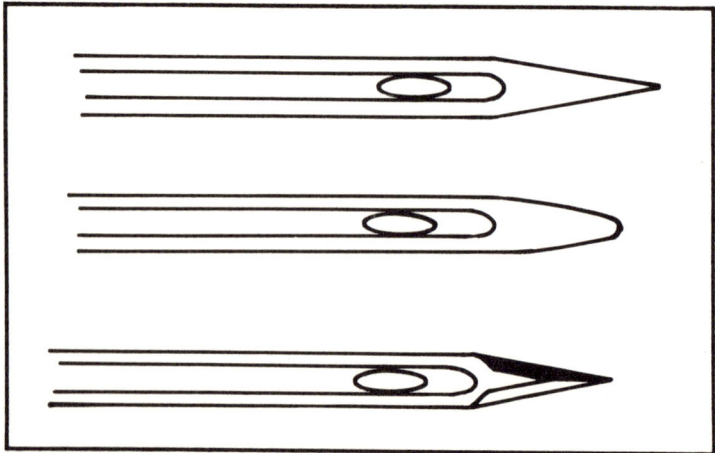

Fig. 5-7. Regular sharp-point needle (top); ball-point needle (center); and wedge-point needle (bottom).

fabrics, yet makes a hole that tends to close back and reduces the risk of stitches tearing the fabric.

Needles that fit a particular machine are available not only with choice of point types, but also in a range of sizes. The size of needle chosen for a particular sewing job depends on the weight and characteristics of the fabrics being sewn. In general, the needle should be fine enough to penetrate the fabric without making a hole larger than is necessary, yet have a large enough eye so that the thread does not fray or break. You will want to use the smallest size needle that will work with the thread and fabrics being sewn. The heavier the fabrics, the larger the needle size that should be used. The heavier the thread, the larger the needle size that should be used.

Table 5-1 is a guide to needle sizes for use with various weights of fabrics and thread sizes.

The needle is set in the needle-holding clamp so that the groove on the needle is facing the thread guide on the needle bar. The needle must also be the correct length and style for the particular machine. Check to make certain that the needle is straight and sharp (except for ball-point needles, which have a slightly rounded point).

To install a needle in the machine, first bring needle bar to its highest point by turning the *balance* or *hand wheel* slowly by hand. Next, loosen the clamping screw that holds the needle in the needle bar. Use a screwdriver for this. Remove old needle.

Table 5-1. Needle Sizes for Various Fabric Weights and Thread Sizes.

American	Metric	Fabric Weight	Thread Size
9	65	Delicate	100
10	70	Delicate	90
11	75	Delicate	80
12	80	Light	70
13	85	Light	60
14	90	Medium light	50
15	95	Medium	40
16	100	Medium	36
17	105	Medium heavy	30
18	110	Medium heavy	24
19	115	Heavy	20
20	120	Heavy	18
21	125	Heavy	16
22	130	Extra heavy	14
23	135	Extra heavy	12
24	140	Extra heavy	8

Most needles have a flat side on the shank. When inserting the needle into the needle bar, the flat side usually goes toward the right. Needle should be pushed up into the needle bar as far as it will go. Hold needle in place and tighten needle clamping screw with a screwdriver. Tighten firmly, but do not overtighten. Do not attempt to use a machine with a needle only part way up into the needle bar clamp. If this is the only way that the machine will make a stitch, the needle is the wrong length or style, or the machine is out of adjustment.

Some machines use needles with completely round shanks. These are installed in the needle bar so that the short scarf at the eye of the needle faces the point or hook of the shuttle. Needle should be pushed up into needle bar as far as it will go. Hold needle in place and tighten needle clamping screw with a screwdriver. Tighten firmly, but do not overtighten.

Although most upholstery machines will take up to a #24 needle size or larger, many home-type sewing machines will only take needles up to size #18.

The needle should be perfectly straight for proper sewing. Care must be taken not to bend the needle when installing it in the machine. Needles can also be bent or even broken by pulling fabric while sewing or sewing into metal fasteners or other solid materials.

To test the needle for straightness while it is mounted in the machine, place a piece of paper between the presser foot and throat plate, and hold it firmly against the throat plate in one position. Turn the balance wheel by hand so that the needle penetrates the paper, descends to its lowest point, then rises back out of the paper again. Remove the paper. If the needle made a small round hole, the needle is straight. If the hole is oblong, the needle is bent.

Needles can also be tested for straightness when not mounted in the machine. If the needle shank has a flat side, place this against the flat surface. If the needle is straight, there should be a perfectly even space between the needle shaft and the flat surface. If the needle is bent, there will be an irregular space.

If the needle has a round shank without a flat side, roll the round surface of the needle over a flat surface. If the needle is straight, the shaft of the needle will remain the same distance from the flat surface. If bent, the point of the needle will wobble up and down.

Threading the Machine

There are three main threading steps or jobs: bobbin winding, upper threading, and lower threading.

Bobbin Winding. Most sewing machines have a bobbin winder. Because these vary from machine to machine, carefully follow the instructions for using the bobbin winder that came with the machine.

Figure 5-8 shows a typical bobbin winder on an upholstery sewing machine. It is mounted so that the drive pulley is directly in front of the machine belt. The drive pulley should make firm contact with the belt when the thumb latch is pressed down, yet will release from contact with the belt when the bobbin has been wound with the proper amount of thread. The automatic stop mechanism is adjustable for more or less thread on the bobbin, usually by means of a turn screw.

An empty bobbin is placed on the spindle. In most cases, the same thread that is used for sewing will be used for winding the bobbin. Unthread the upper portion of the machine and pass the thread through the tension device of the bobbin winder. Then wind the end of the thread a few times around the bobbin so that it will wind on the bobbin without slipping.

Engage the driving pulley against belt by pressing down on thumb latch. Start sewing machine. With industrial machines, this usually involves two steps: engaging the start button on main switch panel and pressing down on the control with foot.

The bobbin winder should stop automatically when the bob-

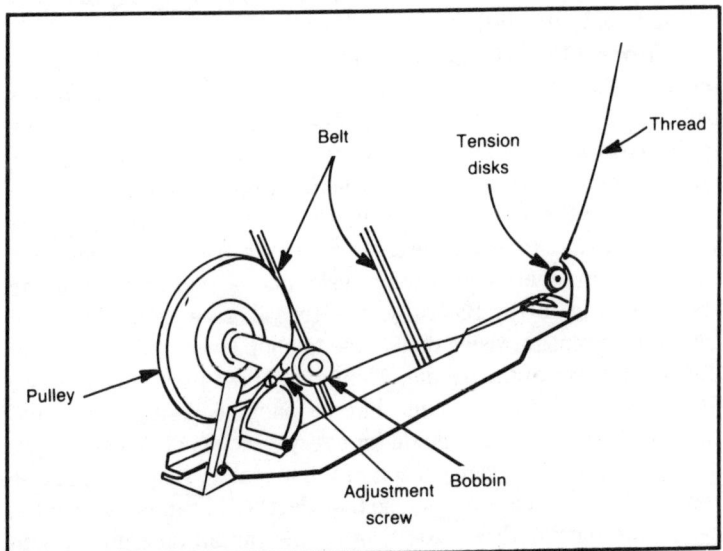

Fig. 5-8. Bobbin winder.

bin has proper amount of thread on it. If it doesn't, adjust turn screw. Usually, the screw is turned inward if more thread is desired; and outward if less thread is desired.

It may be necessary to adjust the tension device, especially if fine thread is used. The finer the thread, the lighter the tension.

The thread should wind evenly on the bobbin. If it winds unevenly, adjust the tension bracket so that the tension device lines up with the center of the bobbin. This is usually accomplished by loosening a screw holding the tension bracket and sliding the tension bracket left or right, as required. When the tension device is in the desired position, retighten the mounting screw.

Commercial upholstery suppliers can usually supply bobbins prewound on paper or plastic spools for upholstery sewing machines. This is convenient, though a little more expensive than winding your own bobbins. If you use the disposable type, make certain that they are wound with the same size and type of thread as you will be using for the upper threading. When machine stitching, the upper and lower threads form identical pattern on lock stitch. Thus, the strength and other physical properties of the bobbin thread should be the same as those of the upper thread.

Home-type sewing machines may have bobbin winding systems that differ considerably from those found on most upholstery machines. Carefully follow the instructions in the manual for the particular machine for winding bobbins and making adjustments on the bobbin winder.

Upper Threading. The threading progression for the upper portion of most rotary shuttle and oscillating shuttle machines is basically the same, although the location and appearance of the parts involved might differ. The instruction manual for a particular machine generally contains a threading diagram.

Figure 5-9 shows the threading of a typical sewing machine with *take-up lever* and *tension disks* on side of arm. Some machines have take-up levers and tension disks on the end of the arm, as shown in Fig. 5-10. Basically, the thread goes from the spool through the tension disks, then to the take-up lever, and then finally down to the eye of the needle. Along the thread path are a number of guides, which vary from machine to machine. As a general rule, there will be at least one guide for every 8 inches of thread travel.

To thread the upper portion of the machine, raise the presser foot. This will release tension so that the thread can be passed between the tension disks. Next, bring the thread take-up lever to the highest position by turning the balance wheel by hand. The top

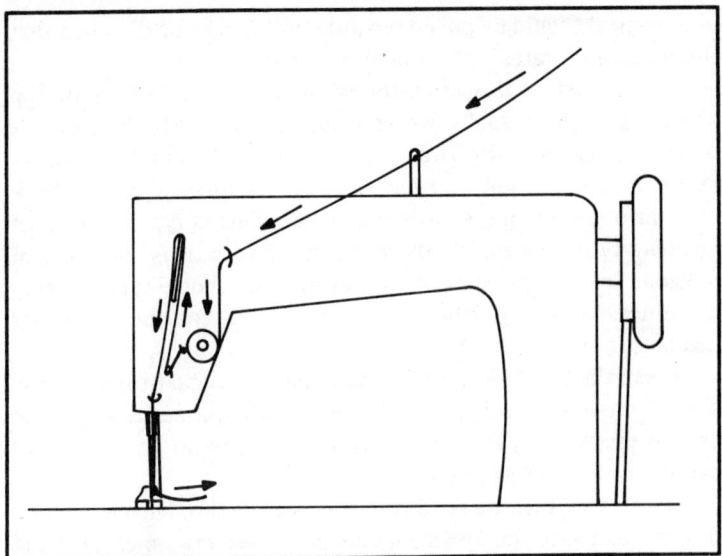

Fig. 5-9. Threading of a typical machine with take-up lever and tension disks on side of arm.

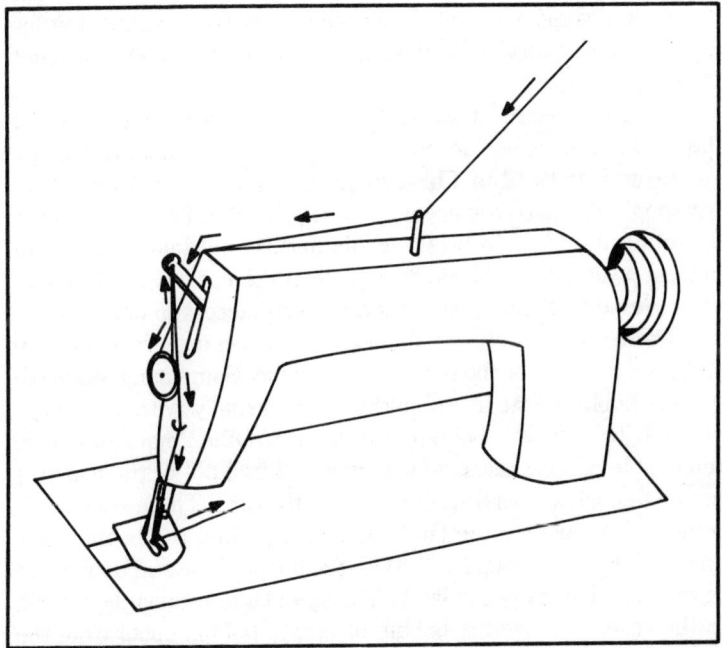

Fig. 5-10. Threading of typical machine with take-up lever and tension disks on end of arm.

71

of the wheel should be pulled toward you. This is the direction that the machine rotates during power operation.

Place spool of thread on thread stand or on spool pin on top of arm. Thread is usually passed through from one to three guides on way to tension disks. Draw thread down and around tension device from right to left on rotary shuttle machines and from back to front on oscillating shuttle machines. This is typical for most heavy-duty machines, but there are many variations and types of tension assemblies in use, especially on home-type sewing machines. Carefully follow the instructions for the particular machine.

Next, the thread is drawn around the thread guard and into the loop of the check spring. The thread usually passes through one or two guides on path upward to thread take-up lever. Thread passes through eye of take-up lever.

The thread then passes downward, usually through one or more thread guides, to the eye of the needle. Most machines have the needles threaded from left to right, but there are a few exceptions, so check the manual for the particular machine. A few older machines with vertical mounted shuttle systems thread from right to left. And some new machines with horizontal mounted shuttles that are located forward of the needle hole are threaded from front to back.

After the needle is threaded, draw out four or five inches of thread through the needle eye. This completes the upper threading.

Lower or Bobbin Threading. To remove the bobbin or bobbin spool to refill or replace it, first turn hand or balance wheel in operating direction to bring needle and thread take-up lever to highest positions and lift pressure foot. If there is any fabric in machine, remove it. Next, open slide plate for access to bobbin area.

There are a variety of bobbin assemblies in use. Follow the instruction manual for the particular machine. Some machines have drop-in bobbins that fit in built-in cases, usually with some type of latch to hold the bobbin in the case. Other machines have removable bobbin cases, which must be lifted out of the machine before the bobbin can be removed from the case. These are usually removed by opening the latch, and then pulling the bobbin case and bobbin out by open latch. With the bobbin case and bobbin out of the machine, close the latch. The open latch retains the bobbin in the case. Remove the bobbin or empty bobbin spool from the case. Either rewind the spool or use another wound bobbin.

Hold bobbin and bobbin case as shown in Fig. 5-11A and slip

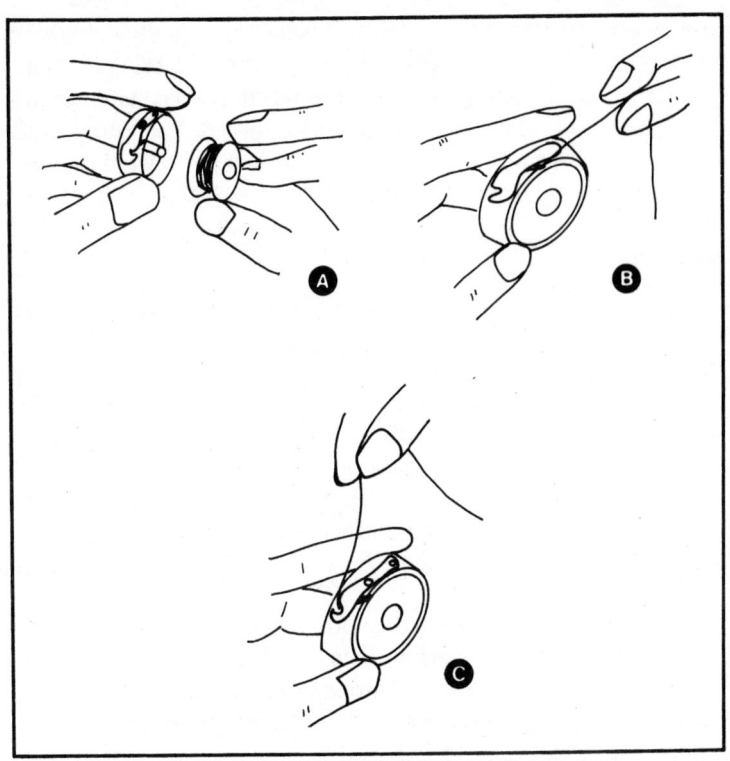

Fig. 5-11. Installing bobbin in machine. Bobbin is inserted in case (A); bobbin thread is pulled into slot (B); thread is drawn under bobbin case tension spring (C).

bobbin into case. Notice direction that bobbin thread is wound. Pull bobbin thread into the slot, as shown in Fig. 5-11B. Then draw thread under bobbin case tension spring, as shown in Fig. 5-11C. The bobbin case can then be inserted back into the machine.

There are also a number of other types of bobbin tension devices in use. For example, some have neither a slot opening nor a tension spring and use a special latch or some other method to control the flow of bobbin thread.

After the bobbin has been threaded and inserted in machine, close the slide plate. The next step is raising the bobbin thread. This is done without fabric in the machine and the presser foot in raised position. Hold needle thread with thumb and forefinger of left hand, as shown in Fig. 5-12A. Turn hand wheel in operating direction of machine with right hand. Continue until needle is all the way down. Then draw it back up. If everything was done properly, a loop of bobbin thread should come up with upper thread, as shown in Fig. 5-12B. Pull on the upper thread to bring up more bobbin thread. Then release upper thread, and pull on loop of bobbin thread to bring up free end of bobbin thread. Then draw both the upper and lower thread ends under the foot and toward the rear of the machine. The thread ends should be at least 3 inches long.

SEWING

The machine should now be ready for sewing. Place fabric under presser foot and lower the foot. Always make sure that the needle will go through the fabric; do not sew unless fabric is under the needle. Always stop sewing before the needle goes off the fabric.

Operating a sewing machine requires considerable coordination. The movement of both hands controlling the fabric must be coordinated with the foot operation of the sewing machine accelerator. Most upholstery machines have a variable speed control. Slight pressure and the machine runs slowly; greater pressure and the machine runs faster.

A suggested starting exercise for anyone who hasn't had experience using a sewing machine is to practice with a piece of scrap fabric about a foot square. Turn on the power switch to the machine. Allow motor to accelerate. Then press foot control to start

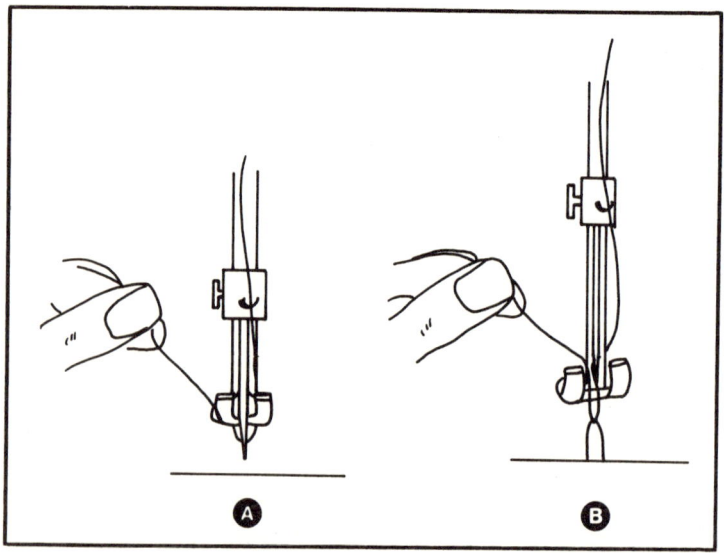

Fig. 5-12. Bringing bobbin thread up: thread is held with thumb and forefinger of left hand (A); loop of bobbin thread is brought up (B).

sewing. Try to press lightly so that the machine sews slowly. This is generally difficult to do at first, as the tendency is to put too much pressure on the foot control and sew at "ninety miles an hour." At first, it might seem that there isn't any speed in between.

When you get near the edge of the fabric, release foot pressure to stop sewing. Fabric can be turned with presser foot down while sewing, but not when stationary. To turn fabric, bring needle to lowest position by turning hand wheel if needle isn't already in this position. The needle can also be brought to lowest position by foot control, but this requires considerable practice before it can be done consistently.

With the needle through fabric and in its lowest position, raise presser foot. Turn fabric to desired new direction. Then lower presser foot. You are then ready to start sewing again.

Try to learn to sew at any desired speed with control. For the first several hours of practice, it might seem that the sewing machine has a mind of its own, but gradually this will change, and you will gain more and more control. The basic idea is to be able to sew at any desired speed and yet be able to stop when you want to, such as when you are about to sew off the fabric.

Figure 5-13 shows the proper hand positions on the fabric for sewing. Always let the machine do the work. Never push or pull the fabric through the machine. The purpose of the hands is to guide the fabric. The sewing machine feed mechanism draws the fabric through the machine.

It is generally most convenient to stitch a seam on the right-hand side of the fabrics, as shown in Fig. 5-13. If the machine has a seam guide, it is usually arranged for sewing in this manner. This method also allows sewing large pieces of fabric without having to fold them up to fit under the sewing machine arm.

Practice sewing two pieces of fabric together with a seam on the right-hand side one half inch from the edges of the fabric. The desired finished or right side of the two pieces of fabric should be face to face. Make a chalk line one half inch from the edge of the back side of the top layer of fabric to use as a guide. The chalk should have a chisel edge. Use a straightedge to make a straight line. When sewing, the right hand guides the fabric to sew along the line; the left hand rests lightly on the fabric. Control the direction of the stitching, but let the machine feed the fabric.

If the sewing machine has a reverse, the start of the seam is usually fixed by first sewing in reverse for a short distance. Then at the edge of the seam, switch to forward and make seam. If the

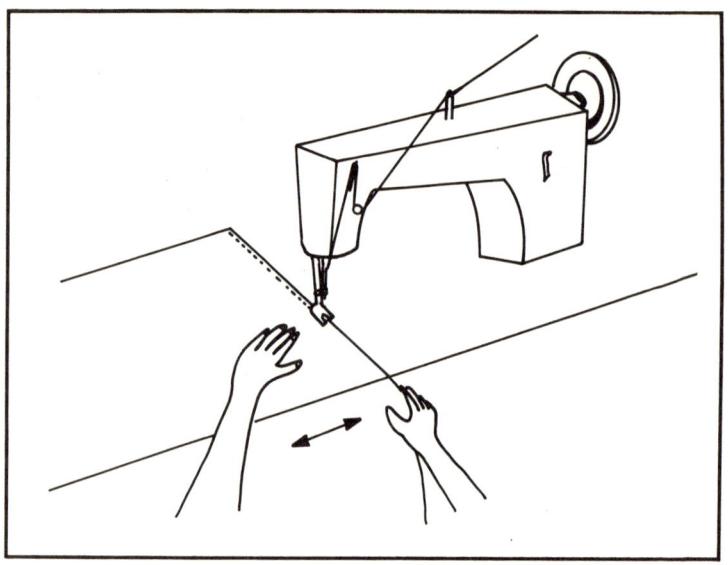

Fig. 5-13. Proper hand position for machine sewing. Stitching is usually done on right hand side of fabric.

machine does not have a reverse, start with the fabric turned around in the machine with the needle centered about 3/4 inch from the edge of the fabric. Then sew to near the edge of the fabric. With needle in lowest position, raise presser foot and turn fabric around. Lower presser foot and then make seam.

End of seam can be fixed by reverse sewing on machines that have reverse mechanisms. After sewing back along the seam a short distance, stop the machine. If the machine does not have a reverse, turn the fabric around in the machine, as detailed above, and sew back along the seam about 3/4 inch.

After seam is completed, stop machine. If needle is not in highest position, turn hand wheel until it is. Then raise presser foot. The presser foot should only be raised when the machine is not operating; never while you are sewing. Pull out three or four inches of upper and lower thread, then cut off threads close to the fabric with scissors or thread cutter. Pull the upper and lower thread ends from the machine under the presser foot and toward the rear of the machine so that you are ready for sewing again.

Next, draw a circle pattern with chalk on a foot square piece of fabric. Use a round object such as a plate or pan as a pattern. Next, place the fabric in the machine so that the needle is directly over one part of the line. Then lower the presser foot. As the fabric feeds through the sewing machine, gently pull it to the right to keep the stitching on the circle line. If done properly, the stitches should closely follow the line. Continue to practice until you can control the fabric to the circle pattern. Remember, guide the direction of the fabric by moving it gently right or left. Do not attempt to push or pull the fabric through the machine.

Next, make a figure-eight pattern on a scrap piece of fabric. Place the fabric in the machine so that the needle is directly over one part of the line. Then lower the presser foot. Grip the fabric as for sewing the circle pattern. Start sewing. This time you will need to pull the fabric gently to either the right or left, depending on what part of the figure-eight you are sewing on. If done properly, the stitches should closely follow the line. Continue to practice until you can control the fabric through the figure-eight pattern. Remember, guide the direction of the fabric by moving it gently right or left. Do not attempt to push or pull the fabric through the machine.

This is similar to sawing with a power jigsaw. The blade remains pointed in one direction. You saw a pattern by guiding the forward part of the wood right or left. You generally have to also push the wood forward at the same time, while the sewing machine does this for you automatically by means of a feed mechanism.

The sewing machine can be thought of as a device that sews straight ahead. The fabric can be turned as desired, but the sewing machine continues to sew straight ahead. You control where this straight-ahead pattern of stitches will be on the fabric by pulling the forward edge of the fabric to the right or left or holding it straight, as required. Notice that if you move the forward edge of the material to the right while sewing, the stitching moves to your left on the fabric. In turn, if you move the forward edge of the fabric to the left while sewing, the stitch pattern moves to your right on the fabric.

Another fundamental technique that should be learned is making turns about a point, that is, the needle. These can be to any desired new direction. For practice, mark the pattern shown in Fig. 5-14 on scrap piece of fabric. Sew along one of the straight lines until the needle is over the exact point where the turn is to be made. You may want to stop a stitch or two short of this point and make the last stitches by turning the hand wheel. At the exact point, you want the needle through the fabric and in its lowest position. Then, with your foot off the accelerator, raise the presser foot. Turn the fabric to the desired new direction. Lower the presser foot. Then continue sewing along new line. Continue practice with remainder of pattern.

If the sewing machine you are using doesn't have a reverse feature, this same method can be used for fixing the beginning or end of a stitch by backtracking. Sewing a few stitches in the reverse direction helps to ensure that stitches won't pull loose so that the seam opens up. This also makes it unnecessary to tie off the seam by tying knots in top and bottom threads by hand.

Of course, if the sewing machine has a reverse feature, this can be done by starting forward of desired beginning of seam in reverse. When needle reaches desired beginning of seam, switch to forward and continue sewing. At the end of the desired seam, switch to reverse and backtrack along the seam for a short distance.

The same thing is accomplished on a machine without a reverse feature, although it takes longer and is less convenient, by reversing the fabric in the machine from the desired direction for sewing the seam. Sew a short distance along desired seam line to desired start of seam. When needle reaches this point, take your foot off accelerator, use hand wheel to bring needle through fabric to lowest position in sewing cycle if it isn't already there, raise presser foot, and turn fabric all the way around until it faces direction for sewing desired seam. Next, lower presser foot, sew the seam. At end of seam, take foot off accelerator, use hand wheel to bring needle through fabric to lowest position in sewing cycle if it isn't already there, raise presser foot, and turn fabric all the way around until

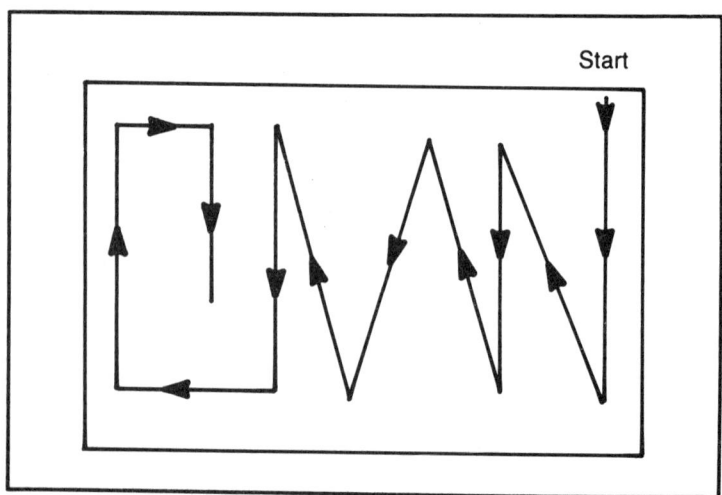

Fig. 5-14. Pattern for practice sewing.

it faces direction for backtracking along seam. Lower presser foot. Sew a short distance beside original seam.

Fixing the ends of seams should be practiced until it becomes habit. If this is not done, there is a much greater possibility of seams opening up on canvas and upholstery projects.

The importance of correct needle and thread size for the particular fabric being sewn has already been pointed out. Stitch length is another related factor. Almost all modern sewing machines allow adjustment of stitch length, usually by a dial or lever control. As a general rule, the heavier the fabric, the wider the spacing of stitching. For lightweight fabrics such as those typically used for boat and recreational vehicle curtains, 10 to 12 stitches per inch is generally about right. For heavier fabrics, 6 to 10 stitches per inch is typical. About 6 stitches per inch is generally used for vinyl coated fabrics to reduce the risk of tearing the material and to make fewer needle holes.

Before sewing a fabric, test and, if necessary, adjust the combination of needle, thread, and stitch length by sewing sample layers of the fabric. If possible, use the same number of layers as you will be sewing. Do not, however, adjust stitch length while the machine is running.

Here are some "do's and don'ts" for operating a sewing machine:

- Do not sew without fabric under presser foot and needle.
- The slide cover over the bobbin area should be closed when sewing.
- Do not run the machine with the presser foot in the raised position.
- Do not raise the presser foot while the machine is running, such as by working knee control.
- Let the machine do the work. Do not attempt to push or pull the fabric through the machine.

Before going into some basic seams, it is important to understand basic sewing machine problems, their cures, and how to make adjustments and simple repairs.

TROUBLESHOOTING, ADJUSTMENTS, AND SIMPLE REPAIRS

In the case of most sewing machines, it usually doesn't take long before something goes wrong. It is uneconomical and usually unnecessary to call a service technician every time something goes wrong. The same applies to making adjustments and simple repairs and routine maintenance.

Upper and Lower Thread Tensions

When the upper and lower thread tensions are correct, the two threads interlock midway between the layers or layer of fabric, as shown in Fig. 5-15. Also, the seam should look the same on both sides of the fabric. If the fabrics pucker, the problem could be that both tensions are too tight.

If the upper tension is too tight or the lower tension is too loose, the lock stitch is incorrectly made, with the upper thread flat on

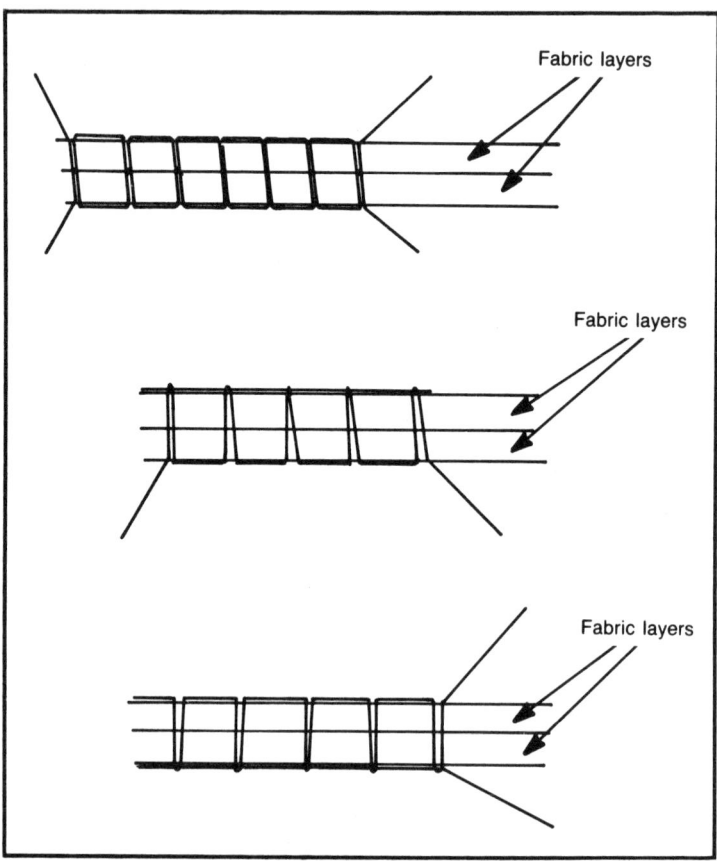

Fig. 5-15. When upper and lower thread tensions are correct, threads interlock midway in fabric (top). Stitching pattern when upper tension is too tight or lower tension is too loose (center). Stitching pattern when upper tension is too loose or lower tension is too tight (bottom).

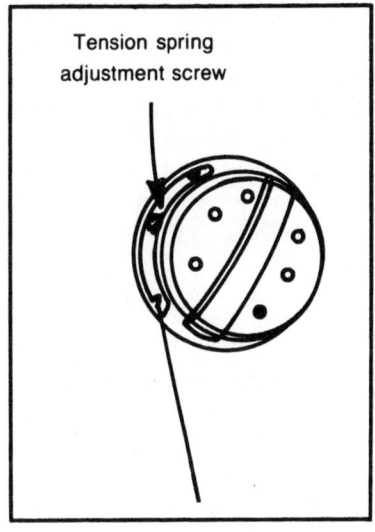

Fig.5-16. Tension spring adjustment screw.

top of the fabric and the lower thread drawn up to the surface to form small knots, as shown in Fig. 5-15.

When the upper tension is too loose or the lower tension too tight, the lock stitch is incorrectly made, with the lower thread flat on bottom of the fabric and the upper thread drawn through the fabric to form small knots on the lower surface, as shown in Fig. 5-15.

Almost every sewing machine has a tension control adjustment for the upper thread, and most machines also have one for the bobbin. In most cases, however, only the upper tension requires adjustment. This is adjusted so that it is balanced with the lower tension to form a perfect lock stitch, that is, with the link formed by each stitch midway between fabric layers.

The upper thread tension is usually adjusted by a dial or thumb nut located on or near the tension disks, although the location varies on different machines. Turning the thumb nut clockwise usually increases the tension; counterclockwise decreases it. With a dial adjustment, a higher number usually increases tension; a lower number decreases it.

If adjustment in stitch tension and balance is not possible by upper tension control, it may be necessary to adjust lower or bobbin thread tension. Adjustment is usually made by a screw on the tension spring of bobbin case (see Fig. 5-16). Thread bobbin case before making adjustment. To increase tension, turn screw clockwise. To decrease tension, turn screw counterclockwise. Use a small blade screwdriver for turning screw. If there are two screws on tension spring, adjustment is made by turning the screw nearest the center of spring, not the one on the end.

Before starting canvas or upholstery sewing, test tension adjustment by sewing the type of fabric and same number of layers as will be used. If tension is incorrect, make necessary adjustments. Usually, this can be accomplished by upper tension adjustment alone. In some cases, an adjustment in the lower tension will be necessary.

Feed Dogs and Presser Foots

The correct amount of presser foot pressure is important for even feeding and correct stitching without damaging the fabric. The presser foot functions to hold the fabric being sewn against the throat plate and feed dog with the required pressure for the formation of a good needle thread loop and so that the feed dog (and walking foot on machines with this feature) will feed the fabric through the machine at the desired distance between needle penetrations.

The amount of pressure required depends mainly on the weight of the fabric being sewn. As a general rule, the lighter the weight of the fabric, the less pressure required by the presser foot. The heavier the weight of the fabric, the greater the pressure required by the presser foot. This applies to the weight of all layers of fabric being sewn together.

Correct pressure gives stitches that are even in length and tension (assuming proper thread tension adjustments) and does not damage the fabric. Too much pressure can cause top layers of fabric to slip while bottom layers gather up, often with stitches of uneven length and tension. Too little pressure can result in poor control over guidance of fabric layers, skipped or uneven stitches, and even the pulling of fabric into the bobbin area.

Correct pressure allows the operator to swing the fabric while continuing to sew without raising the presser foot. This freedom of operation is very important. The main point is that the presser foot pressure can be too little or too great, and proper adjustment is important.

Most machines have a pressure regulator for adjusting the pressure exerted by presser foot. The adjustment may be by means of a dial, a push bar with a lock-release collar around it, or a screw-type regulator. On the dial-type, turning the dial to a higher number gives greater pressure; to a lower number gives less pressure. On the push bar-type, increase pressure by releasing collar lock, push down on push bar, and lock collar in place. In turn, when pressure bar is brought up, pressure is released. Screw-type regulators are usually turned counterclockwise to decrease pressure and clockwise to increase pressure.

Actually, it is two forces, the presser foot and the feed dogs, that must work together to produce correctly stitched seams. The feed, whether a common drop feed mechanism or a walking foot, is controlled by the stitch length regulator that moves the fabric into position for each stitch. For short stitches, the fabric moves only a short distance between each stitch. For long stitches, the fabric moves a longer distance between each stitch. The fabric is stationary when the needle penetrates the fabric. The feed also functions to hold the layers of fabric taut during the formation of stitches.

The pressure exerted by the presser foot, which serves to hold the fabric layers so that they move evenly during stitch formation, is *downward* (Fig. 5-17). This pressure is supplied by a spring. This can be adjusted by the pressure regulator, as detailed previously.

The feed serves to move the fabric under the presser foot. In the case of the common drop feed mechanism, the force is *upward*. With a walking foot, there is also a downward force. The stitch length regulator controls the feed.

The interaction between the feed and pressure is vital for proper stitch formation. Both the feed and the presser foot serve to hold the fabric taut while the needle and thread penetrate the fabric. As the needle comes downward, the feed dog drops downward away from contact with the fabric, leaving only presser foot contact with the fabric.

As the needle is drawn out of the fabric, the feed dog is moving forward without contact with the fabric. The presser foot maintains contact with the fabric.

As the needle leaves the fabric, bringing the stitch with it, the feed dog moves upward to contact the fabric, while the presser foot maintains contact with the fabric.

While the stitch is being set into the fabric layers, the feed dog interacts with the presser foot to advance the fabric one stitch length and to hold the fabric taut.

A walking foot is essentially an upper feed dog that works in conjunction with the lower feed dog. This generally improves the feeding of heavy canvas and upholstery fabrics.

The feed dogs seldom require height or position adjustment.

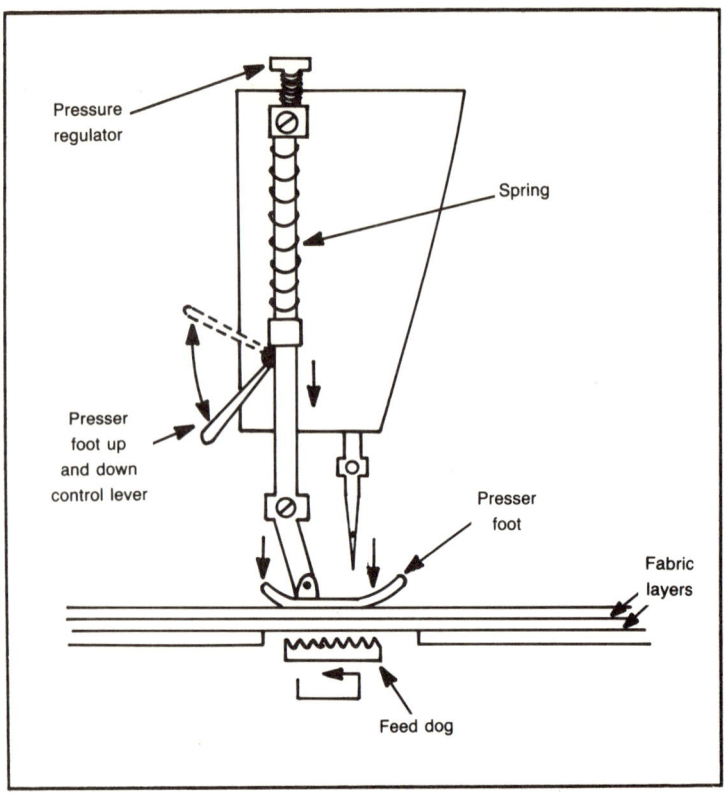

Fig. 5-17. Pressure exerted by presser foot during stitching is downward.

There usually isn't any simple control for making adjustments, so if adjustments are required, this job is generally left to an experienced sewing machine mechanic.

A variety of presser foot types are available. Figure 5-5 shows a straight stitch foot, which is generally best for straight stitching even when using a machine with zigzag stitching capabilities. A zigzag presser foot can also be used for straight stitching. A zipper or piping foot (Fig. 5-5) is useful in canvas and upholstery work for sewing close to zippers and piping.

Presser foots are attached and changed in various manners. A screw attachment is typical. Some machines have snap-in-place attachment.

There are also a number of related attachments, such as *roller foot feed assist attachment* and *buttonhole attachments.* I have found a *binder attachment,* which positions the fabric and binding so that they are simultaneously positioned and fed through the machine for stitching together, and a *seam gauge* (Fig. 5-18), which is attached to the machine bed and can be adjusted desired distance from needle for use as a guide, to be useful for canvas and upholstery work.

Cleaning and Oiling

To properly maintain a sewing machine and ensure flawless operation, regular cleaning and lubrication is essential. For cleaning, a solvent such as kerosene can be used. This can be applied with a small stiff paint brush or toothbrush. You also need soft clean rags.

A quality, brand name sewing machine oil should be used. Follow instructions that come with the machine for oiling. Most machines have a number of *oil holes*. In general, oil should be added after about ten hours of machine use. There will also be a number of points where one metal surface rubs against or turns against another metal surface where oil should be applied. Always wipe excess oil up with a rag so that it will not collect dust and dirt. Do not apply oil to tension disks or springs. The instruction manual that comes with the particular machine should be followed as to where to and not to apply oil. Do not go overboard on oiling. Too little oil can cause excess noise and wear, but too much oil can cause gumming up and serve as a trap for dirt and grit.

When dirt and grit does collect, or the oil gums up, clean with solvent. Wipe dry with clean soft rag. Then apply fresh oil.

Tools

A few tools are required for servicing and simple repairs.

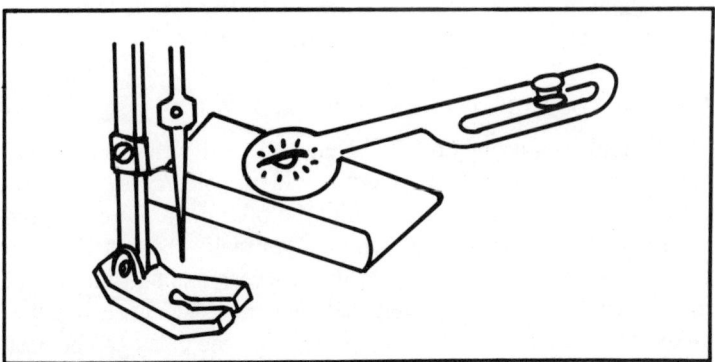

Fig. 5-18. Seam gauge.

Screwdrivers. A variety of sizes and types of screwdrivers is useful. You will at least need a small, narrow screwdriver that will fit the screw for adjusting the thread tension spring on the bobbin case and a larger screwdriver about 6 inches long with a 3/16-inch wide blade.

Pliers. A variety of sizes and types of pliers is useful. Small long-nosed pliers will find many uses.

Hammers. A light hammer is useful.

Pointed Objects. A long pin and a small awl are both useful.

Knife. A small knife will find many uses. This can be a pocketknife or a small knife with a wood or plastic handle fixed to blade.

Tweezers. Tweezers are useful for a variety of jobs, such as clearing thread from behind a bobbin case and so on.

You will probably need other tools, but these can be added as a need develops. The above will serve for most routine servicing and some minor repair work.

Timing a Sewing Machine

If the sewing machine gets out of time, that is, the interaction between the needle and shuttle is off, you will probably want to leave the readjustment to a professional sewing machine mechanic. The manuals that come with some machines give adequate instructions for doing this yourself, though. Some machines have timing marks, which makes adjustments fairly easy. The main idea is that the needle must be in correct position in relation to shuttle hook during the sewing cycle. Correct setting of both rotary hook and oscillating shuttle machines is similar. Usually, after the needle has risen 3/32 of an inch above the lowest point, the shuttle hook or point should be 1/16 inch above the top of the eye of the needle and just opposite the center line of the needle.

Troubleshooting

A number of problems may be encountered with a sewing machine that will slow down canvas and upholstery sewing. By troubleshooting—that is, identifying the problem and making the necessary corrections or adjustments yourself—these delays can be kept to a minimum. On the other hand, if you don't know how to solve the problem and have to call on a professional sewing machine mechanic to take care of the problem, the delay can be both long and expensive.

The purpose here is to point out some of the most common sewing machine ailments and how to make necessary repairs and adjustments.

Needle Thread Breaks. Most common causes are needle being inserted backwards and needle being threaded backwards. Check to make certain that needle groove faces the thread guide on the needle bar. If not, loosen screw clamp, turn needle so that groove faces the thread guide on the needle bar, and then tighten screw clamp. This applies to most machines, but check the manual for the particular machine to make certain that this applies.

Make certain that the needle is threaded correctly. Check the manual for the particular machine. Most machines have the thread passing through the eye of the needle from left to right, but there are some exceptions, especially on older machines. Some late model machines with a horizontal mounted shuttle thread from front to back.

Another cause of the needle thread breaking is that the thread is caught on the spool or spindle or somewhere along the path to needle. With the presser foot raised and the thread take-up lever in the highest position, make sure that the thread can be pulled freely out of the eye of the needle. If not, determine where the thread is catching and make corrections as required.

The needle should be all the way up into the clamp. If not, this could be cause of needle thread breaking. Loosen clamp, push needle all the way up into clamp, and retighten the clamp.

The needle thread might be breaking because the needle size is too small for the thread being used. Replace needle with a larger size or use smaller thread.

Rough areas on thread guides and needle eye sometimes cause thread to break. Repair or replace thread guides. Replace needle.

The needle might be bent or the point might be blunt. Insert new needle if this appears to be the problem.

Too much tension on the upper thread might cause the thread to break. Loosen tension by adjusting tension control of tension disks.

The machine might not be threaded correctly. Make certain that thread follows correct path from spool to needle.

The problem might be with the thread itself. It might be too weak, of irregular shape, or too large for the needle being used. Replace inferior thread with quality thread.

A more serious problem is a bent needle bar. If needle does not pass through center of hole in throat plate, this might be the problem. If needle bar is bent, it usually needs to be replaced, a job that is best left to a professional sewing machine mechanic.

Check for possible rough or burred places on presser foot, needle eye, throat plate, and shuttle hook or point.

Bobbin Thread Breaks. Most common cause of bobbin thread breaking is incorrect threading and not inserting bobbin case properly. Check this first.

Another cause of bobbin thread breaking is that the bobbin thread tension is too tight. Loosen tension by adjusting screw on tension spring.

Winding the bobbin too full does not allow it to revolve freely in bobbin case, which can cause the bobbin thread to break. Remove some of the thread from the bobbin and see if this cures the bobbin thread breaking problem.

An accumulation of dirt and lint in the bobbin case can also be cause of bobbin thread breakage. Remove case and bobbin from machine. Remove bobbin from case. Clean case with kerosene. Dry thoroughly. Then install bobbin in case and case in machine.

Rough areas around the needle hole in throat plate might be the problem. Smooth hole with fine file or replace throat plate, as required.

The bobbin spool might be bent or damaged. If this appears to be the problem, try a new bobbin. Or the bobbin case could be damaged, the repair of which is usually best left to a professional sewing machine mechanic.

The problem might be the bobbin thread itself. It might be too weak or of poor quality. Replace inferior thread with quality thread.

Needle Breaks. In some cases the cause is obvious, such as accidentally sewing into a metal fastener. Forcing fabric under the needle can cause needle breakage from it striking throat plate. Allow the machine to feed the fabric; do not attempt to pull it through.

A loose or improperly fastened throat plate or presser foot can also cause the needle to break. This could allow the needle to strike the throat plate or presser foot. Cure problem by making certain that throat plate and presser foot are properly installed.

A bent needle can also break from striking the throat plate or presser foot. Install new needle.

Problem might be using too fine a needle for the fabric being sewn. Try a larger size needle.

The needle point might be blunt. The needle can break because it is unable to penetrate the fabric. Replace needle.

Needle might be improperly installed in machine. Make certain that it is inserted all the way up into the needle clamp on the lower end of the needle bar.

When a needle breaks, remove the remainder from needle clamp and install new needle. If cause of needle breaking is unknown, turn machine by hand and make certain that needle does not hit anything.

Needle Unthreads. The most common cause is that insufficient thread is pulled through the needle before seam is started. Pull at least three inches of thread out before starting seam.

The machine can also come unthreaded when the machine is out of top thread. The problem may actually be breaking the thread in the eye of the needle. Follow steps given above for "Needle thread breaks."

Stitches Are Uneven Lengths. Make certain that you are allowing the machine to feed the fabric, without pulling it through the machine or holding it back. Another cause is too little or too much pressure on the presser foot. Adjust as necessary.

On machines with a stitch regulator screw, the screw may be loose, allowing control to vibrate. Correct problem by tightening stitch regulator screw to desired position.

The teeth on the feed dog might be dull or worn. Repair or replacement is usually best left to professional sewing machine mechanic.

Skipped Stitches. The most common cause is the wrong type or size of needle for the particular machine. Use needle recommended for the particular machine.

Inserting the needle backwards or not all the way up into the clamp can also cause skipped stitches. Make certain that the needle is installed properly.

A blunt or bent needle can also cause skipped stitches. Replace needle.

The eye of the needle can clog with lint or sizing from fabrics. Either clean the needle or change it.

There might not be enough pressure on the presser foot. Adjust presser foot.

Some machines tend to skip stitches when operated at an uneven speed. Try steady sewing speed.

Pulling fabric through feed or holding it back can also cause skipped stitches. Practice correct sewing techniques, as detailed previously.

Still another cause is using upper thread that is too heavy or of uneven thickness. Use quality thread of the correct size for the needle being used and fabric being sewn.

Loops on Top of Fabric. If the needle or upper thread lies flat on the top of the fabric and the lower thread forms loops there, the cause is likely to be that upper tension is too tight and/or lower tension is too loose. Adjust thread tensions until they are correctly balanced, as detailed previously.

Other possible causes are bent or damaged bobbin case tension spring and accumulation of lint or pieces of thread under bobbin case tension spring.

Loops on Underside of Fabric. If the bobbin or lower thread lies flat on the underside of the fabric and the upper thread forms loops there, the cause is likely to the that upper thread tension is too loose or lower thread tension is too tight. Adjust thread tensions until they are correctly balanced, as detailed previously.

Other possible causes are accumulation of dirt, lint, or pieces of thread between tension disks, grooves cut into the tension disks up upper thread, a bent or damaged bobbin spool that does not revolve freely in bobbin case, and timing problems in the sewing cycle, such as needle cycle out of time with loop taker and feed dog operating too early.

Loose Stitches. If the stitching is loose, the most likely cause is that the machine is not correctly threaded.

The problem could also be in the upper tension or thread take-up mechanisms. Repair generally involves replacement of defective parts and is usually done by a professional sewing machine mechanic. The problem can also be using too light or too heavy upper thread. Use quality thread of the correct size for the fabric being sewn and the needle size being used.

Fabric Does Not Feed Properly. If the layers of fabric do not feed evenly, the pressure of the presser foot might be too light or too heavy. Increase or decrease pressure by making adjustment as detailed previously.

Sewing canvas and upholstery fabrics with a common drop feed mechanism could be inadequate. A walking foot feed is highly recommended. Various feed attachments available for most machines can also be helpful.

With large pieces of heavy fabric, work the fabric to the machine so that the fabric does not bind or hang up on the sewing table or elsewhere and is free to feed. It may also help to sew more slowly.

If the fabric does not feed in a straight line, the presser foot may be loose or bent. If loose, tighten mounting screw. If bent, it might be possible to straighten it, but replacement is usually called for.

The pressure of the presser foot might be too light or too heavy. Adjust as necessary.

Other possible causes are bent needle and pushing or pulling fabric instead of letting machine do feeding. The problem could also be a defective feed mechanism. Repair or replacement is generally best left to a professional sewing machine mechanic.

Fabric Puckers When Stitched. There are many possible causes. Stitch length may be too short. The thread might be too heavy for the fabric or the needle too large or coarse. The stitch tensions might be unbalanced, or the bobbin could be wound unevenly. The feed dog could be out of time, the adjustment of which is usually best left to a professional sewing machine mechanic.

Fabric Is Marked or Damaged During Sewing. If marks from teeth of feed dog show on fabric, the pressure of the presser foot might be too heavy. Adjust as required. If this does not cure problem, the feed dogs could be set too high or damaged. Adjustment or repair is generally best left to a professional sewing machine mechanic.

If fabric is snagged or has holes around the stitches, the cause might be a needle with a blunt or burred point or the wrong type of point for the fabric being sewn. Replace needle. Another possible cause is a burr on presser foot, feed dogs, or by the needle hole in throat plate. Smooth area or replace damaged parts.

Heat generation is another cause of fabric damage. This is caused by friction between needle and fabric, especially when sewing certain types fabric. Possible solutions are to use special needles that reduce areas of contact, the use of needle lubricants, and the use of thread lubricants.

Machine Problems. If the sewing machine motor will not run, the most likely problem is that the cord is not plugged in or is not plugged into a live plug outlet. Plug in a lamp to see if you have a live outlet.

On most upholstery machines, there is a power switch that must be turned on. Often, there is a "start" button and a "stop" button. The foot accelerator or treadle might be jammed or have a poor connection with power source.

If the above do not seem to be the problem, there could be a broken or loose wire in the circuit, or the problem might be in the motor itself. Repair is generally left to a professional sewing machine mechanic.

If the motor runs, but the hand wheel does not turn, thread might be caught or jammed in the bobbin case area. Remove tangled thread. Turning hand wheel back and forth by hand will usually help to loosen thread. Tweezers can be used for removing pieces of thread. After thread has been removed, add a drop of sewing machine oil to the bobbin case housing, and run the machine without thread or fabric for a couple of minutes. This will help to clear out any remaining thread, lint, or dirt. Wipe oil from bobbin area with soft clean rag before installing bobbin.

It should be noted that some machines have motors that run continuously; the foot control operates a clutch drive that turns the belt that goes to the power head. On other machines, the foot control is a variable speed switch that starts the motor. When the foot is released, the motor shuts off.

If the motor runs, but the needle does not move even though the hand wheel turns, problem is most likely in the link between the main drive shaft and needle bar. Repair is generally best left to a professional sewing machine mechanic.

If hand wheel turns and needle moves, but fabric does not feed, the presser foot might not be in "down" position or the stitch regulator might be set at zero. A more serious problem is a malfunction of feed dog mechanism. Repair is generally best left to a professional sewing machine mechanic.

If hand wheel, needle, and fabric move, but no stitch is formed, the problem could be that the thread has come out of the needle, the needle is threaded in wrong direction, or it is inserted backwards or not pushed all the way up into the clamp. The needle could be the wrong length. Use the needle recommended for the particular machine. Other possible causes are the machine is incorrectly threaded, the bobbin is empty, the bobbin and/or bobbin case are incorrectly inserted, or the timing of the machine is off. If the problem is in the timing, repair is usually best left to a professional sewing machine mechanic.

If the machine runs noisily, the machine probably needs cleaning and oiling. There also might be a specific cause, such as a bent needle hitting against throat plate or presser foot, presser foot is loose, or bobbin case might be loose. Try to locate from where noise is coming. Then look for a loose part or something rubbing or hitting.

SEWING BASIC SEAMS

Although there are many possible seams that can be made by straight stitch sewing, only a few of these are commonly used for canvas and upholstery work. Practice these seams with a variety of canvas and upholstery fabrics.

Plain Seam

The plain seam is a basic method of joining two pieces of fabric together (Fig. 5-19). The two pieces of fabric are sewn together in a plain seam with the right sides placed facing each other. After the fabric is sewn, the material is turned so that the seam edges of the pieces of fabric will be on the wrong side.

Although there is no set rule, a plain seam is usually placed 1/2 inch from the edges of the pieces of fabric. A seam gauge can be used as a guide, but experienced sewing machine operators can usually make a half inch plain seam accurately without a gauge. Some machines have seam guidelines etched on the throat plate, as shown in Fig. 5-20. Masking or adhesive tape can be placed the desired distance from the needle hole for use as a seam guide.

Practice making straight plain seams. Fix the start and end of the seam by backtracking. If machine has reverse feature, use this. Otherwise, turn fabric around, stitch a 1/2 inch, turn, and begin seam. In a well-made seam, the stitching is straight and the same distance from the edge the entire length of the seam.

Next, practice making a plain seam around three sides of matched squares or rectangularly shaped pieces of fabric. Begin by fixing seam at start. Then sew seam along one side. Stop sewing 1/2 inch from end. If needle is not in lowest position, turn hand

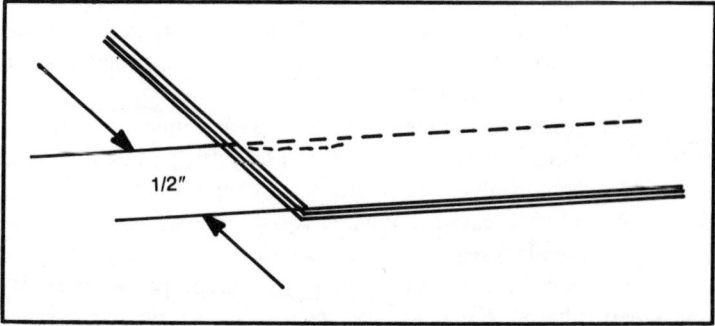

Fig. 5-19. Plain seam is usually 1/2 inch from edge of fabric.

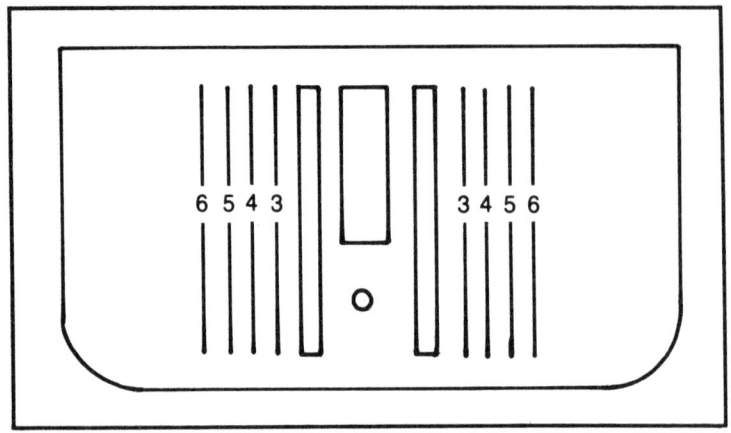

Fig. 5-20. Seam guidelines etched on throat plate.

wheel until it is. Needle should be through fabric 1/2 inch from edge. Raise presser foot. Turn fabric to new sewing direction. Lower presser foot. Then sew next straight section of seam, stopping 1/2 inch from edge. Make turn as detailed above. Then sew last straight section. Fix end of seam by backtracking. Cut off thread near fabric, then turn right side out. You should have a sack shaped bag with the cut edges of the fabric inside.

Next, practice a curved plain seam. This will require more careful guiding of the fabric as it passes under the needle to keep the seamline the same distance from the edge of the fabric. Fix both start and finish of seam by backtracking.

Next, sew a sack with a rounded bottom. Fix the start of the seam by backtracking. Then make a plain seam, guiding the fabric carefully around the curved portion. Try to keep the seamline the same distance from the edge of the fabric all the way along the seam. Finish by backtracking and then cutting off threads near the fabric. Then turn right side out. You should have a rounded sack with the seam edges inside.

The plain seam is widely used in canvas and upholstery work, especially when the raw edges of the fabric can be hidden, such as inside a cushion cover. The plain seam does place the strain on the stitches when stressed. If a water resistant or waterproof seam is required, the plain seam will tend to allow water through the join of the fabrics even if the holes where the thread passes through are sealed. There are many situations where both sides of fabrics will be exposed, making a plain seam undesirable, as the edges will tend to come unravelled.

Hems and Tablings

Hems and *tablings* are used to protect and reinforce the edges of fabrics. A simple hem is formed by folding the edge of the fabric and then sewing the layers together with a straight stitch, as shown in Fig. 5-21. This method is not ordinarily used however, as it still leaves an exposed edge on the fabric that can come unravelled. Of course, this might be okay if the edge of the fabric is selvaged (woven so that it will not ravel) or heat sealed (nylon, polyester, and acrylic fabrics can all be heat sealed). The usual method, however, is to turn the hem under again.

Practice sewing a turned-under or rolled hem. Although the width of hem can be as desired, first practice a 3/4-inch hem made by folding a 1 1/4 inch edge of fabric over, then 1/2 inch under again, as shown in Fig. 5-22. The seam is then made through three layers of fabric. Fix both the start and finish of the seam by backtracking.

If desired, the hem can be doubled, sewn by making a second straight stitch about 1/8 inch from the first one.

Next, practice sewing a cut tabling in place. Cut a strip of fabric 1 3/4 inch wide the length of the hem. On each side, fold 3/8 inch under. Also fold the fabric that is being hemmed so that 3/8 inch turns back, as shown in Fig. 5-23. Sew seam along the edge through four layers of fabric first. Fix both the start and finish of the stitching by backtracking. Next, sew inner seam.

It may be difficult at first to make straight seams exactly the

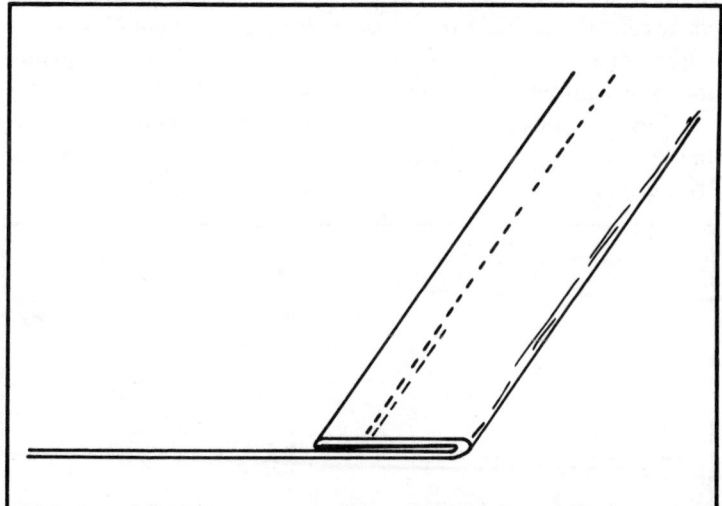

Fig. 5-21. A simple hem.

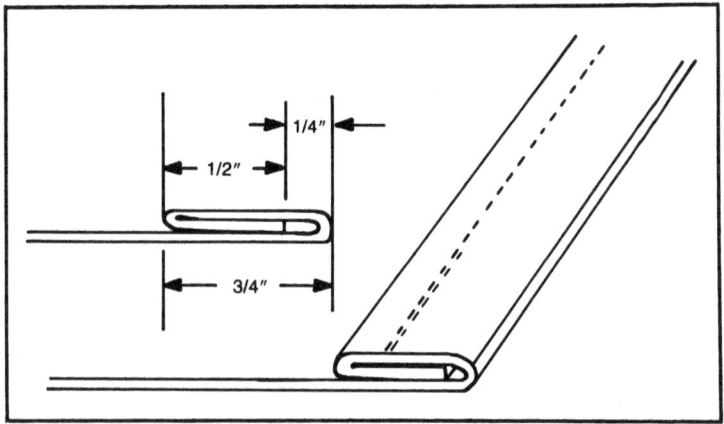

Fig. 5-22. Hem with 1 1/4-inch edge folded over and 1/2 inch turned under.

same distance from the edge. Marking guidelines on the fabric may be helpful.

Another method is to use *tape binding* to form a hem. This is available in a variety of widths, but 5/8 inch width is commonly used for canvas and upholstery work. The binding tape has selvaged or sealed edges, so the edges do not need to be turned under. Simply fold the binding in half over the open edge of the fabric, as shown in Fig. 5-24. Then sew in place with a straight stitch.

Although this may not be as strong as a folded hem or cut tabling, it is neat and simple to sew in place and is satisfactory for many canvas and upholstery uses. A binder attachment for the sewing machine, described previously in this chapter, further simplifies the ease with which binding can be sewn in place.

Binding tape can be the same color as, or a different color than, the fabric being hemmed. A contrasting color often gives a neat trim effect.

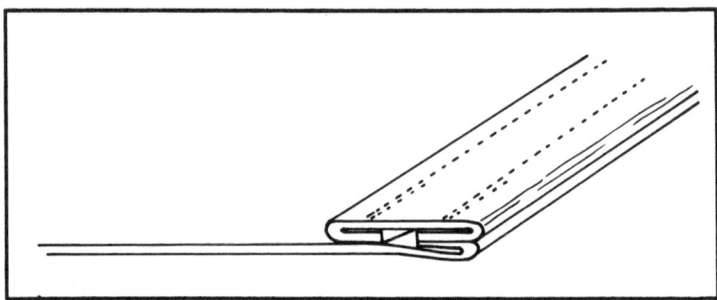

Fig. 5-23. Cut tabling.

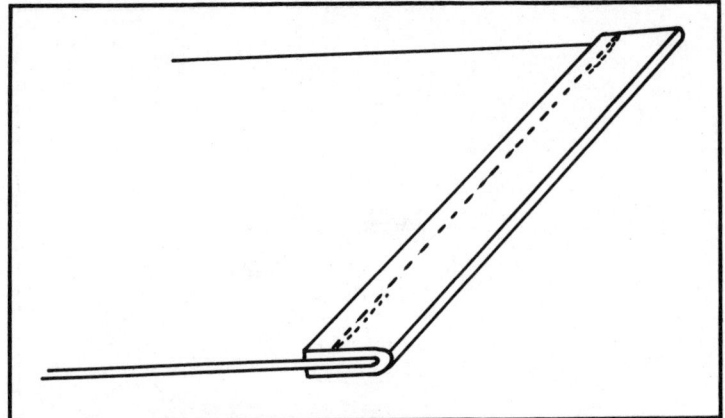

Fig. 5-24. Binding tape sewn over edge of fabric to form hem.

Flat-Felled Seam

A *flat-felled seam* is frequently used to join two pieces of fabric together, as shown in Fig. 5-25A. Begin by sewing a plain seam 1/2 inch from the edges of the fabric as shown in Fig. 5-25B. Then trim one edge, as shown in Fig. 5-25C. Fold long edge over 1/4 inch or as desired, then flatten and sew, as shown in Fig. 5-25D. This forms an extremely strong seam with raw edges of fabric neatly hidden.

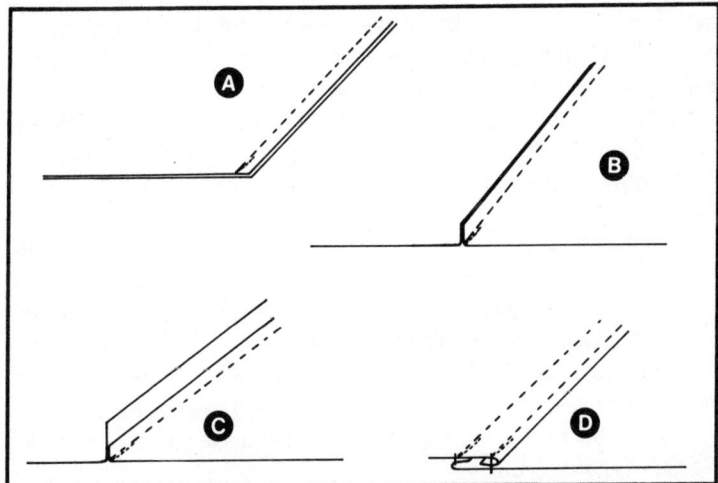

Fig. 5-25. To make a flat-felled seam, begin by sewing plain seam 1/2 inch from edges of fabrics (A); spread fabric out flat (B); trim one edge (C); and flatten fabric and sew second row of stitching (D).

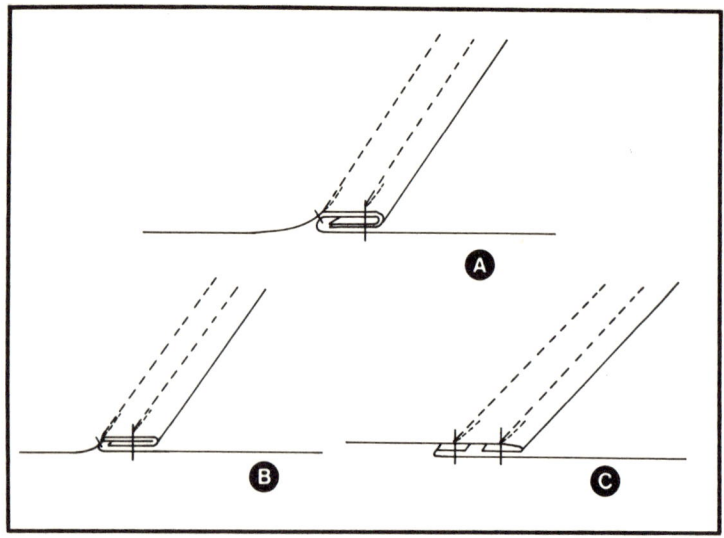

Fig. 5-26. Flat-felled seam with second row of stitching through five layers of fabric (A); with second row of stitching through four layers of fabric (B); and flat-felled seam formed with lap joint (C).

An alternate method is to fold both layers of fabric under without first trimming one edge and then make stitch through five layers of fabric instead of three, as was done previously (Fig. 5-26A). Still another method is to trim one layer of fabric at the point where the other layer will turn under, then sew through four layers of fabric, as shown in Fig. 5-26B. The three-layer method gives the flattest seam, but the four- and five-layer method can give added strength, assuming that the sewing machine used is capable of handling this thickness. When the four- and five-layer methods are used, an extra stitch is often made midway between the first two stitches.

A flat-felled seam can be formed by joining the fabrics end to end with a *lap joint*, with the edges turned under, as shown in Fig. 5-26C. This allows both stitches to pass through three layers of fabric. Because of the difficulty of making a straight stitch line and handling fabric under the arm of a sewing machine on the first stitch, however, this method is not ordinarily used, except with special double needle machines, which have a special feed for making this type of seam.

Piping or Cording

Piping and *cording* (Fig. 5-27) is often used to strengthen and protect stitches and give a neat trim effect. Piping can be purchased preformed, ready for sewing, or you can make up your own by sewing cording into a strip of fabric, as shown in Fig. 5-27. In order to match the 1/2 inch from edge seam allowances normally used in sewing, strips should be 1-inch wide (two times 1/2 inch) plus the distance it takes to go around the cord. In most cases, 1/8-inch diameter nylon or polyester cord is about right. Make test strip to see how much fabric it takes to go around the cord by sewing a strip, then removing stitches and measuring the distance between stitch holes.

There are several methods used for joining strips of material: a plain seam at right angles (which is not recommended because of too many layers of fabric in one area); a plain seam at a 45 degree angle, as shown in Fig. 5-28; and with a lap joint, as shown in Fig. 5-29. The choice depends on the particular job being done and the type of fabric being used.

Binding tape can also be used for covering the cording. Because this is available in rolls in long lengths, this will keep joints to a minimum or even eliminate them.

You will need a zipper or piping foot on the sewing machine so that you will be able to sew the seam close to cord, as shown in Fig. 5-5.

If you make up your own piping from cord and fabric strips or binding tape, first sew in the cord, as shown in Fig. 5-27. The piping, whether you use the kind already made up or form your own, is usually first sewn to one layer of fabric, as shown in Fig. 5-30. Fix the start and finish of the seam by backtracking. Sew seam close to the cord.

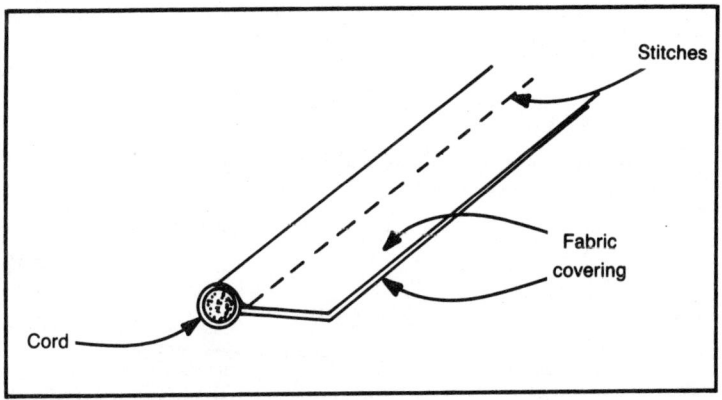

Fig. 5-27. Piping or cording.

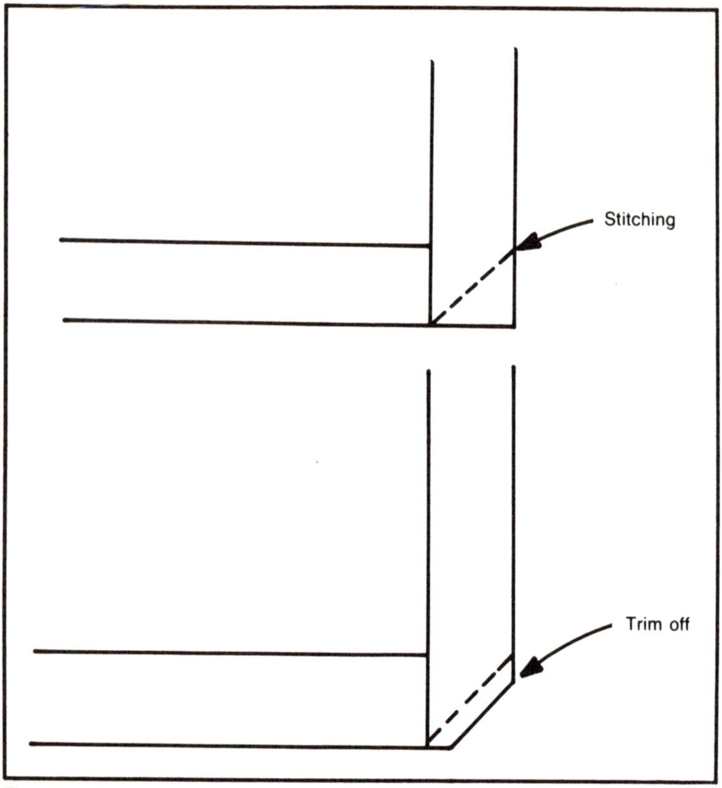

Fig. 5-28. Plain seam at 45-degree angle.

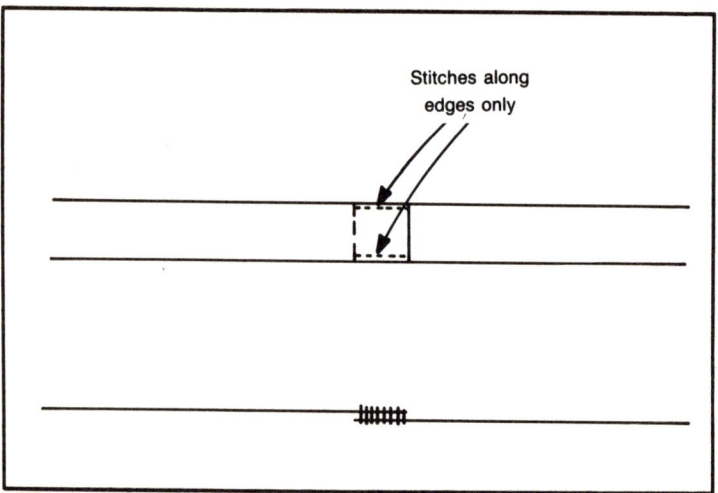

Fig. 5-29. Lap joint.

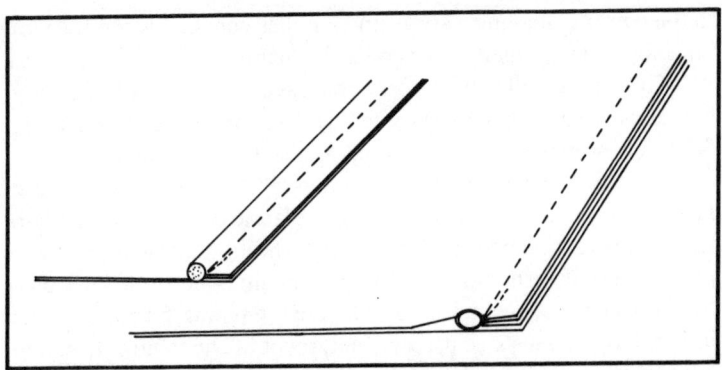

Fig. 5-30. Piping is first sewn to one layer of fabric (left); then second layer of fabric is sewn to piping and first layer of fabric.

Next, place the right side of the second piece of fabric face to face with right side of layer of fabric with piping sewn in place, as shown in Fig. 5-30. Line up edges of fabric and make a straight seam close to the cord in piping. Fix both the start and finish of the seam by backtracking.

After sewing is completed, turn fabric right side out so that cord is on top. Pull the fabrics to check the stitching. A common mistake is not to sew close enough to the cording, leaving a space and stitches showing when the fabric is pulled taut across the seam.

This is essentially a plain seam reinforced with piping or cording. When used on cushion covers, it reinforces the stitching, adds strength, and gives a neat finished appearance. It is also frequently used in canvas cover seams.

There are many situations where it is desirable to install piping around curves. Practice this by cutting two matching pieces of fabric to pattern shown in Fig. 5-31.

Next, sew piping to one layer of fabric, as shown in Fig. 5-31. Stitching should be close to the cord and the same distance from the edge of the fabric all the way around. The edges of the cord covering fabric and the fabric that piping is being sewn to should all line up.

Next, place right side of second piece of fabric face to face with right side of layer of fabric with piping sewn in place. Line up edges and sew seam close to cord. Fix both the start and finish of seam by backtracking.

After sewing is completed, turn fabric right side out so that cord is on outside and fabric ends are inside. Pull fabric at seams to check stitching. A common mistake is not to sew close enough to the cording, leaving a space and stitches showing when the joining fabrics are pulled taut across the seam.

The piping will usually form gradual curves without difficulty, but darts are usually necessary for sharper curves, as shown in Fig. 5-32. These make sewing around a corner much easier.

A square corner may also be desirable. Practice with scrap fabrics. First, sew piping to one layer of fabric up to the point where turn is desired. Needle should be down through fabric in the exact point where a turn is desired. If the needle is not in lowest position, turn hand wheel until it is. Cut dart in piping fabric as shown in Fig. 5-33. Then raise presser foot, pivot fabric to new direction, lower presser foot, and continue stitching in new direction. Then sew second piece of fabric in place.

After sewing is completed, turn fabric right side out so that piping cord is on outside and fabric ends are inside. Pull fabrics on each side of seam to check stitching. A common mistake is to sew away from the cording, leaving a space and stitches showing.

Other Basic Seams

The above seams are those used extensively in canvas and

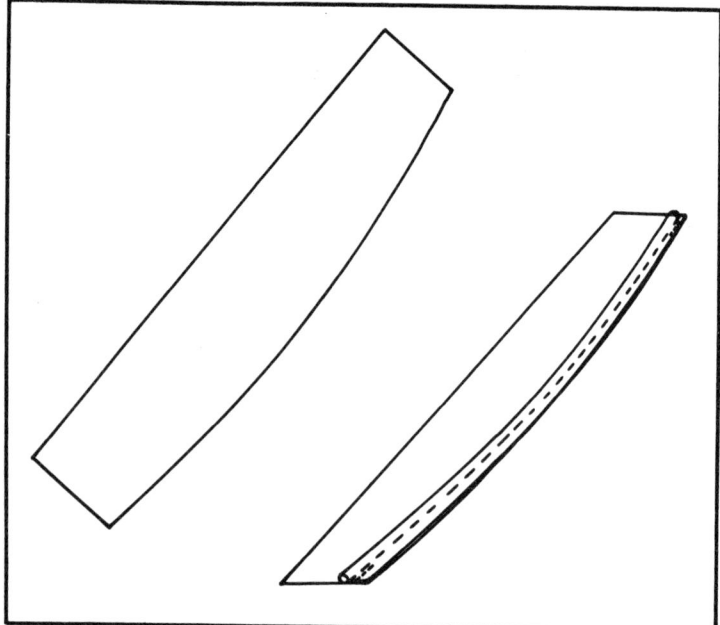

Fig. 5-31. Fabric pattern (left) and after piping is attached to one layer.

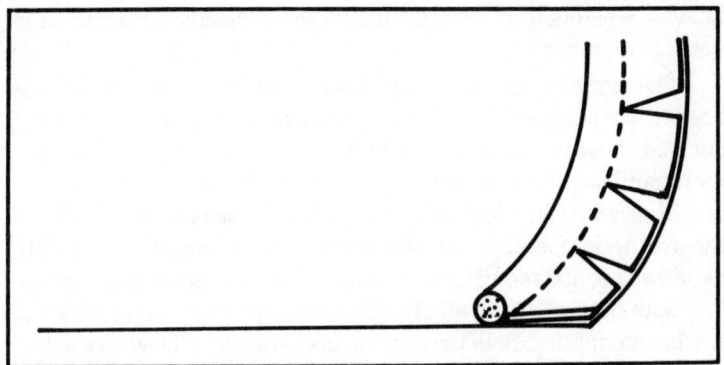

Fig. 5-32. Notches are cut in piping fabric for sewing around sharp curves.

upholstery work. These should be practiced until they can be done properly. Quality sewing is extremely important for professional canvas and upholstery work. Additional seams, most of which are variations of the above seams, are covered in later chapters.

SEWABILITY OF FABRIC

It quickly becomes apparent that some fabrics are easier to sew than others. Fabrics are woven from yarns that are made from natural or synthetic fibers, or a combination of natural and synthetic fibers.

Natural fibers that are commonly made into fabrics include cotton, linen, silk, and wool. Of these, only cotton is widely used for boat and recreational vehicle canvas and upholstery work. Cotton fabrics are generally fairly easy to work with and sew. Cotton canvas, however, generally is much heavier than a synthetic canvas with the same strength, which makes it necessary to work with

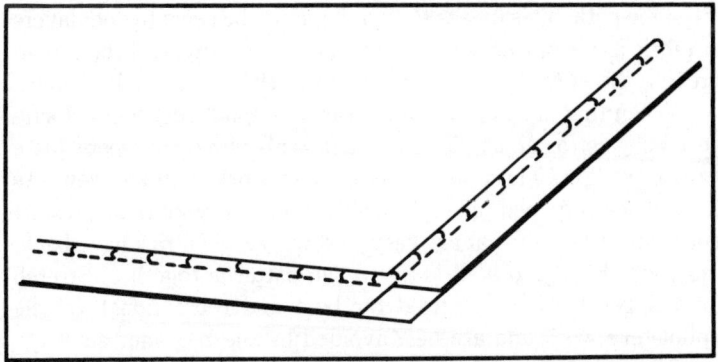

Fig. 5-33. Notch is cut in piping fabric for making square corner.

heavier weights (and greater thicknesses). Needle penetration is generally quite good.

The synthetic or man-made fibers include rayon, acetate, triacetate, spandex, nylon, polyester, and acrylic. It should be pointed out that these are generic names. In some cases, trade names are more familiar. For example, DuPont calls their polyester Dacron, and Monsanto Chemical Company calls their acrylic Acrylan®. Of the synthetic fibers, only nylon, polyester, and acrylic are widely used for boat and recreational vehicle canvas and upholstery fabrics.

Both natural and synthetic fibers are spun into yarn, which is woven into fabrics. Both the specific fiber used and the weave determine the suitability for canvas and upholstery projects and the sewability of the fabric.

Three basic weaves are in common use: *plain, twill,* and *satin.* The plain weave is generally the strongest and most often used for boat and recreational vehicle canvas and upholstery work. The yarns that run lengthwise are known as the *warp.* The crosswise yarns are known as the *weft* or *filling.* Twill and satin weaves are sometimes used for boat and recreational vehicle upholstery fabric.

Acrylic canvas fabrics are generally fairly easy to sew. Nylon and polyester fabrics vary from fairly easy to sew to quite difficult, depending on how close the weave pattern is and the type of finish applied.

The sewability of more open weave upholstery fabrics varies greatly. Try sewing samples before purchasing a large quantity for an upholstery project.

Coating natural and synthetic fabrics with vinyl or other plastics can greatly increase the sewing difficulties. Wide stitches are generally used, as close stitching generally weakens the fabric. With some vinyl upholstery fabrics, only one seam can be made along the same path. This means that piping must be sewn to both layers of fabric at once, without first sewing it to one layer. If the thread breaks, the stitching is started again in the same needle holes.

When first starting out in canvas and upholstery work, I suggest using cotton or acrylic canvas that is about 8-ounces-per-square yard in weight. These are fairly easy to work with and sew. As experience is gained, go on to woven upholstery fabrics. To start with, select fabrics that are easy to sew. Some fabrics have backings, which help to hold loose weave patterns together. Stretch fabrics generally aren't used for boat and recreational vehicle upholstery work and are best avoided by the beginner anyway.

Then go on to the more difficult vinyl coated fabrics. Begin with a cotton backed vinyl upholstery fabric. Vinyl and other plastic materials without fabric backing should not be used for upholstery work, except for clear vinyl material for flexible windows (see Chapter 2).

Finally, go on to vinyl-coated canvas fabrics, which are generally more difficult to sew.

The main idea is to learn how to operate a sewing machine, first by using easy to sew fabrics so that you can concentrate on operating the machine and making basic seams. Then gradually work up to more difficult fabrics as you gain skill and experience.

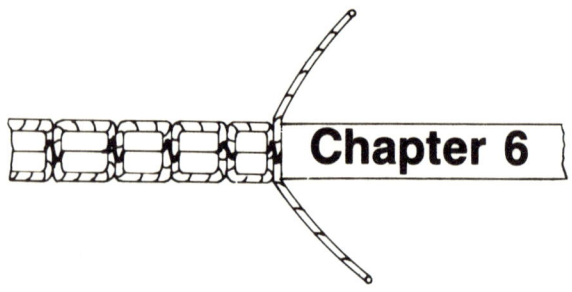

Chapter 6

Patterns and Cutting

Another important aspect of canvas and upholstery work is making patterns, marking them on fabrics, and cutting them to desired size and shape. A main difference between the work of a beginner and a professional is that the professional's work fits. Cushion covers are tight and wrinkle free. Canvas tops fit snugly to the frames. Where necessary, patterns are properly aligned.

Of course, all this takes practice and experience, but even a beginner can achieve good results by learning the fundamental techniques for making patterns and cutting fabrics. Progress will be more rapid than trial and error learning. In this way, you can practice sound and proven techniques right from the start.

By the same token, it should be pointed out that there is no one method that is best for everyone. I have observed professional workers, for example, who use a variety of approaches for making a pattern for cushion covers, often with equally good results. In general, I suggest that you try all of the methods detailed in this book before deciding the method that you want to use.

MAKING AND TRANSFERRING PATTERN MARKINGS

There are several possible methods for making a pattern either directly on fabric to be used or on paper or some other material and then transferring the pattern markings to the fabric. One method is to use the old fabric as a pattern for the new. If you are replacing worn cushion covers, for example, you rip the seams of the old covers, and use the fabric pieces as patterns for marking and cutting the new pieces. There are some problems, however. You will need old covers that fit and are in good enough condition to use as a pattern. If you want to make modifications, such as to make the new cushions thicker, this will have to be taken into account. With some fabrics, shrinkage will have to be taken into consideration. Still, this method is useful, either by itself or supplemented by other methods.

Another method is to use the item to be covered as a pattern for direct transfer to fabric or paper or some other pattern material. Examples of this are using the foam cut to shape for a cushion or the frames for a canvas top set up in position. This method is useful even when you don't have the old cover or top or are making original ones. You cut the foam to fit (see Chapter 14), then you use the foam as a pattern for marking and cutting the fabric. Or you make up and install the frames for a canvas top. With the frames in place, you use them as a pattern for marking the new fabric.

A third method is to take measurements, then transfer these to the fabric or paper or other pattern material.

Using Old Canvas and Upholstery as Pattern

If the old canvas or upholstery fits and is in good enough condition to give you a pattern, this may be the best way to go. Before ripping seams apart, first mark all pieces so that you will know what goes where. Also note any changes that need to be made. The marking can be done with a felt tip marking pen. In most cases, I do the marking on the wrong side. The right side of the pattern fabric will then be placed face to face with the wrong side of the new fabric. The pattern will then be marked on the wrong side of the new fabric, which is usually facing outward (top or bottom) when the sewing is done on a sewing machine.

A seam ripper is useful for ripping out the seams, but use care. Avoid tearing the fabric. The idea is to remove the thread stitches, while leaving the fabric intact.

As an example for our purposes here, we will assume that you have a piece of fabric, shaped as shown in Fig. 6-1, that you want to duplicate on a new piece of fabric. This will be placed right side down on the wrong side of the new fabric, as shown in Fig. 6-2. On printed and coated fabrics, determination of right and wrong sides is easy. On single color fabrics, look for the more attractive side. This is generally the right side. Some fabrics are identical on

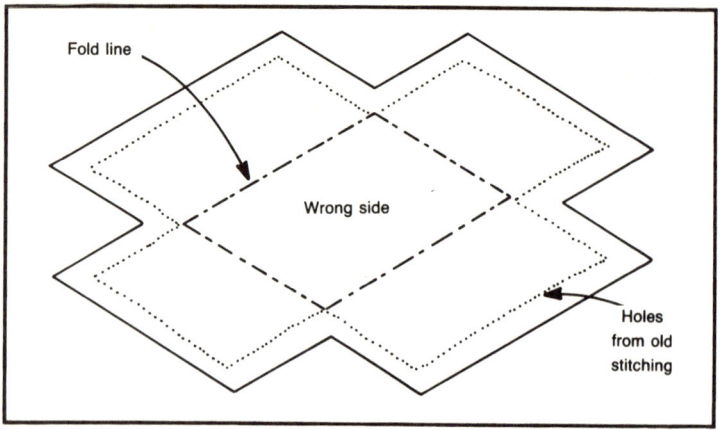

Fig. 6-1. Old fabric.

both sides, and the choice is arbitrary, but you will have to keep in mind which side is to be the right side.

To make the best use of the new fabric, the pattern should lie in a certain direction in relation to the weave and in a position that keeps waste when cutting to a minimum. For now, it is assumed that you have the pattern fabric placed where you want it on the new fabric. The next problem is to transfer the pattern.

The outside outline can be made by marking around the pattern. Both fabrics should be spread out flat. This is best done on a cutting table, but can also be done on a floor. Both fabrics should

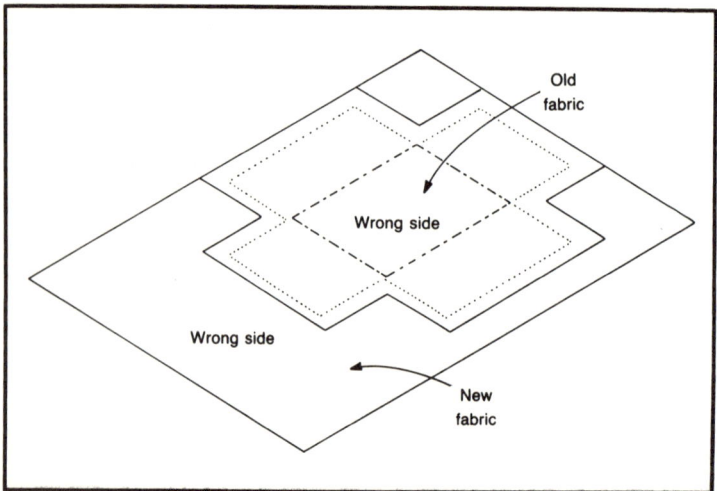

Fig. 6-2. Using old fabric as pattern for new fabric.

be stretched out equally. It may be helpful to pin the fabrics together around the edges.

Marking can be done on most fabrics with chalk. Yellow chalk is often used. This is usually sharpened to a chisel point with a knife. Chalk fabric pencils can also be used. Regardless, a sharp point is required so that a thin line can be made close to the edge of the pattern fabric. Washable marking pens can be used on some fabrics on the wrong side, but try this on a scrap piece to make sure that the ink will not soak through the fabric to the right side.

For straight edges, place a straightedge rule along the edge on top of the pattern fabric. Then mark the line on the new fabric, using the straightedge as a guide.

The next problem is to mark where the stitches go. If these are a set distance from the edges of the fabric, such as a standard 1/2 inch, the seam lines can be measured, marked off, and drawn on the reverse side of the new fabric.

Another method is to use fabric *tracing paper* and a *tracing wheel* (Fig. 6-3). The tracing paper is placed between pattern fabric and the new fabric. The tracing wheel is then rolled over the seam lines. For straight lines, mark with the tracing wheel against a ruler.

Tracing paper specially formulated for use on fabrics is available in a selection of colors. Use the kind that will not stain and is waxless and greaseless.

Make marks to indicate where the new fabric goes in relation to pieces to be joined to it, or which is the front, back, and so on. You should now have the pattern on the new fabric, ready for cutting as detailed later in this chapter.

Using Item to be Covered as Pattern

This is a reverse approach. This time, instead of using the old

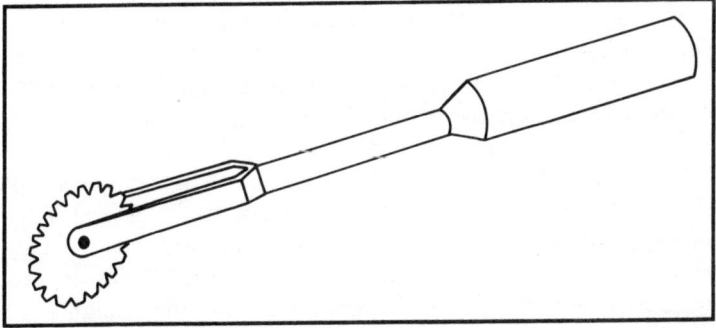

Fig. 6-3. Tracing wheel.

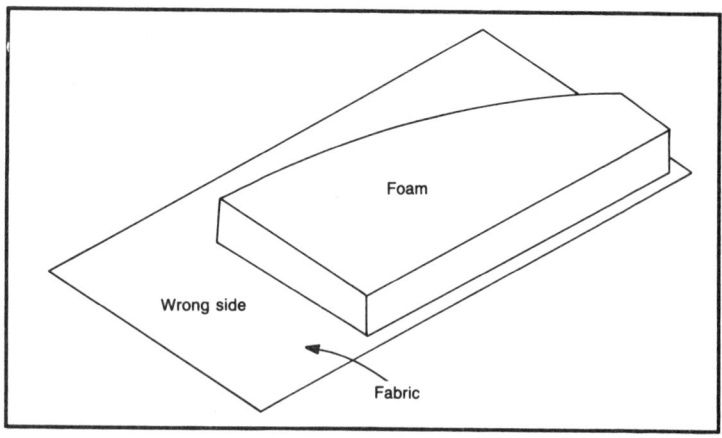

Fig. 6-4. Foam placed on fabric for use as a pattern.

fabric, the item covered is used as a pattern. As an example, assume that you already have the foam padding shape from a cushion. This might or might not have been previously covered with fabric. Although there is a variety of methods for covering cushions (see Chapter 14), a common method is to use a separate piece of fabric for the top, another for the bottom, and a separate strip to go around the edges, which may be more than one piece joined together to make the necessary length.

For our example here, we will only be concerned with the top piece of fabric. The pattern for all pieces can be made similarly.

Place the new fabric on the cutting table right side down. Place the foam top side down on the fabric in desired position. Placement should be made on basis of grain of fabric and to keep waste to a minimum.

With the foam in position on the fabric, as shown in Fig. 6-4, mark a line on the wrong side of fabric all the way around the foam. This is generally the seam line. The stitching is generally done a certain distance, usually 1/2 inch, from the edge of the fabric, so this distance must be added to the seam line all the way around on the fabric to get the pattern for cutting. The pattern already marked will be the *stitching line*.

Measure desired distance outward from stitching line in at least three places for a straight line, usually near each end and in the middle, and then line up a straightedge with these marks. If the marks don't agree, determine why and make necessary adjustments. Make a line on the fabric following the straightedge.

For curved areas, measure off a number of marks and then

mark in line by hand. *Curve battens* with weights can also be used, but this precision is seldom required. Remember, you will be sewing along stitch lines. Reasonable accuracy is required, though, because you may not be able to see the stitch line, if it is on bottom layer of fabric when joining two pieces.

Which brings up an important question: how much can the pattern be off? This depends on many things, but in most cases plus or minus 1/32 inch should not have much effect. Larger errors may start to show up in the finished results. Thus, accurate pattern marking is extremely important if professional results are to be achieved. Always try to mark the pattern as accurately as possible. Although adjustments may be possible later, it's best to get it right the first time.

Make marks to indicate where the new fabric goes. In this case, it's the "top." Also mark other reference points, as required. You should now have the pattern on the new fabric, ready for cutting.

This same concept can be applied to a variety of situations. For example, the wheel of a recreational vehicle can be used as a pattern for making a fabric wheel cover. Or the frames for a canvas top can be used as a pattern. Set frames in position, place fabric over frames, and make necessary pattern marks. This method of pattern making is covered in detail where it applies in later chapters. For now, it's important to understand the general differences between this method and using old fabric as pattern.

Using Measurements for Pattern

Professional canvas and upholstery workers generally place more faith in measurements than either of the other methods described above. Even when they use one of the above methods, they usually double check it with measurements. Let's look at some examples.

For a wheel cover, a piece of fabric is usually required to fit one side of the tire, plus 1/2 inch extra all the way around for the seam. Measure the radius, then add 1/2 inch to this. Connect marking chalk to a string. Measure off radius from chalk on string. Hold string on fabric at this point and mark off circle. If desired, shorten radius 1/2 inch and mark off second circle inside first. This will be the stitching line.

This method requires a reference point to relate whatever is being used as a pattern (or is being fitted) to the fabric. In the above example, the reference point was the center of the wheel and the center of the circle on the fabric.

This is simple with a circle, square, or even a rectangle, but becomes more complicated with more complex shapes. For example, you may want to make a canvas cover to fit over an object shaped as shown in Fig. 6-5. You will need two lines that cross at right angles to each other as reference points. If the object is symmetrical, center lines are often used. If the object has an irregular shape, it might be better to have reference lines elsewhere, such as along a straight edge. Regardless, the principles are the same.

It is important that the two reference lines are at right angles to each other. Use a square to mark these. Check this carefully: a mistake here means everything will be off.

You may want to transfer the pattern directly to the fabric or to paper, which can be checked before transferring the pattern onto the fabric. Either way, the next step is to mark the two reference lines on the fabric or paper at right angles to each other. Make certain that you have enough room, including space for seams at the edges.

Next, transfer necessary measurements from object to fabric or paper. Whenever you take measurements, do not trust them to memory. Write them down on a scratch pad or in a notebook. For the above example, measure distance on object from crossline on centerline to one end of object. Then transfer this measurement to the fabric or pattern, marking it with a short line across the centerline. Do the same thing for the other end. Then repeat along the crossline in each direction from the centerline.

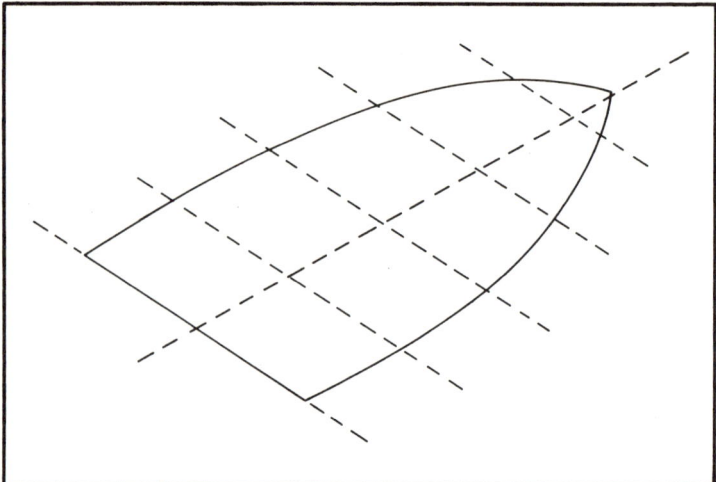

Fig. 6-5. Reference lines for making pattern.

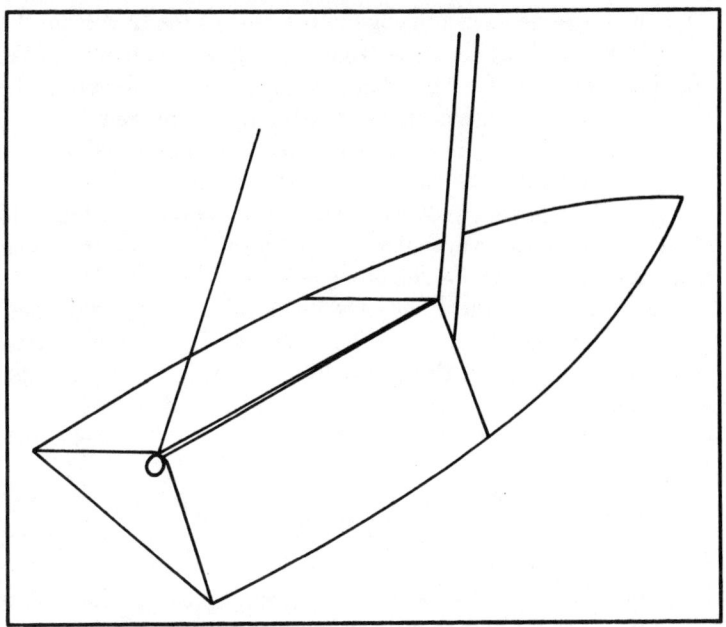

Fig. 6-6. Sailboat cover that goes over boom tent fashion.

Additional measurements may be required for the complete pattern. Measurements should be in relation to the reference point where the two lines cross at right angles. For example, it might be desirable to measure a certain distance forward on the centerline from the reference point, say 2 feet. Then measure the right angle distance using a square to determine the right angle to one edge of the object. This measurement is then transferred to the fabric or paper in the same manner.

Select key points for making measurements. For example, if the object is a flat surface with four straight sides, all you really need is the locations of the four corners. Once these have been transferred to the fabric or paper using the method detailed above, use a straightedge to mark straight lines connecting the points.

In a similar manner, more complex patterns can be made. I have found that most canvas and upholstery fabric patterns are simple ones, even though they may appear complicated at first. Consider the case of a boat cover that is to go over a boom, as shown in Fig. 6-6. A single piece of fabric or sections of fabric sewn together to form a single flat piece, can be used in tent fashion. The boom forms the centerline. A centerline can also be made on the fabric. From here, it is a simple manner to make a series of right angle measurements to the edge of one side of the boat from the centerline at various distances from a crossline, which in this case could conveniently be the forward or aft (backward) edge of the desired cover. Because each half of the cover from the centerline will be the same or symmetrical, measurements need be taken to one side only. After the pattern has been marked on half the fabric, it can be transferred to the other half by folding the fabric in half. If a paper pattern is used, simply turn the paper over, and you have the pattern for the other half.

In most cases, these measurements are for stitching lines. Before cutting the fabric, you will need to add edges for the seams. If plain seams are used, this is usually 1/2 inch all the way around. Other seams and hems require varying amounts of additional fabric. This must be carefully taken into account before making a final pattern line for cutting.

Most patterns will consist of stitching lines, folding lines, and lines for cutting, in addition to any reference lines. It is important to have a system for keeping track of which are which. One method is to make stitching lines a series of short dashes, folding lines a series of long dashes, and cutting lines a connected line. Another method is to make all lines connected lines and to code the lines where there might be confusion. In most cases, the outside line will be for cutting, and it will be obvious which lines are for folding and stitching. Mark only the ones where errors might be made, but don't trust these to memory. Make necessary notes on fabric, paper pattern, or in a notebook.

Using measurements to make a pattern is mainly simple logic. Although it is also possible to take measurements at various angles from the reference point where the centerline crosses the crossline at right angles, this involves accurate measurement of angles, something that is often difficult to do under actual canvas and upholstery working conditions. For this reason, I have found it usually best to stick to the right angle scheme detailed above.

Other Methods of Patterning

Throughout this book, methods for making patterns for specific projects are explained. In some cases, such as for duffel bags, specific patterns are given. These can be followed exactly or modified to fit your special requirements. In other cases, such as sail covers, general patterning is covered, but this must be adapted for the particular job at hand. There is no one pattern; the cover must fit the particular sail and spars.

The three main methods for making patterns given above are by no means the only possibilities, but most others are variations or combinations of the above. As a general rule, I recommend the simplest and most direct method. Although there are certainly situations where it is desirable to first make a paper pattern, transfer this to cardboard, then transfer this to the fabric, each separate transfer can add error to the lines. So, when possible, eliminate unnecessary steps.

In some cases, it's possible to fit the fabric almost directly by putting fabric in the position where it will be used, making the necessary marks, and even cutting the fabric in place. You can even temporarily join fabrics with pins or by hand sewing a basting (temporary) stitch in place.

Whenever possible, double the triple check patterns on fabric before cutting fabric. With the pattern marked, put the fabric in place where it will be used. This will sometimes make pattern errors apparent. Check measurements in a number of different ways. For example, if an object to be covered is rectangular, take a corner to corner measurement. Check this out on the pattern marked on the fabric. If the measurements don't agree, go back and find out where the mistake is.

In situations where you are uncertain about an exact measurement, use one that will give a little extra fabric rather than possibly too little. It's usually easier to make adjustments later by removing fabric than it is by having to add fabric.

Sloppy patterns usually mean a poor fit. It generally takes years of experience to consistently get a perfect fit, but don't use this as an excuse. Always try for the best fit possible. As has been pointed out, there is no one best method for making patterns, at least the experts don't agree on one. If possible, spend some time watching various professional canvas and upholstery workers at work. Study both the methods and the results. Look for methods that you can use in your own work. Don't be afraid to experiment. This is usually best done with scrap materials, not on an actual job.

You may get an opportunity to observe work being done at a canvas or upholstery factory. You may see stacks of fabric being automatically cut in a stack. Sewing will probably be at top speed. You may get ideas here for your own work, but be careful. These methods are for mass production, for making a profit, and do not necessarily result in the best possible canvas and upholstery work. Besides, they will probably be using machinery and equipment unavailable to most do-it-yourselfers.

LAYING OUT PATTERNS

Fabrics are usually sold by the yard in linear measure. Some fabrics are available only in one width; others are available in choice of two or more different widths. The edges of the fabrics are usually selvaged or fixed in some other way so that they will not unravel. After the fabrics are cut, however, this feature is usually lost, although some fabrics that are vinyl-coated or have special backings will not unravel even when cut, or at least resist unravelling.

There are many variables to consider in laying out patterns of fabrics. A first consideration is what fabric or fabrics to use. Recommendations for each canvas and upholstery project are given in later chapters. In general, the fabric chosen will depend on the particular project, personal preferences, how much you can afford to spend, what's available, and other factors.

Next, after the fabric has been chosen, you need to determine how much of it you will need. Take careful measurements. The amount of fabric required will depend on how the patterns are laid out on the fabric. These should be arranged on the fabric to keep waste to a minimum. At the same time, the patterns must be placed correctly in relation to the warp (lengthwise grain) and weft (crosswise grain) of the fabric. In general, the fabric has greatest strength on the warp or lengthwise grain. Next greatest is on the weft or crosswise grain. Weakest are diagonal angles or *bias*. These factors should be kept in mind when laying out patterns on fabric.

On some fabrics, approximately an inch of fabric along each selvaged edge will not be useable. I have found that the complete width of most boat and recreational vehicle canvas fabrics can be used, at least for seam allowance, however.

If it will be difficult to get more of the same fabric, purchase a little extra to make certain you will have enough. Also, cutting mistakes are always a possibility, so you might want extra fabric in case this happens. Extra fabric can also be useful to have on hand for possible future repair work.

Once you have the fabric on hand, you need to determine which is the right side and wrong side before laying out patterns. The patterns and cutting lines are usually marked on the wrong side of the fabric.

The individual patterns are arranged on the fabric in the proper directions in relation to the weave patterns and positioned in such a manner so as to keep waste to a minimum. On some fabrics, color design patterns will need to be matched on separate pieces of fabric. I suggest that you select fabrics that will make this unnecessary until you have gained considerable experience.

In most cases, no matter how you arrange the patterns, there will be some extra fabric off the patterns. When you have a choice, try to have these of a useable shape.

Some fabrics have weaving and/or color defects in one or more areas. These should either not be used, the defective areas located off the patterns, or the defective parts used in areas where they will not show.

CUTTING

After you have the cutting lines marked on the fabric and have checked the measurements and patterns over carefully, you are ready for cutting. You will need scissors or shears for this (see Chapter 3). Some synthetic fabrics can also be cut with a hot knife. This method also seals the edges. Similar cuts made with scissors or shears can have edges sealed by moving the raw edge back and forth near a candle flame until loose threads melt together. Try this on a scrap piece of the fabric first . . . and do not breathe the fumes.

None of the projects detailed in this book require heat sealed edges. Instead, edges are hidden, such as inside cushions (Fig. 6-7), turned under, or protected by a binding. Cutting with a hot knife and heat sealing edges will not be considered further in this book. It should be mentioned, however, that these methods are commonly used in sailmaking, an area that many canvas and upholstery do-

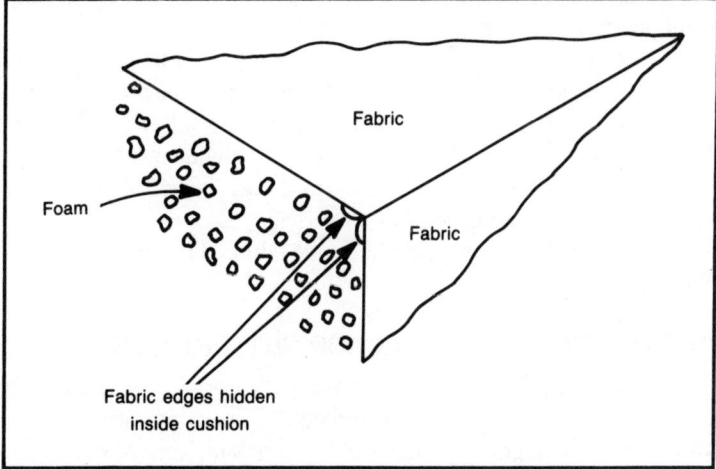

Fig. 6-7. Fabric edges of plain seam hidden inside cushion.

it-yourselfers branch off into. From this point on, it will be assumed that fabric cutting will be done with scissors or shears unless otherwise indicated.

With the pattern correctly marked on the fabric, usually on the reverse or wrong side of the fabric (although some canvas and upholstery workers prefer to mark patterns on the right side of the fabric), spread the fabric out on cutting table or clean smooth floor.

Because not leaving enough fabric for seaming allowance, folding under for hems and flat-felled seams, and other uses is a common error, make a last minute check of this.

Next, cut the fabric with scissors or shears, carefully following the cutting line. Rest the edge of the scissors on the cutting table or floor.

In canvas and upholstery work, most cutting will be along warp or weft lines. Usually, the pattern lines will follow a thread line in the fabric. A limited amount of cutting will be on a diagonal or bias. There will also be curves, circles, and various other cutting lines. Regardless, carefully cut along the cutting line.

Some patterns are symmetrical. The fabric can be folded in half, then the cutting can be done through both layers of fabric at once. This method is useful for some of the projects detailed in this book.

There are a number of situations where you will need strips of fabric of various widths, such as for making piping and sides for cushion covers. These are usually cut either lengthwise or crosswise on the fabric. A first step for a crosswise cutting is to straighten the end of the fabric. This is generally done by marking a line along a weft or crosswise thread or yarn or at right angle to the edge of vinyl-coated fabrics. The fabric is then cut along the line with scissors or shears. Other methods that can be used on some fabrics are tearing or drawing out a thread and following the line it leaves. Lines for lengthwise cutting can usually be measured from the edge of the fabric, but make certain that these follow a warp or lengthwise thread or yarn.

Cutting lines are then laid out on the fabric. The cutting is done with scissors or shears.

ORGANIZING PATTERNING AND CUTTING WORK

A common problem is keeping everything organized. You don't have to do all of the patterning and cutting work at once. For example, if you are going to make covers for a number of cushions, you might want to do the patterning, cutting, and even the sewing of one complete cushion cover before going on to the next one, and so on. This is especially useful if you have a variety of shapes and sizes of cushions.

If you do the patterning for a number of cushion covers at once, be sure to code not only where the parts go, but also which cover they belong to. This can be done by letters or numbers, as desired.

Keeping fabrics clean can be a problem. The cutting table should be clean. If the cutting is done on the floor, paper can be spread over the floor to help keep the fabric clean.

FITTING

In spite of careful measuring and patterning, there will be times when, after sewing, it doesn't fit. It's too big or too small. In some cases, adjustments can be made. The seam can be ripped out, fabric cut off, and a new seam made. If there is too little fabric, a whole section may have to be ripped out and replaced with a larger piece of fabric. On some fabrics, seams can be ripped out and resewn without damaging or weakening the fabric; on the other fabrics, you have to get it right the first time or else start over again with new fabric. For example, removed stitching holes will clearly show on vinyl upholstery fabric. If resewing is done along an old stitch line, the fabric will be greatly weakened if the needle does not go through the same holes, and this is quite difficult to accomplish.

KITS

Some canvas products are available in kit form with the patterning and cutting already done for you (see Suppliers section).

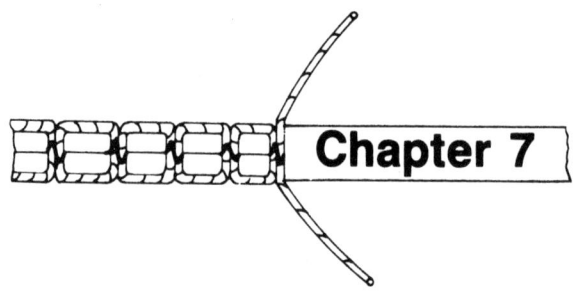

Chapter 7

Fasteners and Adhesives

There are two basic ways of securing canvas and upholstery fabrics in place: permanently, and removably, so that they can be taken apart. Canvas and upholstery fabrics can be glued or held in place by means of staples or other mechanical fasteners that are not easily removed. Fasteners that can be easily taken apart include zippers, Velcro®, snaps, hooks, twist fasteners, elastic, draw strings, and tie-down cords and ropes. Some fasteners, such as screws, might fall in either category, depending on how they are used.

Canvas and upholstery work frequently requires a base of support, such as frames and fittings for awnings and canvas tops. To this point, patterning, cutting, and sewing basics have been covered. Skills and techniques for installing fasteners, frames, and fittings and using adhesives are another important aspect of canvas and upholstery work.

PERMANENT FASTENINGS

By permanent is meant not intended to ordinarily be removed or opened, rather than being attached so that they can never be taken apart again. Upholstered paneling is a case in point. Usually, there is a means for later removal for recovering or repairs either to upholstered panel or to the area behind paneling.

Adhesives

Many fabrics can be attached to wood, metal, and a variety of plastics by means of adhesives. In some cases, even pieces of fabric are joined by gluing, although this is the exception rather than the rule.

Special fabric adhesives are available in liquid and spray form. The strength of the bonding will depend on the particular adhesive, the fabric, and the surface it is being glued to.

Some adhesives are applied to one or both surfaces, and the fabric is set in place immediately. Others are contact cements, which are applied to both surfaces and allowed to dry a certain length of time. When the two layers of contact cement are placed together, they immediately bond.

When using fabric adhesives, always follow manufacturer's directions carefully. Observe any health and safety precautions. Some of the adhesives in spray cans are particularly dangerous to use. In general, you will need to work in a well-ventilated area.

Always test the adhesive on a scrap piece of the fabric before using it on the actual job. Make certain that the adhesive will not soak through the fabric and show on the right side. Make sure that the adhesive gives an adequate bond between the fabric and the surface to which it is being glued.

When gluing, use paper and masking tape to keep glue from unwanted areas. Have rags handy for cleaning up any spilled or excess glue.

Sometimes, gluing is reinforced by using mechanical fasteners like staples or tacks.

Staples and Tacks

Staples and tacks are sometimes used to attach fabric to wood. A typical example is covering a piece of wood with fabric, folding the fabric around the edges, and fastening the fabric to the wood with staples or tacks. This is frequently used for attaching fabric to a wood paneling and sometimes for attaching cushion covering to wood pieces, as detailed in later chapters.

Because recreational vehicles and, especially, boats are often used in harsh environments, staples and tacks should be of noncorrosive metals, such as stainless steel or *monel*.

Heavy-duty *staple guns* are available for driving staples. A *tack hammer* can be used to drive tacks. Incidentally, even if sterilized tacks are used, I don't recommend putting them in your mouth. Swallow a tack and you can spoil the day, to say the least.

The number and placement of staples and/or tacks depends on the particular job, but the staples and/or tacks should hold the fabric firmly in place. The joint is often reinforced by using an adhesive, as detailed above.

Staples and tacks are sometimes used to fasten fabric to various types of construction cardboard and fiberboard, but this often doesn't hold very well.

Other Mechanical Fastenings

Screws, bolts, and other mechanical fasteners are also widely used. These are generally used indirectly, however. For example, the fabric is often first fastened to a backing piece of wood or other material with adhesive, staples, tacks, or other means. This panel is then fastened in place, by means of screws, bolts, or other mechanical fasteners, as shown in Fig. 7-1. Special washers (Fig. 7-2) are often used to protect the fabric and give a better appearance.

Various types of wood, metal, and plastic trim strips are often used in a similar manner. There are many possibilities here.

TAKE-APART AND OPENING FASTENERS

There are many of these. Some, such as zippers, allow you to

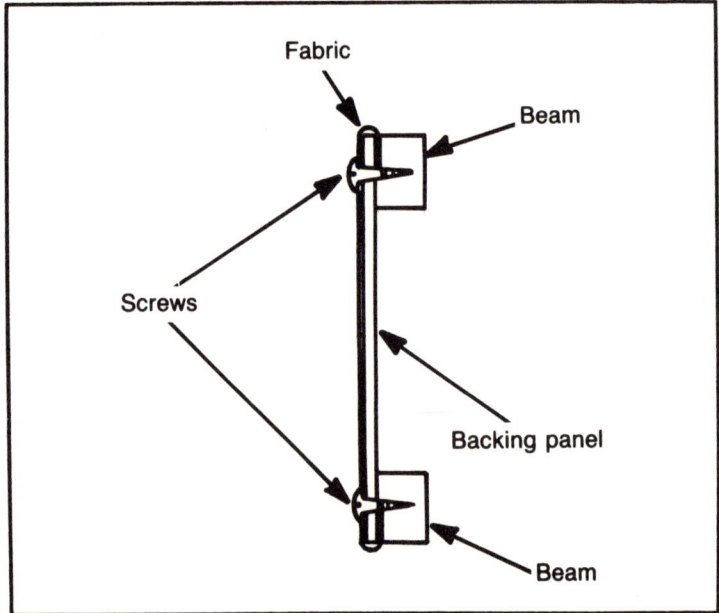

Fig. 7-1. Backing panel covered with fabric is fastened to beams with screws.

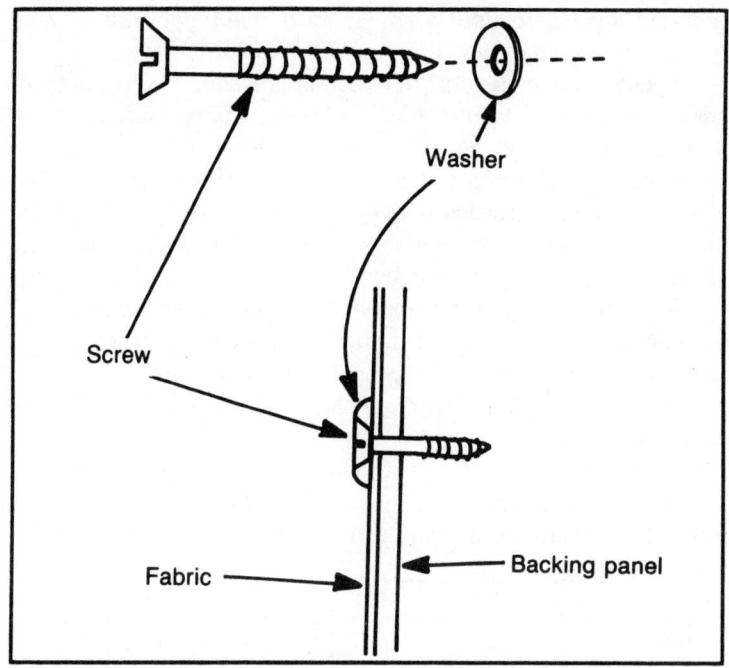

Fig. 7-2. Special washer protects fabric and gives better appearance.

open and close a section of fabric. Snaps, twist fasteners, and hooks can be similarly used or for fastening fabric to a wood, metal, or rigid plastic surface. These fasteners are basically used in canvas-to-canvas or canvas-to-something else applications. Canvas is frequently secured in place by cords or ropes, either sewn to the canvas or tied to a grommet, ring, or fabric or webbing loop sewn or otherwise attached to the canvas.

Although these are considered take-apart and opening fasteners, parts of the fasteners are usually permanently fastened to the fabrics or elsewhere. For our purposes here, drawstrings and elastic are opening fasteners.

Zippers

There are two basic types of zippers to consider, the *separating* and the *nonseparating*. Each type has specific uses in canvas and upholstery work.

The separating zipper comes apart at the bottom. It is the type commonly found on jackets. It is used in canvas and upholstery work when it is necessary to separate the fabrics when the zipper is open. This type is used when it is desirable to join and be able to completely separate two pieces of fabric.

Nonseparating zippers are closed at one end. This is the type commonly used for trouser flies. In canvas and upholstery work, it is used when only one end of the zipper needs to separate, as for an opening flap in a canvas side curtain. This type of zipper is also commonly closed at both ends when all that is needed is an opening with neither end having to separate, as in a carrying bag or an opening in a fabric cushion cover.

Regardless of the type required, I recommend the use of heavy-duty plastic zippers, because metal ones, including brass, tend to corrode and break quickly, especially on boats, where a damp atmosphere is likely. Many recreational vehicles also face similar environmental conditions.

There are a number of methods for sewing zippers to fabric. One method is to sew the zipper tape directly to the turned-under edge of the fabric, as shown in Fig. 7-3A. The zipper should be

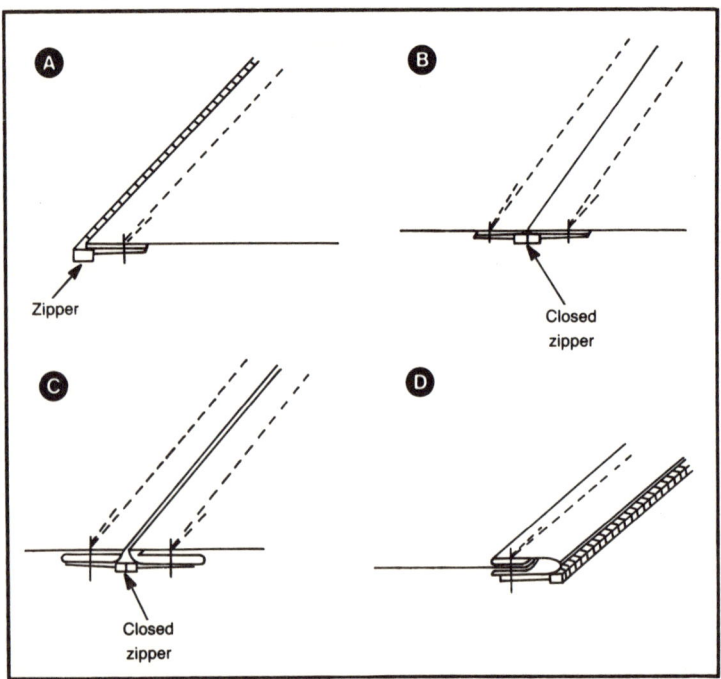

Fig. 7-3. Several methods of applying zippers: zipper tape sewn directly to turned-under edges of fabric (A); zipper sewn in place so that fabric edges just meet (B); zipper tapes sewn to hems with turned-under edges (C); and zipper installed to fabric strip with turned under edges (D).

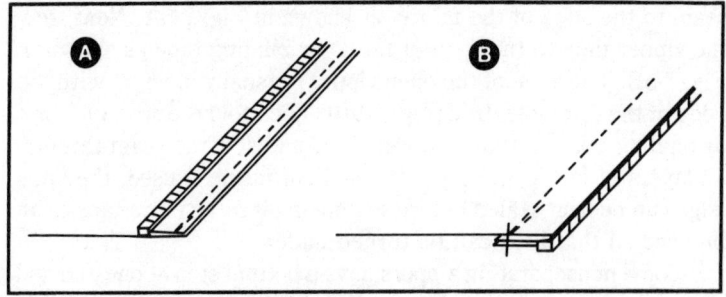

Fig. 7-4. Method for installing zipper.

zipped. The edges of the fabrics at the opening are usually placed so that they just meet, as shown in Fig. 7-3B. Use a zipper presser foot for machine sewing. Sew one side first. Then sew other side.

A similar method is to have the edges of the hem folded back under again, as shown in Fig. 7-3C and D. Another method is to first sew the zipper tape to the fabric right side to right side, as shown in Fig. 7-4. Then fold fabric as shown so that the fold extends to the center of the zipper. Then sew hem in place. This is generally done first to one piece of fabric, then to the other.

The above methods require fabric for the fold or hem. These are often installed first, before measuring the fabric for the rest of the pattern. It is often desirable to install a zipper directly at the edges of a cut in the fabric. This can be accomplished by using binding tape or a strip of fabric as shown in Fig. 7-5. First, sew the strip of fabric or binding tape right side to right side in a plain

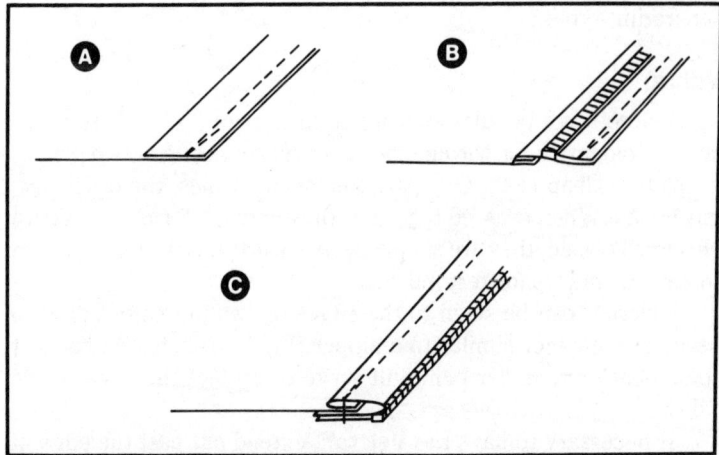

Fig. 7-5. Method for installing zipper using a strip of fabric.

seam to the edge of the fabric, as shown in Fig. 7-5A. Next, sew the zipper tape to the strip of fabric or binding tape as shown in Fig. 7-5B. The edge of the open zipper is usually lined up with the edge of the original fabric (Fig. 7-5B). Then fold the strip of fabric or binding over as shown in Fig. 7-5C and sew the seam through all layers of fabric and tape. If a strip of fabric is used, the open edge can be heat sealed before sewing in place, or extra fabric can be used so that hem can be turned under.

Some nonseparating zippers have a bottom stop at one end and top stops at the other so that the slider will not come off the ends of the zipper. When a zipper is purchased by the foot from a roll, however, it doesn't have these stops. The ends can be secured by whipstitching. This method can also be used for shortening a zipper. In addition, stop tabs are often sewn in place.

Separating zippers are sold in various lengths. When unzipped, the half with the slider and tab has stops on both ends so that the slider will not come off. The other half has a stiffened end for insertion into the slider and a stop on the other end. When installing this type of zipper, care must be taken to position the halves correctly.

Most zippers only have a tab on one side. For canvas work, it is frequently desirable to be able to open the zipper from either side. Zippers are available with tabs on both sides, often called *double slide*, that allows this.

By whipstitching one or both ends, separating zippers can be turned into nonseparating zippers. The reverse, however, is not true. Nonseparating zippers cannot ordinarily be converted to separating type.

Velcro®

Velcro® is a popular alternative to zippers. Velcro® is a registered trademark for woven tape fasteners consisting of two mating strips (see Chapter 2). One part has loops or piles, the other part has hooks. When pressed together, they engage, forming a secure closure. To open, they are simply peeled apart. It can easily be sewn to canvas and upholstery fabrics.

Velcro® can be sewn to the edges of two pieces of fabric to serve in a manner similar to a zipper (Fig 7-6). A folded back or folded-back-and-under hem will serve to protect the edge of the fabric.

If necessary to have the Velcro® extend out past the edge of the fabric, a strip of fabric or binding tape can first be sewn to the

Fig. 7-6. Velcro® sewn to fabric pieces.

fabric. The Velcro® is sewn to this.

Velcro® can also be used to hold cushions and other items in place. One part of the Velcro® is sewn to the cushion. The other part of the Velcro® can be stapled or glued to wood or attached to metal or plastic surfaces by using appropriate adhesive.

Velcro® fasteners can also be used for holding light covers, mosquito nets, and a variety of other canvas and upholstery items in place. They are easily removed and put back in place thousands of times. This is versatile material, and you will probably think of many uses for it.

Snap Fasteners

Snap fasteners (Fig. 7-7) can be used to secure two pieces of fabric together or a piece of fabric to some other object. These have many uses in canvas and upholstery work, as when joining canvas side curtains to canvas tops and holding cushions in place.

There are two basic parts, the *socket* or female and the *stud* or male. The socket or female part should always be the outside or opening part. Sockets and studs are easy to install in canvas fabric. A hole is made in the fabric for the shaft of a special button or eyelet. The socket or stud fits over this. A special die and punch is used to set them. The button or eyelet and fabric are set in die, the socket or stud is set in place and tapped with a hammer. Buttons are used with sockets and studs with eyelets.

A variety of setting tools is available, including the die and tap described above, and special vise pliers. There are also expensive

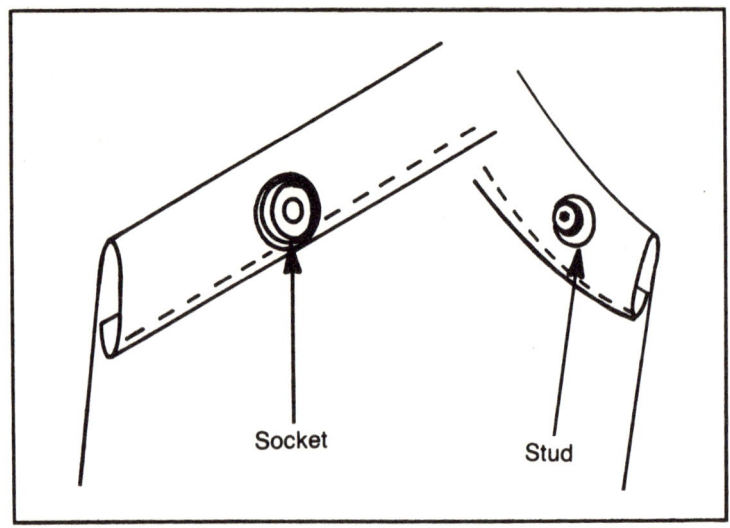

Fig. 7-7. Snap fastener has socket and stud parts.

shop tools, but the inexpensive die and tap sets will suffice for the projects detailed in this book.

The studs are also available with screws, both wood and self-tapping, and machine screws (Fig.7-8). These can be used for attaching the studs to wood, metal, and plastics. Because there is considerable stress on these fasteners, whenever practical, I suggest the use of machine screws rather than wood or self-tapping screws. When fastening to fiberglass, use machine screws and backing washers. Caulking should be applied to the threads to prevent possible leaking. Slide sockets for use on straps (Fig. 7-9) are also available.

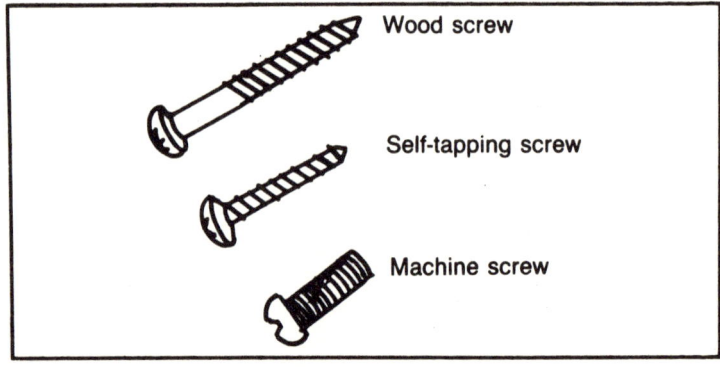

Fig. 7-8. Snap studs for fastening to solid objects.

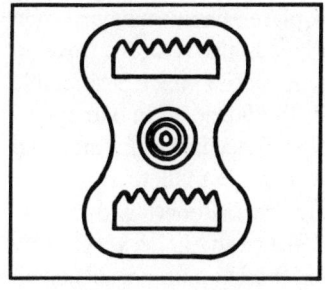

Fig. 7-9. Slide socket for use on strap.

The main advantage of snap fasteners as compared to Lift-the Dot and Common Sense fasteners described below is that they do not stick out very far. Although snaps hold fairly well in shear, in tension they tend to come apart or open. Snaps are also less expensive than other fasteners.

Lift-the-Dot Fasteners

Lift-the-Dot fasteners protrude more than snaps, but they are generally more secure. These consist of a socket and a stud (Fig. 7-10. The socket has prongs that pass through openings in the fab-

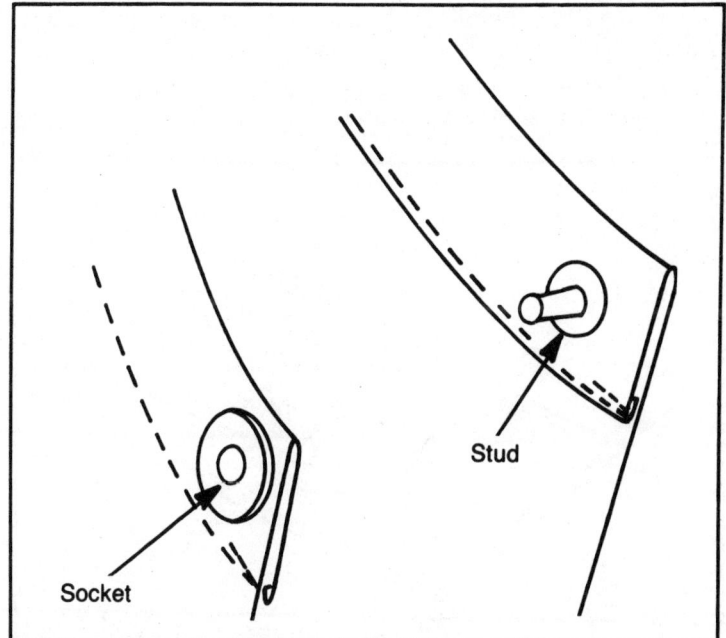

Fig. 7-10. Lift-the-Dot fastener.

ric and then through holes in a clinch plate. The prongs are then bent over to hold the parts in place. A hole is also required through the fabric for the stud to pass through. A special punch is available to make the prong and socket holes in the fabric all in one operation. To use, first mark location for socket. Place fabric on soft wood surface. Position punch, and tap with a wood mallet.

It is also possible to install Lift-the-Dot fasteners without the special punch by marking and cutting the prong holes with a tiny bladed screwdriver. This takes longer, though, and doesn't do as neat a job. If a large number of these fasteners are to be installed, by all means get the punch. If done with a screwdriver blade, a socket hole can be cut through the fabric after clinch plate has been installed.

After holes have been made, slip socket prongs through holes. Install clinch plate on prongs, as shown in Fig. 7-11. Place face of socket on solid surface. Bend prongs inward with a screwdriver or other appropriate tool.

There are two types of studs available for installation in fabric. One type has two prongs and a clinch plate (Fig. 7-12). A special punch is available to make the two prong holes, or a tiny bladed screwdriver can be used. After making the holes, insert the prongs through the fabric. Install clinch plate over prongs. With the clinch plate pushed up tight, bend the prongs inward to secure the stud in place, as shown in Fig. 7-12.

Another type of stud has an attached eyelet (Fig. 7-13). A round

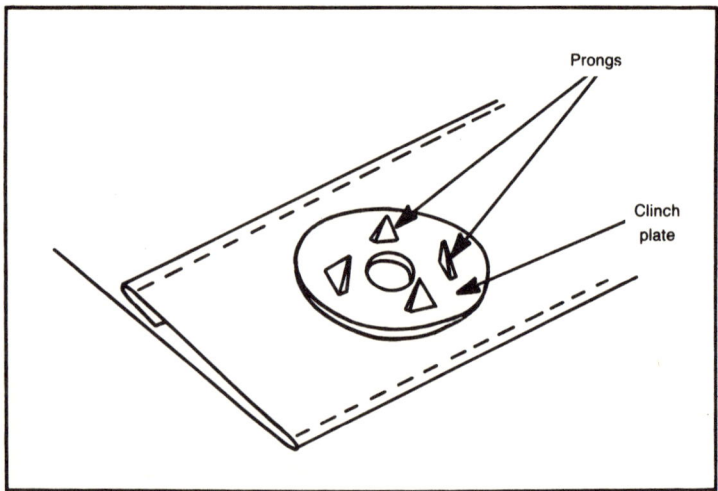

Fig. 7-11. Clinch plate is installed over socket prongs.

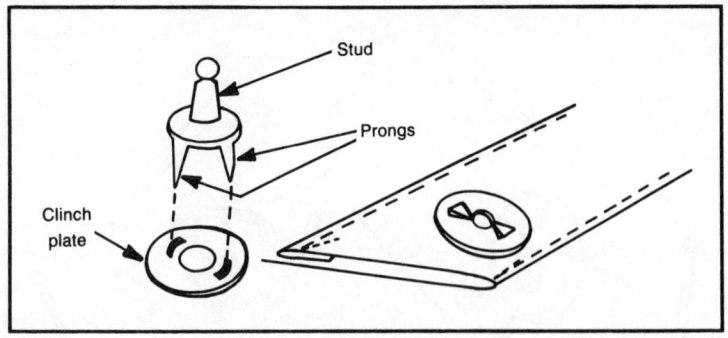

Fig. 7-12. Lift-the-Dot stud and clinch plate for installation in fabric. Prongs are bent over to secure stud to clinch plate.

hole is punched in the fabric, and the eyelet is passed through this. A special washer is placed over this, and a special attaching tool is used to set the eyelet.

Studs are available for attachment to solid surfaces by means of wood screws, self-tapping screws, and machine screws (Fig. 7-13). A special hand screwdriver is available for installing these. Studs that hold either a single socket or two sockets are available.

Common Sense Fasteners

Common Sense fasteners are twist-type fasteners with considerable holding power (Fig. 7-14). They do protrude a considerable distance, but if this can be tolerated, these are the fasteners to use. There are two basic parts, a stud and an eyelet. The eyelet is always installed in fabric; the stud can be installed

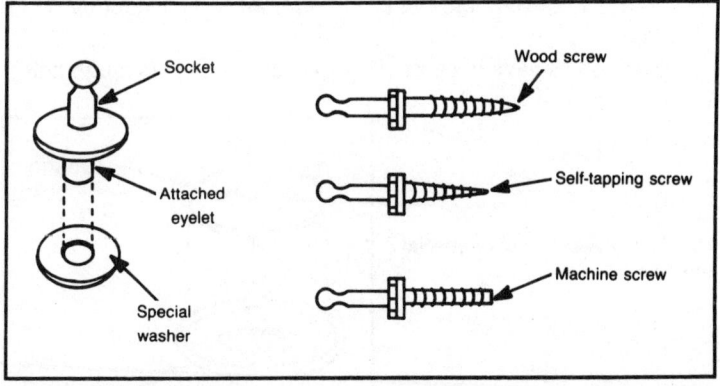

Fig. 7-13. Stud with attached eyelet, and Lift-the-Dot studs for attachment to solid surfaces.

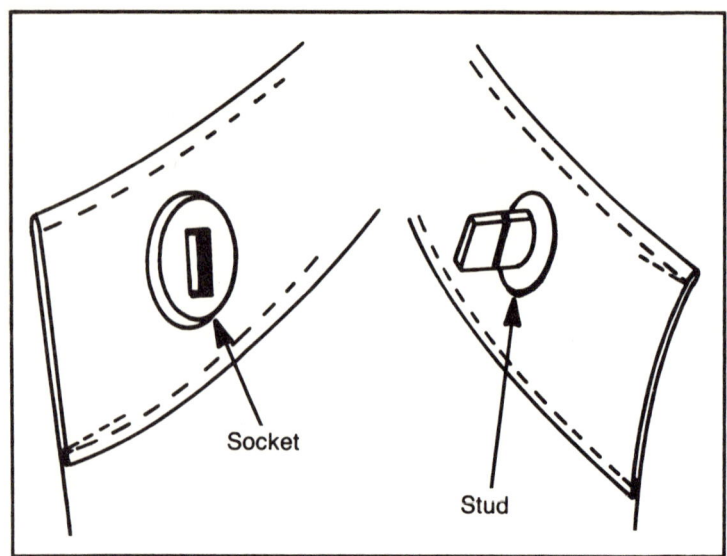

Fig. 7-14. Twist or Common Sense fastener.

in fabric or to solid surfaces. Studs are available for holding a single eyelet or two eyelets stacked on each other.

Eyelets require special washers (Fig. 7-15). A special cutting punch is available that cuts the four prong holes and the stud hole in the fabric all in one operation. To use, first mark location for eyelet. Place fabric on soft wood surface. Position punch and tap with a wood mallet.

It is also possible to punch the four prong holes with a tiny bladed screwdriver. First, mark desired location, then punch the four holes. The stud hole can be cut later after the eyelet has been installed.

After holes have been made, slip eyelet prongs through holes.

Fig. 7-15. Eyelets require special washers.

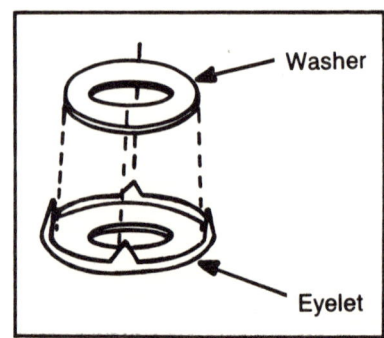

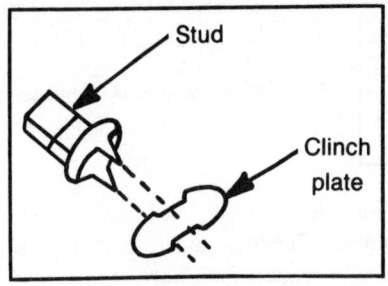

Fig. 7-16. Stud with clinch plate.

Place special washer between prongs. Place face of socket on solid surface. Bend prongs inward with a screwdriver or other appropriate tool.

There are two types of studs available for installation in fabric. One type has two prongs and a clinch plate (Fig. 7-16). A special punch is available to make the two prong holes, or a tiny bladed screwdriver can be used. After making the holes, insert the prongs through the fabric. Install clinch plate over prongs. With the clinch plate pushed up tight, bend the prongs inward to secure the stud in place.

Another type of stud has an attached eyelet. A round hole is punched in the fabric, and the eyelet is passed through this. A special washer is placed over the eyelet on the side of the fabric opposite the stud. A special tool is used to set the eyelet.

Studs are available for attachment to solid surfaces. These are available with wood screw (Fig. 7-17A), self-tapping screw (Fig. 7-17B), machine screw (Fig. 7-17C), and with a two-hole base (Fig.7-17D) for attachment to solid surface by means of screws, rivets, or bolts. A special hand screwdriver is available for installing the screw-type studs. The studs are available for holding a single eyelet or two eyelets stacked on top of each other.

Hook and Eye Fasteners

Hook and eye fasteners (Fig. 7-18) are sometimes used for

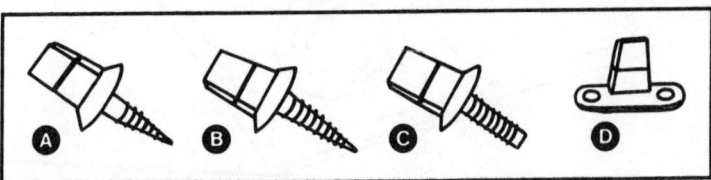

Fig. 7-17. Stud with wood screw (A); stud with self-tapping screw (B); stud with machine screw (C); and stud with two hole base (D).

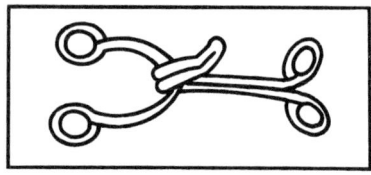

Fig. 7-18. Hook and eye fastener.

canvas closures, as on boom covers on sailboats, but I don't recommend this. The savings over Common Sense fasteners is small, and Common Sense fasteners generally work much better.

The hooks and eyes are generally hand sewn to the fabric. Sometimes, they are riveted to the fabric and a backing washer. In either case, it is also a good idea to back up the fabric with an extra layer of fabric.

Grommets

Grommets (Fig. 7-19) are frequently installed in canvas and upholstery fabric for the attachment of ropes, shock cords, and hooks, and sometimes to allow air to escape.

Grommets are available in a variety of types and sizes from about 1/4 inch up to 5/8 inch and larger. They are available in steel (not recommended for boat and recreational vehicle use) and brass (recommended). Punch cutters are available to make the holes for installing grommets. After the correct size hole is made, one part of the grommet is passed through the hole. The other part of the grommet is slipped in place on the opposite side of the fabric. Special setting dies are available to set the grommet parts.

It is generally a good idea to use a backing layer of fabric in areas where grommets are to be installed. A frequent problem with

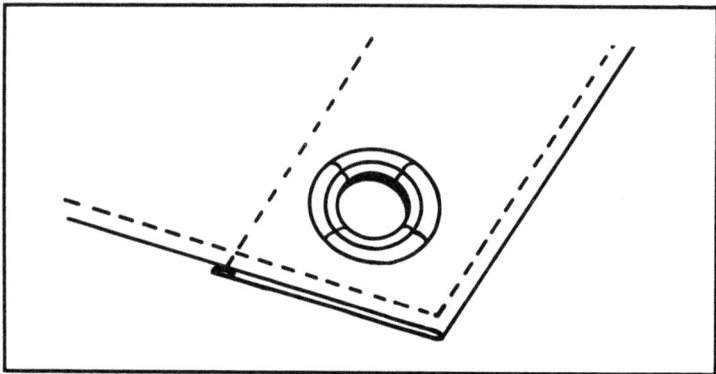

Fig. 7-19. Grommet installed in fabric.

grommets is that they tend to tear out of the fabric. Reinforce the fabric and use enough grommets for tie downs so that the stress will be spread to a number of areas of the fabric.

Webbing

Webbing is sometimes sewn to canvas fabric for use as tie downs, as shown in Fig. 7-20. If heavy stress is to be placed on the loops, reinforce the canvas with an extra layer of fabric where the webbing is to be sewn in place.

Webbing is usually easy to sew with an upholstery sewing machine and is available in cotton, nylon, polypropylene, and polyester in a variety of widths. Nylon or polyester is usually recommended for use on boats and recreational vehicles. Webbing generally comes in rolls and is sold by the foot or yard. It usually has considerable strength. One brand of one-inch wide polyester webbing has a test strength of 1,200 pounds and one-inch wide nylon a test strength of 2,000 pounds. The nylon has more stretch than polyester. Select webbing for a particular use on basis of whether or not stretching is desirable. Webbing is also used for handles and straps on bags, to reinforce fabric, and in a variety of other ways.

Although a variety of sewing patterns can be used to sew webbing to canvas, a rectangle with diagonal cross stitches is frequently used, as shown in Fig. 7-20.

Cords and Ropes Sewn to Fabric

Small braided nylon cord is easily machine sewn to fabrics for use as tie downs, as shown in Fig. 7-21. The cord flattens out under

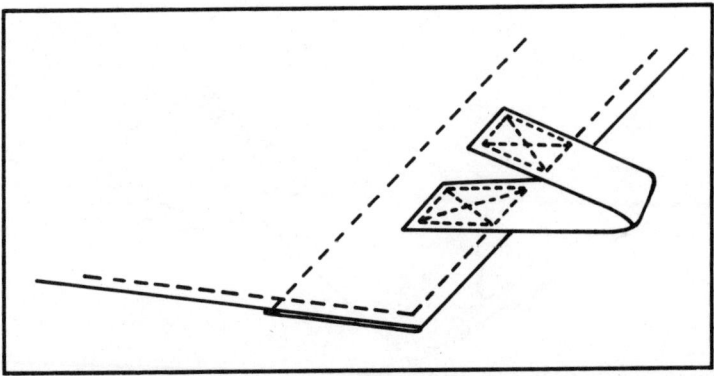

Fig. 7-20. Webbing sewn to fabric for use as tie down. Note "X" stitching pattern for sewing webbing to canvas.

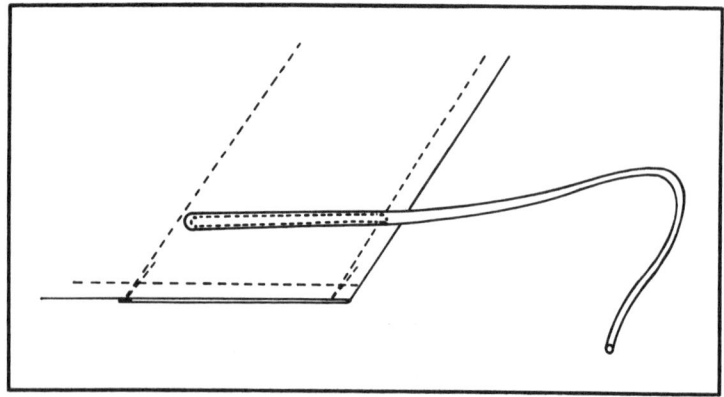

Fig. 7-21. Braided cord sewn to fabric for use as a tie down.

the presser foot, making stitching easy. This makes ideal tie downs when only light stresses will be involved. It is a good idea to use a backing layer of fabric to reinforce the fabric.

Heavier ropes are sometimes sewn to canvas, usually by hand sewing. This seems to be a carry-over from the old days and doesn't seem to be used much anymore. The main problem is that the rope is usually much stronger than the fabric, and when load is placed on the rope, the fabric tends to tear.

D-Rings

Sometimes, D-rings are attached to fabric directly by hand sewing (generally not recommended), as shown in Fig. 7-22, or in-

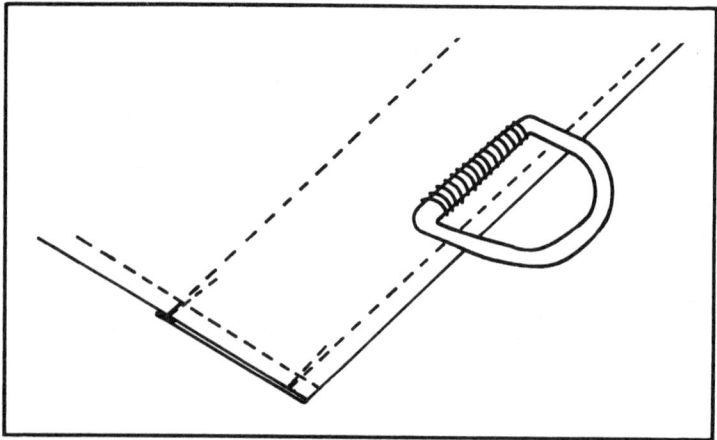

Fig. 7-22. A D-ring sewn directly to fabric.

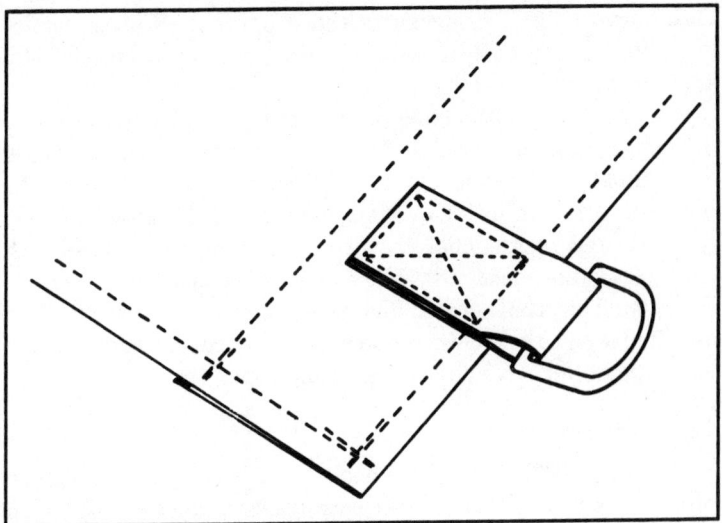

Fig. 7-23. Webbing attachment of D-ring.

directly by using webbing (a much better arrangement), as shown in Fig. 7-23.

Draw Strings and Ropes

Draw strings and ropes are frequently installed in hems to close bags and hold down covers. The basic installation is to sew a casing in the fabric with an opening to the outside. A large safety pin or wood spike can be attached to the end of the cord or rope to feed it through the casing. Draw strings form a simple closure and hold down system for many canvas items.

Elastic and Cord

Elastic tape and cord can be used instead of a draw string to hold a number of canvas items in place. Elastic tape can be sewn to fabric. Shock cord is frequently installed in a casing, and the ends of the shock cord connected by special clamps, as shown in Fig. 7-24. The clamps are available in stainless steel for boat and recreational vehicle use. Special pliers are available for setting the clamps.

To sew elastic tape to fabric so that it will draw the fabric together, stretch the elastic as it is being sewn in place. Elastics are usually made from a rubber core yarn covered with natural or synthetic fibers. These are either braided or woven together. Braided elastics have parallel ridges that run lengthwise. Woven elastics are softer. Elastics are available in various widths and are usually sold by the foot or yard.

Shock cord is available with cotton or nylon covering in diameters from 1/8 inch up to 1/2 inch and larger. It comes in rolls and is usually sold by the foot or yard from these rolls. Short lengths of shock cord with spring C-clamps on the ends are also available. For boat and recreational vehicle use, I recommend those with spring C-clamps made of stainless steel rather than the more common plated or plastic coated high tensile steel. These shock cords are often used as hold down devices for canvas covers, and for many uses, they offer advantages over using rope.

Cover Hooks

There is often a need for hooks on a boat or boat trailer to secure canvas covers. These are usually best when through-bolted in place.

FRAME SUPPORT SYSTEMS

Many canvas items require frame support systems. Recrea-

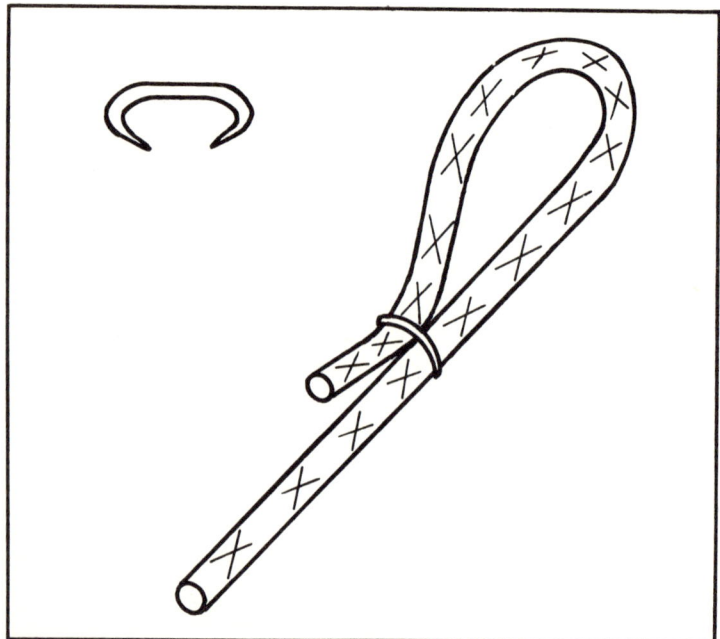

Fig. 7-24. Crimp ring for joining shock cord.

tional vehicle awnings and cabanas frequently have a system of metal frames and fittings for supporting and holding the canvas in position. Canvas tops for dune buggies and other similar recreational vehicles and boats frequently use a system of frame supports and fittings. These often fold so that the top can be raised or lowered. Arches and bow frames are frequently used under rain covers to give the necessary slope for water to run off.

Frames for both boats and recreational vehicles are typically made of aluminum or stainless steel tubing. In some cases, standard steel tubing is used, but this tends to rust and thus is not recommended for boat and recreational vehicle use. Plastic tubing and pipe, such as PVC, is sometimes used for frames and battens.

A tube bender is used to bend aluminum and stainless steel tubing. If only a limited amount of work is to be done, you may want to borrow or rent a tube bender or have someone else who has one do the bending for you. Inexpensive tube benders will suffice for aluminum tubing, but you need a substantial bender to handle stainless steel.

The outside diameter of aluminum tubing used for frames is usually 3/4 inch. The outside diameter of stainless steel tubing is commonly either 7/8 inch or 1 inch.

Several fittings are available for use with tubing, and these generally make welding unnecessary. The fittings are made from aluminum, brass, standard steel (not recommended), stainless steel, bronze, and a variety of plastics. Typical fittings include *end fittings* (Fig. 7-25A), *jaw slides* (Fig. 7-25B), *mounting fittings* (Fig.

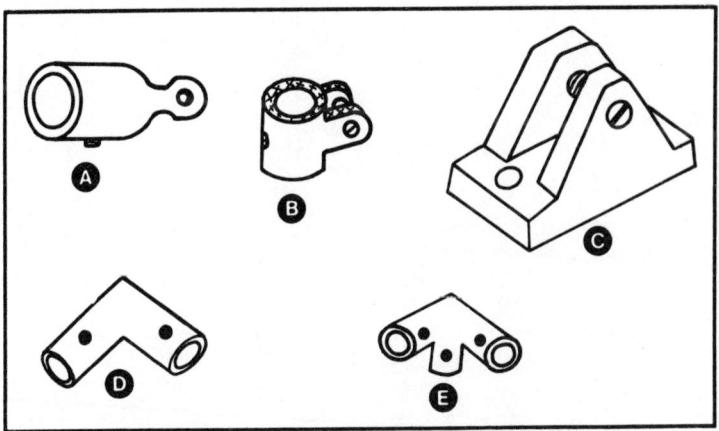

Fig. 7-25. Various frame support system hardware: end fitting (A); jaw slide (B); mounting bracket (C); elbow (D); and three-way corner (E).

7-25C), *elbows* (Fig. 7-25D), *three-way corners* (Fig. 7-25E), and a variety of others.

Most of the fittings have set screws for attachment to tubing. The tube bender is used to bend tubing to desired shape without collapsing the walls of the tubing. The tubing can be cut with a hacksaw, but considerable care is required to obtain a straight cut unless a jig is used. A *tube cutter* will make this work easier and give a clean straight cut. Mounting brackets and fittings are usually through-bolted to boats and recreational vehicles.

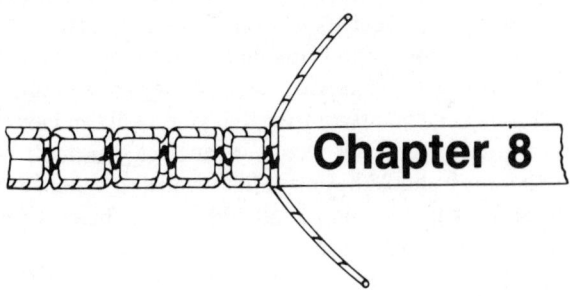

Chapter 8

Overall Planning

To this point, basic skills and techniques for boat and recreational vehicle canvas and upholstery work have been covered. These will allow you to make the specific canvas and upholstery items detailed in the chapters that follow.

To successfully carry out a canvas or upholstery project requires, in addition to mastering basic skills and techniques, careful overall planning. You have to put it all together.

SELECTING A PROJECT

First, you will need to decide on a specific project. This will probably be something that needs to be done on your boat or recreational vehicle.

A first project should be limited in scope so that you won't be overwhelmed by it. Even if you have in mind an extensive overall project, such as replacing all of the canvas or upholstery work in a boat or recreational vehicle or doing all of the fabric work for an original interior, you should tackle it in steps or stages.

Select a logical starting project. If you plan to make covers for cushions and seats, curtains, a wheel cover, and a cover for the top carrying rack for your recreational vehicle, decide which job you want to do first. In some cases, this will be decided for you, as something must go in before something else. But in many cases the items are independent of each other, and you can do them in any order that you want. For example, on a sailboat, the mainsail cover is independent from the winch covers and tiller cover. Although you may want to use the same fabric for all of these and purchase this all at once, you can make each item individually.

Try to select a project that is simple and straightforward for a starter. Not all canvas and upholstery items are of equal difficulty. Begin with an easy one that can be done in a reasonably short period of time. You should try to match your skills and experience with the job. Although you won't advance if you don't try new things, experience should be added in easy doses. Whenever possible, new skills and techniques should be practiced with scrap materials, not on an actual job.

The project should be such that the finished item will be successful, and you will be proud of it. Even if it doesn't turn out very good, as sometimes happens with first attempts, it's better if this is a small simple cover that didn't require much fabric than, say, a canvas top that is complicated and requires considerable material.

There are really two main aspects: how difficult or complicated the project is and how much of it there is. A hem or casing around a large boat cover may be the same as used on a small cover, but there will be a lot more of it on the large cover. The same seam is machine sewn in each case, but the large cover is going to require a much longer seam and will require a lot more time to complete the job.

ORGANIZING A PROJECT

Once you have selected a specific project, you need to plan and organize how you are going to carry it out. This involves a number of steps: decide the best way to do the job; determine required fabrics and other materials; purchase materials; make the necessary patterns and transfer these to fabrics; cut fabrics; sew fabrics; and make necessary installation.

Best Way to Do the Job

You should first learn the basic skills and techniques presented up to this point in this book. Specific projects are detailed in later chapters. I suggest that you read through all of this material once. Then return to the section relating to the specific project you have in mind. In most cases, more than one method is presented for accomplishing the same thing; there are several methods for making and mounting curtains. Study the advantages and disadvantages of each method as they apply to the specific job you have in mind, and decide how you want to do it.

The method selected should, when possible, take advantage of your special skills and interests. One method may require more machine sewing and less of something else; another method may require less sewing and more of some other type of work.

Do you have the necessary skills and techniques for doing the job right? If not, learn them first. It's important to have confidence that you can finish the project successfully before you begin.

The particular method you select for doing a project will also depend in part on the tools and equipment you have available. When you have a choice of two kinds of fabric, you may choose one over the other because the sewing machine you have available will not handle the other one.

There is usually a general method for doing the project. You will often have a number of other choices relating to types of seams to be used, arrangement of pieces of fabric, joining of fabrics, and so on. Make diagrams on paper of the possibilities, and then decide the way you want to go.

Although a number of methods for accomplishing the various projects are detailed in this book, they are not the only ones. You may come up with a better method for your particular purposes. This is the creative part of canvas and upholstery work.

Fabrics and Other Materials

For most projects, you will have a choice of fabrics and other materials. You will need to consider suitability for the particular project, quality, durability, and cost. The choice of color and pattern design of fabrics is also important. Materials and supplies are covered in Chapter 2.

When selecting colors and pattern designs, keep in mind all work that is to be done. Interior decoration is especially important in both boats and recreational vehicles. Color schemes and design patterns play an important role here, so make your selections accordingly. For exterior covers and other canvas work, light colors are generally chosen so that they will reflect more sunlight and remain cooler underneath.

After deciding what fabrics and other materials are to be used, determine how much you will need. Take careful measurements and, if you can afford it, purchase a little extra. A frequent problem is getting part way through a job and then discovering that you don't have enough fabric to complete the job.

Make a list of everything required so that you can have everything on hand before you start a project. This also includes thread and needles for the sewing machine, binding tape, zippers, fasteners, and whatever else is required for the particular job. Of course, you may already have some of the materials on hand.

Purchase Materials

After you decide what you will need and how much, the next step is to purchase it. This is generally most conveniently done at stores in the area where you live, assuming that they have what you need. This can, however, be the expensive route. Mail order can save you considerable money, even when you figure in the cost of shipping. You do have to plan further ahead, however, as you will have to wait until you receive your order.

Make Patterns and Transfer to Fabric

Methods for measuring, marking, and transferring patterns to fabric are given in Chapter 6. This is an important step, and care should to taken to avoid mistakes, because they can be costly. The basic idea is to measure twice (or three or four times) and cut once. Well, you can always cut off more, but *un*cutting is best left to magicians.

Although all steps are important, this is the one that frequently means the difference between sloppy and professional looking results. Take your time and do it right.

Mark and label all parts so that you will know where they go in relation to other parts, the position of seams, and where reinforcements are to go. Make notes to help you avoid errors. Don't trust these to memory: write them down.

Cutting

Cutting is generally fairly easy, sometimes too easy. Check everything over again before cutting the fabrics. Keep fabrics clean and organized.

Sew Fabrics

The next step is usually to do the sewing, although this varies depending on the particular project. Also, you may do some of the sewing, then trial fitting, some additional pattern marking and possibly cutting, then more sewing, and so on. But don't lose control.

If you make a seam in the wrong place, it may be possible to rip it out and then sew again in the correct place. Some fabrics are more forgiving in this aspect than others. If you use vinyl upholstery fabric, be careful, because too many needle holes can cause the fabric to tear, and needle holes in an exposed area generally show.

A common mistake is not to fix the beginning and ends of machine stitches by backtracking. If you don't fix the seams, there is a much greater chance that they will open later. Remember, on many canvas and upholstery projects, the seams are the weakest point in the system.

Sewing on the seamlines of the patterns is important for quality work. Wavy and uneven seams often give the finished project a sloppy appearance.

Installation

Some canvas and upholstery items require additional installation; others don't. It may be necessary to install fasteners to hold canvas or upholstery in place, to install foam padding inside cushion covers, or to do a number of other jobs.

QUALITY OF WORK

You will want to produce the kind of finished work of which you will be proud. This may not happen on the first project, although it can if you plan and organize everything carefully and take the time and trouble to do each little job right. The professional canvas and upholstery worker has generally had years of experience, but most do-it-yourselfers have the advantage of not having to consider time as money.

Try, and then try again. The quality of your work will probably improve greatly with experience. You can learn from your mistakes, too. When you finish a piece of work, examine it carefully. See what is wrong with it. The problem may have been in the sewing, cutting, patterning, or some combination of these. Try to improve on any weaknesses when you do future projects.

Try to break each project into a number of small jobs rather than one great big one. Then do each little job right. The result will be quality work. On the other hand, if you let little mistakes creep in here and there on the little jobs, these can accumulate to the point where the total project turns out to be a mess.

Most do-it-yourselfers have to make do with less than the ideal in the way of tools, equipment, and work areas, but with care, high quality work is usually still possible.

INTRODUCTION TO THE PROJECTS

In the following chapters, similar projects have been grouped together in the following categories: bags and carrying cases, covers, awnings and enclosures, canvas tops and side curtains, mosquito screens and netting, cushions and seats, upholstered panels and headliners, curtains, and carpets. In some cases, a specific project could have been placed in more than one category, and the choice was made arbitrarily.

Some projects apply specifically to either boats or recreational vehicles. Others apply to both. Some of the boat projects are only for power boats; others are only for sailboats. The term recreational vehicles is being used very broadly here to include campers, motor homes, travel trailers, vans, pickup trucks, dune buggies, and a variety of other similar vehicles that make use of canvas and upholstery work or items. Naturally, only some of the possibilities can be covered, but you can probably adapt these to fit a variety of specific requirements. Also, the skills and techniques can be used to replace or modify existing canvas and upholstery work.

The projects have been organized by categories rather than difficulty, although bags and carrying cases, a good starting point, has been placed first. This will give good experience in a variety of techniques. The remainder of the projects can be approached in any order desired.

It is assumed that you are thoroughly familiar with all the material presented up to this point in this book and that you have mastered the basic skills and techniques.

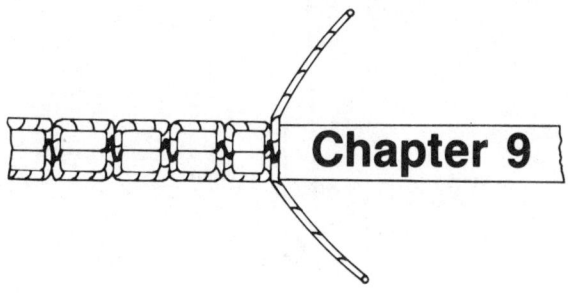

Chapter 9

Bags and Carrying Cases

Many bags and carrying cases can be made from fabrics, and these are popular with boaters and recreational vehicle users. They make ideal starter projects, because they are usually carry-on items that are not attached to the boat or recreational vehicle.

Three basic types of bags and carrying cases are considered here: open top bags with carrying handles, bags with drawstring closures at one end, and zipper closed bags with carrying handles.

OPEN TOP BAGS WITH HANDLES

These are easy to make, useful bags (Fig. 9-1). They resemble shopping bags. They are sometimes called *flat bags* because the most common type fold flat when empty, although the bags can also be square, rectangular, or round, as desired.

These bags can be used to store all kinds of things, including small sails that are folded flat after each use, and as shopping bags. The size and shape of a particular bag depends on its intended use.

The bags can be made from a variety of fabrics, including cotton, nylon, acrylic, and polyester. Cotton, nylon, or polyester webbing can be used for carrying handles, or you can make handles from strips of fabric.

A flat bag can be made from a single piece of fabric, as shown in Fig. 9-2. Dimensions can be as desired. Leave a seam allowance, usually 1/2 inch, for making plain seams on both sides of the bag. The pattern shown is for folding the hem over twice so that the

Fig. 9-1. Open top bag with carrying handle.

edge of the fabric will be hidden. If desired, a single fold can be used.

Begin by laying out pattern on wrong side of fabric, including seam and folding lines. Then cut fabric.

Machine sew hems in each end of fabric, as shown in Fig. 9-3. Hems are usually folded inward from right side of fabric, but they can also be folded outward if a double fold is used so that the edge

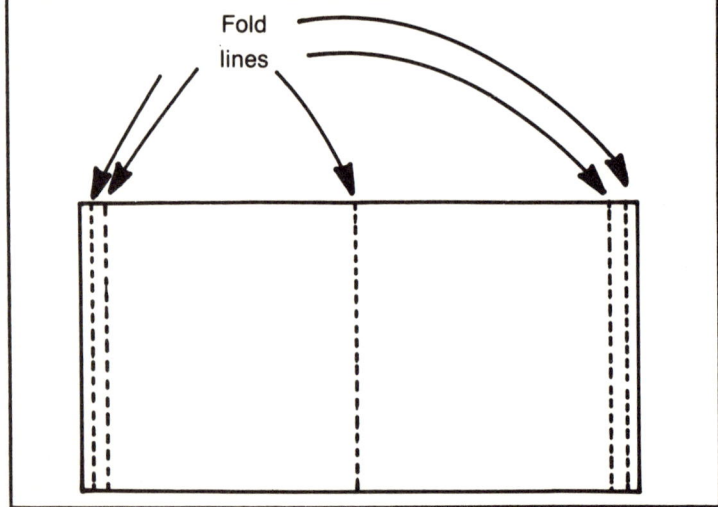

Fig. 9-2. Pattern for making flat bag.

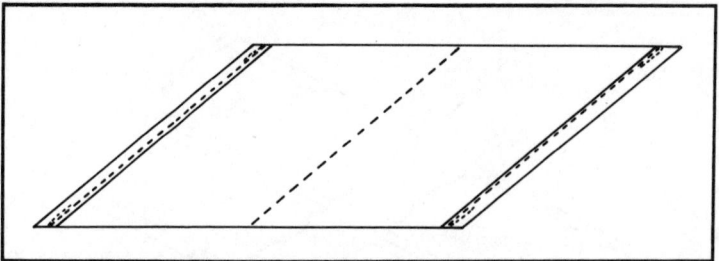

Fig. 9-3. Hems are sewn on each end.

of the fabric will be hidden. Keep in mind which side will be the right side and which will be the wrong side of the finished bag.

The handles are usually sewn in place next. Webbing from about 1 inch to 1 1/2 inch is about right for most bags, or you can make a handle from a strip of fabric the required length of the handle. A 4 1/2-inch wide strip will give a finished handle 1 3/4-inch wide by using a 1/2-inch seam allowance. Fold the fabric right side to right side, and make plain seam along one side with a 1/2-inch seam allowance, as shown in Fig. 9-4. Then turn right side out, using a wood dowel to work one end of the fabric through. Then flatten tube with seam in center of one side and flaps folded outward, as shown in Fig. 9-4. Turn ends under 1/2 inch and make seam 1/8 inch from edge, as shown in Fig. 9-4. Continue sewing around edge, 1/8 inch from sides, as shown in Fig. 9-5. Handle

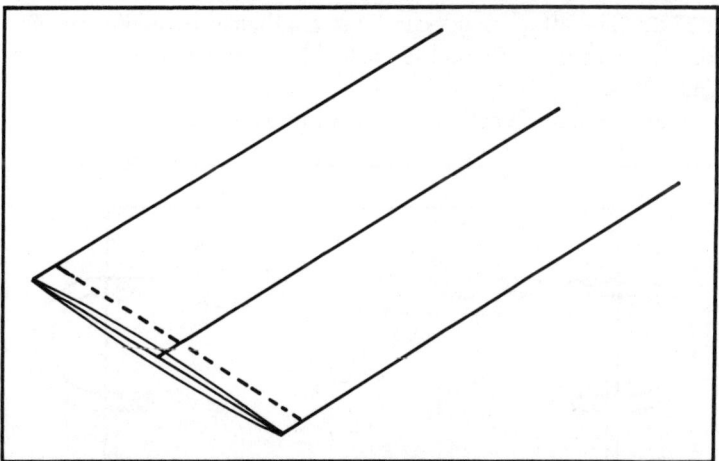

Fig. 9-4. Seam is sewn with 1/2-inch seam allowance. The tube is flattened with seam in center and flaps outward, and ends are turned under 1/2 inch and seam is made 1/8 inch from edge.

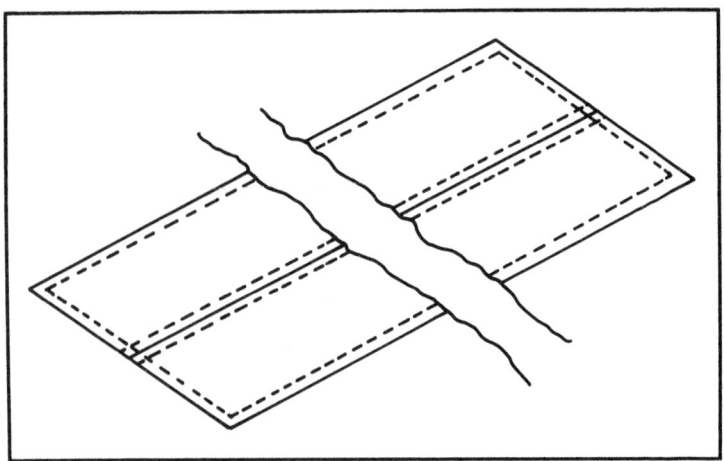

Fig. 9-5. Stitching around edge of handle and on each side of centerline.

should be desired length, plus 1/2 inch, before closing second end. Next, make two more stitches, 1/8 inch outward on each side of center, as shown in Fig. 9-5. These will each be through three layers of fabric, the outside layers and the flap. If desired, additional rows of stitching can be made.

One possible arrangement of handles is shown in Fig. 9-6. These are sewn to the outside of the fabric and should extend three or more inches from the edge. This attachment is usually adequate for carrying light loads provided that heavy fabric was used to make the bag. The attachments can be strengthened by adding a reinforcing layer of fabric on the back side, which will be inside the finished bag.

Regardless of whether standard webbing is used or you make

Fig. 9-6. Handles sewn to right side of fabric.

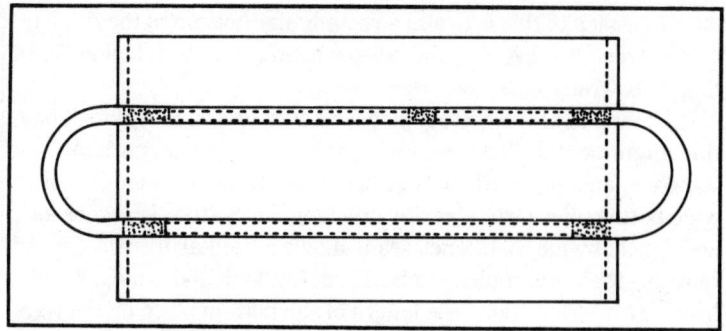

Fig. 9-7. Handles formed from single loop.

the handles from strips of fabric, a rectangular stitching pattern with an "X" inside is generally used to attach the handles.

If heavy loads are to be carried, it's a good idea to have the handles extend on down and around the bottom of the bag. The two handles will then be formed from a single loop with an inch or so overlap for joining the ends. The loop is then sewn to the right side of the fabric, as shown in Fig. 9-7. Because the straps extend around the bottom of the finished bag, they help protect the bottom of the bag from wear.

Next, fold the fabric together with the wrong side on the outside and make a plain seam along each side of the bag. Be sure to backtrack the start and finish of each seam to fix the ends. Turn the bag right side out. This completes the construction of a basic flat bag with an open top.

If desired, the plain seam along the sides can be strengthened by turning the 1/2-inch edges under and sewing another seam along this. This also hides the raw edges of the fabric.

A similar bag can be made with a rectangular bottom, (Fig. 9-8).

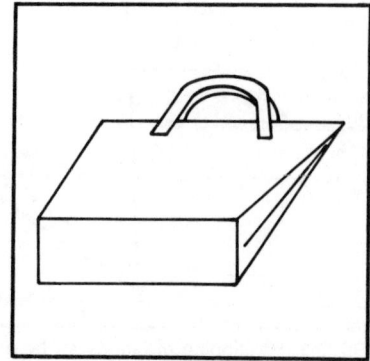

Fig. 9-8. Bag with rectangular bottom.

One approach to this is to add a rectangular bottom to the flat bag, as constructed above. Cut the bottom open along the fold line. Turn fabric to wrong side out.

The width of the bottom piece can vary. For a fairly small bag, this might be 2 or 3 inches; for a slightly larger bag, perhaps 5 or 6 inches; and so on. If the flat bag was 18 inches wide, a 3-inch wide bottom piece would make a rectangular bottom 12 inches long and 3 inches wide. A 1/2-inch seam allowance left all the way around requires the bottom piece to be 13 inches long and 4 inches wide. Mark a centerline along the length of the bottom piece on the right side.

The sewing is done with the wrong side of the bottom facing downward on the bed of the sewing machine. Starting at the centerline of one side of the bottom piece, position and line up the upper portion of the bag as shown in Fig. 9-9. Position fabric under sewing machine needle at centerline and lower presser foot to fabric. Edges of upper and lower fabrics should line up exactly.

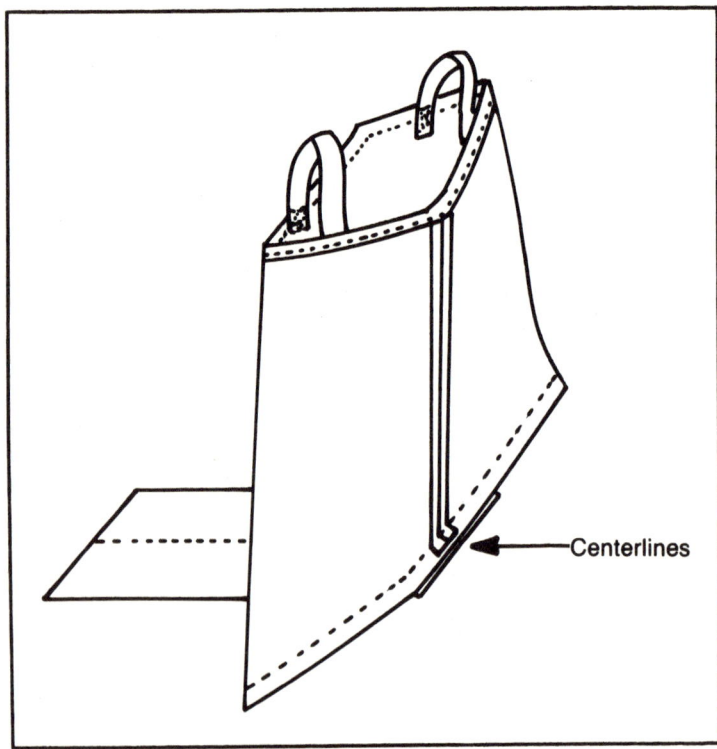

Fig. 9-9. Positioning of fabrics for sewing.

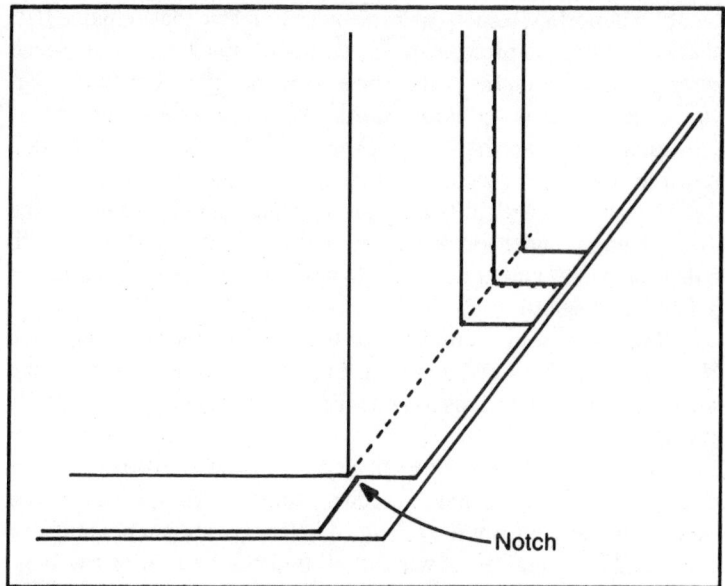

Fig. 9-10. Cut dart in upper fabric at corner.

Sew seam to 1/2 inch from edge. Needle should be in lowest position through fabric, 1/2 inch from edge. Raise presser foot. Cut dart in upper fabric (Fig. 9-10). Turn fabric to new sewing direction. Sew to 1/2 inch from next edge. Repeat turning procedure as detailed for first corner. Sew next seam. Continue sewing all the way around and overlap start of stitching an inch or so.

If desired, the plain seam around the bottom can be strengthened by turning the 1/2-inch edges under and sewing another seam along this to upper fabric only. This makes a flat-felled seam.

Turn the bag right side out. This completes construction of an open top bag with a rectangular bottom.

Another method for accomplishing essentially the same shape bag is to make the front, back, and bottom from a single piece of fabric and the end pieces from two separate pieces of fabric as shown in Fig. 9-11. When marking pattern, don't forget to allow for seam allowances. Next, sew side pieces in place with a plain seam, starting in center of bottom. Complete this seam to top of bag. Then go back to the bottom center. Start an inch or so back over first stitching, and sew in opposite direction to top of bag. If heavy fabric is used, you may want to cut a notch to make the corners. With lighter fabrics, this usually isn't necessary.

It is important to note that the piece of fabric that remains flat, in this case the end piece, is the lower fabric for sewing and is placed wrong side down on the bed of the sewing machine. The fabric that turns the corner is the upper fabric. If this is done in reverse, it is difficult to make the corner properly. After one end has been sewn in place, sew second end using same method.

If desired, the plain seams can be strengthened by turning the 1/2-inch edges under together either inward or outward (but do both sides the same) and sewing another seam along this. This makes a flat-felled seam.

Next, sew hem around top of bag. This is usually done with the edge turned inward and folded twice. If desired, the hem can also be made outward, as long as the fabric is folded twice to hide the raw edge.

Turn the bag right side out and sew handles to bag, as was done before for a flat bag. Handles should extend at least a few inches downward from top of bag. A better arrangement is to have the handles extend on down and around the bottom of the bag.

A similar bag can be made with an oval shaped bottom instead of a rectangular one. One approach to this is to add an oval bottom to a flat bag, as constructed previously. Cut the bottom open along the fold line, and turn fabric to wrong side out.

The next problem is making an oval pattern for the bottom that will fit. As an example, an oval bottom will be fitted to a flat bag that is 18 inches across. Because a true oval is difficult to pattern,

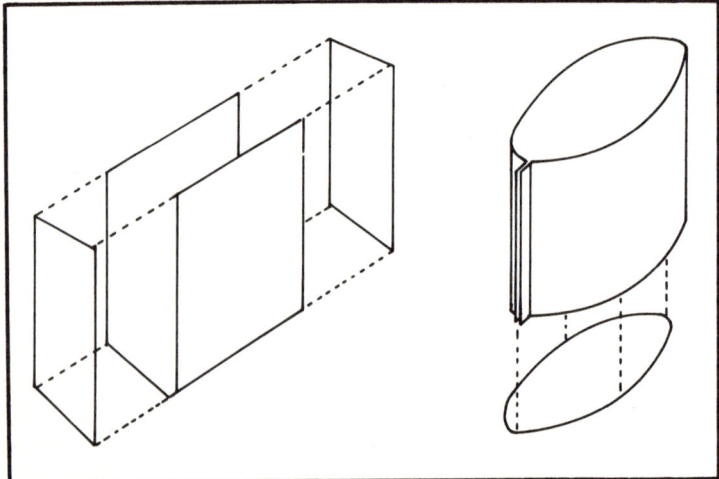

Fig. 9-11. Two alternate patterns for bag.

half circle ends and straight sides are usually used. Suppose you want the bottom three inches wide at the center. You would then use circles with 3-inch diameters. The problem is how far apart to place them to give the required 36 inches around the bottom seam line. The circumference or distance around a circle is 3.14 times the diameter. For our example, 3 × 3.14 equals 9.42 inches. This is also the distance around the two half circles. The 9.42 is then subtracted from 36 inches to give twice the required distance between the centers of the circles, or 26.58 inches. Divide this by 2, and we get 13.29 inches, the correct distance to place the centers of the circles apart when the pattern is laid out. Notice that this gives the stitching line. A 1/2 inch extra is added all the way around as seam allowance, making 4-inch diameter circles on each end for marking the cutting lines. These circles have the same center points as the 3-inch circles. Draw straight lines connecting the sides of the circles for stitching and cutting lines.

The next step is to cut the fabric along the cutting line. Then mark a centerline along the length of the bottom piece on the right side. Use chalk or another marking device that can be easily removed from the fabric later, because this will be on the outside of the finished bag.

The sewing is done with the wrong side of the bottom piece of fabric facing downward on the bed of the sewing machine. Starting at the centerline of one end of the bottom piece, position and line up the upper portion of the bag. Position the two layers of fabric under the sewing machine needle at centerline and lower presser foot to fabric. Edges of upper and lower fabrics should line up exactly.

Start sewing seam. Cut darts in upper fabric to sew around curve. Then continue sewing down straight side. Sew around half circle, cutting darts in upper fabric. Continue sewing down straight side. Sew around quarter circle, cutting notches in upper fabric. Continue sewing along start of seam an inch or so to fix the stitching. If everything was done properly, the curves will be smooth and even, and you will have an even match of upper and lower fabrics, with the two original edges of the upper portion lined up with the centerline on the bottom piece. This, of course, may take some practice to achieve, because the edges of the two layers of fabric must be kept exactly lined up and the stitching line kept at 1/2 inch from the edge all the way around. This is generally more difficult to do on curves than straight lines.

If desired, the plain seam around the bottom can be

strengthened by turning the 1/2-inch edges under, usually toward the top of the bag, and sewing another seam along this to make a flat-felled seam.

Turn the bag right side out. This completes construction of an open top bag with an oval (actually rectangular with half circle ends) bottom.

Another method for accomplishing essentially the same shape bag is to make the upper portion from a single piece of fabric, and join this together and to a bottom piece, as shown in Fig. 9-11.

The pattern for fitting the bottom to the upper fabric can be done the same as before, or you may want to reverse the procedure and start with a bottom piece and fit the upper fabric to this. On the bottom fabric, you will have a seam or stitching line of known diameter a known distance (center of circle to center of circle) apart. Multiply the circle's diameter by 3.14. This is the distance around the two half circles on the pattern. Add twice the distance from center of one circle to center of other circle to this to get the distance around stitching line on bottom piece. The cutting line is 1/2 inch outside the stitching line all the way around.

Use the distance around the stitching line for marking pattern for the upper piece. This will be the distance from seamline to seamline on the upper piece. Add a 1/2-inch seam allowance on each end and on the bottom. Allow necessary fabric for hem at the top.

Check measurements before cutting. After cutting, first sew hem in place. Usually, the hem folds will be on the inside of the finished bag, but they can be on the outside.

Fold upper fabric in half, right side facing right side and join edges with plain seam and fabric edges lined up and 1/2-inch seam allowance. If desired, this seam can be strengthened by folding the seam allowance fabrics in half and to one side. Then sew a seam along this. This makes a flat-felled seam.

Next, sew upper fabric to bottom fabric. Bottom fabric should be wrong side down on the bed of the sewing machine. Line up seam on upper fabric with centerline on one end of bottom piece. Position the layers of fabric under sewing machine needle and lower presser foot to fabric. Edges of upper and lower fabrics should line up exactly.

Start sewing seam. Cut notches in upper fabric for sewing around curve, as in previous project. Then continue sewing around curve and along straight side. Sew around half circle, cutting darts in upper fabric. Continue sewing along straight side. Then sew around quarter of circle, cutting darts in upper fabric, to start of seam. Sew an inch or so along start of seam to fix the stitching. If everything was done properly, the curves will be smooth and even, and you will have an even match of upper and lower fabrics. This, of course, may take some practice to achieve, as the edges of the two layers of fabric must be kept exactly lined up and the stitching line kept at 1/2-inch from the edge all the way around. This is generally more difficult to do on curves than straight lines.

If desired, the plain seam around the bottom can be strengthened by folding the seam allowance fabrics in half and both together to one side. Then sew a seam along this to make flat-felled seam. Usually, the fabric is folded and sewn to upper fabric portion of bag rather than to bottom piece.

Turn the bag right side out. Sew handles to bag, as for a flat bag. Handles should extend at least a few inches downward from top of bag to give adequate stitching area. A better arrangement is to have the handles extend on down and around the bottom of the bag.

The upper portion of the bag can also be made up from four pieces of fabric: two side pieces and two end pieces. This complicates the construction, however.

BAGS WITH DRAWSTRING CLOSURES

This type of bag is often called a *ditty* or *sail bag*. It's also a common design for laundry bags. These bags can be made of many shapes and sizes and from a variety of fabrics, depending on your particular needs. Fabrics can include cotton, nylon, acrylic, and polyester. The cord for drawstrings can be cotton, nylon, or polyester. Bags used for storage of sails are usually made from nylon.

A simple flat construction is often used for laundry bags, but most bags have round bottoms. Square bottoms are sometimes used.

A simple flat bag can be made from a single piece of fabric. Figure 9-12 shows the basic pattern. This can be made in desired dimensions. Allow 1/2-inch seam allowances on both sides and the bottom. Allowance for the casing in the pattern shown is 1 3/4 inch beyond the desired dimensions of finished bag, but this can be changed to fit your particular needs. The corners are cut off as shown in the pattern.

The first step is to hem the corner cuts, as shown in Fig. 9-13. The fabric is folded 1/4 inch, then 1/4 inch again to the wrong side

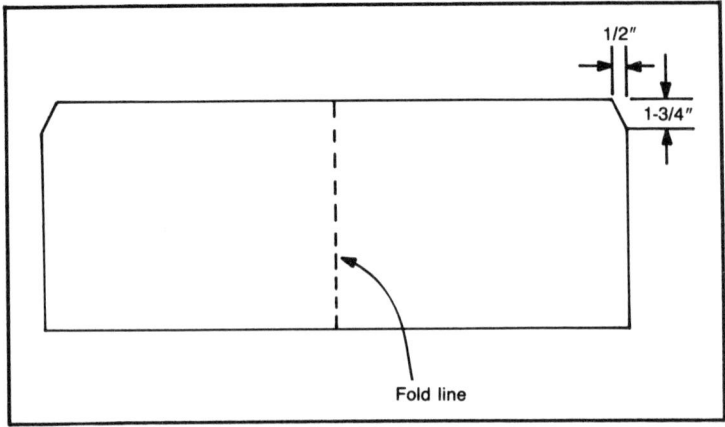

Fig. 9-12. Pattern for drawstring bag.

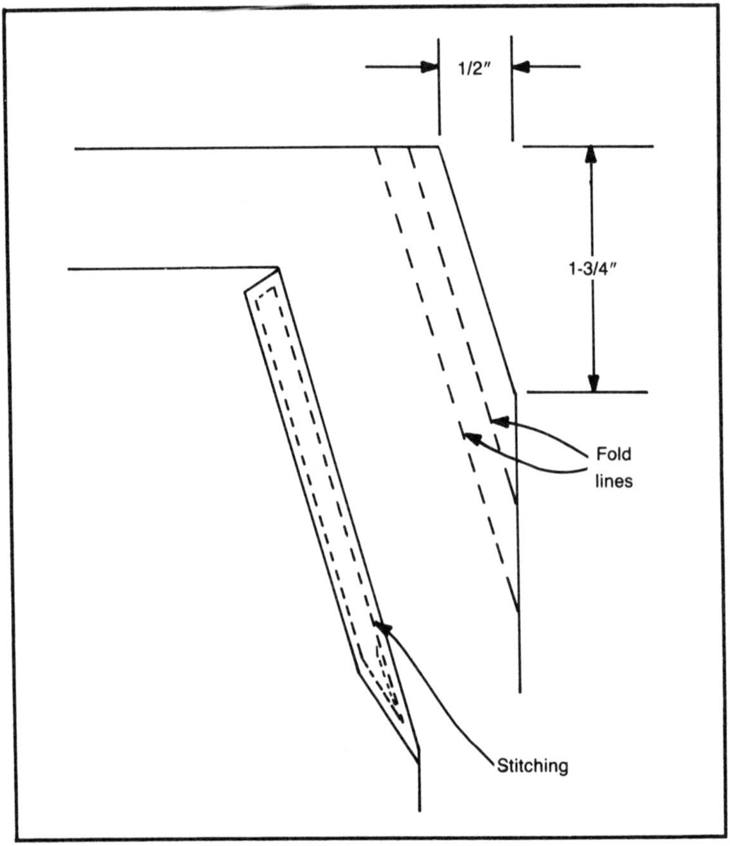

Fig. 9-13. Fabric is folded and hemmed.

of the fabric, which will be the inside of the finished bag. Make two stitch lines with sewing machine, as shown.

Next, fold 1 3/4 inch of fabric over, then 1/2 inch under again, to form casing (Fig. 9-14). Sew seam as shown, backtracking at both start and finish to fix seam. Seamline should be 1/8 inch from inside edge. Then make second seam 1/8 inch outward from this.

Next, fold fabric in half from side to side with right sides face to face. Sew plain seam across bottom. Make square corner 1/2 inch from edge. Continue sewing along side to edge of fabric. Both start and finish of seam should be fixed by backtracking. If desired, the two seam allowance flaps can be folded together to one of the fabrics and the raw edges of the fabric turned under. Sew a seam along this to one layer of fabric only. To do this, roll the fabric back out of the way as you sew. Notice that this does not shorten the dimensions of the finished bag, as would be the case if the folded layers were sewn to both layers of fabric.

Opinions vary on the need for flat-felled seams. I use them extensively, as they greatly reinforce the seam and hide the edge of the fabric. They are easy to sew in place. Also, I like the double stitch appearance.

Turn the bag right side out. Attach a safety pin or wood spike to the cord and feed this into the drawstring opening and around through the casing. Then tie the ends of the cord together with an overhand knot. This completes the construction.

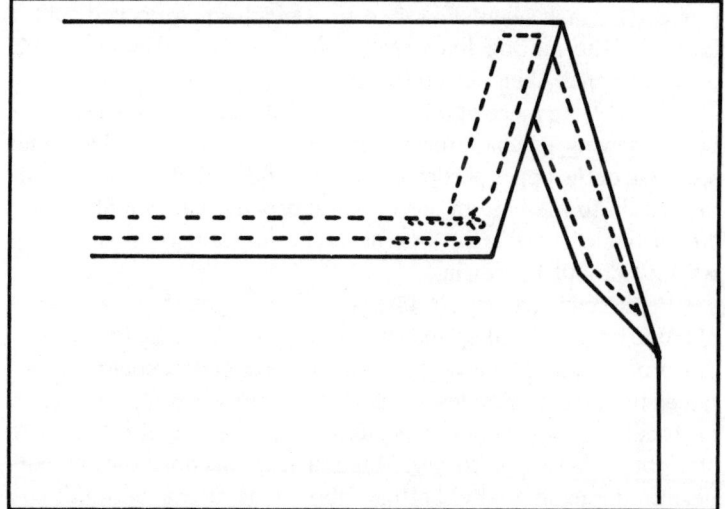

Fig. 9-14. Casing is formed.

An alternate method for constructing the casing is to have the opening for the drawstring through two grommets spaced close together. First sew up bottom and side of bag without first sewing casing. Then install grommets in fabric. Grommets should be of a size that allows the cord to pass through easily. Pass cord through grommets as it will go in finished bag and tie ends together with overhand knot. Fold casing over 1 3/4 inch and then turn edge under 1/2 inch. Sew casing seam 1/8 inch from edge of folded under fabric. Then make second row of stitches 1/8 inch above this. Keep cord inside casing and away from stitching as seams are made. Casing can be sewn with bag turned wrong side out or right side out, but make certain that the casing is folded inward to the wrong side of the fabric so that it will be inside the finished bag.

The above method uses two grommets, but a single grommet that allows both ends of cord to just pass through can also be used. A large knot can be made in the ends of the cord to keep them from being pulled back inside the casing.

A square bottom can be installed in the above bags, if desired. Construction is the same except that a seam is not made across bottom, as was done previously. To make pattern for bottom piece of fabric, lay upper portion of bag out flat and measure distance from folded edge to seamline. Divide this distance by two. This will give the length from stitch line to stitch line for the bottom piece. For example, suppose the distance from edge to seamline of upper fabric is 20 inches. Dividing this by two gives 10 inches. Using a 1/2-inch seam allowance, an 11-inch square is laid out on fabric as the cutting line for the bottom piece. Double check measurements, then cut fabric along cutting line.

The bottom piece of fabric is placed wrong side downward on bed of sewing machine for sewing to upper portion of bag. The seamline of the upper portion can be positioned at any desired point in relation to the bottom piece, but is usually placed midway between two corners or at a corner. The upper portion should be wrong side out for sewing.

Begin sewing at any starting point. The edges of the two pieces of fabric must be lined up and an even 1/2-inch seamline maintained. At corner, stop sewing 1/2 inch from edge. Needle should be positioned through fabric to lowest point. Raise presser foot. Cut a notch in corner of upper fabric. Turn fabric to new sewing direction. Sew straight seam to next corner. Make turn as was done for first corner. Continue on around bottom fabric in same manner until you reach starting point. Continue sewing over start of stitching for an inch or so to fix seam.

If desired, the plain seam around the bottom can be strengthened by turning the 1/2-inch edges together to the upper fabric and then folding the edges under again and making a seam along this to the upper fabric only. It will be necessary to bunch the fabric up to do this so that the sewing is to the upper fabric only. This makes a flat-felled seam that is much stronger than a plain seam alone.

Turn the bag right side out. This completes the construction of a bag with a square bottom and drawstring top.

A round bottom is most commonly used for drawstring bags. One approach is to fit a round bottom to a completed upper portion of bag, as was done with a square bottom. The problem is to determine the diameter of a circle that will be the right size to fit the upper portion. Because the upper portion is already sewn to form a tube, it is usually best to first consider the diameter of a circle that will give the seamline for bottom piece.

To make a pattern for the bottom piece of fabric, first lay the upper portion of bag out flat. Measure distance from folded edge to seamline, then multiply this distance by two to get distance around seamline. For example, suppose the distance from edge to seamline of upper fabric is 20 inches. Multiplying this by 2 gives 40 inches, the desired distance around the seamline of the bottom circle. The problem is to find the diameter of the required circle. The diameter equals the circumference of the circle divided by 3.14, or 40 divided by 3.14, which equals 12.74 inches. The radius of the circle is half of this or 6.37 inches. With a compass, make a circle with chalk, mark stitch line on fabric. If you do not have a compass, attach a piece of chalk to a string of the proper length. Anchor the string with a tack or pin to the center of the fabric and draw the circle. Then increase radius by a half inch to 6.87 inches and make second circle with same center point. This gives the cutting line. You will have to calculate for the particular folded edge to seamline distance that you have. Double check measurements, then cut out circle following cutting line carefully.

The bottom piece of fabric is placed wrong side downward on bed of sewing machine for sewing to upper tube portion of bag. The upper portion should be turned wrong side out for sewing. Line up the edges of the two fabrics at any desired starting point around the bottom fabric. It doesn't matter where the side seam on the upper tube is, but you may want to start the stitching at this point. To have everything come out right, the edges of the two pieces of fabric must be kept lined up and an even 1/2-inch seamline maintained. Usually, a series of notches are cut in the upper fabric as the sewing progresses. An alternate method is to pin the fabrics together with evenly spaced creases all the way around. Regardless, sew fabrics together all the way around, and overlap seams an inch or so to fix the stitching.

If desired, the plain seam around the bottom can be strengthened by turning the 1/2-inch edges together to the upper fabric and then folding the edges under again. Make a seam along this to the upper fabric only. It will be necessary to bunch the fabric up to this so that the sewing is to the upper fabric only. This makes a sturdy flat-felled seam.

Turn the bag right side out. This completes the construction of a bag with a round bottom and drawstring top.

A somewhat different patterning situation is faced when you have a certain diameter circle for the bottom piece and want to construct the upper tube piece to fit this. To do this, multiply diameter of circle for seamline by 3.14 to get circumference or distance around circle. This will be the width of the bottom fabric from seamline to seamline. Add a 1/2-inch seam allowance to each side of this to determine cutting lines. Sew fabric together to form tube, as before. You may want to sew the casing in the top before doing this. The tube should be the correct size for sewing to the bottom circle.

ZIPPER CLOSED BAGS WITH HANDLES

Figure 9-15 shows a typical zipper bag. These can be in a vari-

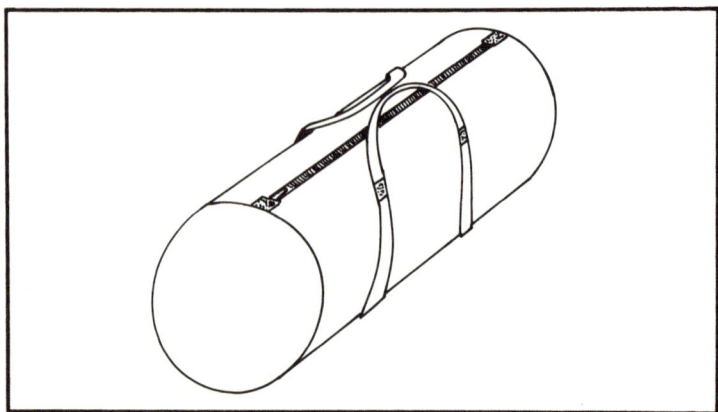

Fig. 9-15. Zipper enclosed bag with carrying handles.

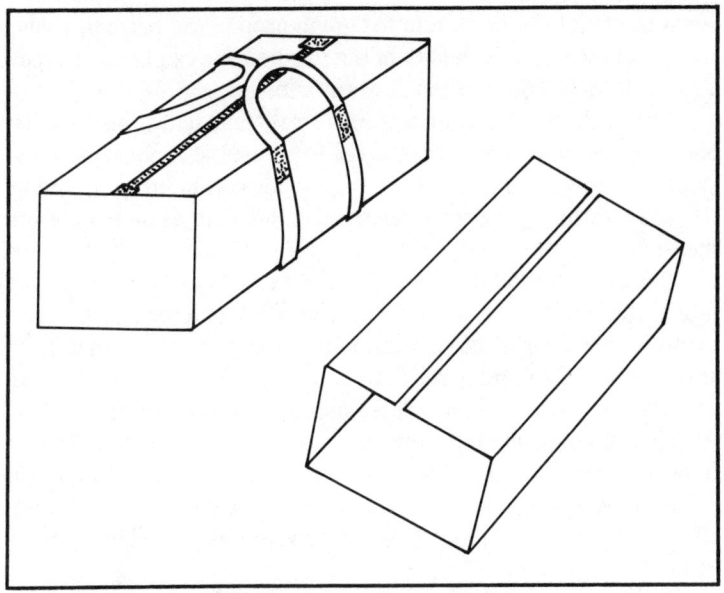

Fig. 9-16. Bag with rectangular end pieces. The bottom, sides, and top are made from single piece of fabric.

ety of shapes and sizes, with or without pockets and so on. They are variously called duffel bags, tote bags, and carryalls. They can be used to carry and store all kinds of gear and equipment. They usually store aboard boats and recreational vehicles much more conveniently than standard hard luggage.

Two basic designs will be detailed here, but these can be modified as desired. Pockets can be added and different strap arrangements can be used. A variety of fabrics can be used.

First, we will consider a bag with square or rectangular ends, as shown in Fig. 9-16. The bottom, sides, and top can be made from one piece of fabric, as shown in Fig. 9-16. An open space is generally left for the zipper so that it can be opened and closed easily. Usually the space between the folded under edges of the two pieces of fabric is about 1/2 inch. If the fabric is turned under 1/2 inch on each side of the fabric, then 1/2 inch again, this means that the fabric can be cut to the desired length total for the bottom, sides, and top of the finished bag, plus 1 1/2 inch.

A quarter of this distance will give the seamline for each side of square end pieces. Before cutting, a 1/2-inch seam allowance is added all the way around. A rectangular pattern for end pieces can be determined similarly. The distance around the seamline should equal the length of the fabric for going around the bottom, sides, and top of the bag. The length of the finished bag can be as desired. To this length, add a 1/2-inch seam allowance to each end.

Although many different zippers can be used, a heavy-duty plastic zipper will generally give the best results. A nonseparating zipper is required, but a separating zipper can be used by fixing the ends of the zipper together so that the slide cannot come off the ends.

Before installing the zipper or the ends to the main piece of fabric, the handles are usually attached. Although the zipper could be positioned as desired in relation to the top of the finished bag, assume that it will go across the center of the top of the bag. If you want it elsewhere, simple adjustments will take care of this.

The handles are typically made from a single piece of webbing sewn into a loop and sewn to the right side of the main piece of fabric. Webbing can be of cotton, nylon, or polyester. For most bags, webbing from about 1 1/2 inches to 2 inches wide is about right.

Other strapping arrangements are possible for carrying handles. If cut ends of webbing are sewn directly to the fabric, use a reinforcing layer of backing fabric. Sometimes, D-rings are attached to the bag by webbing sewn to the bag. The handles and carrying straps are a separate piece of webbing, often with an adjustable strap buckle arrangement.

After sewing handles and/or carrying straps in place, install zipper to fabric ends. The hem is turned under 1/2 inch, then under again 1/2 inch. The edge of this fabric is then lined up 1/4 inch from the center of the closed zipper, as shown in Fig. 9-17. The fabric

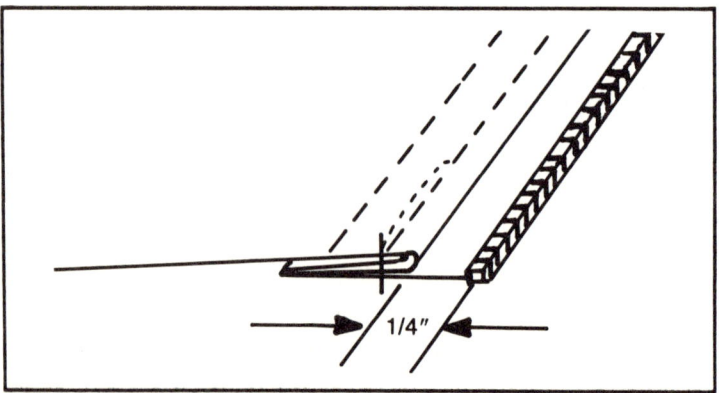

Fig. 9-17. Zipper installation.

is then sewn to the zipper tape. The procedure is then repeated for the other end of the fabric, attaching it to the other half of the zipper. Make sure that the fabrics on each side of the zipper are lined up before stitching.

If desired, a second stitching a short distance from the first can be used. This will serve to reinforce the attachment of the zipper. Alternate methods for attaching zippers are given in Chapter 7.

The ends of the zipper are usually reinforced with square pieces of fabric. These are usually machine sewn across the zipper.

The zipper portion of the bag is turned wrong side out for sewing the end pieces in place. The bottom piece of fabric is placed wrong side downward on the bed of the sewing machine. The zipper part must be positioned so that the zipper will be at the top center of the end piece. Begin sewing at a point lined up with the center line extending from zipper. The edges of the fabrics must be lined up and an even 1/2-inch seamline maintained. At corner, stop sewing 1/2 inch from edge. Needle should be positioned through the fabric to lowest point. Raise presser foot. Cut a notch in corner of upper fabric. Turn fabrics for sewing in new direction. Sew seam to next corner. Make turn as for first corner. Continue on around square in same manner until you reach starting point. Continue sewing over start of seam for an inch or so to fix seam.

If desired, the plain seam around the end piece can be reinforced by turning the 1/2-inch flaps together to the fabric away from the end piece, and then folding the edges under again and making a seam along this to the fabric. It will be necessary to bunch the fabric up to do this so that the sewing is to the main fabric only and not to the bottom piece. This makes a flat-felled seam that is much stronger than a plain seam alone. Follow the same procedure for sewing the other end in place. Turn the bag right side out through the zipper opening. This completes the construction.

The second main type of construction is a bag with round ends, as shown in Fig. 9-15. A basic tube without the ends is constructed in same manner as for a bag with square or rectangular ends. To determine the diameter of circles for end pieces, lay the main portion of bag out flat. Measure distance from folded edge to folded edge on the short side. Then multiply this distance by two to get distance around seamline. For example, suppose the distance across is 20 inches. Multiplying this by 2 gives 40 inches, the desired distance around the seamline of end pieces. The problem is to find the diameter of the required circle. The diameter equals the circumference of the circle divided by 3.14, or 40 divided by 3.14 in this case, which equals 12.74 inches. The radius of the circle is half of this or 6.37 inches. With a compass or chalk attached to a piece of string, mark off circles for two end pieces with this radius. Then increase radius by a half inch to 6.87 inches and make second circles from same center points. This gives the cutting line. Double check measurements, then cut out circles following cutting lines carefully.

An end piece of fabric is placed wrong side downward on bed of sewing machine for sewing to tube portion of bag. The tube portion should be turned wrong side out. Line up the edges of the two fabrics at any desired starting point. To have everything come out right, the edges of the two pieces of fabric must be kept lined up and an even 1/2-inch seamline maintained. Usually, a series of notches are cut in the tube fabric as the sewing progresses. An alternate method is to pin the fabrics together with evenly spaced creases all the way around. Regardless, sew fabrics together all the way around and overlap seams an inch or so to fix the stitching.

If desired, the plain seam around the end piece can be strengthened by turning the 1/2-inch flaps together to the tube fabric and then folding the edges under again. Make a seam along this to the tube fabric only. It will be necessary to bunch the fabric up to do this so that the sewing is to the tube fabric only. This makes a sturdy flat-felled seam.

Follow the same procedure for sewing the other end in place.

Turn the bag right side out through the zipper opening. This completes the construction.

A somewhat different patterning problem is faced when you have a certain diameter circle for the end pieces and want to construct a tube piece to fit this. To do this, multiply the diameter of the circle for seamline by 3.14 to get circumference or distance around circle. For example, a 12-inch diameter gives a circumference of 37.68 inches. This will be the total length of fabric required to form the tube. The distance between fabrics along the zipper should be subtracted from this and the fabric folds for the hems added. In many cases, the distance between fabrics along the zipper will be 1/2 inch, and the required fabric for making the hem folds will be 2 inches. In this case, 1-1/2 inch is added, so the fabric length is 39.18 inches. After sewing the zipper in place, the tube should be the correct dimensions for installing the end pieces.

There are many possibilities for customizing these bags. For example, constrasting color fabrics can be used for tube and end pieces. A separate carrying handle can be installed on one end, as shown in Fig. 9-18. A variety of pockets can be added. Figure 9-19

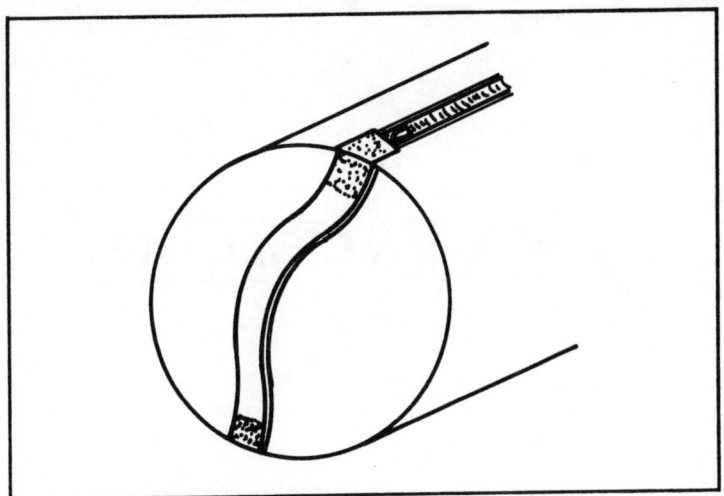

Fig. 9-18. Carrying handle installed on end of bag.

shows a pocket installed between webbing that extends around bottom of bag. The bottom of the pocket is turned under and sewn to the bag. The top is hemmed, and the sides are sewn in place under the webbing. Pockets with zippers are another possibility.

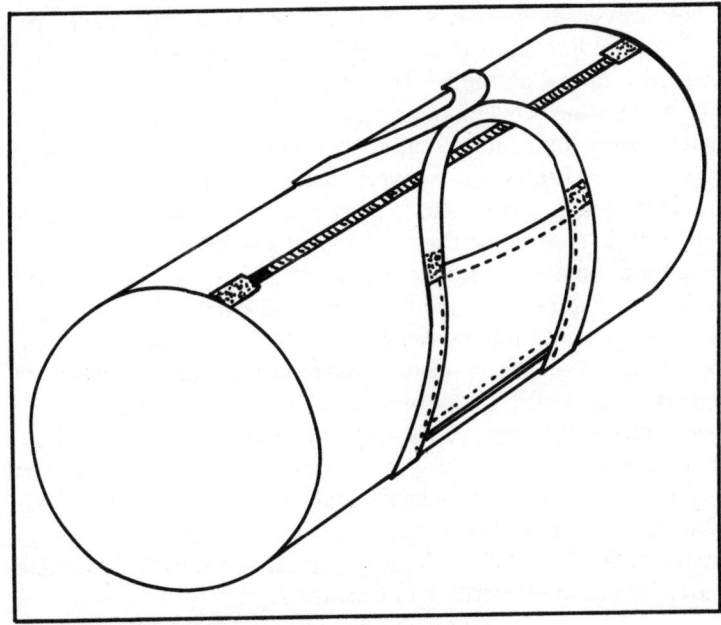

Fig. 9-19. Pocket installed between handle webbing.

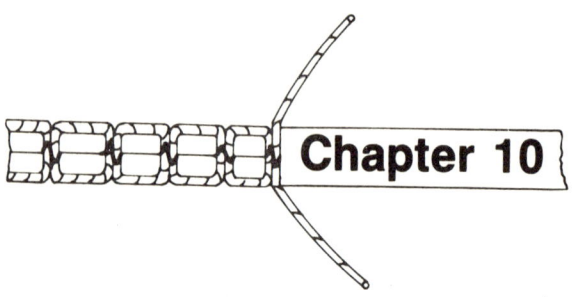

Chapter 10

Covers

Because of the damaging effects of weather conditions on boats and recreational vehicles, especially on certain parts, a variety of canvas covers are useful. These range from small to large. The focus here is to detail some of the most common types of covers. These can easily be adapted and modified to fit your special requirements. For recreational vehicles, spare tire covers, top luggage rack covers, pickup bed covers, and full covers are considered. For boats, winch covers, tiller covers, binnacle and wheel covers, hatch covers, outboard motor covers, sail boom covers, jib (bag-type) covers, fishing chair covers, and full covers are detailed.

In general, the fabrics used must be either waterproof or water resistant. In most cases, the fabrics must also be able to withstand long-term sun exposure. If cotton canvas is used, it should be dry-treated to reduce susceptibility to rot and mildew.

Canvas cover fabrics can be classified as breathing or nonbreathing. Considering all the main factors, acrylic fabric is generally most satisfactory for covers. This fabric is highly water resistant, yet allows sufficient air to pass through to minimize condensation. The nonbreathing-type is usually coated with vinyl or other plastics. These are usually highly waterproof, but condensation can be a problem unless there is adequate air circulation underneath. More details about canvas fabrics and other possible cover fabrics are described in Chapter 2.

RECREATIONAL VEHICLE COVERS

Covers have a variety of uses on recreational vehicles. They not only provide protection from the elements, but can also add a neat finished appearance.

Spare Tire Covers

To save on interior space, many vans and campers have the spare tires mounted on special exterior brackets, leaving the wheel largely unprotected from the elements. A fabric cover is a convenient solution.

Figure 10-1 shows the basic pattern. The seams can be sewn with or without piping, as desired. The covers are usually held in place by an elastic band.

One method for laying out the pattern for a round piece is to place fabric right side down on a clean flat surface. Then place the spare tire on this. Trace around tire with chalk pencil, marking pattern on fabric. This will be the seamline. Mark off desired seam allowance, usually 1/2-inch, outside seamline, as shown in Fig. 10-2.

A second method is to measure the radius of the wheel. Then, using a piece of chalk connected to a string as a compass, mark off circle with this radius on wrong side of fabric. Then add a seam allowance, usually 1/2 inch or 5/8 inch, to mark off the cutting line. Regardless of patterning method, cut out the circle carefully, following cutting line.

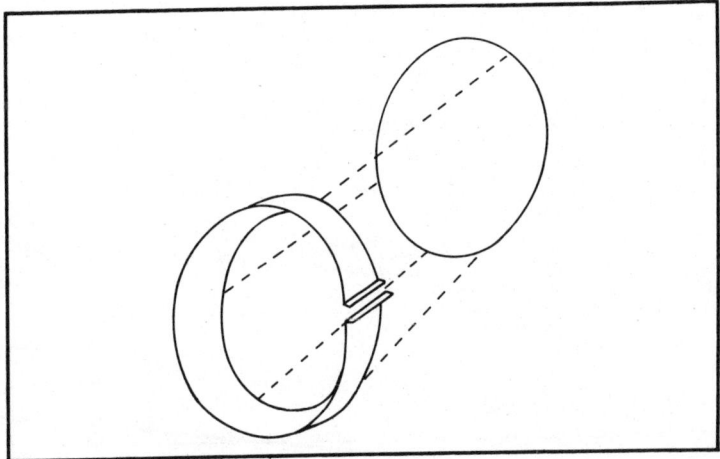

Fig. 10-1. Basic pattern for spare tire cover.

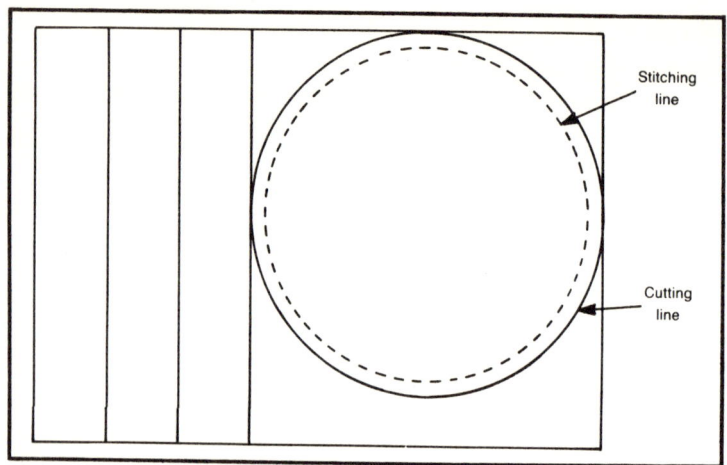

Fig. 10-2. Pattern for tire cover fabric.

Next, pattern the side piece. Measure width of tire tread. Then add seam allowance to one side and 2 1/2-inch allowance on other side for the elastic casing, as shown in Fig. 10-3.

The length of the side piece will be diameter of wheel × 3.14,

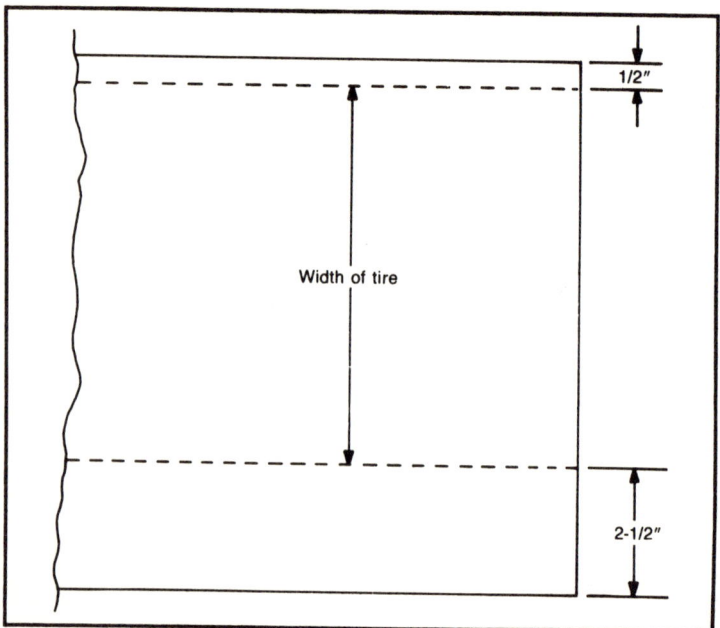

Fig. 10-3. Pattern for side piece.

plus a seam allowance added to each end. For a 14-inch wheel, this would be 14 × 3.14 or 43.96 inches. If a 1/2-inch seam allowance is used, add 1 inch to this. The required length of the fabric is then 44.96 inches. If necessary, join separate pieces of fabric to make this length.

Fold the side piece over right side to right side and make a plain seam to join ends. Fold both flaps over to one side and then one half under. Sew a flat-felled seam in this.

Next, sew casing for elastic on one edge of side piece, as shown in Fig. 10-4. Sew all the way around, except for about an inch, which should be left open for installing the elastic. This will be done later.

The next job is sewing the side piece to the outside circle fabric. Place circle fabric right side up on bed of sewing machine. If piping is to be used, first sew this to outside circle fabric. Cut notches 1 inch apart all the way around on the piping tape. Although you can make up your own piping by sewing fabric over cording, as detailed in Chapter 5, prefabricated vinyl cording, readily available, is generally used for spare tire covers.

Regardless of whether or not piping is used, next sew side piece in place with plain seam. Keep the edges of fabrics even and maintain an equal seam allowance all the way around the circle. Complete seam all the way around and overlap start of stitching to fix seam.

Turn cover right side out. To install elastic band in casing, fasten a safety pin to one end of elastic. Insert pin through space that was left open in casing. Work pin around through casing, pulling the elastic through. Finish with both ends of elastic extending out

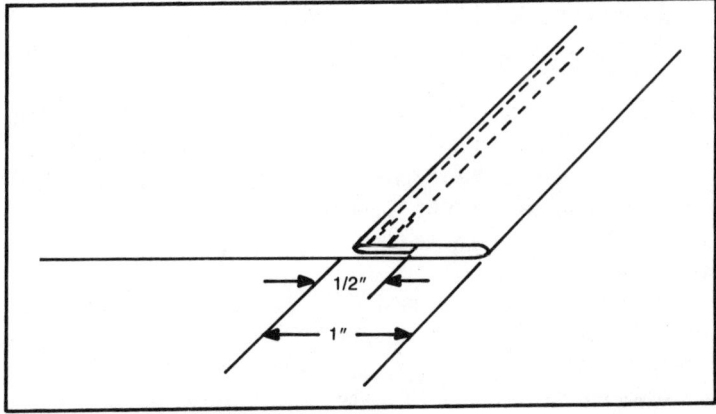

Fig. 10-4. Casing is sewn in side piece.

of small opening left in casing. Install cover on tire and pull ends of elastic until elastic is drawn to desired tightness. Fasten ends of elastic together with a safety pin. Then remove cover and fix the ends of the elastic by sewing through casing and elastic. Remove safety pin.

This completes the construction of a basic spare tire cover. Spare tire covers can be given a customized look by using contrasting colors of fabric for the outside circle and the side pieces, sewing letters or designs to the cover, and so on.

Top Luggage Rack Covers

A wide variety of top luggage racks is in use on recreational vehicles. It is very difficult to construct covers for these that work well. The cover must fit tight, yet the size of the loads carried may vary. In wet and rainy conditions, the cover must not only cover the top of the load, but also extend under it if the load is to be kept dry. Loose, flapping fabric when the vehicle is operated at high speed can be a problem.

I've seen a number of attempts to design satisfactory covers, but a plain tarpaulin with grommets or hold down straps placed about a foot apart seems to work about as well as more complicated designs. This provides only limited weather protection, however.

A tarpaulin can be made from a variety of fabrics, coated or uncoated, as desired. The tarpaulin can be flat, box shaped, or shaped to fit over a specific load.

In most cases, the first step is to make up a fabric blank. This is a large piece of fabric made up by joining smaller pieces. Usually, the fabrics will be continuous lengthwise, but will be joined sideways to give the necessary width.

The fabrics are usually joined by a flat-felled seam. First, make a plain seam. Then fold both flaps together to one side and turn the edges under, to form a flat-felled seam. An alternate method is to cut one of the flaps off approximately 1/8 inch from the stitching. Then fold the remaining flap over and under the short one. This requires stitching through one less layer of fabric and reduces the bulk of the seam area, but it reduces the strength somewhat.

If a flat cover is to be used, the next step is to add a hem all the way around. Shaped covers should be cut and sewn to shape before hemming.

A wide hem, usually 2 inches or more in width, is usually used. Grommets or hold down straps can be attached to the double fabric of the hem. Spacing the grommets or straps depends on the particular project, but about 10 or 12 inches apart is usually about right.

In use, the cover is generally secured by attaching ropes to the grommets or hold down straps and then attaching the ropes to the rack of the vehicle. Luggage and other items carried should first be securely tied down. Do not depend on the tarpaulin alone to hold them in place.

Pickup Bed Covers

Flat fabric covers are popular for use over pickup truck beds, as shown in Fig. 10-5. These are usually secured by snaps, but Lift-the-Dot and Common Sense fasteners (see Chapter 7) can also be used. They extend out further, but generally hold more securely.

The covers are generally made from vinyl-coated fabrics. In most cases, a single piece of fabric will not be wide enough. Join pieces to make necessary width using flat-felled seams.

Next, take careful measurements from pickup truck bed. Fabric will overlap edges and extend slightly past locations where fasteners are to be placed. Add to this the necessary fabric for making desired hems. An alternate method is to trim the edges with binding tape. In this case, the fabric is patterned and cut to desired finished size.

Cut fabric. Sew hem or binding tape around edges. Regardless

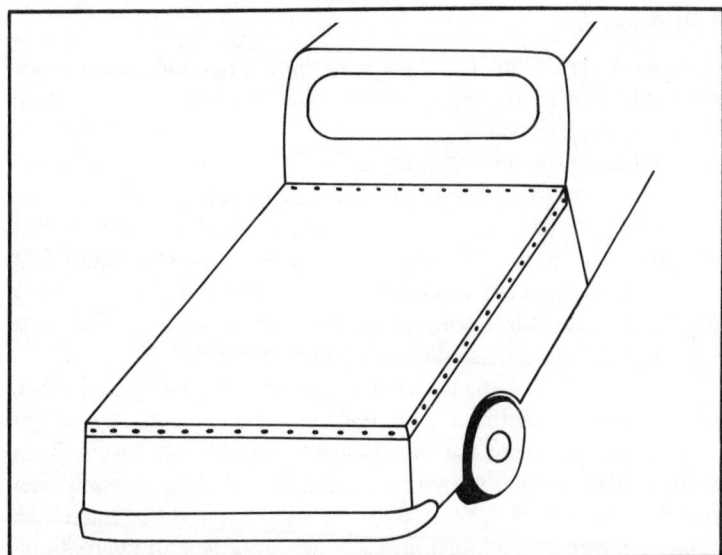

Fig. 10-5. Fabric cover for pickup truck bed.

Fig. 10-6. Canvas cover for small camper.

of whether snap, Lift-the-Dot, or Common Sense fasteners are used, studs are usually first attached to the pickup truck either by means of machine screws installed in tapped holes; through holes with washer, lock washer, and nut; or by means of self-tapping screws. These are usually spaced about 4 inches to 6 inches apart.

Next, carefully mark locations on fabric for sockets or eyelets. Then install these in fabric, as detailed in Chapter 7. When fasteners are connected in place, fabric should be stretched tight. This completes the construction of a pickup bed cover.

Full Covers

Full covers, similar to those used for automobiles, can be constructed to fit many types and sizes of recreational vehicles. A breathing-type canvas is generally used. For most uses, this should be a soft canvas and fairly lightweight. Drawstrings around the bottom are often used to hold the cover in place.

General construction procedure is to first take careful measurements of the recreational vehicle to be covered. Figure 10-6 shows a typical construction for a cover for a small camper. When marking fabrics for cutting, allow for seam allowances. Separate pieces of fabric are usually joined by flat-felled seams.

After desired shape has been achieved, sew casing around bottom. Leave an opening for the ends of the drawstrings. Attach a large safety pin to one end of cord and feed it through casing. Take it all the way around through casing and bring end out through opening. Tie the ends of the cord together with an overhand knot. This type of cover can be custom-made for a variety of recreational vehicles.

BOAT COVERS

A variety of covers can be constructed for boats, including sailboats, powerboats, and rowboats. Some projects, like sail covers, are specific to one type of boats; others, such as full covers, can be used on most types of boats.

Winch Covers

These are useful, yet easy to make. Often scrap materials from another job will be large enough to make a small cover like this. In most cases, a breathing-type fabric is used, and acrylic fabric seems to be the first choice.

Although many designs are possible, I like the double arrangement shown in Fig. 10-7. The inner half cover has elastic around it to hold it securely around the center of the winch. The outside cover then hangs down like a skirt. For our purposes here, we will call these the "inside" and "outside" covers.

First, take measurements of the winch to be covered, as shown

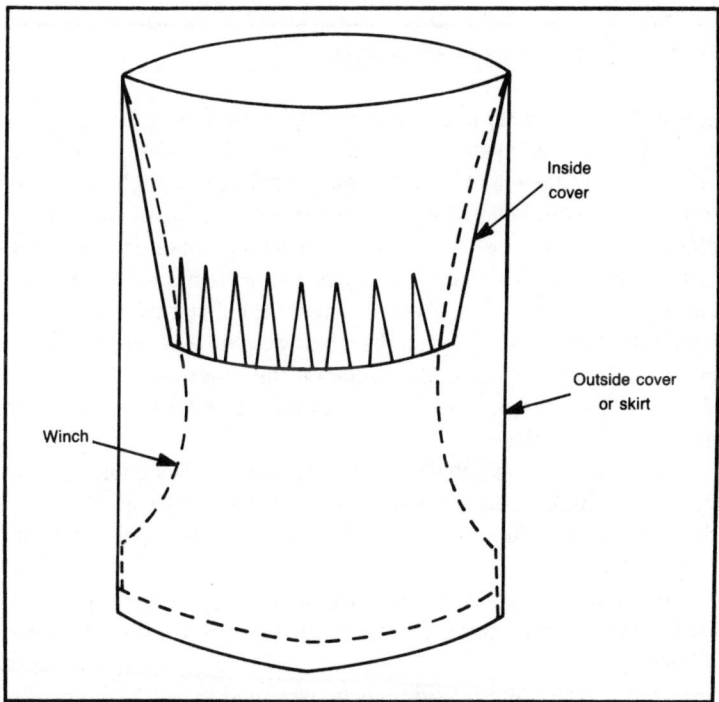

Fig. 10-7. Winch cover with double arrangement of fabric.

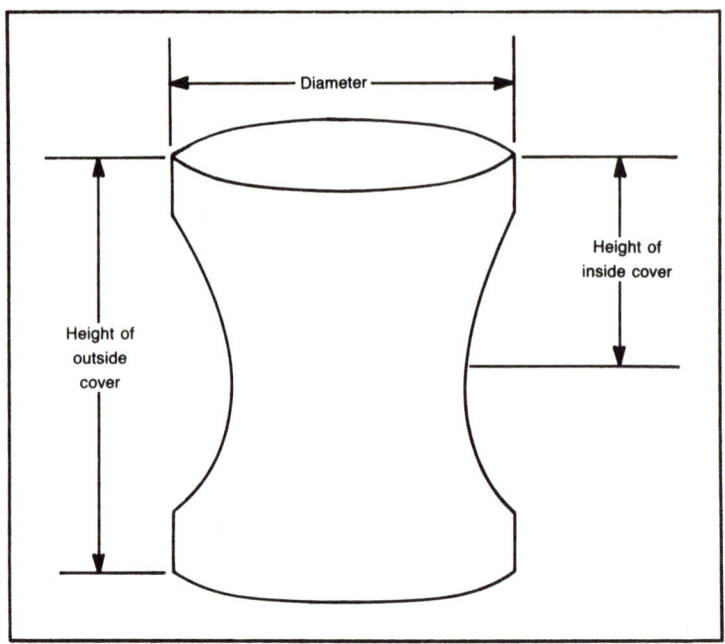

Fig. 10-8. Measurements for winch cover.

in Fig. 10-8. Then lay out pattern on fabric as shown in Fig. 10-9. The length of the inside and outside cover fabrics is the diameter of the winch times 3.14, plus a seam allowance on each end. The top piece is a circle equal to the diameter of the top of the winch, plus a seam allowance. The width of the outside cover is the height of the winch, plus a seam allowance and a hem allowance. The width of the inside cover piece is usually the distance from top of winch to halfway down or slightly below, plus a seam allowance on one side and a casing allowance on the other side. Cut fabric along cutting lines into the three required pieces of fabric: outside, inside, and top pieces.

Next, sew hem in outside piece. Sew stitching along folded edge first. Then make a second row of stitches close to edge of folded over fabric. Sew the casing for elastic in inside piece, as shown in Fig. 10-10.

Join ends of outside piece with plain seam, as shown in Fig. 10-10. Do the same thing for the inside piece, except do not sew across casing.

Leave inside and outside pieces wrong side out. Slip outside piece inside shorter inside piece, as shown in Fig. 10-11. Line up

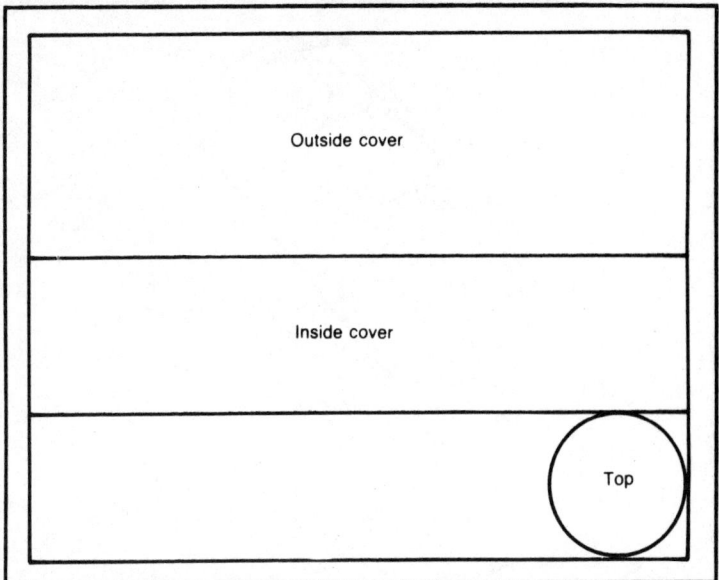

Fig. 10-9. Pattern for winch cover.

edges. Position top piece and pin or staple this to the outside and inside pieces so that the edges of the three layers of fabric line up. Then sew these together with seam allowance, keeping edges flush all the way around.

Fasten a safety pin to one end of the elastic, and feed it through casing. With both ends of elastic extending from opening in casing, pull ends until elastic is of the desired tautness. Finish original

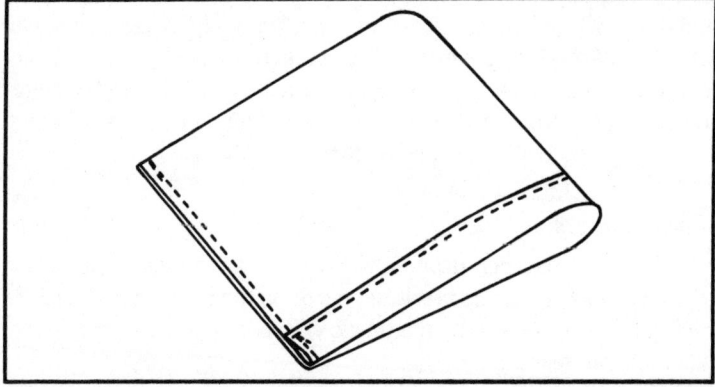

Fig. 10-10. Casing is sewn in bottom edge of inside piece. Ends of outside piece are joined with plain seam.

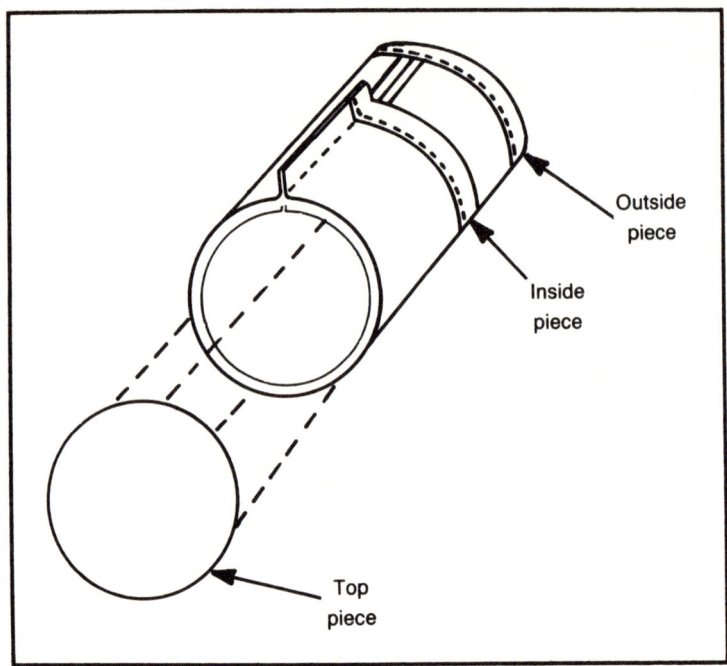

Fig. 10-11. Outside piece is slipped inside shorter inside piece.

plain seam, joining ends of inside piece, and sewing across casing and elastic ends. Make necessary extra stitches to securely fix ends of elastic. Cut off excess elastic.

Turn winch cover right side out. This completes the construction of a basic winch cover. There are many possible variations. For example, binding can be used around the bottom edge of the outside skirt instead of a sewn in place hem. The basic design can also be adapted for covering other similar shapes, such as dome-shaped compasses and so on. Some winches have larger diameter bottoms than tops. Appropriate modifications in the basic winch cover pattern will take care of this.

Tiller Covers

A tiller cover can prolong the life of varnish and other wood finishes. Again, acrylic fabric seems to be the favored material for making these. Generally, the fabric will match that of other covers used on the same boat.

Several tiller types are in use. In most cases, the covers are basically a sock that slips over the tiller (Fig. 10-12); however, the methods for securing the covers in place depends on the particular tiller arrangement.

The basic cover is usually a tube. Take measurements of tiller. Lay out pattern on fabric, as shown in Fig. 10-13A. Allow seam allowance on both sides and one end. The other end, which usually fits over rudder post or rudder, will also be sewn closed, with a pocket left in the bottom for slipping the cover in place. In some cases, elastic bands or drawstrings in casings will be necessary to secure cover in place. Regardless of method, necessary seam, hem, and casing allowances should be taken into account when laying out the pattern.

Cut fabric along cutting lines. Place fabric pieces right side to right side. Sew plain seam, leaving a sock opening, as shown in Fig. 10-13B. Sew hem or casing around sock opening. If drawstring or elastic is to be installed in casing, do not sew across casing. Install drawstring or elastic. If drawstring is used, tie ends of cord extending from casing together with overhand knot. If elastic is used, pull ends of elastic until elastic band is tight, then fix ends

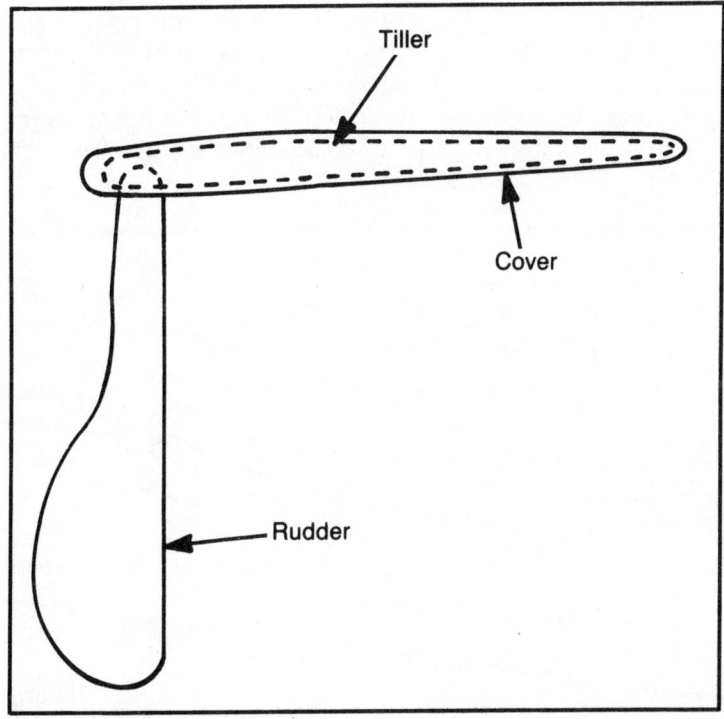

Fig. 10-12. Tiller cover.

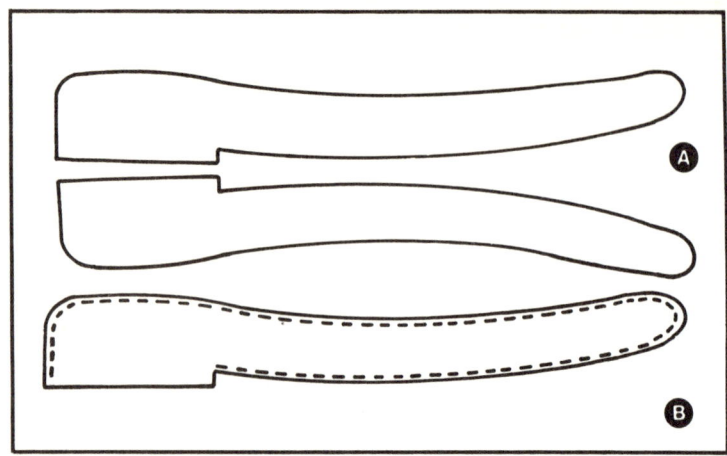

Fig. 10-13. Pattern for tiller cover (A) The two pieces of fabric are sewn together with a plain seam (B).

by sewing. Turn tiller cover right side out. This completes the construction of a basic tiller cover.

Covers for large tillers, especially those with curves, are sometimes made up of four or more separate pieces of fabric, such as is shown in Fig. 10-14. Other variations include using piping in seams and fabrics of contrasting colors for top and sides of cover. The basic tiller cover pattern can also be adapted for making covers for other similarly shaped objects.

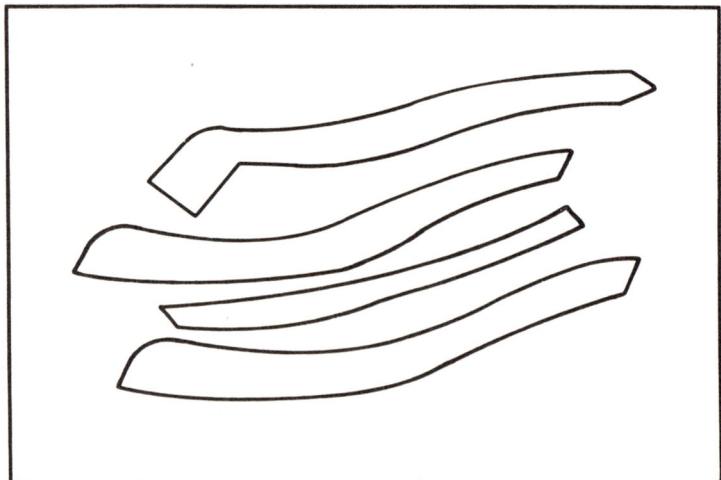

Fig. 10-14. Tiller cover made from four pieces of fabric.

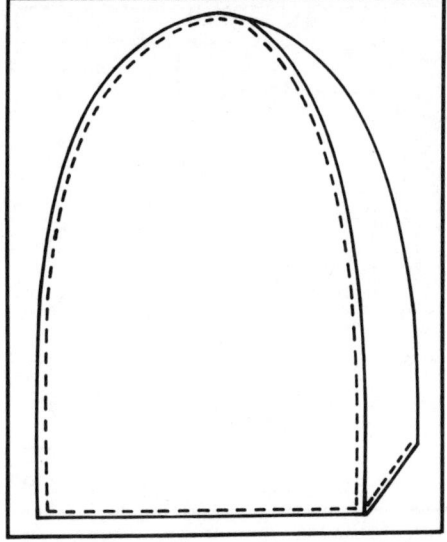

Fig. 10-15. Drop cover for wheel and binnacle.

Binnacle and Wheel Covers

There are many shapes and sizes of binnacles and wheels in use, and a number of possible approaches for making covers for these. One basic approach is to make a *drop cover* that fits over both the wheel and binnacle like a typewriter cover, as shown in Fig. 10-15. The second basic approach is a separate wheel and binnacle cover, which may or may not be joined by a seam (Fig. 10-16). These two basic methods are detailed below and can be adapted and modified to fit your special requirements.

Fig. 10-16. Fitted covers for wheel and binnacle.

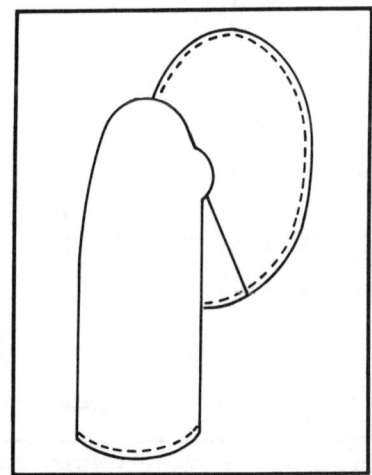

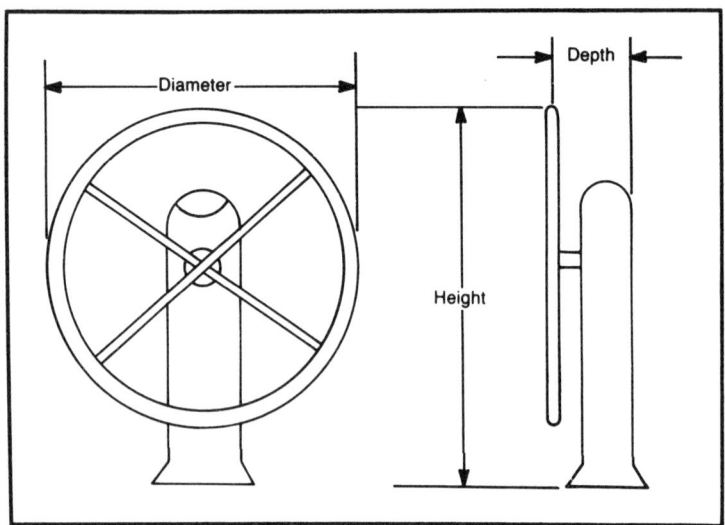

Fig. 10-17. Basic measurements.

Drop Cover. To make a drop cover, first take basic measurements, as detailed in Fig. 10-17. This includes diameter of wheel and distance from cockpit sole or deck, as well as depth of wheel and binnacle.

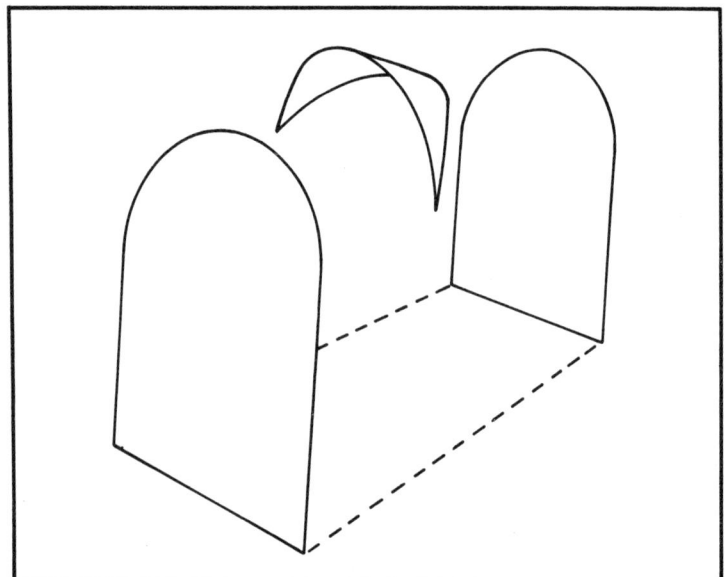

Fig. 10-18. Construction of wheel and binnacle cover with three pieces of fabric.

There are a number of possible ways to make the cover. Figure 10-18 shows a typical construction, with three pieces of fabric. The cover could also be made up of four or five pieces of fabric.

Decide on the method you want to use, then transfer measurements to fabric and lay out pattern. Allow seam allowances for joining separate pieces of fabric and extra fabric for forming the hem around lower edge. Cut fabric.

Place pieces of fabric right side to right side for sewing with plain seams. Seams can be made with or without piping. If piping is used, first sew it to one layer of fabric, using a zipper presser foot on the sewing machine. Then sew second piece of fabric in place.

If plain seams without piping are used, these can be reinforced by rolling the fabric ends together to one side and sewing them to one layer of the fabric.

After sewing upper portion, add hem around bottom. This can be a single fold or double fold of fabric. Turn cover right side out.

This completes construction of a basic drop cover for a wheel and binnacle. There are many possible variations. For example, you may want to add a drawstring or elastic band to the bottom.

Fitted Cover. The second basic approach is a fitted cover, usually in two basic parts: one for the wheel and one for the binnacle. These may or may not be sewn together.

The cover for the wheel requires an arrangement for getting it on and off the wheel, yet it must be held securely when in place. Figure 10-19 shows a typical construction with Common Sense

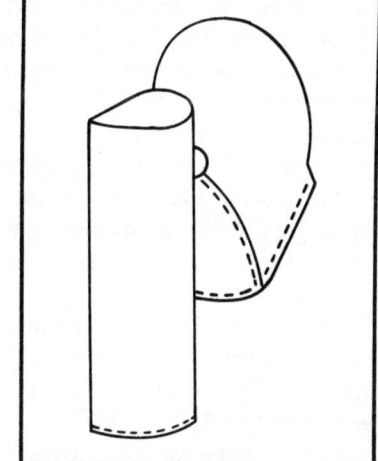

Fig. 10-19. Fitted wheel cover with fasteners.

fasteners. Another possibility is a similar construction with three zippers. If desired, Velcro® can be used instead of zippers.

You will need two round pieces of fabric: one for the aft side of the wheel and one for the forward side, plus ample fabric to join more fabric at the center of the wheel's ring. Seam allowances must be added to each circle. This assumes that the two pieces of fabric will be joined directly. If desired, a separate piece of fabric can be used between these two pieces of fabric to make up the distance across the ring of the wheel. If this method is used, make necessary adjustments in pattern and seam allowances.

If Common Sense fasteners are to be used, make necessary allowances for overlap areas for fasteners, as shown in Fig. 10-19. For zipper and Velcro® construction, make provisions for installing these.

Measure diameter of wheel. Lay out desired patterns on fabric. The marking is usually done on the wrong side of the fabric. Check patterns carefully to make certain that you have allowed for seams, overlaps for fasteners, and so on. Then cut.

Next, sew, including installation of zippers or Velcro® if these are used. Install Common Sense fasteners if this method is used. This completes the construction of the wheel cover, unless you intend to sew it to binnacle cover.

The binnacle cover is usually a drop-type cover with a slot opening to allow you to pass the cover over the wheel shaft. This opening is usually closed below the wheel shaft by Common Sense fasteners, zipper, or Velcro® after the cover is in place.

Binnacles are different shapes and sizes. Custom-make cover to shape of particular binnacle. Figure 10-19 shows a typical cover shape and construction. This is basically a tube of fabric with a round top piece, but some binnacles may have basically square or rectangular shapes. Odd shapes can be taken care of as long as you can get the cover on easily.

Take necessary measurements and lay out patterns on fabric. Allow for seam allowances, hems, casings if drawstrings or elastic bands are to be installed around bottom or other areas, and overlaps for fasteners. Check measurements and patterns over carefully, then cut.

Next, sew seams, including the installation of zippers or Velcro® if these are used. Install Common Sense fasteners if this method is used. If wheel and binnacle covers are to be attached, sew these together.

This completes the construction of a fitted cover or covers.

Similar covers can be designed to fit a variety of other similar shapes.

Outboard Motor Covers

A typical outboard motor cover is shown in Fig. 10-20. This type of cover fits over the upper powerhead portion of the motor, which is the typical arrangement. It's easy to put on and take off, yet gives good protection to the upper and most vulnerable portion of the motor. Full covers and even cover bags can also be designed and constructed, but these are often inconvenient to use and do not seem to be very popular. Our concern here will be with a basic cover for the upper portion of standard outboard motors, but you can design and construct other more complicated types if desired.

In most cases, a breathing-type canvas is used. Acrylic fabric again seems to be the first choice. This type of cover is usually held in place with either a drawstring or a band of elastic or shock cord installed in a casing around the bottom.

The cover is basically a simple fabric bag that fits over the top of the motor. The bag should fit loosely so that it will be easy to put on and take off.

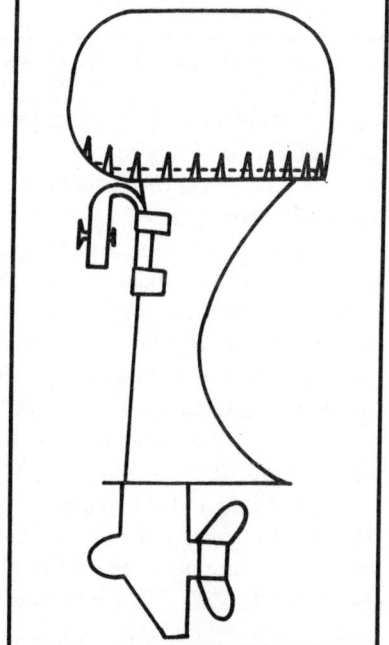

Fig. 10-20. Outboard motor cover.

Fig. 10-21. Patterns for outboard covers.

There are many shapes and sizes of outboard motors. Some outboards are basically round at the top, some square or rectangular with rounded corners, and still others have five or six sides. Figure 10-21 shows some basic shapes and pattern layouts.

To make a cover for a particular outboard, first determine the basic shape of the upper portion of outboard. Decide on the best construction method for cover. Take necessary measurements on outboard motor and lay out pattern on fabric. Marking is usually done on wrong side of fabric. Allow necessary seam allowances for joining separate pieces of fabric. Allow ample fabric for sewing the casing for drawstring, elastic, or shock cord. Check measurements and patterns over carefully, then begin cutting.

Sew seams. Individual pieces are usually joined by plain seams. These can be reinforced by turning both flaps together to one side and then folding the edges in half and under. Sew along this to join the folded layers of fabric to one layer of the cover fabric. This makes a flat-felled seam.

Sew casing around bottom of cover. Leave an opening for installing drawstring, elastic, or shock cord. To install drawstring, elastic, or shock cord, fasten a safety pin to one end and feed it through casing. Have both ends extend out of same opening. If a drawstring is used, tie overhand knot in ends of cord. If elastic is used, stretch elastic the desired amount and then fix ends by sewing through casing and elastic in the area of the opening. If shock cord is used, stretch it the desired amount and connect by crimping shock cord clamps in place to form a band inside casing. Cut off excess shock cord. Sew up opening that was left in casing. This completes construction of basic outboard motor cover.

Hatch Covers

Fabric hatch covers help prevent water from leaking below (some water often manages to find its way through most gaskets) and protect wood hatches, especially varnished or oiled wood, and trim from sun and weather damage.

There are many types, shapes, and sizes of hatches found on boats. Most are some form of hinged box-type or sliding companionway hatches, or variations of these. For our purposes here, we will consider basic box-type covers and covers for companionway hatches and drop boards or doors. These can be adapted for use with other types and arrangements.

Box-Type Hatch Covers. Figure 10-22 shows a typical cover of this type. Snaps, with the sockets attached to the fabric and studs attached to the lower rim of hatch, boat deck, or cabin top, are usually used to secure the covers, although Lift-the-Dot and Common Sense fasteners are sometimes used.

The cover can be made from a single piece of fabric, as shown

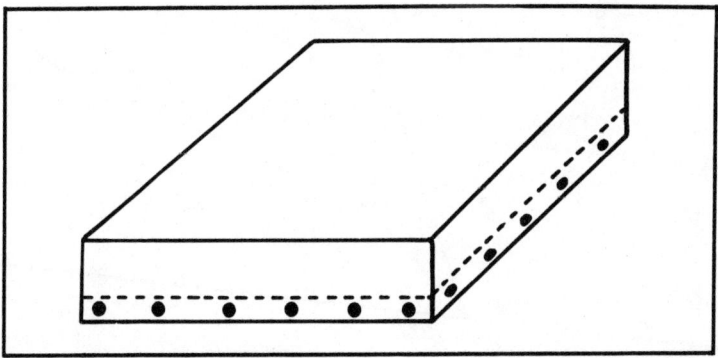

Fig. 10-22. Box-type hatch cover.

Fig. 10-23. Pattern for fabric hatch cover.

in Fig. 10-23. Allow necessary fabric for hem around bottom edge. Hem should be wide enough to allow installing fasteners without passing through stitching.

Take measurements of hatch. Lay out pattern on fabric. Square corners are often made by folding and stitching across folds, as shown in Fig. 10-24. The excess fabric can then be trimmed off. Roll the edges together to one side and sew flat-felled seam for each corner. Next, sew hem in place around the bottom of the cover fabric.

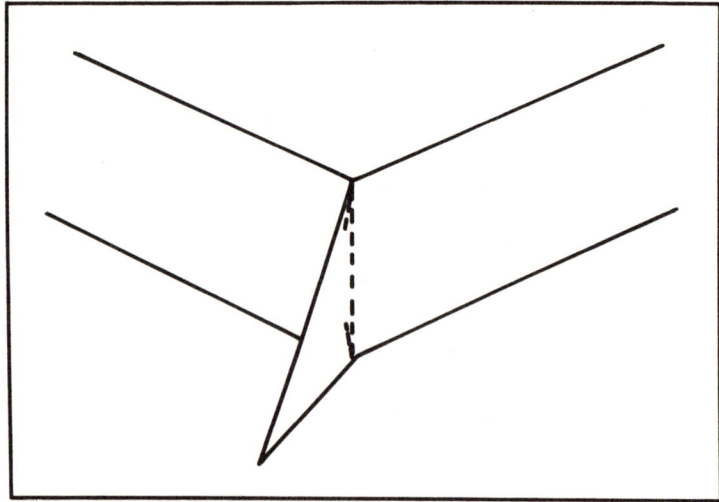

Fig. 10-24. Box corner formed by stitching across folded fabric.

Studs for snaps are generally first attached to lower rim of hatch base, deck, or cabin top. Spacing is usually from about 3 inches to 6 inches apart.

Put cover in place and determine and mark location for snap sockets on fabric. Install snap sockets and buttons, as detailed in Chapter 7. This completes the construction of a basic box-type hatch cover.

A similar cover can be made for skylight-type hatches with angled tops, as shown in Fig. 10-25. The pattern shown is for three pieces of fabric. If desired, however, each flat section can be a separate piece. Lay out patterns from hatch measurements. Allow for seam allowances and ample fabric for hem around the bottom. Cut fabric.

Sew seams, joining fabric pieces with plain seams. Then roll the edges together to one side and sew flat-felled seams. Next, sew hem in place around the bottom of the cover fabric.

Studs for snaps are generally first attached to lower portion of hatch base. Spacing is usually from about 3 inches to 6 inches apart.

Put cover in place and determine and mark location for snap sockets on fabric. Install snap sockets and buttons, as detailed in

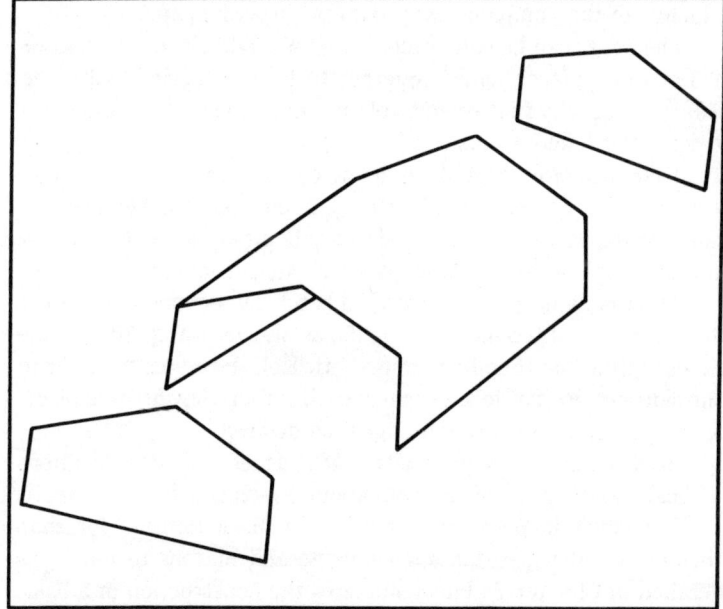

Fig. 10-25. Pattern for fabric cover for skylight-type hatch.

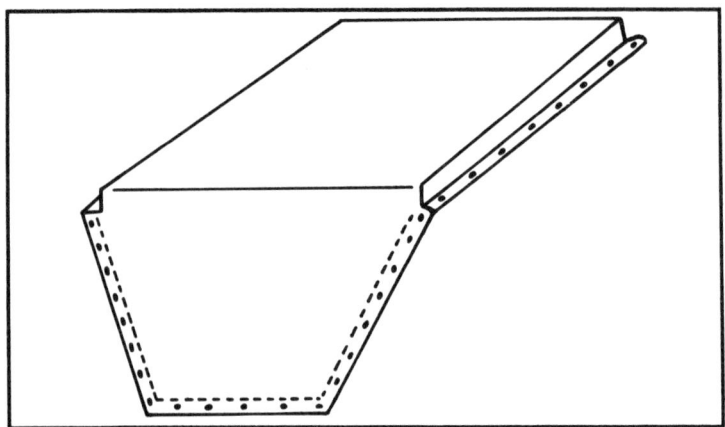

Fig. 10-26. Companionway hatch and drop board cover.

Chapter 7. This completes the construction of a basic cover for a skylight hatch.

Companionway Hatch and Drop Board or Door Covers. A typical cover of this type is shown in Fig. 10-26. The portion of the cover over the sliding hatch can be secured by snaps. The studs are usually attached either to the sides of the sliding hatch or to deck. The companionway drop board part of the cover usually attaches to the companionway trim wood with snaps.

The cover can be constructed from a single piece of fabric, or two or more pieces joined together to form a fabric blank. The seams are usually first sewn as plain seams, then folded and sewn to form flat-felled seams.

Take measurements of hatch and companionway. Lay out pattern on fabric. Folded under hems or binding tape attached to edges can be used, as desired. If folded under hems are to be used, allow necessary fabric for forming these. Next, cut fabric.

The four square corners around hatch can be made by folding the fabric and stitching across folds, as shown in Fig. 10-24. The excess fabric can then be trimmed off. Roll the edges together to one side and sew flat-felled seam in each corner. Sew hems in place, or sew binding tape around edges, as desired.

Studs for snaps are generally first attached to desired locations on boat. Spacing is usually from about 3 inches to 6 inches apart.

Put cover in place, determine, and mark location for snap sockets on fabric. Install snap sockets and buttons to fabric, as detailed in Chapter 7. This completes the construction of a basic companionway hatch and drop board or door cover.

Because different companionway hatch and drop boards or door openings are in use, modifications to the basic design will usually be required to make a cover for a particular boat. It is also possible to make a cover just for the hatch or the companionway opening, or separate covers for each.

Drop Covers for Cockpit and Fishing Chairs

Covers can be made for a variety of cockpit and fishing chairs. Figure 10-27 shows a typical example. Drawstrings or elastic cord bands around the bottom edges of covers are frequently used to secure the covers in place. The covers are usually loosely fitted for easily slipping them in place and removal.

A breathing-type canvas fabric is usually used. Acrylic generally seems to be the first choice for fabric to use for these covers.

To make a cover for a particular chair, first take measurements. Determine the number of separate pieces of fabric to be used to form the desired shape. Lay out the patterns on the fabric. Allow for seam allowances to join the pieces of fabric and ample material for forming the casing or hem around the bottom edge of the cover. A typical pattern is shown in Fig. 10-28.

Before cutting, check measurements and pattern carefully. If everything looks okay, cut fabric.

Next, sew pieces of fabric together, first with plain seams.

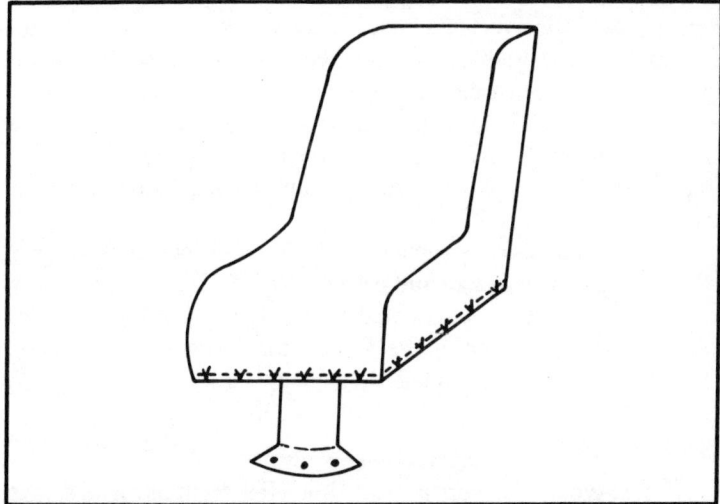

Fig. 10-27. Chair cover.

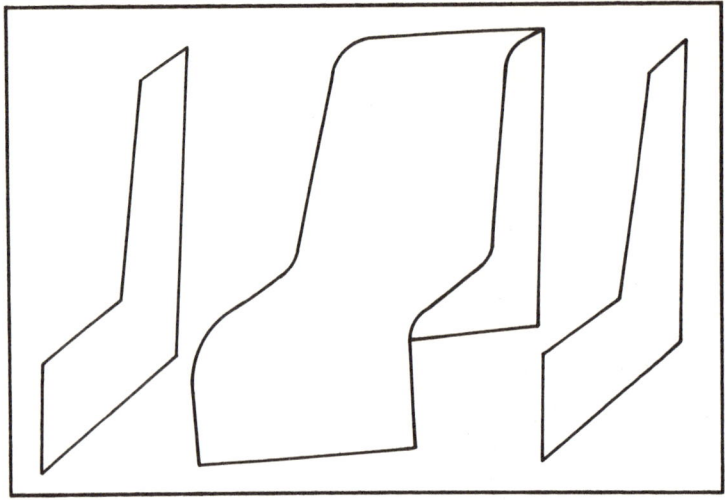
Fig. 10-28. Pattern for chair cover.

These can then be flat-felled by rolling the edges together to one side and sewing a seam along this to one layer of fabric.

If no drawstring or elastic is required around bottom, sew hem in place. For drawstring or elastic band, sew casing around bottom of cover. Leave an opening for installing drawstring, elastic, or shock cord. To install drawstring, elastic, or shock cord in casing, fasten a safety pin or similar object to end and feed it through casing. Have both ends extend out of same opening. If a drawstring is used, tie overhand knot in ends of cord. If elastic is used, stretch elastic desired amount and then fix ends by sewing through casing and elastic in area where opening was left in casing. If shock cord is used, stretch it the desired amount and connect shock cord by crimping shock cord clamps in place to form a band inside casing. Cut off excess shock cord. Sew up opening that was left in casing.

This completes construction of a basic cover for a cockpit chair or seat. This basic design and pattern can be adapted to a variety of types and styles of chairs and seats. Notice that these are intended only as weather covers. Covers for the chairs themselves, that is, upholstery, are detailed in Chapter 14.

Boom-Type Sail Covers

Boom-type sail covers provide protection from ultraviolet rays and keep rain out. This allows sails to be stored under the covers without removing them from the booms for storage inside the boats. The covers also give a boat a trim appearance. They are used not only for mainsails and mizzens, but also for jibs and staysails that have club booms.

A breathing-type fabric should be used for these so that condensation will not form underneath. Acrylic seems to be the first choice of fabric for sail covers.

Generally, the sails are lowered and furled to the booms with the mast sail slides still in the tracks or the jib shackles still in place on the stays. The covers are then shaped to fit over the sails and booms in this arrangement, with the forward section of the covers going around the mast or stays. Figure 10-29 shows a typical mainsail cover. A typical cover for a staysail with a club boom is shown in Fig. 10-30. Because there are differences in the patterning for the covers, these are treated separately below.

Fig. 10-29. Mainsail cover.

Fig. 10-30. Cover for staysail with club boom.

Mainsail and Mizzen Sail Covers. We will first consider covers over booms that attach to a mast. The lowered and furled sail forms a basic shape (Fig. 10-31). Figure 10-32 shows a basic cover to fit this shape. A cord is used to secure the cover around the mast above the lowered sail. Fasteners hold the cover closed forward of the mast and below the boom behind or aft the mast. Although a variety of fasteners can and have been used, Common Sense fasteners seem to work best and are only slightly more expensive than some of the less satisfactory alternative methods, such as hooks and eyes, snaps, and zippers. These sail covers are often secured at the aft end of the boom to keep them from sliding forward, usually with a tie down cord or other arrangement.

There are two basic patterns commonly used to make boom type sail covers. The first method uses one piece of fabric folded over the top of the furled sail and boom, with added fabric sewn

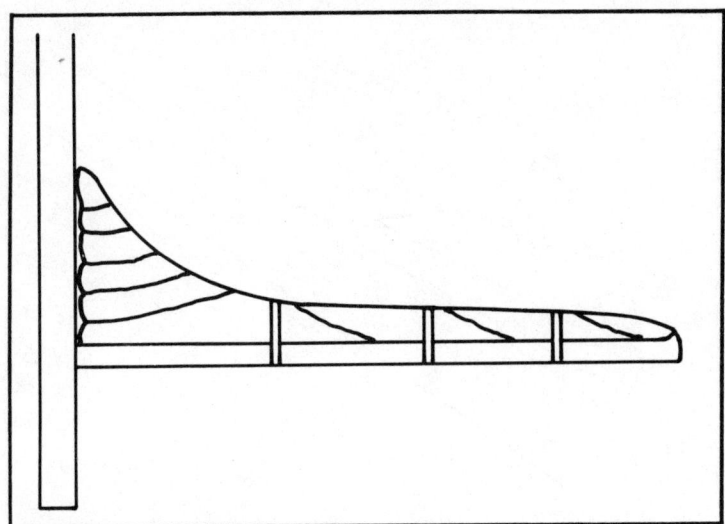

Fig. 10-31. Furled mainsail.

to the forward section, as shown in Fig. 10-33. This method has the advantage of not having a seam at the top of the cover for most of its length. For larger covers, however, a single piece of fabric may not be wide enough to accomplish this.

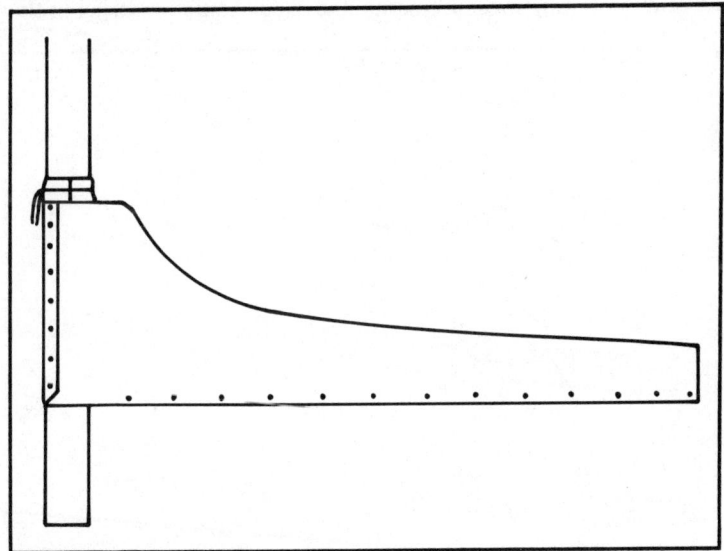

Fig. 10-32. Cover for furled mainsail.

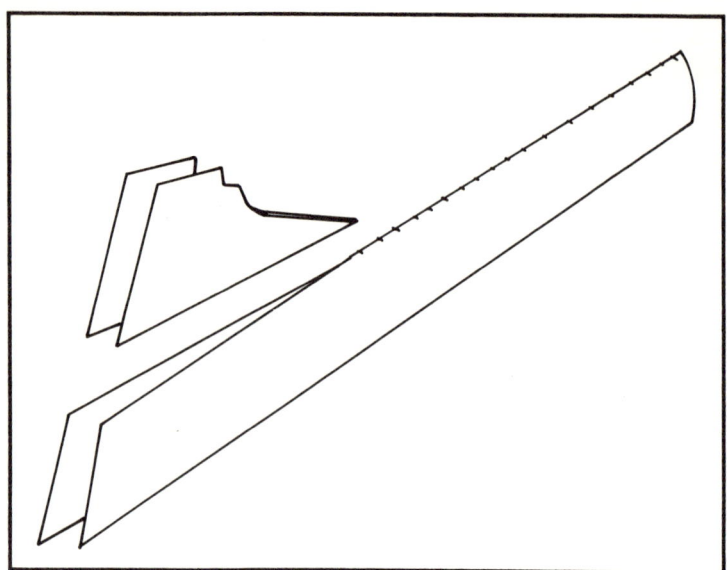

Fig. 10-33. Basic pattern with main fabric folded over sail.

A second method requires a seam along the full back of the cover, a shown in Fig. 10-34. This method is commonly used for larger size sail covers.

Before taking measurements, the sails should be furled in the

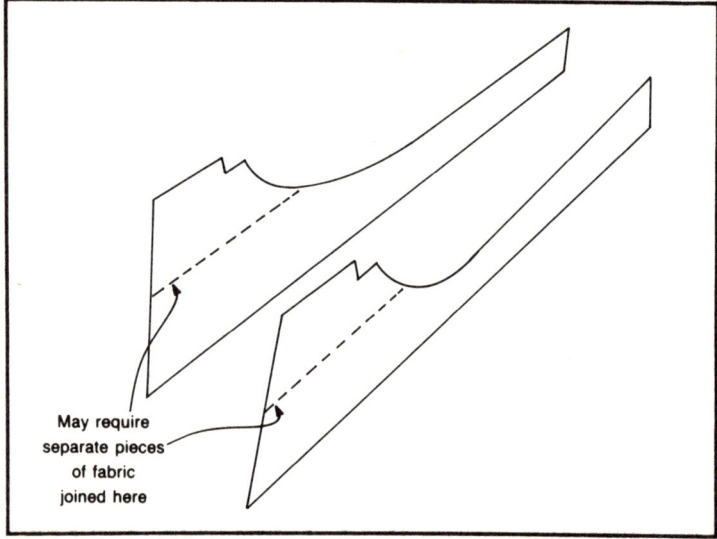

Fig. 10-34. Basic pattern with separate fabric pieces for each half of cover.

normal manner. If you have an old sail cover that fits properly, this can be used as a pattern. If it fits too tightly or loosely, it may still be possible to use it as a pattern by making necessary adjustments.

To use an old sailcover as a pattern, mark pieces so that you know where they go in relation to each other. Unless it is obvious, also mark right and wrong sides. Then open all seams. Use a seam ripper for this.

The fasteners can also be removed. In some cases, these will be in good enough condition that they can be used again on the new cover; in other cases, they will require replacement with new ones.

Next, transfer all seamlines, folding lines, and cutting lines from old fabric to new. One method for doing this is to use tracing paper and a tracing wheel, as detailed in Chapter 6. Place new fabric right side down on the cutting table. Place old fabric right side down on top of new fabric. Place tracing paper between fabrics. Use tracing wheel to go over seam, fold, and cutting lines on old fabric to transfer these marks to the new fabric.

Before doing any cutting, check pattern and mark lines on new fabric for stitching, folding, and cutting. Make desired modifications if old cover did not fit properly. Then cut.

If you don't have an old cover, or it won't give a satisfactory pattern, measurements can be taken directly from the sail furled in place. Make certain that the sail is furled in the manner that you normally do it. A common mistake is to do a better than normal job of furling the sail to make measurements for the cover. This can result in a cover that will be too tight to fit over the sail when it is furled the way you normally do it.

Opinions vary on how tight a sail cover should fit. Some will fit even when the sail is merely bunched up and tied with straps around the boom. Others will only fit properly when the sail is actually well furled. In most cases, you can't have a good fit both ways. You may be able to compromise somewhere in between. In any case, it's important that a sail cover be easy to put on and take off.

Measurements are essentially the same regardless of which one of the two basic patterns is used, except that seam allowances will have to be allowed in the latter pattern for joining the two main pieces of fabric together.

Starting from the forward edge of the mast, measure back along the boom and place small pieces of masking tape on the boom to mark off set distances, such as every 2 feet. Place a piece of masking tape on forward section of mast even with bottom of boom.

Boom should be in the position where the sails will be furled when sail cover is to be used. Then place two other reference marks above this on the mast, one at highest area of sail in lowered position and the other level with the point where the furled sail curves rapidly upward.

Using a tape, measure around the furled sail and spars at the location of each masking tape marker. Sketch pattern on scratch pad and write down the measurements.

Next, transfer these measurements to fabric. Add 2 inches to edges of each piece of fabric that extends below boom or forward of mast for fasteners. Then add an additional 2 1/2 inches for hem folds. An alternate method is to omit the 2 1/2 inches and use binding tape instead to cover the raw edge of the fabric.

Figure 10-35 shows a sample pattern for sail cover with main aft part made from one piece of fabric. Figure 10-36 shows alternate pattern when two pieces of fabric are used. The first method requires two separate pieces of fabric be joined to the main piece to form the upper forward section of the cover. These are generally cut extra large, then sewn to the main part. Usually, plain seams are sewn first. These are then flat-felled.

If the second patterning method is used, separate pieces might or might not be required. The fabric might be wide enough with-

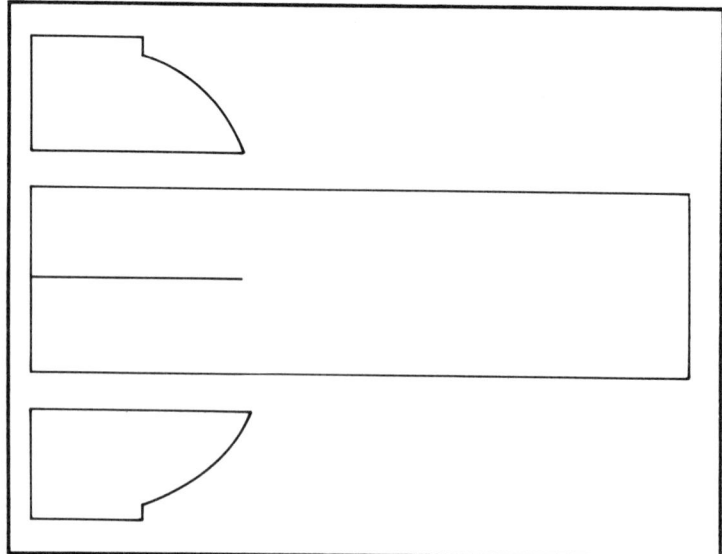

Fig. 10-35. Fabric pattern for sail cover with main part made from one piece of fabric.

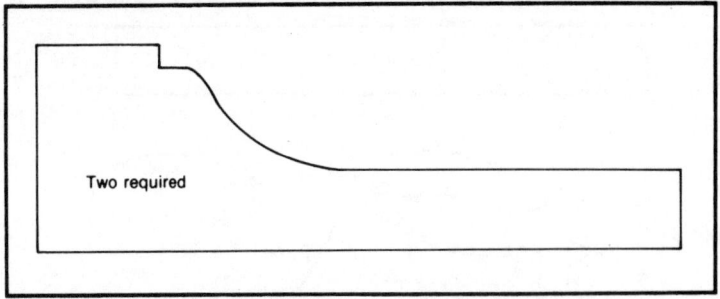

Fig. 10-36. Pattern for making sail cover in half sections.

out these. If required to make the necessary height, sew these to the main pieces of fabric. This will form a fabric blank for each side of the cover. Usually, plain seams are sewn first and then flat-felled. Mark pattern from measurements for patterning and cutting slope. Allow seam allowances.

If the first method is used, sew seam to form slope area in fabric. With the fabrics right side to right side, first sew plain seam in place. Then flat-fell the seam to give added strength to the stitching.

If the second patterning method is used, stitch along entire backbone of cover to join the two halves. With the fabrics right side to right side, first sew plain seam in place. Then flat-fell the seam to give added strength to the stitching.

Turn covers right side out and try them in place over furled sails. The remainder of the construction is the same for both patterning methods.

Check fit. If everything looks right, sew hems in bottom and forward sections.

Next, pattern and cut fabric for mast collar, as shown in Fig. 10-37. The length of the collar should be approximately 1 1/2 times the circumference of mast.

Sew hems all the way around collar. The collar is then sewn to upper forward portion of sail cover, as shown in Fig. 10-37. A tie cord is then sewn to the collar, as shown. Cord should be polyester rather than nylon or cotton.

Next, hem aft end of cover. If tie cord is to be used, sew this in place.

It may be necessary to add special covers for winches and other protrusions, such as shown in Fig. 10-38. Lay out patterns on fabric. Cut fabric and sew as necessary. Then make cutouts on main cover and sew the special cover in position.

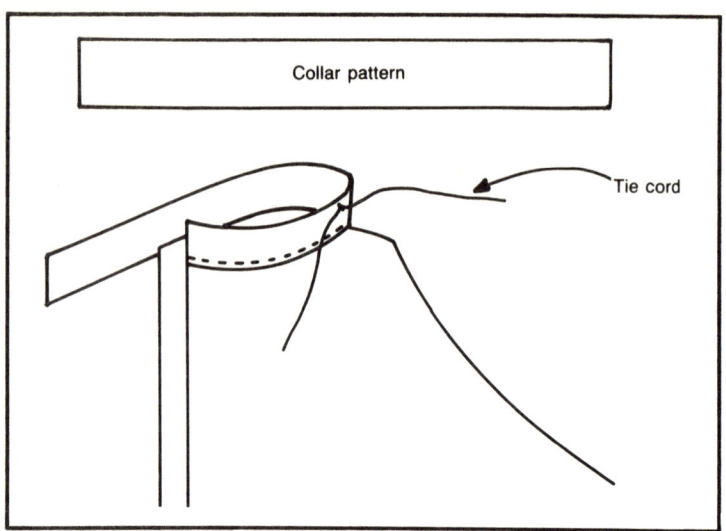

Fig. 10-37. Mast collar pattern.

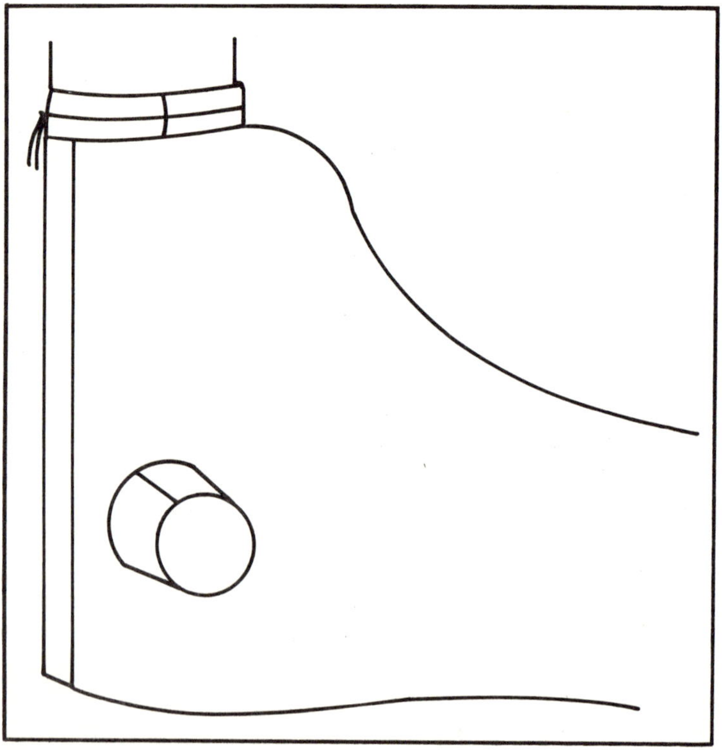

Fig. 10-38. Special added cover for winch.

Before installing fasteners in cover forward of mast and below boom, try cover on again and make certain everything fits correctly. Make any required corrections.

Mark location for each fastener. In most cases, Common Sense fasteners are used. Install these as detailed in Chapter 7. All of the studs are generally installed on one side of the cover and all the eyelets on the other. Check this carefully, because it's easy to make a mistake here. Fasteners are placed in all corners of cover and from about 4 inches to 12 inches apart, as desired.

This completes the construction of a basic boom-type sail cover. There are many possible variations, of course. Other types of fasteners, such as hook and eye or zippers, can be substituted.

Jib Boom-Type Covers. Construction is essentially the same as for mainsail and mizzen sail covers, except that the forward section fits over a wire stay that generally angles aft instead of being vertical like the typical mast.

The collar that goes around the stay is quite small. The forward section of cover is cut at the same angle as stay. Sew hem in place as for mainsail and mizzen sail covers. Then install fasteners in place. This completes construction of a basic jib boom-type cover.

Jib Bag-Type Covers. Foredeck bag-type covers for jibs (Fig. 10-39) are becoming increasingly popular. These allow jib storage without unshackling the jib, a considerable convenience when cruising in a sailboat. Interior space on most sailboats is limited, and this allows on-deck storage. The jib is also ready to hoist quickly by simply removing the cover bag.

Although there are many possible patterns for these bags, I like those shown in Figs. 10-40 and 10-41. It's essentially a bag with a collar that has a tie to secure it around the stay, and fasteners to secure the opening forward of the stay and jib shackles.

The jib should fit easily into the bag so that it will be easy to put the cover on and take it off. Although perhaps not essential, small grommets can be installed or other small openings can be made along the bottom of the bag so that any water that happens to get inside the bag can drain out. The aft end of the cover bag can be attached to a bow rail or held up by the halyard.

Because it is difficult to estimate the size of a bag required for a particular jib with the sail bunched up on deck, using a jib bag that is about the right size as a pattern makes sense. With the jib shackled to stay, fit jib into jib bag. Hold opening of bag up to stay. Determine if bag should be made larger or smaller and where any changes should be made.

Fig. 10-39. Foredeck bag-type jib cover.

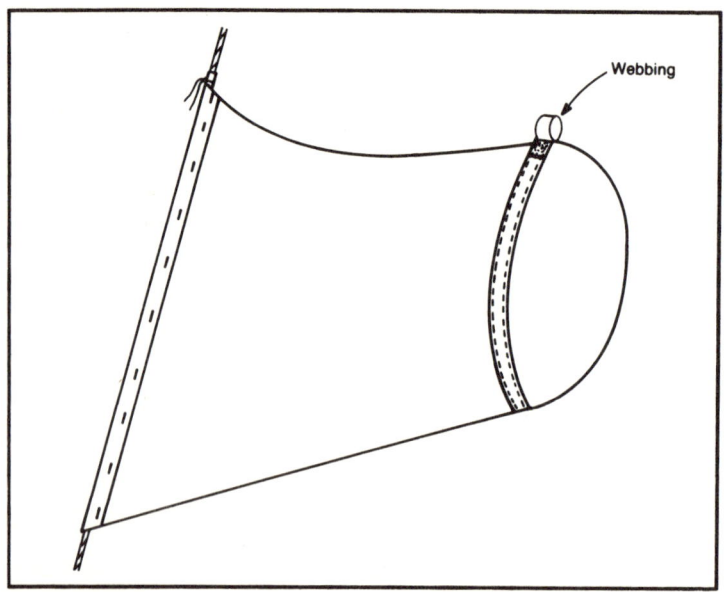

Fig. 10-40. Pattern for foredeck bag-type jib cover.

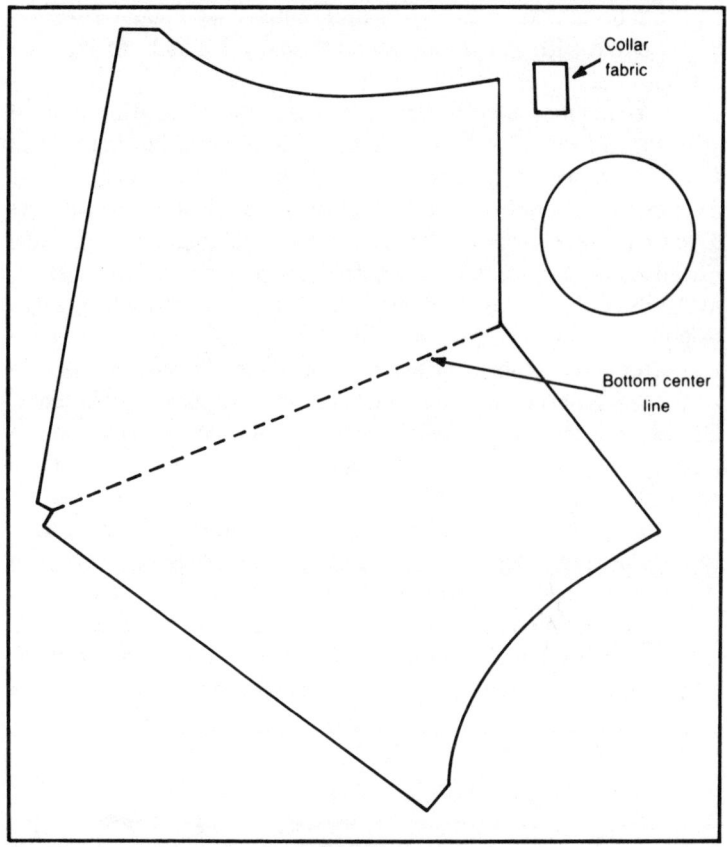

Fig. 10-41. Fabric patterns for foredeck bag-type jib cover.

Figure 10-41 shows a typical pattern. Mark pattern for a particular jib on fabric, taking measurements from jib bag. The jib foredeck bag should be made from a breathing-type canvas. Acrylic fabric seems to be the first choice of material for these cover bags.

When marking pattern, allow seam allowances and ample fabric for hems and fasteners. Check all measurements before cutting. End piece shown is round, but this can also be oval or rectangular if desired.

One method is to fit a round end piece to a sewn loop of fabric. Lay the fabric out flat, and then measure the distance across from stitching in seam to other edge of fabric. Double this length to determine circumference of circle for required stitching line. To determine diameter of required circle, divide the circumference by 3.14. Half of the diameter is the radius for laying out the required circle on the fabric. Then, using the same center point, make a second larger circle with a seam allowance, usually 1/2 inch, to give the cutting line.

A second method is to determine the required length of a piece of fabric to form a loop which fits a circle piece of fabric that has a specific diameter. Multiply diameter of seamline circle by 3.14. This gives the required length of fabric to form loop from seamline to seamline. Add a seam allowance to each end to get cutting lines. Because the loop of fabric required for a foredeck bag tapers, measurements are made a seam allowance length away from edge of fabric.

After cutting fabric pieces, first join ends of main piece of fabric to form tapered loop, as shown in Fig. 10-42. Sew a plain seam. Usually, this is then flat-felled by rolling both flaps together to one side and then sewing a seam along this to one of the layers of the main piece of fabric.

Next, place end piece wrong side down on bed of sewing machine. Position tapered end of tube piece of fabric for sewing to this; it should be turned wrong side out. Pin or staple the two layers of fabric together for sewing plain seam around circle. If this is done, sewing is usually possible without cutting notches in upper fabric. Keep edges even and the same distance from edges as seam

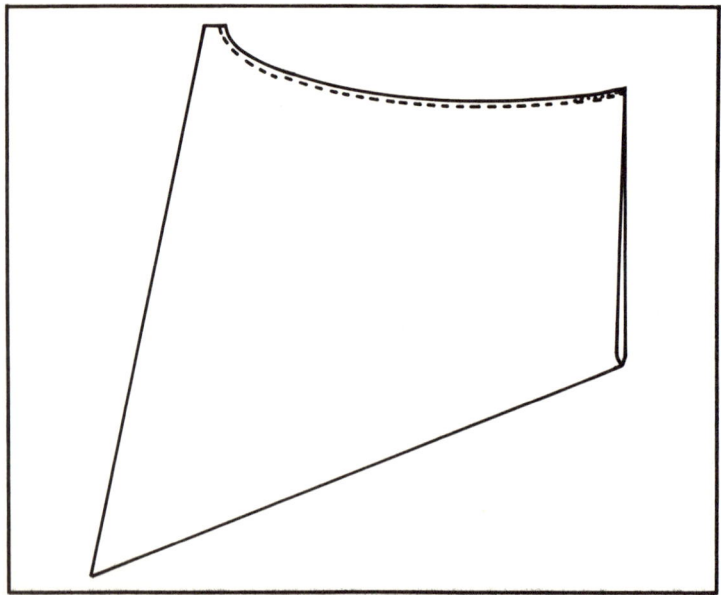

Fig. 10-42. Seam is made to join ends of fabric to form tapered loop.

is made all the way around. Overlap start of stitching to fix the seam.

Next, pattern and cut fabric for collar for going around stay, as shown in Fig. 10-43. Only a short length is required, usually about 2 inches. A tie cord is then sewn to the collar. Cord should be polyester rope rather than nylon or cotton.

Sew hems in forward section of cover bag. Edge of fabric is usually folded back 2 1/2 inches, then 1/2 inch of this is turned under.

Try cover bag on before installing fasteners. Make any necessary adjustments. Mark location for each fastener. In most cases, Common Sense fasteners are used. Install these as detailed in Chapter 7. All of the studs are generally installed on inner layer of the cover and all of the eyelets on the outer flap. Check this carefully, because it's easy to make a mistake here. A fastener is placed at the top and bottom and from about 4 inches to 6 inches apart in between.

A strap to tie the aft end of the bag to a bow pulpit or to hoist it by a halyard is usually attached to bag, as shown in Fig. 10-43. Reinforce back side of fabric in area where straps are to be sewn in place with extra fabric layer. Webbing is usually used for the strap. Polyester is generally the first choice, but nylon will usually give satisfactory results. Sew webbing in place with a rectangular pattern with an "X" pattern inside. This completes construction of a basic foredeck cover for a jib.

Another pattern is shown in Fig. 10-43. This is constructed from a single piece of fabric for the main portion of the bag. A collar for going around the stay can be added, as shown. If desired, a handle made from webbing can be sewn to aft edge.

Estimate size of bag required by measuring around jib when shackled to stay and folded and shaped as it will go into bag. Fold fabric in half, right side to right side. Lay out pattern on one layer of fabric. Allow seam allowance along aft edge and ample fabric to overlap stay and form hem for attaching fasteners on forward edge. Cut fabric along cutting lines.

Sew hem in place along luff (forward) edges. Then sew plain seam along aft edge. This can then be flat-felled.

Next, pattern and cut fabric for collar going around stay. Only a short length is required, usually about 2 inches. Sew collar to main fabric. A tie cord is then sewn to the collar to tie it around stay. Polyester cord is usually used rather than nylon or cotton.

Try cover on before installing fasteners. Make any necessary

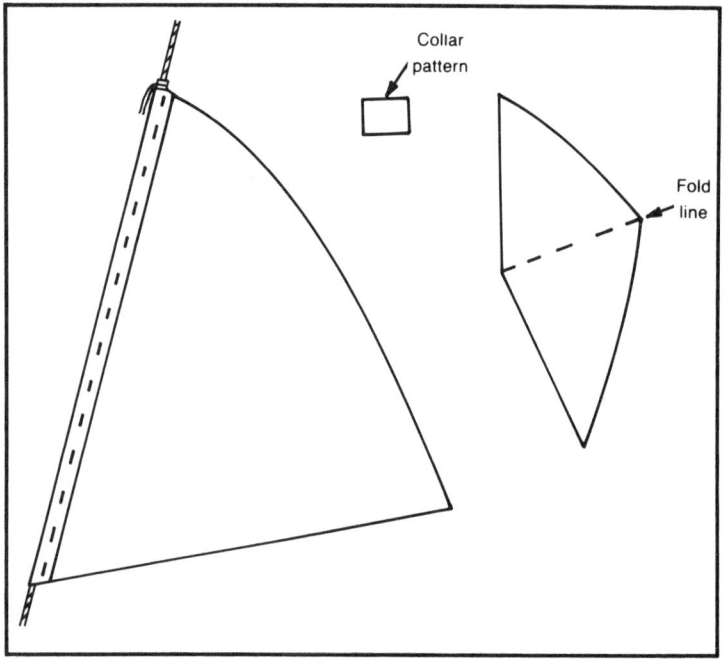

Fig. 10-43. Alternate pattern for foredeck bag-type jib cover.

adjustments, then mark location for each fastener. In most cases, Common Sense fasteners are used. Install these as detailed in Chapter 7. Spacing is usually from about 4 inches to 6 inches between fasteners with a fastener at the top and bottom. All of the studs are generally installed on one side of the cover and all of the eyelets on the other.

If desired, sew webbing handle on aft edge of bag. This completes the construction.

If desired, grommets can be installed in bottom of foredeck jib bags as drain holes. Use small grommets and space them from about 6 to 12 inches apart along the bottom of the bag.

Boat Covers

Full and partial boat covers can protect a boat from the damaging effects of sun, water, and dirt. Covers are used on a variety of types and sizes of boats. Covers can be used while boat is in the water or ashore on a cradle or boat trailer. They are suitable for covering boats between uses or for long-term storage.

There are a number of possible approaches to making boat

covers, which are usually custom fitted to the particular boat. The approach here is to construct a basic boat cover, then modify this as necessary for special situations and types of boats.

In general, breathing-type fabrics should be used unless special provisions are made to prevent condensation underneath. Specially treated cotton boat canvas is the most commonly used fabric for boat covers, but if you can afford the extra cost, boat acrylic canvas often works better.

A basic fabric blank can be constructed first. This is necessary, because in most cases a single piece of fabric will not be large enough for the entire cover. The fabric blank can be formed by running the individual pieces of fabric across the boat, lengthwise, or a combination of these positions.

Fabric that extends across open cockpits and other areas must be supported by bows or other means so that water will run off and not form in puddles. Manufactured versions are available, or you can make up your own. If bows or other means of support are required for the particular cover, these should be set up before measurements are taken for the cover.

If you have an old cover that fits, and you want to make a new one, one approach is to use the old cover as a pattern. Open the seams in the old cover after carefully marking assembly locations. A seam ripper can be used to open the seams. The pattern can then be transferred to new fabric by using tracing paper and a tracing wheel or other means. Then cut fabric and sew together in the same manner the old cover was assembled. Make necessary modifications to correct any defects or problem areas in the old cover.

In most cases, however, it won't be that simple, and you will need to make up a fabric blank. We will assume that you will be running the individual pieces of fabric across the boat, for our purposes here, but the same principles can be applied for running the fabric pieces lengthwise or a combination of directions.

The fabrics most commonly used for boat covers come in widths from about 24 inches to 40 inches. The wider widths will mean less seams and should be used when you have a choice.

First, measure the centerline length of the boat, measuring over cabin tops, windshields, and any other obstructions that the finished cover will pass over. If a standard overhang of 8 inches from the rail is desired, allow 12 inches extra all the way around. Thus, 2 feet would be added to the centerline length. Allowing for seam allowances to join pieces of fabric together, determine the number of sections that will be required. Mark the seamlines along the centerline. This can be done with masking tape placed on a cord tied from bow to stern. Be sure to allow for the forward piece to extend 12 inches beyond the bow and the stern piece to extend 12 inches beyond the stern. If the cover is to pass over the boom of a sailboat, be sure to take this into account.

At each seamline mark and measure distance across boat from rail to rail. Write down the measurements on a diagram, such as is shown in Fig. 10-44. Add 12 inches additional on each end over rail to rail distance on each section of fabric. Mark lengths on fabric and indicate where pieces go in relation to each other. Cut fabric to these lengths.

The pieces of fabric can then be sewn together to form a flat blank of material. The excess fabric can be taken up later to take care of windshields, transom corners, and so on, as detailed below in this chapter.

A second approach is to pattern and shape the pieces of fabric before joining them together into a single unit. This, of course, is more difficult to do.

Regardless of method used, join pieces of fabric first with plain seams. The seams are usually then reinforced by folding both flaps together to one side and sewing two seams through these and one layer of the fabric. You can also fold the flaps together to one side, turn under and sew one or two seams through this to one layer of the fabric. You might prefer to cut one flap off a short distance beyond the stitching, fold the fabric, and sew one or two rows of stitches to join these with one of the layers of fabric. Strong stitching methods are required, because considerable stress will be placed on the seams of most boat covers.

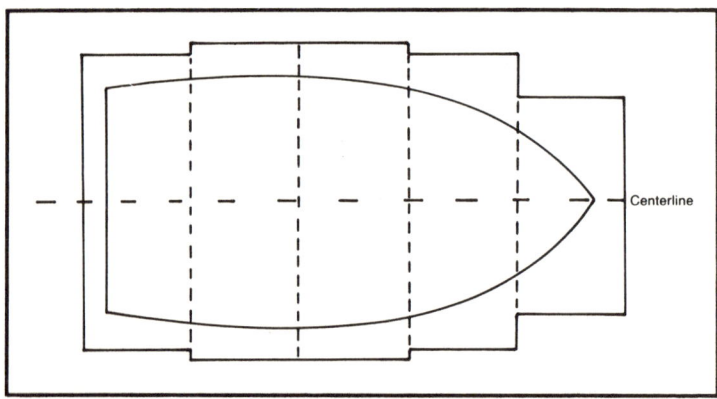

Fig. 10-44. Fabric blank for boat cover.

If flat method is used, drape cover over boat. Take up excess fabric in areas of windshields, corners, and so on by folding darts in fabric. Mark these with chalk. This is usually done on the right side of the fabric, even though the fabric will be refolded to the opposite side for sewing the darts.

Sew darts with plain seams first. Small folds of fabric need not be cut off. Simply fold them over, and sew them to one of the pieces of cover fabric. Larger folds of fabric can be cut off at a seam allowance distance from the stitches and the edges flat-felled.

After the basic cover has been shaped to fit contours of boat, put the cover in place. Measure and mark 8 inches below rail all the way around for location of hem or casing.

In most cases, a casing with a draw cord is used. In this case, add 2 inches all the way around and make second cutting line on fabric.

Cut off excess fabric all the way around. Sew 1 1/2 inch casing with 1/2 inch of fabric turned under all the way around, except for small opening for draw cord. The opening should be reinforced with a hem. Because it is somewhat difficult to feed the cord through such a long casing, the cord is often laid in place as the casing is sewed. Casing should be double- or even triple-stitched.

Alternate methods for securing covers include snaps, Lift-the-Dot and Common Sense fasteners, and elastic cord band inside a casing, as well as grommets, webbing loops, and ring attachments for tie downs to a boat trailer or cradle. Still another method is to sew up canvas bags, fill these with sand, sew up the tops, and sew the bags to the bottom edges of the cover. These weight bags will serve to hold the covers in place under most conditions. The size of the bags depends on the size of the boat cover. Smaller bags can be used for smaller covers and larger bags for larger covers.

Covers for sailboats present special problems in that they must go around masts, rigging, and so on. These covers usually also fit over the booms, as shown in Fig. 10-45.

A cutout slot is usually made for the mast. A collar and tie-off line is fitted. The collar is sewn to the cover. Flaps of fabric are added to the slot that allows the cover to slip around mast, as shown in Fig. 10-45. Fasteners are added to this to secure the cover in place. Slots for chainplates and rigging can be made by cutting fabric and sewing hems and flaps in place.

If the boat has a backstay or boom end topping lift, a slot can be cut for this. A collar with tie off cord is added to this. Flaps are sewn in place for fasteners. Common Sense fasteners are usually

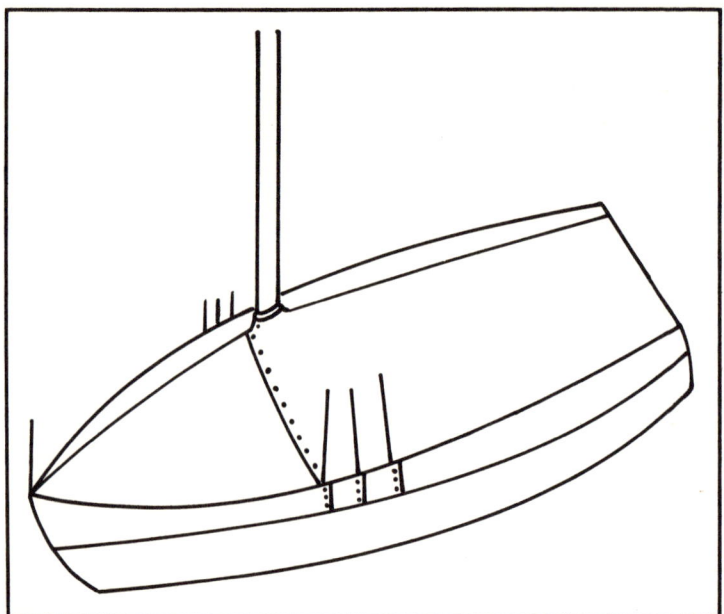

Fig. 10-45. Sailboat cover.

used to secure the flaps.

The above covers are full boat patterns, but partial covers, as from windshield back on power boats and boom covers from mast back on sailboats can be constructed similarly. Covers for dinghies and tenders, whether carried aboard right side up or upside down, can also be fabricated.

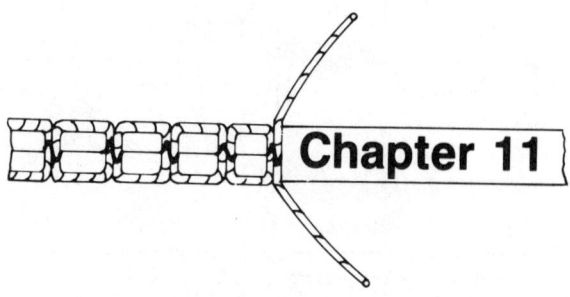

Chapter 11

Awnings, Enclosures, and Weather Cloths

A variety of awnings and enclosures are useful for recreational vehicles. For boats, awnings or sun canopies, enclosures (not including side and stern covers associated with canvas tops, which are detailed in Chapter 12), and weather cloths are popular. Because there are hundreds of possibilities for these items, the focus here will be on the main styles, with suggestions for variations and modifications.

RECREATIONAL VEHICLE AWNINGS AND ENCLOSURES

Many awnings, with or without connected enclosures, are used with travel trailers, campers, motor homes, and other recreational vehicles.

Awnings

A typical awning is shown in Fig. 11-1. Some of these are removable for storage; others can be rolled up in a special casing like a venetian blind.

Various types of framing are used for supporting the awnings and holding them in desired position. Because the design of hardware for awnings is quite complex, the coverage here is limited to replacing existing canvas awning fabrics.

The basic idea is to use the old fabric as a pattern for the new awning. You may want to use the same kind of fabric for the new

211

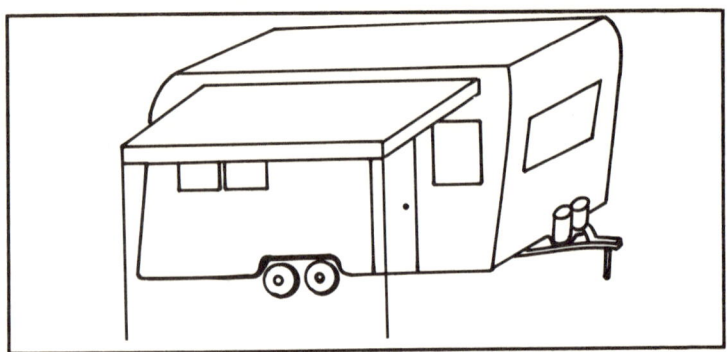

Fig. 11-1. Recreational vehicle awning.

awning, or switch to some other type. Acrylic seems to work well for awnings. Some awning systems will require using approximately the same weight of fabric, such as for fitting in roll up systems; for other awnings this is not an important consideration.

Remove old fabric from recreational vehicle. If awning is a roll-up-type, it may be necessary to disassemble the housing to remove awning. Remove frames and other fittings.

Mark arrangements for joining separate pieces of fabric, then open all seams. A seam ripper can be used for this. Transfer patterns to new fabric. Tracing paper and a tracing wheel can be used on many fabrics. After patterns have been marked, check all measurements, then cut fabric into required pieces.

Sew pieces together. Usually, the same type seams as were used on the old awning will be used on the new. Sew in necessary hems and casings. When sewing has been completed, install any fasteners and connect awning in roll up brackets or other attachments. This completes the basic construction.

In general, I suggest that only factory designed bracket systems be used for awnings that will be used in folded up positions on moving recreational vehicles, because improper design and construction could present a safety hazard. Removable awnings that can be carried inside recreational vehicles are sometimes designed and constructed by advanced do-it-yourselfers.

Enclosures

Tentlike enclosures (Fig. 11-2) are sometimes used in connection with awnings. These may be simple fabric walls or complete enclosures with canvas floors.

Figure 11-3 shows a method for attaching wall panels to awn-

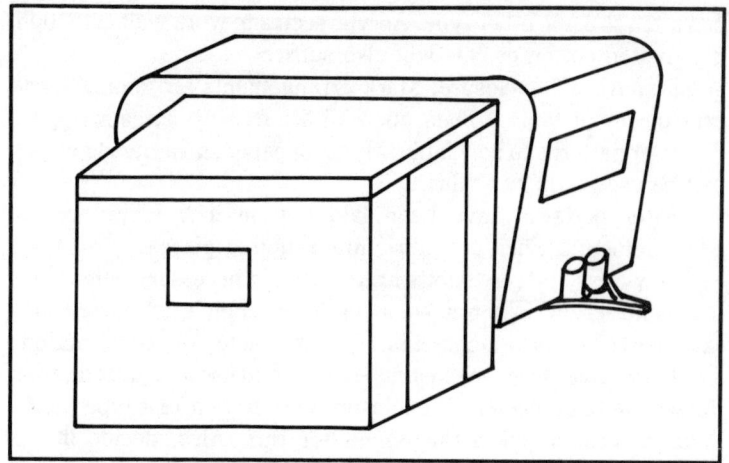

Fig. 11-2. Awning with tentlike enclosure.

ing fabric by means of Common Sense fasteners. Notice that the eyelets are generally placed on the awning fabric and the studs on the enclosure fabric. This arrangement keeps water from leaking through the joint, because the inside enclosure fabric extends above the eyelet openings so that any water that gets through the eyelets simply runs off on the outside of the enclosure fabric.

If you have an existing canvas enclosure and can use this as a pattern for the new one, construction is greatly simplified. The basic idea is to use the old fabric as a pattern for the new enclosure. You may want to use the same kind of fabric for the new enclosure,

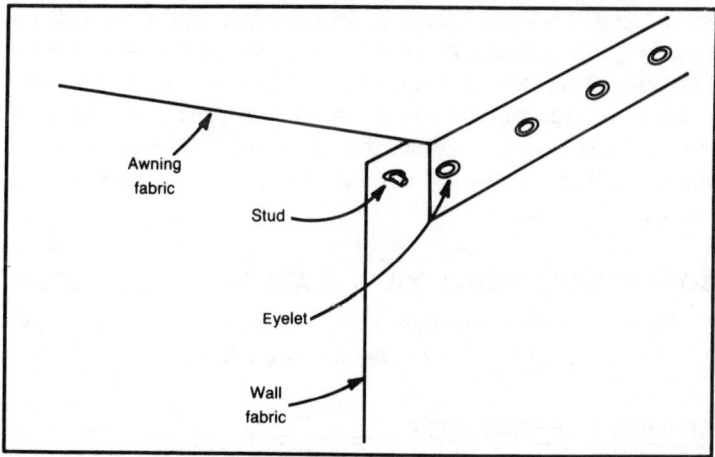

Fig. 11-3. Arrangement of twist fasteners.

or switch to some other type. Acrylic seems to work well, although dry-treated cotton canvas will also suffice.

Remove old enclosure. Mark arrangements for joining separate pieces of fabric. Then open all seams with a seam ripper. Transfer patterns to new fabric. Tracing paper and a tracing wheel can be used on many fabrics.

After patterns have been laid out on new fabric, check measurements. Then cut fabric into required pieces.

Sew fabric pieces together. Also sew in necessary hems, casings, and so on. When sewing has been completed, install any fasteners or other attachments. This completes the construction.

If you don't have an existing enclosure to use as a pattern, first determine basic design. If enclosure is to have a tent-type fabric door, determine the arrangement for this. Also, decide if the enclosure will have a floor.

Take necessary measurements and lay out pattern on fabric. After all patterns have been laid out on fabric, check all measurements over carefully. Then cut fabric into required pieces. Sew pieces of fabric together. Add necessary hems, casings, and so on.

When sewing has been completed, install any fasteners or other attachments. This completes the basic construction.

There are many possible variations for enclosures. Windows are frequently added. Transparent flexible vinyl can be sewn to canvas fabrics, and there are many approaches to installing this. One method is to mark the desired window opening on fabric. Pattern and cut plastic window material 1 inch larger than this all the way around. Then sew this to enclosure fabric with seam approximately 1/4 inch from edge of window plastic all the way around. Then cut out window opening. Use binding tape over the cut edge and sew seam through binding and window plastic, as shown in Fig. 11-4A. Alternate methods include turning cut edges of opening under (Fig. 11-4B) and sewing tablings over window plastic overlap inside enclosure (Fig. 11-4C).

BOAT AWNINGS, ENCLOSURES, AND WEATHER CLOTHS

Many different awnings or sun canopies, enclosures, and weather cloths are useful canvas items for boats.

Awnings and Enclosures

Awnings, with or without side flap enclosures, are frequently

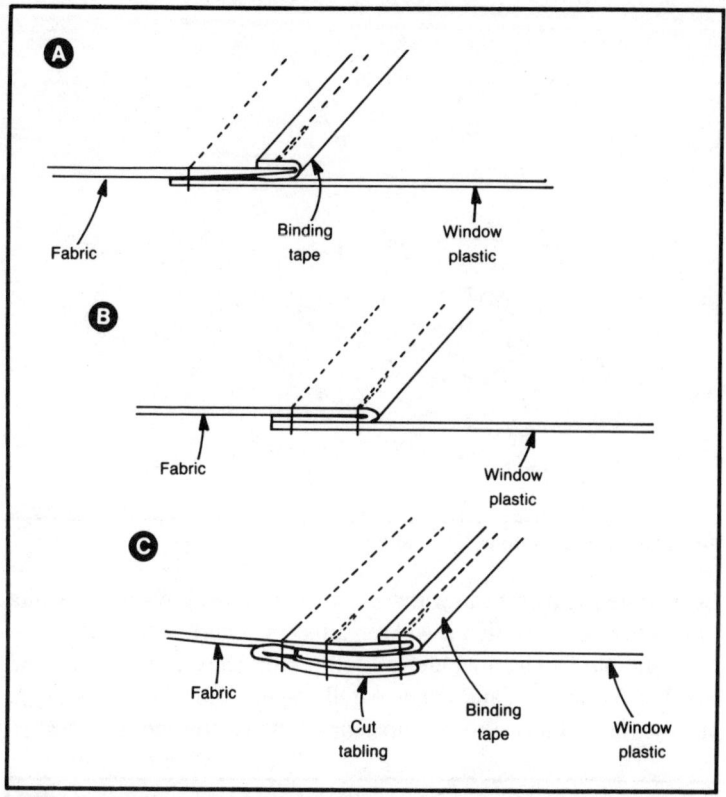

Fig. 11-4. Installing window vinyl: installation of window plastic with binding tape (A); window plastic is sewn to turned-under edge of fabric (B); then cut tabling is sewn over plastic overlap (C).

rigged over boat cockpits, especially sailboats. Figure 11-5 shows a typical awning or sun canopy without side flaps; Fig. 11-6 has side flap enclosures. There are many possible variations.

We will first consider a basic awning for a sailboat. The awning goes over the boom, as shown in Fig. 11-5. There are casings in the forward and aft edges of the awning for awning poles, which are rigged with tie downs to the boat. A hook for attaching a main halyard to the center of the awning top is frequently provided.

Awnings provide shade and can give protection from rain. If enclosures are added, as detailed later in this chapter, they can also provide privacy. An awning should provide maximum sun coverage, yet be easily stowed. Although this type of awning can be used while underway under power, it must be removed before using the mainsail. Thus, it should be easy to put up and take down. It should

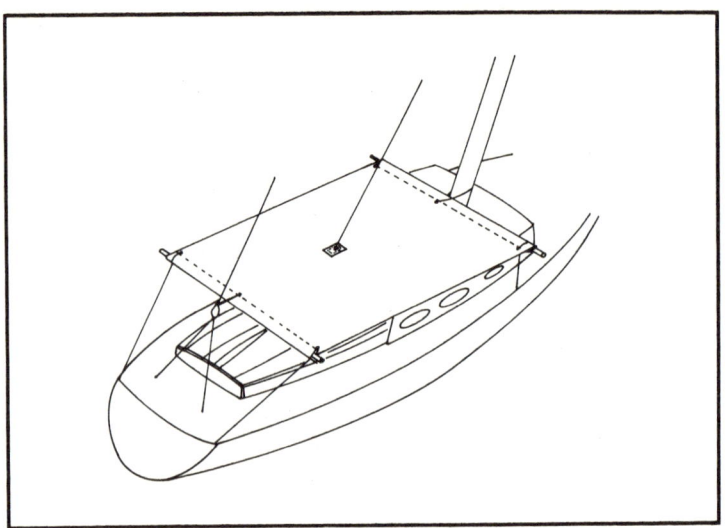

Fig. 11-5. Awning without side flaps.

be mounted so that it can withstand strong winds. It should be white or of a light color so that it will remain cool underneath on hot days.

Suitable fabrics include treated cotton canvas, polyester and acrylic boat fabrics, and vinyl-coated polyester fabric. I have found the synthetic fabrics to be superior to the cotton fabrics because

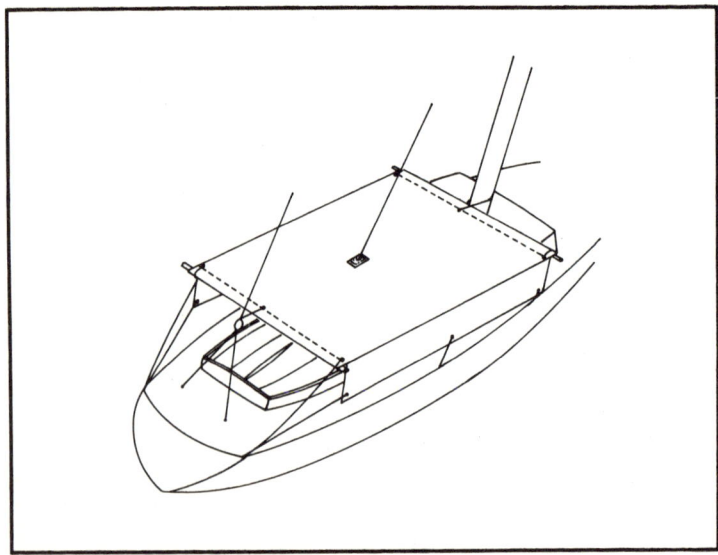

Fig. 11-6. Awning with side flaps.

of their generally better resistance to rot and mildew. The acrylic- and vinyl-coated polyester fabrics usually have the best resistance to sunlight. The vinyl-coated polyester fabric generally offers the best waterproofness and the coated side, which is placed on top of the awning, is easy to clean.

We will first consider a basic flat awning. Although the size of an awning for a particular sailboat can vary, it is typical to have it extend the length of the boom and to have it extend outward at least as wide as the boat's cockpit coamings. Even wider is better.

After the size of the finished awning has been decided on, you will need a blank this size, plus a 6-inch casing allowance on each end and a 3-inch hem allowance on each side. The panels of fabric necessary to form the blank can be joined crossways or lengthwise, whichever will best take advantage of the width of panels you are using. To join the pieces, first sew plain seams. These should then be flat-felled.

Once you have the basic blank, sew a hem along each side. To do this, fold 3 inches of fabric over and make a seam 1/4 inch inward from fold. Then fold 1/2 inch of flap under and make seam along this. It may be desirable to double stitch this seam.

Next, sew casings for awning poles at each end. Begin by folding a 6-inch end of fabric over toward desired underside of finished awning. Then sew a row of stitches 1/4 inch inward from fold. Then fold 1/2 inch of flap under and make two rows of stitches along this. This leaves openings for inserting awning poles.

Awning poles can be aluminum, wood, or plastic, as desired. Telescoping aluminum awning poles are available to permit easy storage.

Six tie downs are generally required, as shown in Fig. 11-7.

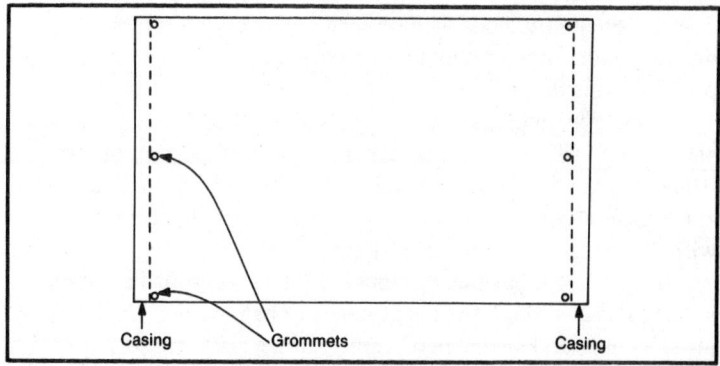

Fig. 11-7. Location of grommets for tie downs.

These can be grommets or D-rings secured by webbing. These should be located inside the inserted awning poles, as shown.

A D-ring secured by webbing sewn to the fabric is often attached to the top center of the awning for mounting the main halyard. The awning should be reinforced underneath in the area of attachment with an extra layer or two of fabric.

Figure 11-5 shows a completed awning set up on a boat. The tie down ropes can be attached to cleats or other convenient attachment points on the boat.

Partial, and even full, side flaps are sometimes added to awnings, as shown in Fig. 11-6. The flaps can be sewn to the awning. Grommets can be installed in the lower edge of flap or D-rings secured to the fabric by webbing can be used. These are used for tie down ropes to secure the panels to the boat. Braided cords or 1/2-inch webbing can be sewn to awning top and underside approximately every 3 feet. The side panels can then be rolled up and secured to the awning by these cords or pieces of webbing by tying the ends together.

Similar front and back panel flaps can also be used. These are sewn to the awning.

Clear plastic windows are sometimes used in these enclosures. Transparent flexible vinyl is frequently used. There are many approaches for installing this. One method is to mark desired window opening on fabric. Pattern and cut plastic window material 1 inch larger than opening line all the way around. Then sew the plastic window to the fabric with a seam approximately 1/4 inch from edge of window plastic all the way around. Wide stitches should be used. Next, cut out window opening in fabric. Use a binding tape folded over raw edge of fabric and make seam through binding, fabric, and window material all the way around the window. Alternate methods include turning cut edges of fabric around opening under, and sewing tablings over exposed edges of window plastic on inside of fabric.

Tent-type awnings placed over sailboat booms (Fig. 11-8) are another possibility. Make up fabric blank roof portion of awning. Allow 3-inch hem allowances on sides and forward end and a seam allowance on aft end. Sew 2 1/2-inch hem around the three sides, with 1/2 inch of fabric turned under.

If boat has a backstay or boom end topping lift, a means for getting these through the cover needs to be provided. A slot opening with flaps and fasteners (Common Sense fasteners seem to work best) can be used to secure it in place.

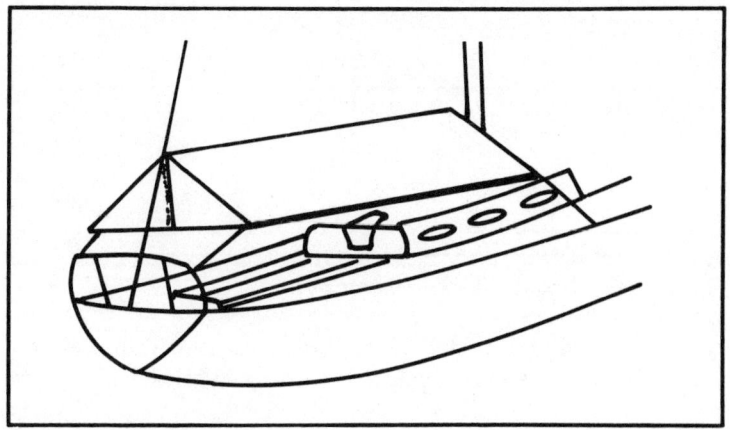

Fig. 11-8. Tent type awning.

Pattern and cut pieces of fabric for aft section of awning, then sew them to the main piece of fabric and make necessary hems. Tie down grommets or D-rings held by webbing sewn to fabric are then added to awning.

Side flaps that extend down over stanchions and lifelines can be added if desired. Foredeck awnings are another possibility.

For power boats, a variety of awnings can be rigged. Actual framed canvas tops, as detailed in Chapter 12, are generally used.

Because boat awnings and enclosures are frequently removed, storage bags, as detailed in Chapter 9, are handy for stowage below.

Weather Cloths

Weather cloths (Fig. 11-9) also called *spray dodgers* and *splash*

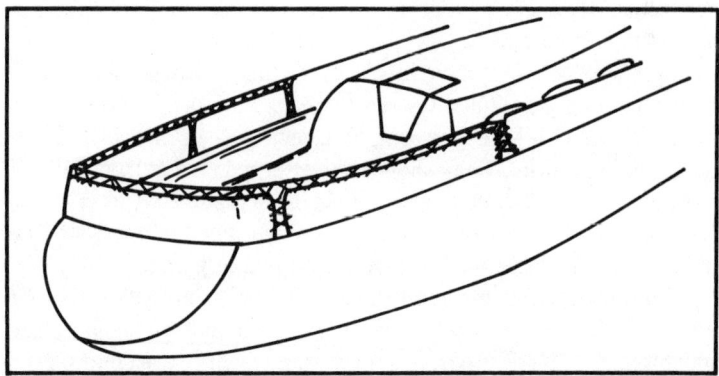

Fig. 11-9. Weather cloths.

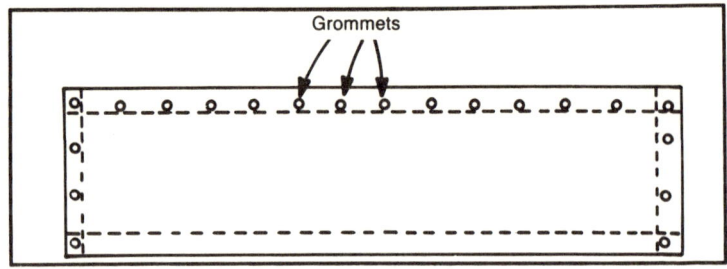

Fig. 11-10. Rectangular shaped weather cloth.

curtains, are used in cockpit and bridge areas of both power and sail boats to reduce spray and add security and privacy. They are usually secured to stanchions, rails, and lifelines by means of ropes laced through grommets in the fabric and around stanchions, rails, and lifelines or other fittings.

Weather cloths can be made from treated cotton boat canvas, acrylic, or vinyl-coated polyester fabrics. Most weather cloths are rectangularly shaped (Fig. 11-10), although some have curved sections. Hems are sewn all the way around. Grommets are usually installed approximately every 6 inches along the top and ends of each section of the weather cloth. Grommets are also attached along bottom in locations where there is something to tie down to or something can be installed for this purpose. Weather cloths can be attached to wood, metal, and fiberglass by snaps or other fasteners, with one part of each fastener placed in the fabric and the other part on the fixed surface.

To make weather cloths for a particular boat, first decide where you want them. They frequently run from about midship all the way aft, often on around a stern pulpit. Bridge areas on power boats are frequently enclosed all the way around except for areas of ladder exits and so on.

Next, take measurements. Mark these down along with diagrams on paper. Then lay out patterns on fabric. Allow 3-inch hem allowances all the way around. Check measurements and patterns over carefully. They should be patterned so that they will not quite reach the rails, stanchions, and lifelines that the weather cloths will be laced to. In areas where snaps or other fasteners will be used, allow necessary fabric for overlaps and hems.

Cut fabric, then sew hems in place. Install grommets and other fasteners. Lacing is usually done with a light continuous line. Use half hitches. In some areas, it is more convenient to use short pieces of rope for individual grommets.

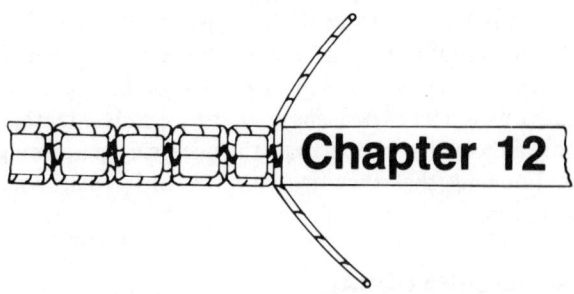

Chapter 12

Canvas Tops, Side and Stern Curtains

The construction of canvas tops for boats and recreational vehicles is probably more complex and difficult than any of the other projects detailed in this book. When I first got started in canvas and upholstery work, by taking an adult education course in upholstery a number of years ago, my main purpose was to make a canvas top for a 21-foot powerboat that I owned at the time. The top frames were on the boat when I purchased it, but the canvas top itself was missing. I was simply unaware that canvas tops were all that difficult to make.

In the upholstery class, everyone started with a series of practice projects, the main purpose of which was to learn machine sewing techniques. These took about 8 hours to complete. I then launched immediately into the construction of the boat top.

The instructor was well versed in the upholstery of household furniture, but showed little knowledge or interest in a canvas boat top other than to say that I was free to go ahead with the project.

I spent considerable time running around looking at boat tops in dealer's showrooms, boat shows, marinas, boat yards, and wherever else I could find boats with tops on them. I wanted to see how these tops were constructed.

Then I set to work on the top for my boat. I spent about 20 hours on the actual construction, with a considerable amount of that time used up thinking about what to do next. The end result was that I had a functional boat top. Although far from perfect, it looked pretty good, and perhaps more important, I knew that I could make the next one better. Over the years, I made a number of additional canvas tops of various types with progressively better and better results, before I began to hear the reasons why amateur do-it-yourselfers should not attempt these. Statements like "mathematically figured curves" were frequently applied.

I think this is a lot of nonsense. There are simple methods that will enable almost anyone to handle the necessary patterning without ever knowing that they are working with "mathematically figured curves."

CANVAS RECREATIONAL VEHICLE TOPS AND SIDE CURTAINS

Canvas tops, with or without side curtains, are used on some recreational vehicles, including Jeeps and dune buggies. In my opinion, canvas tops for land vehicles have proven largely unsatisfactory. The advantages of being able to fold them back so that the vehicle can be used with the top up or down and to be able to store a removed top in a small space is, it seems to me, offset by the fact that, at the speed most vehicles are operated, the canvas tops must routinely withstand the equivalent of gale force winds. Add to this the difficulty of keeping water out, especially where the top joins doors or side curtains, and it's easy to see why substitute tops for these vehicles, such as those made from molded fiberglass, are becoming so popular.

Design and framing for these tops is generally quite complicated, but replacing the fabric portion of tops, at least those of simple construction, should be possible for many do-it-yourselfers. Although a variety of fabrics can be used for tops, those with vinyl coatings are popular. These are often described as laminated convertible top material.

To make a new top using an old one as a pattern, remove fabric portion of old top from vehicle. This may be easy or quite difficult, depending on the particular top. Mark the location and arrangement of individual parts of old top. Then open up the seams. A seam ripper can be used for this.

Transfer patterns to new fabric, including cutting, folding, and seaming lines. Check all patterns and measurements over carefully, then cut.

Sew. Usually, the same types of seams as were used on the old top will be used on the new one, but you might be able to improve on some of these. For example, if a plain seam was used on the old top, you might want to reinforce this with a flat-felled seam on the new top.

After sewing is completed, install any fasteners or other items to canvas. Then install top back on vehicle.

The design, framing, and construction of side curtains for these tops is generally also quite complicated. Replacement of the fabric portion of side curtains, however, at least those of simple construction, should be possible for many do-it-yourselfers. In most cases, the same kind and weight of fabric as is used for the top is also used for the side curtains.

To make a new side curtain using an old one as a pattern, remove side curtain from vehicle. Then remove fabric portion of side curtain from framing. Some side curtains are simple snap-on affairs and don't have any framing.

If the fabric portion is more than one piece, mark the location and arrangement of pieces. Then open up the seams. A seam ripper can be used for this.

Transfer patterns to new fabric, including cutting, folding, and seaming lines. Check all patterns and measurements over carefully before cutting.

Next, sew seams. Usually, the same types of seams as were used on old side curtains will be used on the new ones. In some cases you may be able to improve on these.

After sewing is completed, install fasteners and other fittings. If side curtain has framing, install fabric on or over this.

If you want to attempt both the design and construction of original canvas tops and/or side curtains, the material presented below in this chapter should be helpful. The manufacturers of recreational vehicles that use canvas tops and side curtains may be able to supply plans and/or kits. Write to the specific manufacturer for information and details.

CANVAS BOAT TOPS AND SIDE AND STERN CURTAINS

Although several types and styles of canvas boat tops are in use, most fall in one of three basic categories: convertible tops that attach to a fixed windshield (Fig. 12-1), *dodgers* (Fig. 12-2), and *Bimini tops* (Fig. 12-3).

Before attempting to design and construct an original top for a boat, it's usually a good idea to first replace the fabric on an existing one, using the old one as a pattern. Complete constructions, including frames and fittings, are not really all that difficult once you understand the basic techniques.

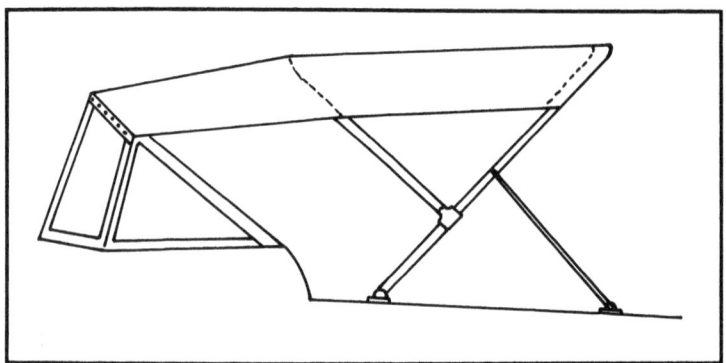

Fig. 12-1. Canvas top attached to fixed windshield.

A variety of side and stern curtains are used with these tops. The construction of these is generally relatively easy compared to that of tops.

Replacing Fabric Portion Using Old Top as Pattern

Begin by inspecting old top. Does it fit properly? If not, determine what changes are required. Mark areas where alterations are needed on the old fabric so that the changes can be made when marking patterns on the new fabric.

If old top is dirty, it can be washed while in place on the boat. This will help prevent transferring the dirt to the new fabric dur-

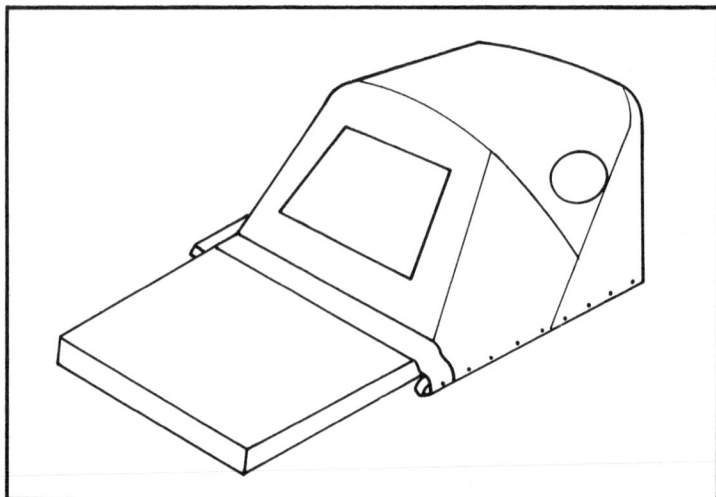

Fig. 12-2. Dodger.

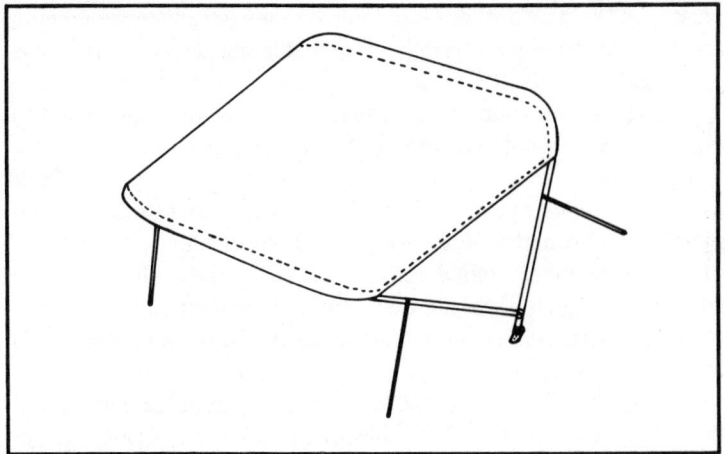

Fig. 12-3. Bimini top.

ing patterning. I do not recommend washing an old top in a washing machine. I once tried this. I put in a dirty top that was a useable pattern. I took out a clean useless one. Whatever was holding the fabric together was washed away.

Mark location and arrangement of separate pieces of fabric on old top. Open seams on old top. A seam ripper can be used for this. Transfer patterns to new fabric, including cutting, folding, and seaming lines. Tracing paper and a tracing wheel can be used for this on most fabrics. In most cases, you will probably want to use the same kind of fabric as was used for the old top or boat acrylic or vinyl-coated fabric. Treated cotton canvas is sometimes used.

Next, sew seams. Usually, the same types of seams, hems, casings, and so on, as were used on old top will be used on the new one, or you might want to improve on these. You might be able to remove the fasteners from an old top and reuse them on the new one. In other cases, you will need to replace them with new ones. In either case, carefully mark the locations for fasteners, then install.

This completes the construction of a canvas boat top using old top as a pattern, except for installation of flexible plastic window material. Transparent flexible vinyl is frequently used and is easy to machine sew to canvas fabrics. There are many approaches to installing windows. One method is to mark the desired window opening on fabric. Pattern and cut plastic window material 1 inch larger than this all the way around. Then sew this to inside of top fabric with seam approximately 1/4 inch from edge of window plastic all the way around. Use long stitches to reduce weakening and tearing the plastic from having needle holes spaced too close together.

Next, cut out window opening in top fabric, taking care not to cut into plastic window material. A binding tape can be used over raw edge of top fabric around cutout. Fold the binding tape in half over fabric edge and sew through binding tape, top fabric, and plastic window material. Alternate methods include turning edges of top fabric under around cutout and heat sealing edge of cutout so that binding tape will not be required to protect edge. To dress up the appearance on the inside, tablings can be sewn in place. This completes the construction.

If modifications of present top, framing system, fasteners, windows, or other features are desired, follow instructions in appropriate sections below in this chapter.

Replacing Side and Stern Curtains Using Old Patterns

Begin by inspecting old items. Do they fit properly? If not, determine what changes are required to correct these problems. Mark areas where alterations are needed on old fabric so that the changes can be made when marking patterns on the new. Mark location and arrangement of separate pieces of fabric. Then open seams with a seam ripper.

In most cases, the curtains are made from the same kind of fabric as the canvas top. Acrylic- and vinyl-coated fabrics are commonly used. Treated cotton canvas is sometimes used. Transfer patterns to new fabric, including cutting, folding, and seaming lines. Tracing paper and a tracing wheel can be used for this on most fabrics. Check all measurements and patterns over carefully before cutting.

Next, do the sewing. Usually, the same types of seams, hems, casings, and so on as were used on old side and stern covers will be used on the new ones, but you might be able to improve on these. Double stitching, with the stitches placed from about 1/8 inch to 1/4 inch apart, is usually a good idea. This way, the strength of a seam does not depend on a single row of stitches.

You might be able to remove the fasteners from old side and stern covers and reuse them on the new ones. In other cases, you will need to replace them with new ones. In either case, carefully mark location for fasteners before installation.

If flexible plastic windows are to be installed, you can install these in the same manner as in the old side and stern curtains, or you can follow instructions given above in this chapter for replacing fabric portion of tops using old top as pattern. This completes the construction.

If extensive modifications are required, or you want to change the design or arrangement of side and/or stern curtains, follow instructions in appropriate sections below in this chapter.

Top Frames and Fittings

Many canvas top framing systems have been used. These can be fixed or arranged so that the top can be folded down to a position on the windshield or elsewhere on the boat. Most framing systems now used employ two frames made from metal tubing, as shown in Fig. 12-4. One of the frames attaches to the boat, usually by means of special fittings. The other frame, which is usually shorter, attaches to the first frame, usually by means of special fittings. For our purposes here, we will call the frame that attaches to the boat the main frame and the one that attaches to this the secondary frame. Keep in mind that these names are being used here for descriptive purposes; no standard terminology is in use.

The tubing usually used for the frames is either aluminum or stainless steel. If aluminum tubing is used, it should be bright dip-anodized to reduce the problem of oxidation. Aluminum tubing is

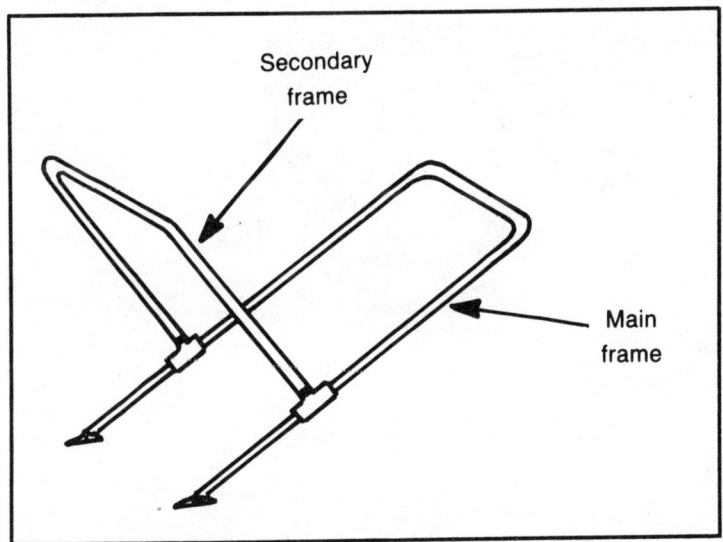

Fig. 12-4. Framing system.

satisfactory for many tops, but stainless steel is much stronger. Aluminum tubing is much easier to cut and bend. It is also less expensive. These factors should be considered in making a selection. In general, stainless steel results in a stronger and more durable framing system, but the lighter and less expensive aluminum tubing will suffice for many installations.

Both aluminum and stainless steel tubing are available with 3/4-inch, 7/8-inch, and 1-inch outside diameters. These are the three sizes commonly used for top frames. They are also the sizes for which standard top fittings are available.

The tubing is generally sold in straight sections up to about 20 feet in length. A tube bender, such as shown in Fig. 12-5, can be used to bend the tubing to desired shape. Mark areas where bends are to be made in tubing. If a bend is required in the center, this is usually done first. Then work outward from this to the ends, making each bend first on one side and then the other. Trace pattern of tubing from centerline outward on one side on paper, cardboard, or other suitable surface, then use this as a template for matching bends on other half.

In general, tubing walls will collapse if you simply attempt to bend the tubing without the use of a tube bender or other special means, as by heating the tubing.

There are many cases where it is necesary to cut the tubing. A tube cutter (Fig. 12-6) generally works best for this. The device

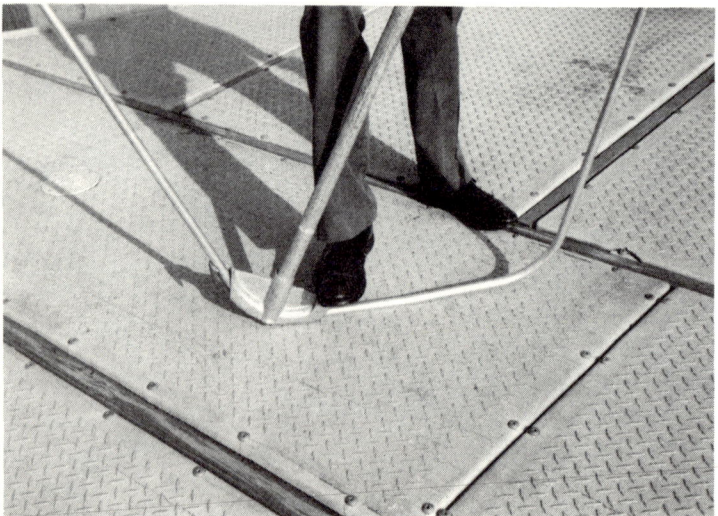

Fig. 12-5. Tube bender.

228

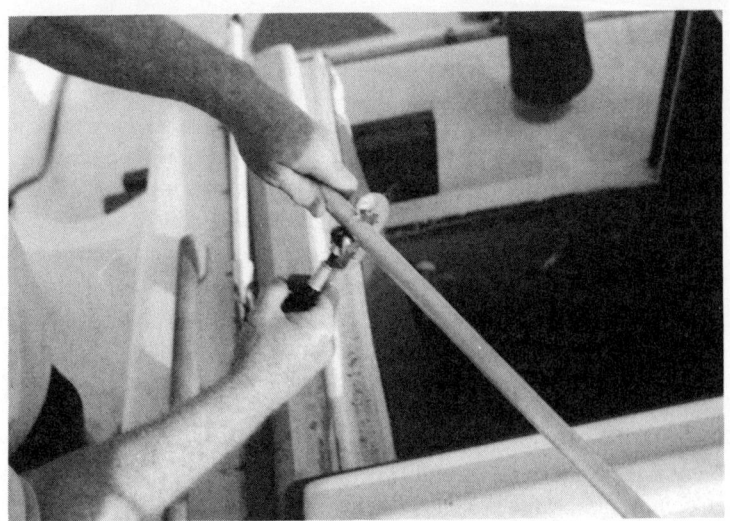

Fig. 12-6. Tube cutter.

has a cutting wheel and two guide wheels or rollers in a clamping arrangement. Open the clamp and place over tubing. Line cutting wheel up with mark for desired cut. Tighten clamp. Turn cutter around tubing. Gradually tighten clamp after every turn or two until device cuts tubing in two.

A variety of standard fittings are available for top frames. These are made from regular steel (not recommended for boat use), aluminum, brass, stainless steel, and even plastic. In general, I recommend the use of aluminum fittings for use with aluminum tubing and stainless steel fittings for use with stainless steel. The stainless steel fittings are expensive, though, and if cost is an important consideration, you may want to use less expensive chrome-plated brass fittings with stainless steel tubing. Low cost plastic fittings are available, but I have not had much luck with these. Perhaps better quality plastics will be used for these in the future, making them more suitable.

End fittings (Fig. 12-7A) fit over or inside the ends of tubing. Their purpose is to give an eye that can be used to attach other fittings. The end fittings that slip over the tubing are called *slip-on eye fittings*. They usually have set screws to secure them to the tubing. The end fittings that slip inside the tubing generally have a groove on the part that slips inside the tubing. A crimp in the tubing, as made with a center punch over the groove area, is used to secure the fitting inside the tubing. This seems to work well as long as the fitting fits snugly inside the tubing. This type of fitting is made of aluminum for aluminum tubing.

Jaw slides (Fig. 12-7B) fit over frame tubing for the attachment of end fittings. This is the usual method for joining the secondary frame to the main frame (Fig. 12-4), thus allowing the two frames to be folded together, which in turn is part of the system that allows the top to be up or folded down against windshield, hatch, or elsewhere. Jaw slides generally have a set screw to secure the fitting to the tubing and a bolt arrangement in the jaw (one side is usually threaded) for connecting the jaw to an end fitting.

There are two main types of fittings for mounting the main frame to the boat: the hinge or *camel back* (Fig. 12-7C) and the side mounting bracket (Fig. 12-7D). These brackets are attached to the boat in an appropriate location, usually by through bolting. Use large backing washers and lock washers and nuts or locking nuts. In some cases, these brackets can be mounted to wood with screws.

Most of the brackets have the mounting bolts for the end fittings on the main frames either vertical or perpendicular to the mounting plates, but angle hinge brackets are also available. This allows you to mount brackets on a flat surface and have the mounting bolt for the end fitting at an angle. One type has a 10-degree angle.

Whether to use a hinge, camel back, or side mounting bracket depends on the particular boat and top frames. One particular method will usually prove more practical.

Most top arrangements require at least two hold down straps

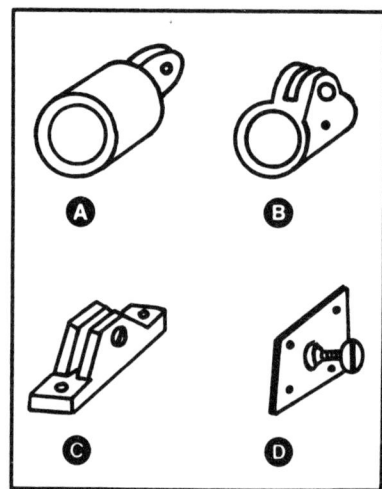

Fig. 12-7. Fittings for top frames.

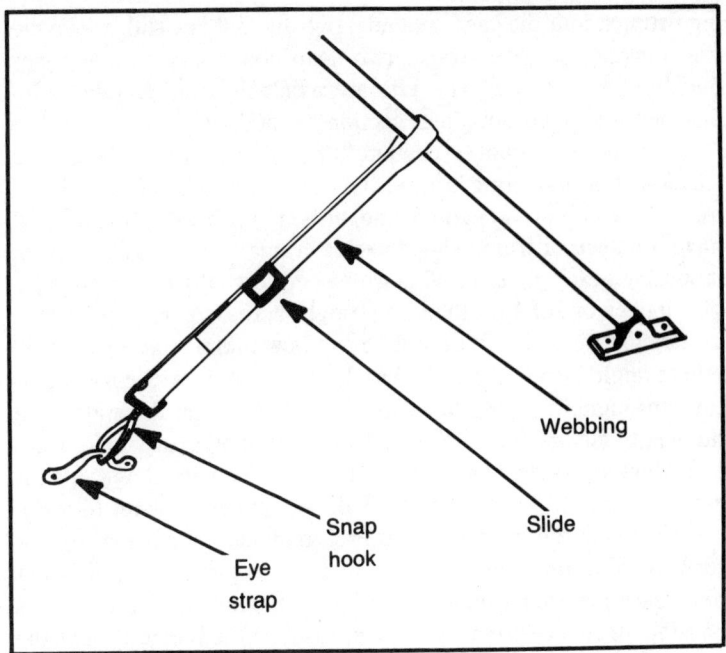

Fig. 12-8. Hold-down strap arrangement.

for securing the top when up, as shown in Fig. 12-1. Bimini tops require four straps, as shown in Fig. 12-3.

An *eye strap* (Fig. 12-8) is usually mounted to the boat in an appropriate location for connecting each strap. The eye straps are usually through-bolted to the boat. Use large backing washers and lock washers and nuts or locking nuts. In some cases, eye straps can be mounted to wood with screws, although this isn't generally recommended because considerable stress is placed on the straps, and the screws could pull out. Whenever possible, use through bolting.

Snap hooks (Fig. 12-8) usually attach to the eye straps. The end opposite from the hook has an opening to pass the webbing through. Usually, 3/4-inch or 1-inch wide nylon or polyester webbing is used. This goes around the frame tubing. The ends of the webbing are joined by a slide, which allows easy adjustment of the webbing. The eye straps are usually mounted in a position so that the straps will form a 90-degree angle with the frame tubing.

Adjustable top frames that will fit mounting brackets from 80 inches to 100 inches apart are available. The tubing is bright dip-anodized aluminum. The frames come in kit form with the following fittings: four die cast eye ends, two die cast jaw slides, two die cast hinges, two eye straps, two snap hooks, and two adjuster buckles for webbing. The kits are available from Defender Industries, Inc. (see Suppliers section for address).

The frames should be custom fitted to the particular boat. The location of the mounting brackets on a particular boat will also determine the width of the main frame, although you will probably still have a choice of frame shape. Some frames go straight up from mounting brackets, have 90-degree bends (usually over a distance of 6 inches or so), and then go straight across at the top. Others go straight up at the sides, but have a bow in the cross piece. Still others angle inward from the brackets. Others have a curved pattern throughout. The choice for a particular top depends on a number of factors, including which gives the most space underneath and which looks the best. A bowed cross piece will allow slope for water to run off; flat tops tend to allow puddles of water to form.

How high the frames should extend upward and backwards or forward also depends on a number of factors. You will want necessary headroom underneath, yet will want the top as low as possible to reduce wind resistance, to allow the boom to clear the top, and so on. How far the top frames should extend back and forward is another important consideration. It generally works best if the main frame and secondary frame form 90-degree angles with each other when the top is set up, but this isn't absolutely essential. It's usually also best to have the frame cross pieces meet when the frames are folded together. This may not be essential for a particular top as long as the frames can fold out of the way in some other arrangement. For tops that connect to a fixed windshield, the frames usually fold together and rest on top of the windshield.

This means that there are a number of angles and length to fiddle with when trying to determine what is right for a particular top. Make a mock-up by tying up pieces of aluminum tubing and other available materials in position on the boat. From this, determine the length and shape of the frame pieces.

Once you have the frame pieces shaped and cut to desired length, install fittings to boat and frame pieces. With the pieces assembled, tie ropes to the frames and boat to hold the frames in position for measuring and patterning fabric for top. A dodger setup is shown in Fig. 12-9.

Before going on to the fabric portion of the tops, however, it should be pointed out that top frame mounting brackets are sometimes fastened to special wood pieces that also have fastener

Fig. 12-9. Dodger frames held in position by ropes.

studs attached, as shown in Fig. 12-10. It is important to understand this, as the wood must go in place before the mounting brackets are positioned and fastened down.

The patterning, construction, and fasteners for each basic type of top are best treated separately.

Canvas Top Attached to Fixed Windshield

This type of top is popular for use on powerboats. Figure 12-11

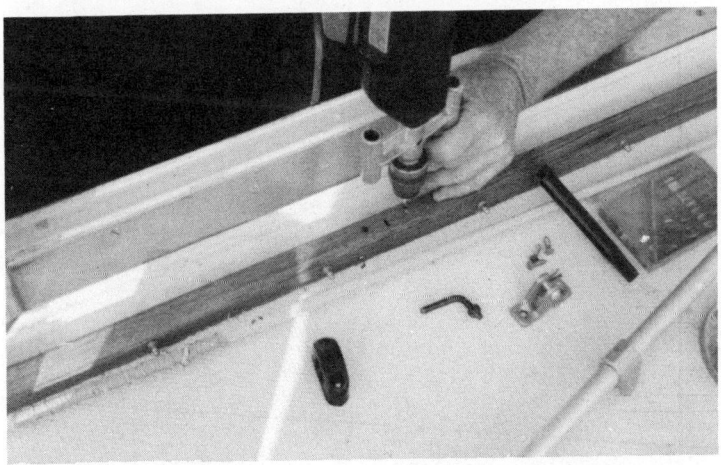

Fig. 12-10. Top frame mounting bracket being installed on wood piece.

233

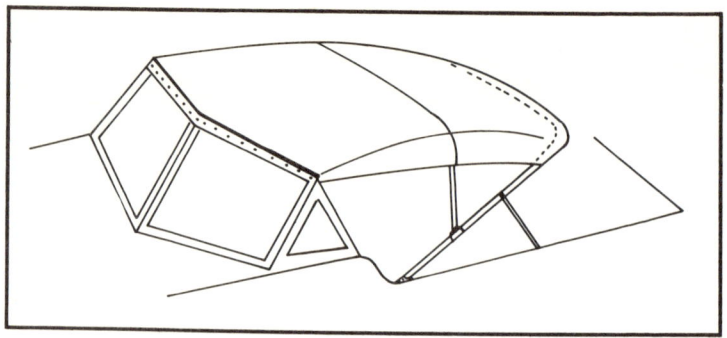

Fig. 12-11. Canvas top attached to fixed windshield.

shows a typical setup. The forward edge of the top overlaps the windshield frame and is attached to the frame by snap, Lift-the-Dot, or Common Sense fasteners. Although any of these will work, there are advantages and disadvantages to each type (see Chapter 7). Snaps protrude the least, but they also tend to have less holding power than the other types. Lift-the-Dots stick out further, but they tend to hold the fabric in place better. The Common Sense or twist-type protrude outward, and some people do not like their appearance, but they tend to hold the fabric in place better than the other types. They are available as plate-mounted studs with two holes for through-bolt fastening to the windshield frame.

The studs are mounted to the frame of the windshield. The sockets or eyelets are installed in the forward edge of the top fabric.

The main part of the top fabric consists of two separate pieces of fabric sewn together, as shown in Fig. 12-12. The forward piece extends from the windshield attachment aft to the secondary frame. The second piece starts at the secondary frame and extends on back to the main frame, often with an overlapping flap with fasteners (socket or eyelet portions) installed for attachment of stern covers

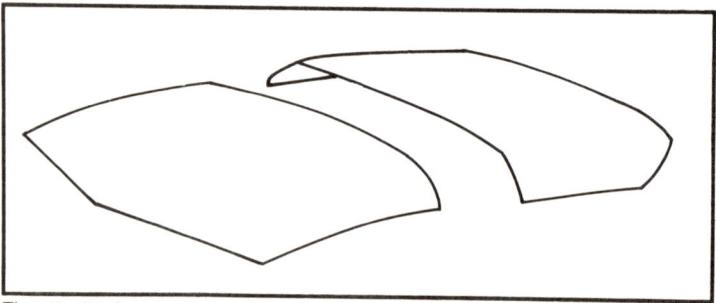

Fig. 12-12. Canvas top consists of two main pieces of fabric.

and/or top extensions (these projects are both detailed later in this chapter.

The sides of the top fabric are usually hemmed and often have fasteners (socket or eyelet portions) for attachment of side curtains.

The top frames usually pass through sleeves or casings sewn to the underside of the top fabric. The forward one is usually a separate piece of fabric sewn in place. The aft one can be either a separate piece of fabric sewn in place, or the main piece of fabric can loop around the frame tubing and be sewn to the main piece of fabric.

There are many approaches to measuring and patterning fabric portions of tops to fit a particular set of frames. The method that I prefer is to tie the frames in position with three cords: one from the center of the top of the windshield, and one straight back from each corner of the windshield, as shown in Fig. 12-13. The ropes must be securely tied in place so that the top frames will not shift during the patterning process.

You will need a fabric blank large enough for each of the two main fabric sections of the top. The fabric can be treated cotton boat canvas (generally least desirable), acrylic fabric, vinyl-coated fabric, or other suitable materials. In some cases, a single piece of fabric will be large enough for each blank. In other cases, it will be necessary to join pieces of fabric. If the fabric panels are run across the top from one side to the other, it will usually be possible to use a single piece of fabric for each main section of the top. If you do have to make seams, these can be across the top from side to side or lengthwise in a symmetrical pattern, with a seam along the center line.

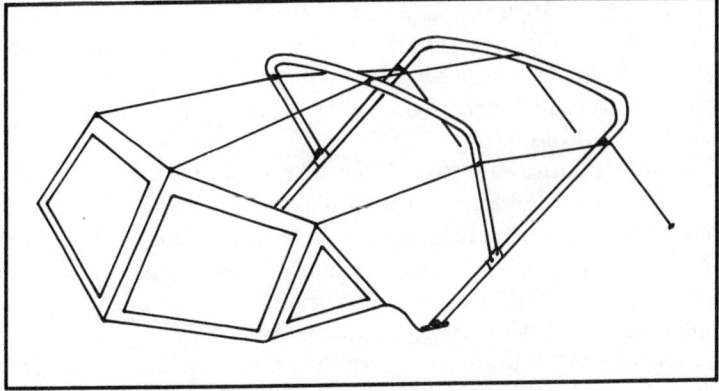

Fig. 12-13. Frames are tied in position with three ropes.

First join the pieces of fabric with a plain seam. If the flap edges of both pieces of fabric have selvaged edges adjacent to the seam, the two flaps can be folded together over to one of the pieces of fabric and two rows of stitches can be made along this. The edges of the flaps can be folded under again, if desired, and two rows of stitches sewn over this. This method is especially useful with cut fabric edges, as it hides the edges and keeps them from unraveling.

Once you have the two fabric blanks, decide how you want the fabric pieces to go on the top. Mark them with chalk so that you won't get mixed up. By some code, indicate forward section, aft section, top side, bottom side, and front and back edges of each piece. Also, mark a centerline on the fabric. This will be used as a reference line and will be lined up with cord tied between frames and windshield.

A decision should be made on how far the sides of the top fabric should extend down. A typical pattern line is shown in Fig. 12-11. When possible, this should follow the lines of the boat so that the top will look like it belongs there. Then tie a cord from windshield to secondary frame and on to main frame following this pattern. Tie a matching cord on the opposite side of the boat. On the actual fabric blanks, you will need to overlap the cords by at least 2 inches on each side for a hemming allowance.

Before joining the two main pieces of fabric in the area of secondary frame tubing, the two pieces of fabric must first be patterned and cut to shape along the edges to be joined. Begin with the forward piece of fabric. Put it in place over the windshield, secondary frame, and cords. Line up the centerline on the fabric with the centerline cord. Fabric should overlap furthest point forward along top of windshield by at least 3 inches, which is required for overlap and hem for fasteners. The back edge should extend at least a 1/2-inch seam allowance beyond the center of the secondary frame tubing, at a point 2 inches below the cord marking the desired finished side of the top.

Smooth forward section of top fabric out and hold it in position with large clothespins, safety pins, weights, and other props and clamps. The idea is to have the fabric positioned as it will be in the finished top. Then carefully make a line on top of the fabric with chalk or a soft lead pencil following the centerline of the top and outside edges of the secondary frame tubing.

After line has been made, remove fabric from boat and spread it out on a table or other flat surface. The pattern line will be the stitching line. Construct a cutting line 1/2 inch from this. Then cut fabric along this line.

Next, place the aft piece of fabric in position over the secondary frame, main frame, and cords. Line up the centerline on the fabric with the centerline cord. Fabric should overlap 1/2 inch at furthest point forward of centerline on top of secondary frame tubing. This will usually be at the center of the top of the frame. Fabric should overlap at least 2 inches at furthest point aft of centerline on top of main frame tubing. Again, this will usually be at the center of the top of the frame.

Smooth fabric out and hold it in position with large clothespins, safety pins, weights, and other props and clamps. The idea is to have the fabric positioned as it will be in the finished top. Then carefully make a line on top of the fabric with chalk or soft lead pencil following the centerline of the top and outside edges of the secondary frame tubing.

After line has been made, remove fabric from frames and spread it out on a table or other flat surface. The pattern line that was marked on the fabric will be the stitching line. Measure and mark 1/2 inch from this a cutting line. This will give a 1/2-inch seaming allowance. Cut the fabric along this line.

The two pieces of fabric are now ready for sewing together. For our purposes here, the top side of the fabric will be called the right side; the underside will be called the wrong side. Place the two pieces of fabric together right side to right side. The aft piece of fabric is usually placed on the bottom for sewing.

The seam is usually started at the centerline and is done outward to one edge of the fabric. Keep the edges of the fabrics lined up and stitch an even 1/2 inch from the edge. Continue seam to edge of fabrics. The method of starting in the center and sewing outward to one side allows exact line up of centerlines on the two pieces of fabric, something that is extremely difficult to do if you start at one edge and sew all the way across.

After a plain seam has been sewn from centerline to one side, return to centerline. Reverse the direction. Start back a short distance over the old stitching. Then sew a plain seam to side. The same fabric that was downward against the sewing machine bed should be downward throughout; you will be sewing once with the seam allowance fabric to the right in the sewing machine, and once to the left.

When done properly, the two pieces of fabric will be joined evenly without creases. You can check this by draping the fabric over the frames, windshield, and cords, positioning fabric as it will be in finished top. The seam should fit the curve of the secondary frame tubing. If not, necessary corrections should be made at this time.

When everything looks correct, the flaps of the seam allowance fabric are folded together over to either the forward or aft fabric and both edges are turned under together. Two rows of stitching are then run down this to form a flat-felled seam. An alternate method is to cut 1/4 inch off the underneath flap before turning the edge of the upper layer under and stitching to form a flat-felled seam.

Once this seam is completed, put the fabric in place over the frames, windshield, and cords. Line up the centerline of the top fabric with the centerline cord.

Smooth the fabric out and attach it temporarily in place with clothespins, safety pins, weights, and other props and clamps, positioning the fabric as it will be in the finished top.

Then mark with chalk or soft lead pencil a line on the wrong side of the top fabric on each side of the secondary frame tubing. The purpose of this is to give a pattern for placement of the casing or sleeve for the frame tubing to pass through.

The length of the casing or sleeve can vary, but usually extends to about the start of the frame tubing corner bend on each side.

There are several possible methods for constructing sleeves or casings for the frame tubing. Figure 12-14 shows one method. This method works well as long as the frame tubing is straight or has only a slight curve in the section that passes through sleeve or casing. First, make seam in folded over fabric to form loop. This should allow the tubing to fit inside, with a little extra space. Leave a 1-inch seam allowance on one side and 1/2-inch on the other. Pattern fabric for this width. The length should be desired length of sleeve or casing, plus 1-inch hemming allowance on each end. Before sewing lengthwise seam, sew hem in each end. Fold 1 inch of fabric over toward wrong side, then 1/2 inch of this under. Sew two rows of stitches through this. Repeat on other end. Next, fold fabric over to form loop, with right side outward on loop. Make plain seam, as shown. Stitching is 1 inch from edge of long flap and 1/2 inch inward from edge of short flap.

Mark center of sleeve or casing with centerline. Sew sleeve or casing to top fabric's wrong (under) side. Start in center. Position sleeve or casing with flaps as shown just aft of the felled seam

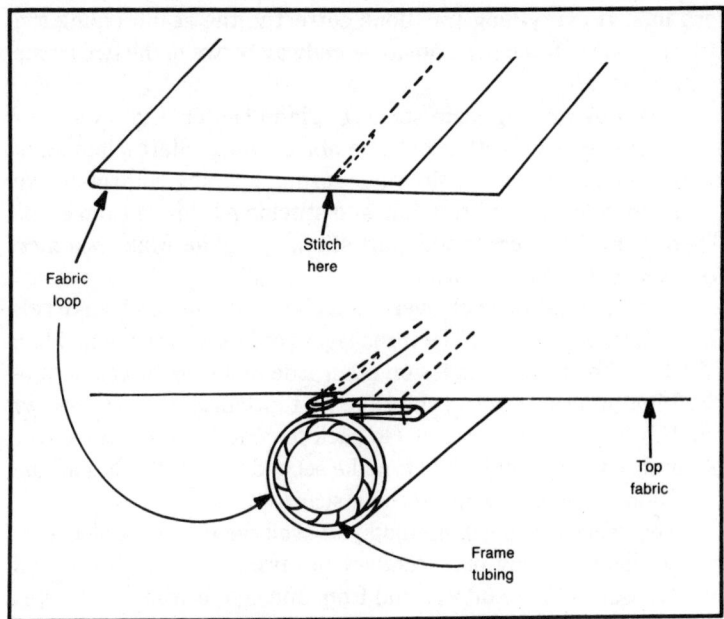

Fig. 12-14. Method for making casing for secondary frame tubing.

used to join the sections of top fabric. Casing seam should follow curve of seam joining top sections. Begin stitching in the center, and sew to one side. Then go back to center and start again, sewing seam to other side. Then make second row of stitches all the way across.

Figure 12-15 shows another method for making a sleeve or casing. The sleeve or casing strip of fabric should be patterned to the same curve as the frame lines patterned on the fabric. This should also be the same curve as the stitching joining the two sections of top fabric. The casing should be wide enough to allow the frame tubing to slip through without bulging the top fabric, as shown. Add 1 inch width to each side for hemming and stitching, as shown. If the frame line pattern curves, a wider piece of fabric is required, as shown. The length should be the desired length of sleeve or casing, plus 1-inch hemming allowance on each end. Cut fabric to pattern. Sew hem in each end. Fold 1 inch of fabric over toward wrong side, then 1/2 inch of this under. Sew two rows of stitches through this. Repeat on other end.

The two pattern lines on the wrong (under) side of the top fabric should be the diameter of the tubing (outside diameter) apart. Make additional lines 1/4 inch and 3/4 inch outward from each pattern line. If everything was done correctly, the seam joining the two sections of top fabric should be midway between the two frame pattern lines.

Begin by making plain seam. Begin in center. Line center of sleeve or casing up with centerline of top fabric. Start stitching in center and sew to end of sleeve or casing, keeping edge of sleeve fabric lined up with pattern line and stitching 1/2 inch from edge. Then go back to center and start stitching again. Make seam on to other side of fabric casing.

Next, fold fabric back over seam allowance flap and make two rows of stitches through the three layers of fabric, as shown. Then fold 1/2 inch of fabric under on other side of sleeve or casing fabric. Line up center with centerline on top fabric and sew row of stitches to one end of sleeve. Go back to center and continue row of stitches to other side. Next, make second row of stitches all the way along casing to reinforce the seam.

Regardless of which method you used for installing sleeve or casing, install casing on secondary top frame. To do this, it will be necessary to take off eye end from one end of frame and ropes

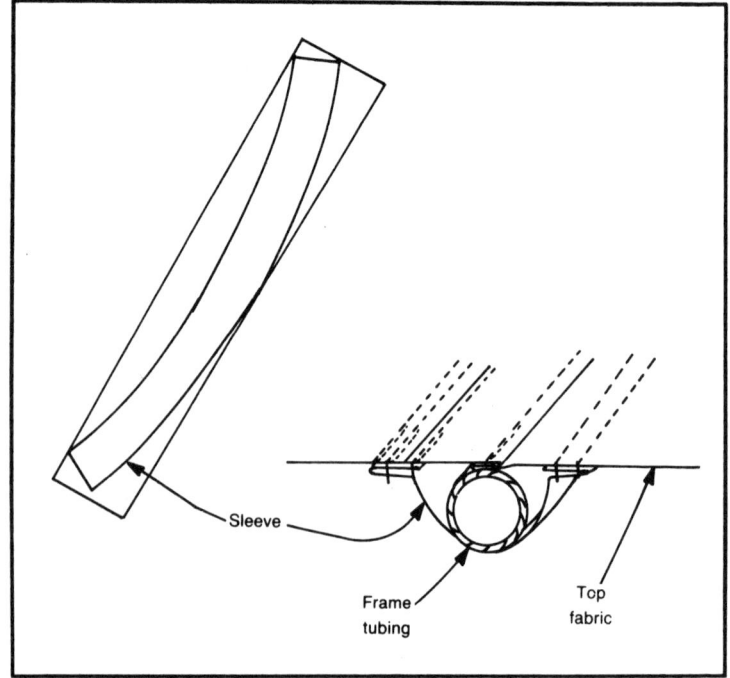

Fig. 12-15. Alternate method for making sleeve.

holding frames in position. Then slip casing over tubing, making sure that you have the forward end of top toward front of boat. You may as well get used to taking the top on and off the frames, as this will be required several more times before the top is complete. As you become more experienced, you can reduce the number of times that you must do this by patterning and sewing a number of steps at one time, but for the first few times, it's better to take things one step at a time, even though it takes longer. Refasten end fitting to frame.

Put the fabric in place over the windshield and main frame with centerlines lined up. Smooth the fabric out and attach it temporarily in place with clothespins, safety pins, weights, and other props and clamps. The idea is to have the fabric positioned as it will be in the finished top.

There are several possible methods for constructing sleeves or casings for the main frame tubing. Unlike the casing for the secondary frame, the one for the main frame tubing usually extends downward over the bends in the tubing to edge of top.

With the fabric in place over the main frame tubing, mark line with chalk or soft lead pencil on wrong (under) side of top fabric following aft edge of tubing. Pattern should continue to sides of top fabric as far as casing will go.

Before removing top fabric, consider type of sleeve or casing to be added. Figure 12-16 shows the pattern and sewing details for

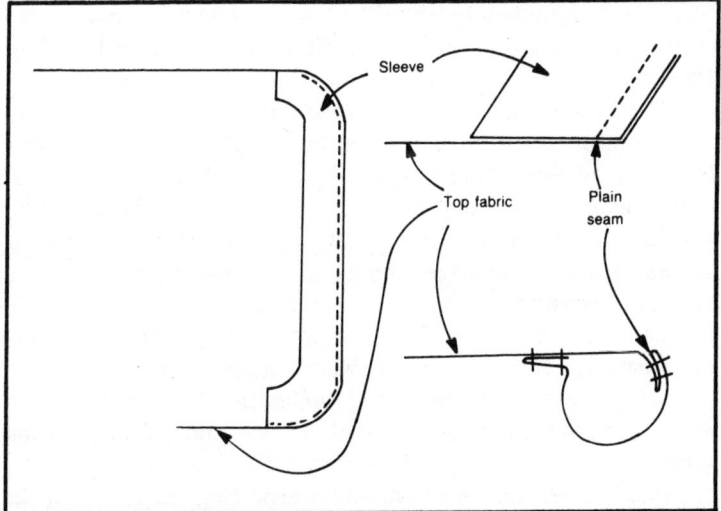

Fig. 12-16. Pattern for sleeve without flap for fasteners.

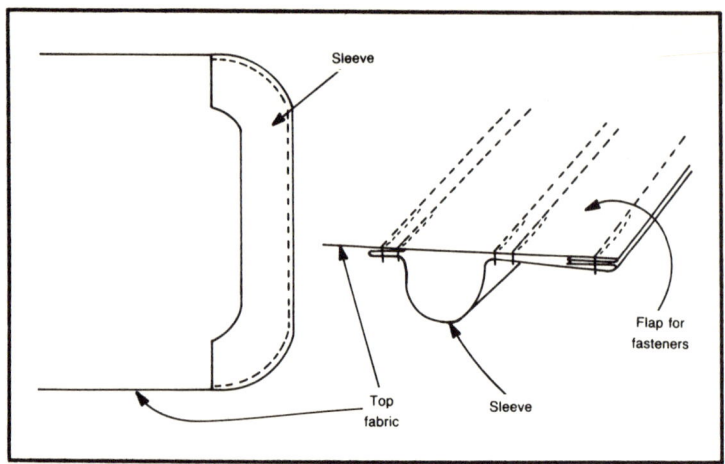

Fig. 12-17. Pattern for sleeve with flap for fasteners.

a casing without a flap for fasteners to attach top extension or stern cover to aft edge of top. The method shown in Fig. 12-17 has a flap for this.

After deciding which type you want on the top, remove top fabric and spread fabric out right side down on a table or other flat surface. If no flap for fasteners is required, as shown in Fig. 12-16, make second pattern line 1/2 inch aft of frame pattern line marked on fabric. This will be the cutting line. It should be parallel to the first pattern line, which will be a stitching line. Then cut along cutting line. If there will be a flap for fasteners, both top and sleeve pattern cutting lines are 2 inches aft of frame pattern line (Fig. 12-17).

The aft edge of the sleeve or casing fabric will have the same aft cutting line pattern as the top fabric. This should be transferred to the sleeve fabric with the pieces of fabric right side to right side or wrong side to wrong side. The sleeve fabric must be wide enough to take care of the frame curves, a 1/2-inch seaming allowance on the aft edge, and a 1-inch hemming and stitching allowance on the forward edge, in addition to the necessary fabric to go around the frame tubing. A 1-inch hemming allowance is required at each end of the sleeve, which extends to and follows the patterns for the edge lines of the top, as shown. Essentially, the sleeve pattern is the same as that of the aft section of the main top fabric.

Pattern and cut the sleeve. Mark centerline on sleeve fabric. Position the aft centers of the sleeve and top fabrics together right side to right side. The shape of the aft edges of the two pieces of fabric should be the same if everything was done correctly. If this checks out, then sew hems in ends of sleeve fabric with 1 inch of fabric folded over to the wrong side and a 1/2 inch folded under. Sew two rows of stitches along each hem.

Then position the aft centers of the sleeve and top fabrics together again right side to right side. Starting in the center, sew a plain seam 1/2 inch from the edge to about 2 inches from desired finished edge of top. The remainder of the seam should be left open to form the hem along the sides of the top.

Go back to the center and start the stitching again, this time sewing to the other side and again stopping about 2 inches from desired finished edge of top.

Install the top back on the secondary frame, as was done previously. Check fit of first seam on sleeve for main frame. Mark areas of any needed changes.

Carefully mark hemline for each side of top. Make a line on the fabric following forward top edge of windshield.

Decide on the type of fasteners to be used to hold the fabric to forward top area of windshield. Snaps, Lift-the-Dot, and Common Sense twist fasteners are the main possibilities. Decide best location on top frame of windshield for installing these. Holes can be drilled in metal frames for self tapping screws, or a tap can be used to make threads inside the holes and machine screws can be used. If the windows are glass, however, care must be taken not to drill into the glass. Usually, drilling into plastic window material will be all right.

If the frame is wood, fasteners can be attached by wood screws. These tend to pull out under the heavy stress of securing the forward edge of the top, however, so through fasteners are recommended. I also like to use through fasteners on metal window frames whenever it is practical.

The studs for the fasteners can be installed on the windshield frame at this time. Usually, they are spaced from about 4 inches to 6 inches apart, with one at each edge.

Mark the area of each fastener on the top fabric. This is for determining the hemline. Locations will be marked again later before actually installing the sockets or eyelets.

It may be necessary to use darts in the top fabric to make the fabric bend smoothly over the windshield frame. Windshield frames that angle in the center and are then straight or nearly straight to the corners usually require one dart in the center and one at each edge or corner, as shown in Fig. 12-11. Fold flaps of fabric and mark the pattern for each dart. Rounded windshields may require a series of symmetrically spaced darts, which can be patterned similarly.

The forward hemline will usually be from about 5/8 inch to 3/4 inch below the fastener centers. Decide on a desired length and mark this on fabric. Next, remove top fabric from secondary frame.

With darts folded so fabric is right side to right side, sew plain seam. If fold of fabric is large or in center, excess fabric can be cut off 1/2 inch from stitching. Small darts and corner darts at sides of windshield are usually simply folded to one side and sewn. Keep the direction of folding symmetrical on the two sides.

Next, redraw forward hemline. Decide on the desired width of hem. This is usually about 3/4 inch to 1 inch. There should be enough space to install fasteners through two layers of the fabric hem. Add to this a 1/2 inch of fabric for turning under. Measure and mark these lines on the fabric. Cut fabric. First sew seam close to hemline fold, then fold 1/2 inch of flap under and make two rows of stitches over this.

Fold fabric in half along centerline and make certain that hemlines for each side of top match. Make corrections as required and redraw lines as necessary. Hem width can be as desired, but should be wide enough to install fasteners for side curtains through the two layers of hem fabric. In most cases a 1-inch to 1 1/2-inch wide hem is used. Add to this a 1/2-inch allowance for turning under to hide cut edge of fabric.

Measure and mark these lines on the fabric. Cut fabric. First, sew seam close to hemline fold. Then fold 1/2 inch of flap under and make two rows of stitches over this.

Alternate methods for making these hems include simply sewing binding tape over raw edge of fabric (this does not provide a very strong base for fasteners, however) and sewing tablings in place.

Continue the seam, which was started to attach the main frame sleeve or casing, the rest of the way to the hemlines at the sides. Then fold both flaps together to the sleeve fabric and sew two rows of stitches through this, as shown in Fig. 12-16. Next, fold sleeve to form fabric loop to go over frame tubing and sew to main top fabric as shown in Fig. 12-16. Use two rows of stitches.

If there is an extension flap for fasteners, continue the plain seam started previously on sleeve to the hemlines at sides. Then fold sleeve and top fabrics right side out. Make row of stitches close to edge through four layers of fabric, as shown in Fig. 12-17. Then make another row of stitches 1 1/4 inch inward from the edge through the two layers of fabric (Fig. 12-17). Make another row of stitches 1/4 inch further inward from this.

Next, fold sleeve to form a fabric loop to go around frame tubing and sew to main top fabric with two rows of stitches, as shown in Fig. 12-17. This should complete the sewing part of the top construction. Install top on frames. Carefully mark locations for socket or eyelet fasteners for the studs mounted on windshield frame. I usually install the sockets or eyelet fasteners with the top in place. Start at center. There will either be a fastener in the center or two fasteners each the same distance from the centerline. Install these first. Then work outward, alternating from side to side. Fabric should be tight between fasteners so that the forward edge will not flap in the wind or when the boat is underway. Continue until all sockets or eyelets are installed. Fasten each one to stud after it is installed.

An alternate method is to mark the location for all sockets and eyelets, then remove top fabric from frames and install fasteners at a workbench. This allows more convenient use of cutting punches.

Connect tie downs to the main frame and connect snap hooks to eye straps. Adjust the slides on webbing to secure top in an up position. This completes the construction of the top, except that fasteners may be added for side and stern covers and aft top extensions, as detailed below in this chapter.

It should be pointed out that, with experience, it should be possible to pattern all the fabric parts for the top in one or two steps, then do all the cutting and sewing before trying the top on. The method detailed above for patterning and fitting the top is generally recommended for beginners, but experienced canvas workers often do this by taking measurements, then transferring these to the fabric.

There is no one way to pattern and construct canvas tops. Study as many top constructions as possible and apply whatever seems useful to your own work. You may even want to experiment with original methods.

Dodgers

Dodgers usually go over companionway hatches, usually on sailboats, and have flexible plastic windows attached to the fabric without fixed windshields. Some dodgers extend outward only to just outside the companionway hatches (Fig. 12-18). Others extend to the sides of the cabin top and/or cockpit coamings. The framing system is similar to that used for canvas tops that attach to windshields, except that the secondary frame forms the curve for the angled forward section of fabric.

Some boats have hatch hoods, which provide a convenient place for the placement of fasteners. Without this hood, the forward section of the top can be fitted with a flap that fits snugly over the sliding hatch, yet still allows opening and closing the hatch. Figure 12-19 shows this arrangement. Still another possibility is to construct a bridge from wood and/or other materials that extends over the sliding hatch. Fasteners are then attached to the bridge.

Fasteners for the remainder of the top can be attached directly to the boat cabin top, sides, and other areas, or fasteners can be attached to wood pieces, which are in turn fastened to the boat. The mounting brackets for the top frames are mounted in various

Fig. 12-18. Dodger that extends outward to just outside companionway.

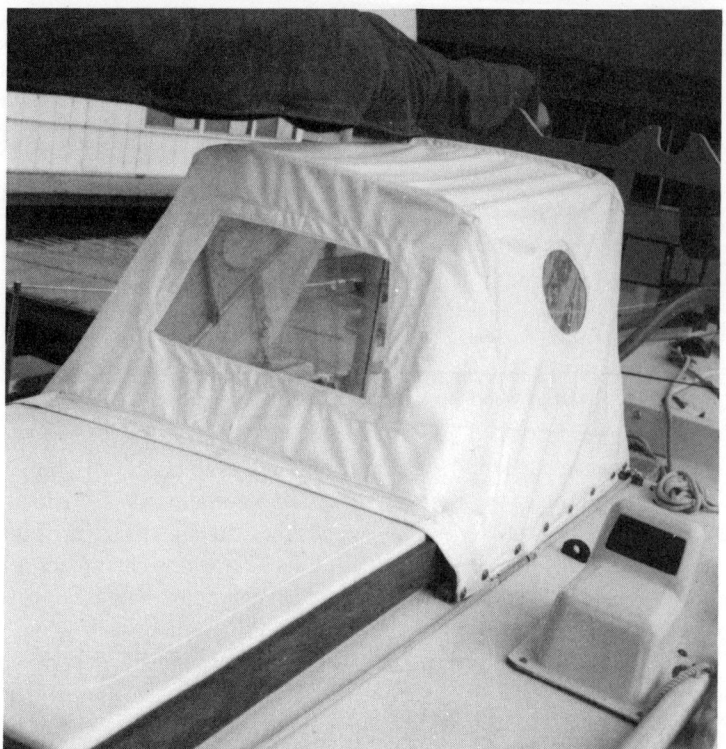

Fig. 12-19. Dodger with flap that allows opening and closing of sliding hatch.

locations, depending on the particular boat and desired top.

Before patterning fabric for top, install frames on boat and tie them with cord in desired finished position. One cord should be tied from frame to frame on the centerline. This will be used as a reference for patterning top fabric.

In general, the main frame should be higher than the secondary frame, and the secondary frame to bottom forward section of planned finished dodger should form a pleasing angle that will look good on the boat.

There are two basic fabric patterns (Figs. 12-20 and 12-21). Decide which is most suitable for your particular application. Regardless of the pattern used, for our purposes here we will call the fabric that goes between the frames the "aft fabric," and the other piece the "forward fabric."

In most cases, a single piece of fabric will be large enough for each of these. In some cases, it will be necessary to join two or more pieces to form a fabric blank. The fabric can be treated cot-

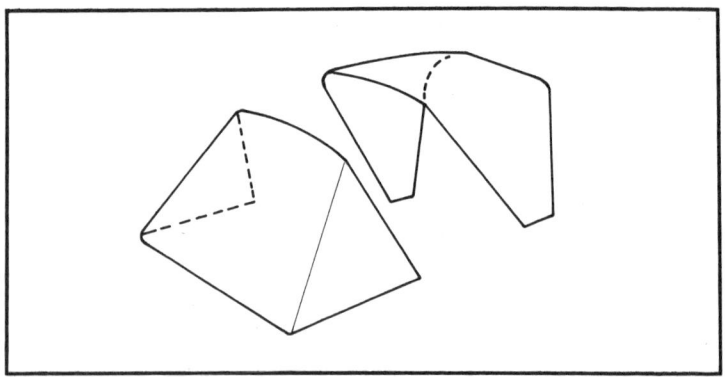

Fig. 12-20. Pattern for top fabrics with seam following secondary frame.

ton boat canvas (generally least desirable), acrylic boat fabric, vinyl-coated top fabric, or other desired suitable materials.

If it's necessary to join pieces of fabric to get a large enough fabric blank for one or both top sections, the seams can be across the top from side to side or longways in a symmetrical pattern with the seam along the center line. First, join the fabrics with a plain seam, then flat-fell this using one of the previously described methods.

Once you have the two fabric blanks, decide how you want to position the fabric pieces for the top. The right side, if there is a difference, should be upward. Mark the fabric pieces with chalk so that you won't get mixed up, and label the fabric pieces as to forward, aft, port, and starboard ends and sides. Also, make a centerline on each piece of fabric with chalk or by other means. This will be used as a reference line and will be lined up with cord

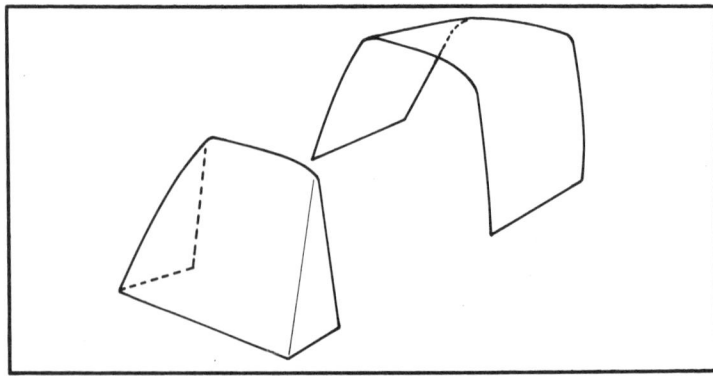

Fig. 12-21. Alternate fabric pattern for dodger.

tied between frames at the centerline.

There are many possible patterning methods. I usually begin by patterning and installing sleeves or casings on aft fabric for frame tubing. Drape aft fabric in place over frames and cords, as shown in Fig. 12-22. You should have at least a 1/2-inch seam allowance from a point horizontally above the furthest aft point on the main frame tubing and from a point horizontally above the furthest forward point on the secondary frame tubing.

Line up the centerline on the fabric with the centerline cord. Smooth fabric out and temporarily attach it in position with large clothespins, safety pins, weights, and other props and clamps. The idea is to have the fabric positioned as it will be in the finished top. Next, mark patterns on the wrong (under) side of the fabric with chalk or soft lead pencil following the forward and aft edges of both frame tubings.

The aft sleeve or casing usually extends downward on each side around the bends in the tubing, as shown in Fig. 12-23. Mark this point on the fabric on each side. This is where the hemlines on each end of the sleeve will be on the finished top.

The forward sleeve or casing usually extends outward on each side to a point just before the start of the main bend. Mark these points on the fabric. This is where the hemlines on each end of the sleeve will be on the finished top.

After pattern lines have been made, remove fabric from frames

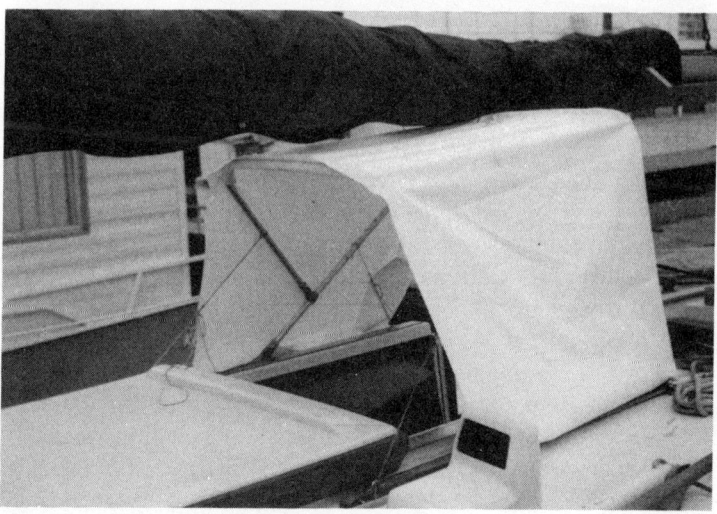

Fig. 12-22. Fabric is draped over frames.

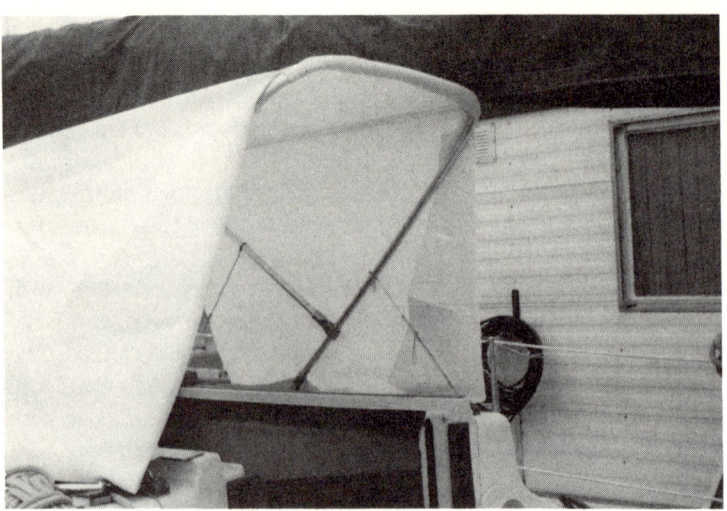

Fig. 12-23. Aft sleeve.

and spread it out right side down on a table or other flat surface. A typical pattern using the above method is shown in Fig. 12-14. Measure and mark cutting lines 1/2 inch aft from aft main frame pattern line and 1/2 inch forward from forward secondary frame pattern line, as shown.

Figure 12-14 shows a method for making the sleeve or casing for the secondary frame. The sleeve fabric needs to be wide enough to go around the frame tubing, plus about 1/2 inch extra. In addition, you will need a 1-inch seam allowance on one side and a 1/2-inch on the other. Pattern a rectangular piece of fabric with this width. The length should be desired length of sleeve, plus 1-inch hemming allowance on each end. Before sewing main seam, sew hem in each end. Fold 1 inch of fabric over toward wrong side, then 1/2 inch of this under. Sew two rows of stitches through this. Repeat on the other end of sleeve.

Next, fold fabric over to form loop, with right side outward on loop. Make a plain seam, as shown in Fig. 12-14. Stitching is 1 inch inward from edge of long flap and 1/2 inch inward from edge of short flap.

Mark center of sleeve. Then sew sleeve on underside of top fabric. Start in center. Position sleeve with flaps as shown in Fig. 12-14, with fold of turned-under flap lined up with aft pattern line of secondary frame. Begin stitching in center and sew to one end of sleeve, following curve, if any, of pattern line. Then go back to center and start again, this time continuing seam to other side. Then make second row of stitches all the way across, as shown in Fig. 12-14.

Figure 12-16 shows pattern details for aft sleeve for main frame tubing. The aft edge of the sleeve fabric will have the same aft cutting line pattern as the top fabric. This should be transferred to the sleeve fabric with the pieces of fabric positioned right side to right side or wrong side to wrong side. The width of the sleeve at any point along its length should be the distance needed to go around the frame tubing in the path shown in Fig. 12-16, plus a 1/2-inch seaming allowance on the aft edge and a 1-inch hemming and stitching allowance on the forward edge. This distance is maintained throughout the length of the sleeve (Fig. 12-16). A 1-inch hemming allowance is required at each end of the sleeve.

Pattern and cut the sleeve fabric. Mark center of sleeve. Position the aft centers of the sleeve and top fabrics together, right side to right side. The shape of the aft edges of the two pieces of fabric, as positioned, should be the same if everything was done correctly. If this checks out, then sew hems in ends of sleeve fabric with 1 inch of fabric folded over to wrong side and 1/2 inch folded under. Sew two rows of stitches along each hem.

Then position the aft centers of the sleeve and top fabrics together again right side to right side. Starting in center, sew plain seam 1/2 inch from edge to one end of sleeve fabric. Go back to the center and start the stitching again, this time sewing to the other side of the sleeve fabric.

Fold seam allowance flaps together to top fabric and sew two rows of stitches through the two flaps and top fabric, as shown in Fig. 12-16. Stop stitching at ends of sleeve fabric. Next, fold sleeve to form a fabric loop to go over frame tubing and sew to main top fabric, as shown in Fig. 12-16. Use two rows of stitches.

Install fabric on frames (Fig. 12-23). It will no longer be possible to use the previous cord tie down system. To insert frame tubing in sleeves, it will be necessary to disassemble framing. After top fabric is installed on frames, reassemble framing. The regular webbing straps can be rigged to hold main frame in position. A similar temporary arrangement of cords can be used to tie down the secondary tubing forward.

The remainder of the patterning and construction depends on the particular boat and desired top arrangement. The next step is usually to pattern the forward fabric. Figure 12-20 shows a typical pattern. Another common pattern is shown in Fig. 12-21.

The forward fabric can be patterned by draping the fabric in place and making necessary pattern marks on fabric. Be sure to add necessary seam allowances and necessary fabric for hems, flaps, and so on. Another patterning method is to take measurements from top frames to boat top and transfer these to the fabric. Frequently, a combination of the two patterning methods is used.

The aft edges of the top below the sleeve may be hemmed or a separate piece of fabric may be sewn in place as a curtain extension. Make necessary pattern marks on aft fabric.

Remove aft top fabric from frames. Cut forward fabric to pattern. Then sew to aft fabric. A plain seam with the pieces of fabric placed right side to right side is usually sewn first. This is usually flat-felled. Next, sew hems in aft edges from end of sleeve to sides of top, or sew extensions in place and sew hems in aft edges.

Install top back on frames. Mark and pattern hemline, flaps, and areas for attachment of fasteners around forward section and two sides of fabric. Figure 12-19 shows a typical flap over a sliding companionway hatch. Also mark patterns for any darts required for fitting top to boat. Remove top from frames and complete sewing of hem and flaps, which might or might not require the patterning and sewing of separate pieces of fabric to the main top fabric.

The next step is usually to install the top back on its frames. Then install fasteners in fabric to mate with those previously installed to boat (Figs. 12-24 and 12-25).

This should complete the construction (Fig. 12-26) except for installing windows. Clear flexible vinyl is frequently used and is

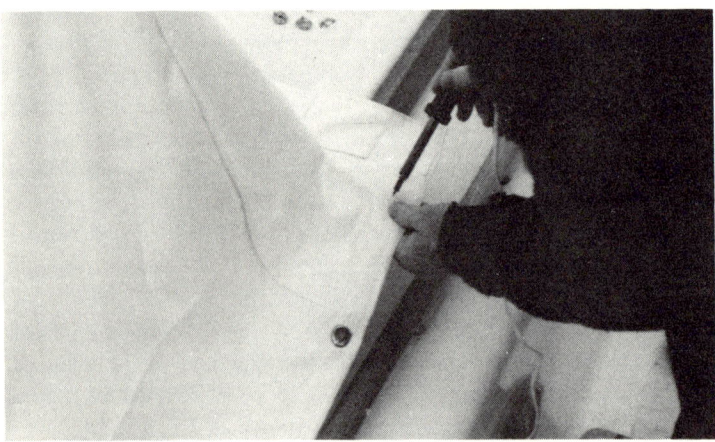

Fig. 12-24. Hole is made for fastener with fine tip soldering iron.

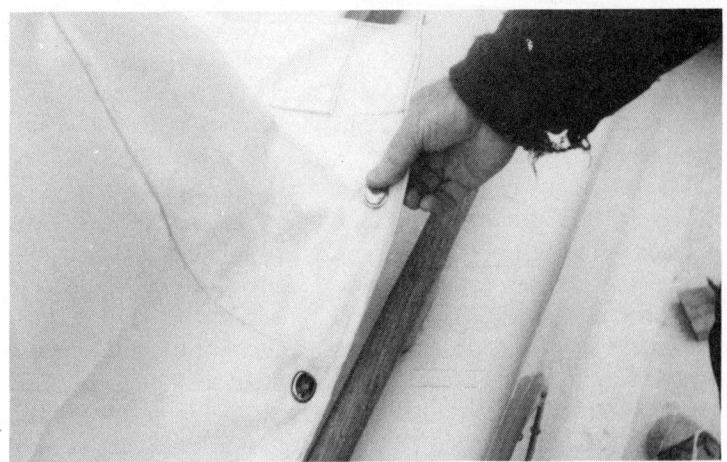

Fig. 12-25. Eyelet in place on fabric.

easy to machine sew to canvas fabrics. Make patterns for desired window openings on fabric, as shown in Fig. 12-27. Then remove top fabric from frames.

Pattern and cut plastic window material 1 inch larger than open-

Fig. 12-26. Construction is complete except for installation of windows.

ing patterns all the way around. Then sew plastic window material to inside of top fabric, with a seam 1/4 inch from edge of window plastic all the way around. Use long stitches to reduce weakening and tearing of window plastic from needle holes spaced too close together.

Next, cut out window opening in top fabric, taking care not to cut into plastic window material. Binding tape can be used over cut edge of fabric around cutout. Fold the binding tape in half over fabric edge and sew through binding tape, top fabric, and plastic window material. Figs. 12-28 and 12-29 show windows installed.

Alternate methods include turning edges of top fabric under around cutout and heat sealing edge of cutout so that binding tape will not be required to protect edge. To dress up the appearance on the inside, tablings can be sewn in place. After all windows have been installed, construction of top is completed.

Bimini Tops

Bimini tops usually have an open front, back, and sides, as shown in Fig. 12-3. Also shown is the typical framing arrangement.

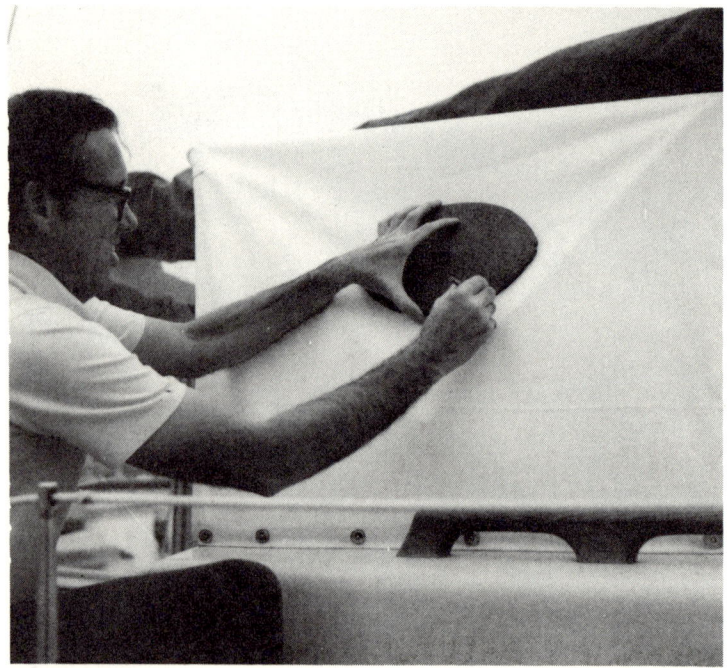

Fig. 12-27. Pattern for window is marked on fabric.

Fig. 12-28. Inside area of completed top.

Only the main frame is hinged to the boat. Four hold down straps are used to secure the top in position. The main frame (the one that extends downward to mounting brackets on the boat) can angle forward or aft, as desired.

Construction begins by setting up frames and tie down straps. Tie a centerline cord between the two frames to hold them in desired position for finished top.

The fabric portion of the Bimini top is simpler and easier to construct than are the two other types detailed above in this chapter. The main part of the top is a single piece of fabric or fabric blank made up of two or more sections of fabric sewn together to form a single flat piece of fabric that is large enough for the top.

Figure 12-16 shows the patterning details for the top when flaps are not required for curtain fasteners at the forward and aft ends. The pattern with these flaps is shown in Fig. 12-17.

Make centerline mark on fabric blank and place fabric in position over frames. Line up centerline on fabric with centerline cord. Smooth fabric out over frames and temporarily attach it in position with large clothespins, safety pins, weights, and other available props and clamps. The idea is to have the fabric positioned as it will be in the finished top. Mark lines on wrong (under) side of fabric with chalk or soft lead pencil, following the forward and aft edges of each frame tubing. Decide on hemlines for sides of top, and mark these on the fabric.

Remove fabric from frames and spread fabric out right side down on a table or other flat surface. If no flaps for fasteners are required, construct lines 1/2 inch further forward than forward frame pattern line and 1/2 inch aft from the furthest aft frame pattern line. These lines are the cutting lines.

If flaps are required for fasteners, similar lines are constructed 2 inches from the frame pattern lines instead of 1/2 inch away, as shown in Fig. 12-17.

The sleeve or casing fabrics will have the same wrong side to wrong side or right side to right side patterns as forward and aft sections of the top. The width of fabric necessary for sleeves in

Fig. 12-29. Completed dodger.

a top without fastener flaps is 1/2 inch for seaming allowance, necessary fabric for going around frame tubing, and 1-inch additional hemming and stitching allowance, as shown in Fig. 12-16. For sleeves that have flaps for fasteners, add 1 1/2 inch additional width to this, as shown in Fig. 12-17. Sleeves should extend outward to hemline on top fabric, plus 1 inch additional on each end for hemming folds.

After patterning and cutting sleeves, sew hems on ends of sleeves. Fold 1 inch of fabric over to wrong side and then 1/2 inch of this under. Sew two rows of stitches through this to form hem. Repeat for each hem.

Next, make cutting lines on fabric 2 inches below hemlines on each side of top fabric. Cut fabric. Fold 2 inches of fabric back to wrong side. Sew row of stitches 1/4 inch from hemline fold. Then fold 1/2 inch of fabric under and make two rows of stitches along this. An alternate method is to cut fabric at hemline and sew binding tape over cut edge of fabric.

After completing hems on both sides of top, sew sleeves to top fabric. Begin with either sleeve. Mark center point on sleeve and line this up with the centerline on top fabric, with sleeve and top fabrics placed right side to right side. Begin in center and sew a plain seam outward to one side. Start in the center again and complete seam to other side.

For sleeves without fastener flaps, make additional seams and rows of stitches as shown in Fig. 12-16. Stitching for sleeves with fastener flaps is shown in Fig. 12-17. After sewing one sleeve, repeat procedure on other sleeve.

This completes the construction of a basic Bimini top, except for tops where fasteners are required to attach curtains, as detailed later in this chapter.

Extension Tops

Extension tops (Fig. 12-30) are frequently used with canvas boat tops that connect to fixed windshields. They are sometimes used with dodgers and Bimini tops.

These usually have a single frame, which is attached to the boat by standard mounting bracket. The frame is usually secured with two tie down straps. The aft edge of the top fabric has a sleeve that fits over the frame tubing; the forward edge attaches to the main top, whether canvas or solid (wood, fiberglass, etc.) construction, by snap, Lift-the-Dot, or Common Sense fasteners. The

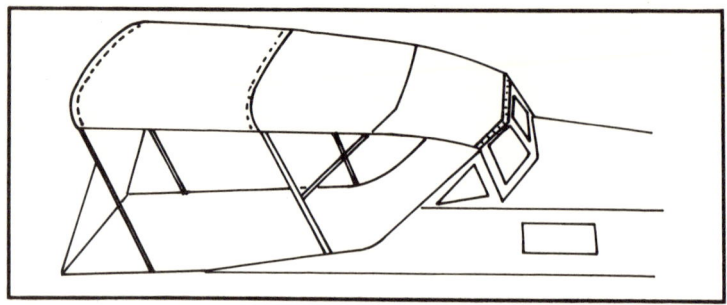

Fig. 12-30. Extension top.

sockets or eyelets are usually located on the main top. The extension fabric goes underneath a flap on the main top, with studs attached upward. The main idea is to form a joint that will not leak. In the arrangements shown, the water tends to run off on the outside of the top fabric.

Construction usually begins by setting up the frame and hold down straps. Use cord or rope to tie frame in desired position for finished top.

A couple of important points: the frame should angle aft sufficiently for the hold down straps to form an effective angle, and the frame should meet aft frame of main top when extension top frame is folded forward.

The forward edge of extension top has the same pattern line as aft edge of main top, as shown in Fig. 12-30. Drape fabric in place and temporarily attach fabric to extension top frame and over aft section of main top. Use clothespins and other clamps and props to hold fabric in position. Trace pattern of aft edge of flap for fasteners on main top on underside of forward edge of extension top fabric.

Remove extension top fabric and lay it out on a table or other flat surface. Measure and mark off cutting line 2 inches forward of pattern line on extension top fabric.

Pattern a 2 1/2-inch tabling to the same pattern line with the tabling fabric wrong side to wrong side on the top fabric, as shown in Fig. 12-31. Cut tabling to pattern. Determine center point by marking from centerline on extension top fabric.

Place extension top fabric wrong side down on bed of sewing machine. Position tabling fabric right side down on extension top fabric. Line up centerpoints and start plain seam, sewing outward to one side. Then go back to center and start seam again, continuing to other side. Figure 12-31 shows the seam. Turn tabling right side out. Sew seam 1/4 inch from edge through the four layers of fabric.

Fold 1/2 inch of tabling under. Make row of stitches through this and top fabric, starting in center and working out to one side. Then go back to center and start seam again, continuing to other side.

Install sockets or eyelets on flap for fasteners on fabric of main top. These are usually positioned from about 3 inches to 6 inches apart, with one at each corner.

Drape extension top fabric back in position. Mark and install fastener studs to connect to fabric tops or sockets or eyelets for attachment to solid tops. Begin in center and work outward, alternating from side to side. If side hem flaps of extension top will be in the area of fastener attachment, do not install corner fasteners at this time. They can be installed after sides of extension top have been hemmed.

Connect extension top to main top by the fasteners. Position aft edge of extension top over extension top frame and temporarily attach fabric to frame tubing with large clothespins or other means. Mark pattern on underside of extension top fabric with chalk or soft lead pencil, following aft edge of frame tubing. Also, mark desired hemline for each side of extension top.

Remove fabric. Check to make certain that hemlines match by folding top fabric in half along centerline. Make any necessary adjustments. Then spread fabric out on table or other flat surface and

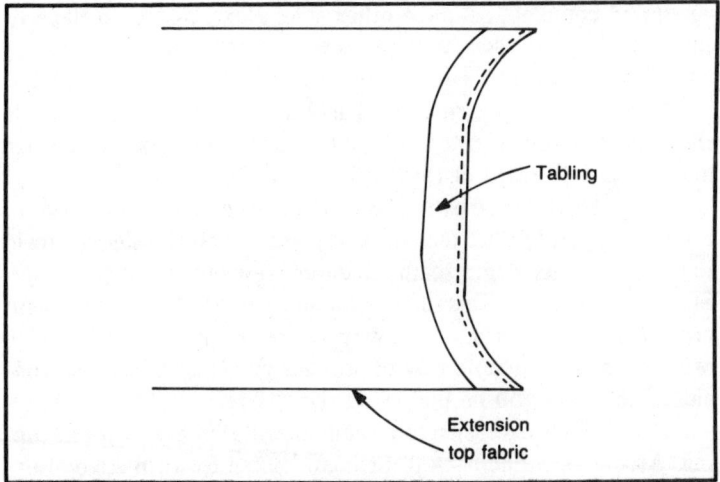

Fig. 12-31. Tabling for forward edge of extension top.

mark cutting lines on fabric 2 inches below hemlines on each side of top fabric. Cut off excess fabric. Fold 2 inches of fabric back to wrong side. Sew a row of stitches 1/4 inch from hemline fold. Then fold 1/2 inch of fabric under and make two rows of stitches along this. An alternate method is to cut fabric at hemline and sew binding tape over cut edge of fabric.

After hems have been completed on both sides of top extension, spread top fabric out right side down on table or other flat surface. Measure off and mark cutting line 1/2 inch aft of frame pattern line. Cut off excess fabric.

The sleeve or casing fabric will have the same wrong side to wrong side or right side to right side pattern as the aft edge of the extension top fabric. Width of sleeve required is 1/2-inch for seaming allowance, fabric necessary to go around frame tubing, and 1-inch additional hemming and stitching allowance, as shown in Fig. 12-16. Because of the curves, it will take a much wider fabric blank than this for the sleeve. Sleeve should extend outward to hemline on top fabric, plus an additional 1 inch on each end for hemming folds.

After patterning and cutting sleeve fabric, sew a hem at each end by folding 1 inch of fabric over to wrong side and then 1/2 inch of this under. Sew two rows of stitches through this to form hem.

Next, sew sleeve to top fabric. Begin by determining and marking center of sleeve fabric. Place sleeve fabric right side to right side on top of extension top fabric. Line up centerpoints. Begin in center and sew plain seam outward to one side. Start in the center again and complete seam to other side. Next, fold both flaps to sleeve fabric, and sew these to sleeve fabric with two rows of stitches, as shown in Fig. 12-16.

Measure and pattern a line 1 inch forward and parallel to aft frame pattern line on underside of top fabric. Then make another line 1/2 inch forward of this in the same manner.

Loop sleeve fabric over to underside of top fabric as shown in Fig. 12-16, and fold 1/2 inch of fabric under. Sew the sleeve fabric to the top fabric. Begin seam in center. Sew outward to one side. Start in center again, this time continuing seam to other side. Make second row of stitches, all the way across, 1/4 inch from first row of stitches. This double row of stitches is required because considerable stress will be placed on the sleeve.

Disassemble extension top frame. Install sleeve over frame tubing. Assemble frame back to fittings. Fasten forward edge of extension top to main top. Install corner fasteners if these were not installed previously. This completes the construction of a basic extension top.

Side and Stern Curtains

Many different side and stern covers are used in conjunction with canvas tops. These are commonly used with canvas tops that attach to fixed windshields, as shown in Fig. 12-32. Bimini tops sometimes make use of curtains that go all the way around. Even some dodgers make use of side curtains and sometimes even stern curtains or covers are attached.

A typical side curtain arrangement for a boat with a canvas top that attaches to a fixed windshield is shown in Fig. 12-32. The curtain goes underneath the canvas boat top, with the fasteners arranged as shown. The forward and lower portion of the curtain goes outside the windshield and coaming. This arrangement is used so that water will run off outside the boat.

A typical curtain is a piece of fabric, shaped to fit, with a hem or binding tape sewn around the edges. Fastener studs that correspond to matching sockets or eyelets in top fabric are used along upper edge of curtain. Sockets or eyelets are usually installed in forward and lower edges of curtain to match the studs attached to windshield frame and boat coaming or other areas of boat.

Flexible plastic windows are usually then installed in curtains. Transparent flexible vinyl is frequently used and is easy to machine sew to canvas fabrics. Make pattern for desired window opening on curtain fabric.

Pattern and cut plastic window material 1 inch larger than opening pattern all the way around. Then sew plastic window material to inside of curtain fabric with seam 1/4 inch from edge of window plastic all the way around. Use long stitches to reduce number of needle holes in plastic.

Next, cut out window opening in top fabric, taking care not to

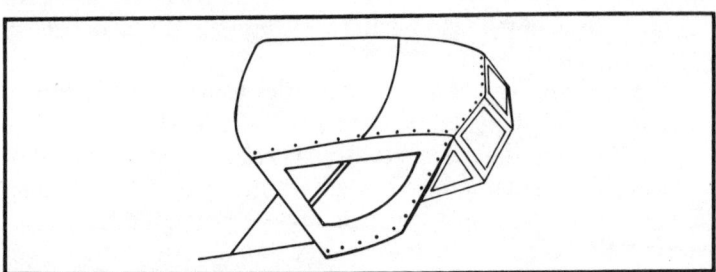

Fig. 12-32. Side curtain arrangement.

cut into plastic window material. Binding tape can be used over cut edge of fabric around cutout. Fold the binding tape in half over fabric edge and sew through binding tape, top fabric, and plastic window material.

Alternate methods include turning edges of top fabric under around cutout and heat sealing edge of cutout so that binding tape will not be required to protect edges. (Most synthetic boat fabrics can be heat sealed.) To dress up the appearance on the inside, tablings can be sewn in place.

An alternate method for making curtains when the curtain will be almost all clear plastic is to sew fabric edges to window plastic. After these fabric pieces have been sewn to all edges of window plastic, the necessary fasteners are installed in the fabric. This type of curtain is frequently used for Bimini tops and installed all the way around.

The above methods for constructing side curtains can be adapted for a variety of specific requirements. A detachable curtain arrangement can be made for dodgers. Curtains can also be constructed for extension tops. They can also be used with a variety of solid or fixed tops. Stern curtains or covers that connect to aft edge of canvas boat top and side curtains are another possibility (Fig. 12-33).

Forward edge of stern cover has the same pattern line as aft edge of top. Tie cords in place. Then drape fabric blank in place and temporarily attach fabric to cords with clothespins. Forward edge should overlap aft edge of canvas top. Trace pattern of aft edge of fastener flap on main top on underside of forward edge of stern cover fabric.

Remove stern cover fabric and lay it out on a table or other flat surface. Measure and mark off cutting line 2 inches forward of pattern line on stern cover fabric.

Pattern a 2 1/2-inch tabling to the same pattern line, with the tabling fabric wrong side to wrong side with the top fabric, as shown in Fig. 12-31. Cut tabling to pattern. Determine and mark centerpoints.

Place stern cover fabric wrong side down on bed of sewing machine. Position tabling fabric right side down on stern cover fabric. Line up centerpoints and start plain seam, sewing outward to one side. Then go back to center and start seam again, continuing to other side. The seam is shown in Fig. 12-31. Turn tabling right side out. Sew seam 1/4 inch from edge through the four layers of fabric.

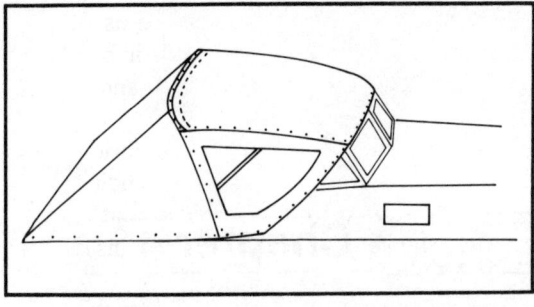

Fig. 12-33. Stern curtain or cover.

Fold 1/2 inch of tabling under. Make row of stitches through this and stern cover fabric, starting in center and working out to one side. Then go back to center and start seam again, continuing to other side. Then make a second row of stitches, all the way across, to reinforce the seam.

Install stern cover fabric back in position and temporarily secure it in place with clothespins and other available clamps and props. Mark and install fastener studs for connecting to canvas top. Begin in center of stern cover and work outward, alternating from side to side.

With main portion of stern cover fastened in place to canvas top, patterns can be made for side pieces. After necessary measurements and patterns have been made, remove fabric and install side pieces.

Then install stern cover back in place. Install fasteners for connecting side pieces to aft edge of side curtains (Fig. 12-33).

Mark hemline along sides and back edge of stern cover. Remove stern cover and mark lines 2 inches outward from hemlines. Cut fabric along these lines. Fold 2 inches of fabric back to wrong side. Sew a row of stitches 1/4 inch from hemline fold. Then fold 1/2 inch of fabric under and make two rows of stitches along this. An alternate method is to cut fabric at hemline and sew binding tape over cut edge of fabric.

After hem has been completed, install stern cover back in place. Install fastener studs to boat, as required. Then install matching sockets or eyelets to stern cover.

This completes the construction of a basic stern curtain or cover. This can be adapted to fit particular requirements. For example, an outboard motor cover can be sewn to the stern cover. Flexible plastic windows can be installed. Plastic zippers can be installed for use as an entrance when the cover is in place. Use the type of zipper that can be opened and closed from either side.

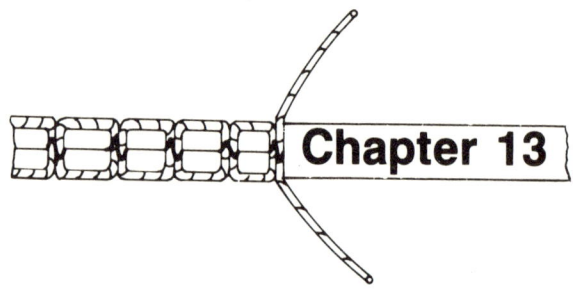

Chapter 13

Fabric Mosquito Screens

Nylon mosquito netting or screening is useful for covering doorways, windows, hatches, and a variety of other openings in boats and recreational vehicles. My first boat trips out into the California Delta were made without any means of keeping mosquitos and other insects from getting inside the boat. This was ample motivation to start thinking of ways to keep them out. As a result, I constructed simple fabric mosquito screens to go over the companionway opening and companionway sliding hatch (Fig. 13-1) and the forward hatch. This has greatly increased the pleasure of Delta cruising for me, and so far I don't believe a single mosquito has gotten inside when the screening was in place.

Another possible solution is mosquito nets placed over berths, but this arrangement seems much less satisfactory than keeping mosquitos and other insects from the entire interior.

I have since become familiar with a number of systems for removable fabric screening and means of securing them to boats and recreational vehicles. Here are some important considerations:

■ Regular aluminum or fiberglass screening in fixed frames should be used whenever practical. These are generally more reliable and durable than the removable fabric type.

■ The fabric screening must be attached or fastened in place in such a way that mosquitos and other insects cannot get through around the edges or fastenings.

Fig. 13-1. Mosquito screens over companionway and hatchway of sailboat.

■ For many applications, it's important that the netting be easy to put on and take off.

■ When mosquito netting is used over doors, there should be a convenient way for getting in and out.

MATERIALS

Nylon mosquito netting is available by the yard in a choice of widths, with 31-inch, 36-inch, and 48-inch widths typical. It is available in white, army green, and a variety of other colors. The netting is easy to machine sew as long as fabric is used on both sides of the netting in area of stitching.

The netting is frequently sewn to fabric, which can be dry-treated cotton canvas (generally least recommended), acrylic, polyester, or nylon, as desired.

Velcro® is frequently used to attach the fabric screening to boats and recreational vehicles. One part is glued or otherwise attached to the boat or recreational vehicle. The other part is sewn to the mosquito netting or to fabric that is in turn sewn to the mosquito screening.

Braided nylon or polyester cording in small diameters (1/8 inch is about right for many applications) can be sewn to the fabric for use as tie down cords. These are usually not sewn directly to the netting, but work well when sewn to fabric that is in turn sewn to the netting.

For some applications, snaps or other fasteners may be desirable. These are not usually attached directly to the netting, but rather to fabric that is in turn sewn to the netting. The same thing applies to zippers.

VELCRO® ATTACHMENTS

A frequently used method for attaching mosquito netting is Velcro®. One part of the Velcro® is glued or otherwise attached around opening to be screened. Figure 13-2 shows an application to the framing of a companionway hatch on a boat. This can be adapted for many other uses. Decide what is the best and most convenient location for the Velcro®. Velcro® is available with pressure sensitive adhesive backing that works well on some surfaces. Special adhesive is also available. Velcro® can be attached to wood surfaces with staples. Rustproof monel staples, available from

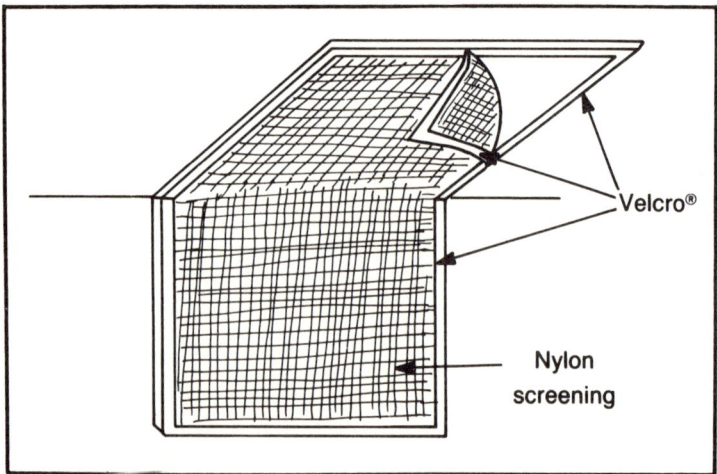

Fig. 13-2. Velcro® attachment of nylon screening to inside hatch and companionway framing.

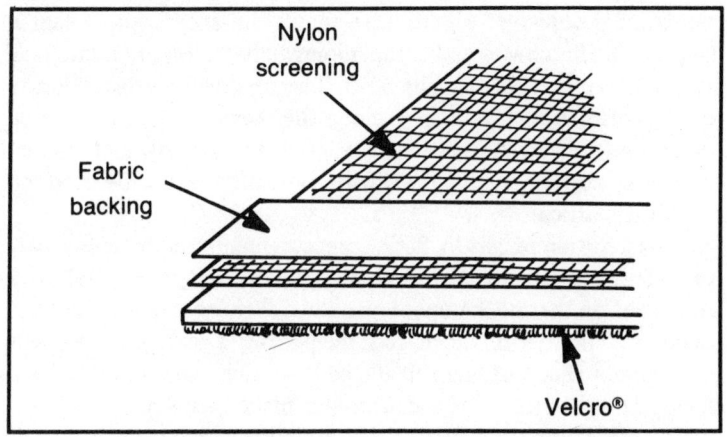

Fig. 13-3. One part of Velcro® is sewn to nylon screening and backing fabric.

marine stores, are recommended.

The other part of the Velcro® is sewn to the nylon netting. Binding tape or fabric can be used as a backing, as shown in Fig. 13-3. This will also give a neat finished look to the project.

There may be situations where it is necessary to join two sections of netting together. Backing fabric or binding tape should be used on both sides of netting lap joint in area of stitching. Use two rows of stitches for each seam.

The materials for this type of screening can be purchased separately. Companionway and hatchway kits with necessary Velcro® and nylon screening are also available. These can be mail ordered from Defender Industries, Inc. (see Suppliers for address).

I have found that this system of screening can be satisfactory for many uses. I haven't had any problems at all with the Velcro® parts where they hook together even after they have been put together and taken apart many times. I have had some problems attaching the back of the Velcro® to fiberglass surfaces with the pressure sensitive adhesive backing with release paper, but special cement available for use with Velcro® tape usually takes care of this problem. It's also important that the screening be installed in such a way that doors, hatches, and so on can still be opened and closed.

TIE DOWN AND SNAP ATTACHMENTS

If large fabric overlap pieces are sewn to the netting, tie downs and/or snaps can often be used to attach screening to boats and recreational vehicles. Figure 13-4 shows the arrangement that I used for the hatchway and companionway hatch on my boat. The basic pattern is shown in Fig. 13-5. The tie down cords are sewn to the fabric. A casing is sewn along the fabric edge at bottom of the companionway for holding a wood dowel or length of rubber hose as a weight to hold fabric down. Snaps could also be used for the same purpose.

Construction begins by taking measurements and making a pattern. The areas of nylon screening should be approximately the same area as that of the openings. The fabric sections should extend a considerable distance from the netting. Location of tie down cords and/or snap fasteners should be in suitable places where there is something to tie to or a convenient place to install a snap.

To sew fabric to netting, a fabric or binding tape backing should be used so that the netting is sandwiched between fabric layers. Outside edges of fabric are hemmed or finished by folding binding tape over the edge of the fabric and sewing this in place. Pattern

Fig. 13-4. Nylon mosquito netting with fabric pieces attached.

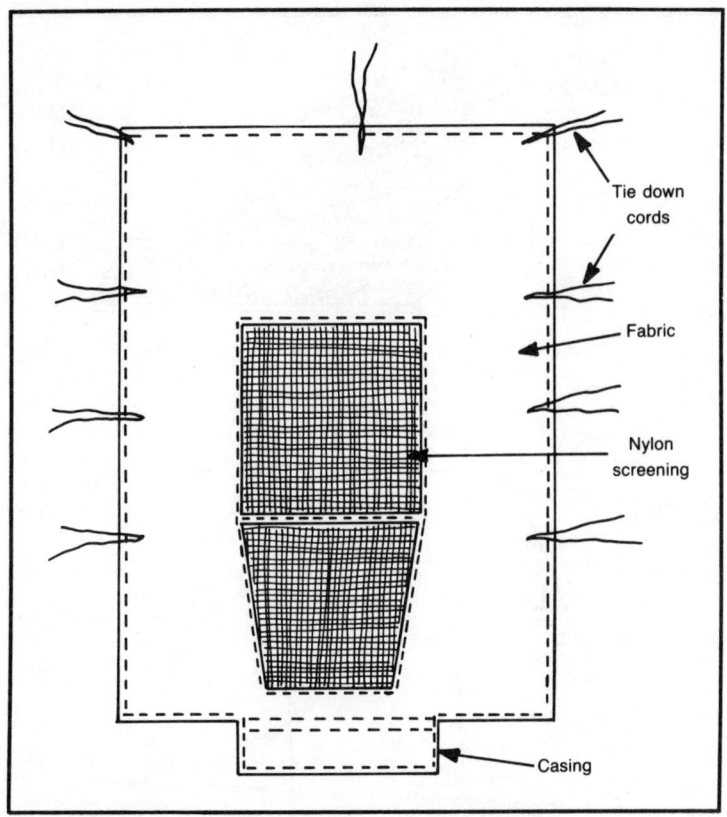

Fig. 13-5. Pattern for hatchway and companionway cover.

and sew a casing in place for a wood dowel or other hold-down weight, as shown in Fig. 13-5.

Sew attachment cords to fabric and/or install snap parts in fabric to match location of snap studs installed on boat. This completes the construction.

Figure 13-6 shows a pattern for a similar screening for a hinged opening hatch. Determine the maximum hatch opening that will be required and pattern the nylon netting for this. This will allow any desired hatch opening up to this maximum.

Pattern locations for tie down cords in areas where there are cleats, stanchions, or other items to tie to.

Construction begins by taking measurements and making a pattern. The fabric sections should extend a considerable distance from the netting.

After patterning is completed, do necessary cutting, then sew-

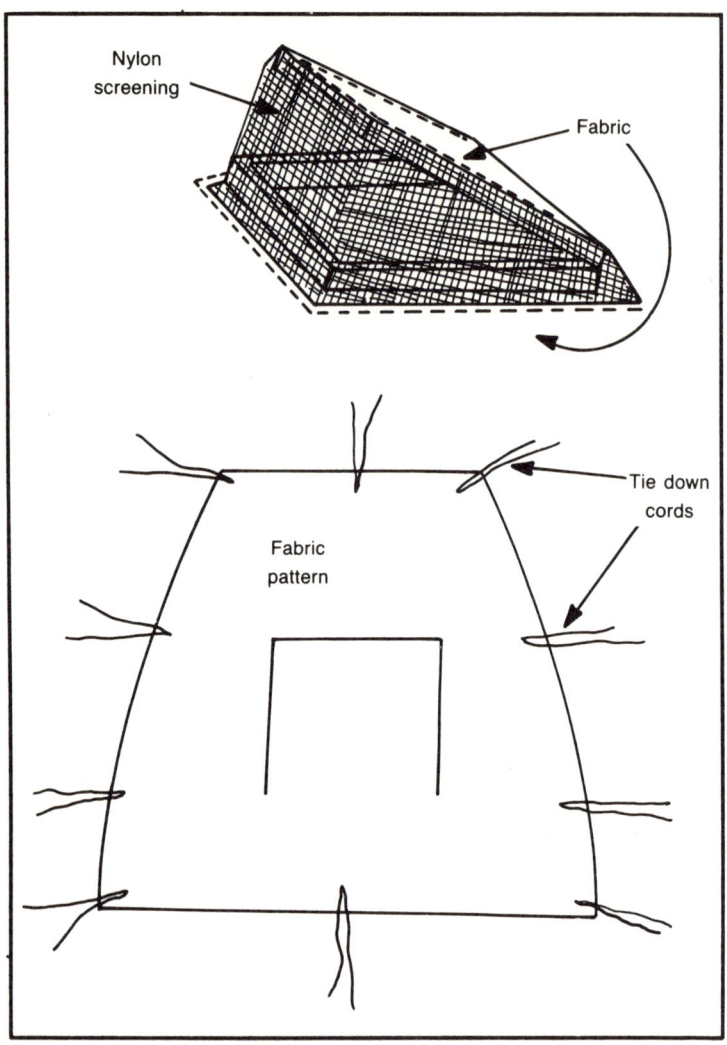

Fig. 13-6. Pattern for cover for hinged opening hatch.

ing. To sew fabric to netting, a fabric or binding tape backing should be used so that the netting is sandwiched between fabric layers. Outside edges of fabric are hemmed or finished by folding binding tape over the edge of fabric and sewing this in place. Sew tie down cords to fabric and/or install snap parts in fabric to match location of snap studs installed on boat. This completes the construction. These basic constructions can be adapted for a variety of boat and recreational vehicle uses.

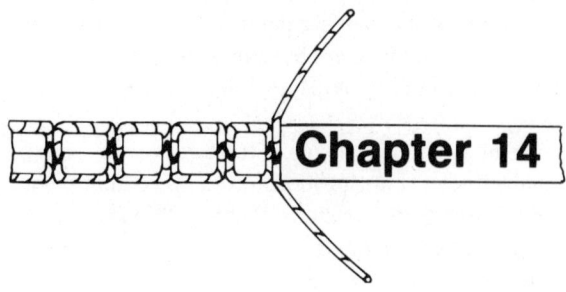

Chapter 14

Cushions and Seat Covers

A variety of cushions and fabric seat covers is used in boats and recreational vehicles. There are many similarities between cushions and seat covers for boats and recreational vehicles, so for our purposes here, these will be treated together, even though there may be some differences. For example, cushions for boats are more often fitted to odd shapes to fit the curvatures of hulls and so on than those for recreational vehicles. In general, foam padding, fabric coverings, and fasteners will be subject to more severe environmental conditions in boats than recreational vehicles. For recreational vehicles, you might be able to use hardware made from standard steel. For boats, it's best to stick to nonferrous metals, such as brass, aluminum, bronze, stainless steel, and monel or plastics. Both boats and recreational vehicles generally face harsh environmental conditions and vigorous use, though, so cushions and seat covers should be designed and constructed accordingly.

Cushions and seats are generally padded with foam or other suitable materials, or some combination of materials. In most cases, the placement, size, and shape of cushions, whether good, bad, or indifferent, was part of the factory design and construction. You will simply be recovering existing items. Some modifications, however, are possible. For example, additional thickness can be added to foam padding. More durable and/or more attractive fabrics can be used for new covers. And so on.

If you are modifying or redesigning the interior of an existing boat or recreational vehicle, you may want to make more extensive changes. Often this involves constructing new cushions of different shapes and designs.

Or you might want to design and install a complete interior in a boat or recreational vehicle. Designing and constructing cushions and making fabric covers for seats will often be an important part of this.

Because of the limited space in the interiors of most boats and recreational vehicles, interior items often serve multiple uses. Seat cushions double as berth cushions. Tables often lower to seat level, and the seat backs go on the table tops to form berths. The possibilities are almost limitless.

Cushions are often separate units, essentially a block or sheet of foam cut to shape with a fabric cover on the outside. These often simply set in place over a bench or other structure made from wood, fiberglass, or other materials. Cushion backs simply set in place and lean back against some solid structure.

Rails, such as shown in Fig. 14-1 are often used to keep cushions from sliding off. Cushion backs are often secured with snap, Lift-the-Dot, and Common Sense fasteners. The studs are attached to the boat or recreational vehicle. The sockets or eyelets are attached to the cushion backs. Another method is to sew one half of Velcro® to cushion fabric, and glue, staple, or otherwise attach the other half to the boat or recreational vehicle.

This type of cushion can have padding sewn inside the cover fabric, or a zipper or other arrangement can be used so that the foam padding can be removed to clean the fabric covers.

Another method for constructing cushions is to use a backing member made from plywood or other material. The foam is then

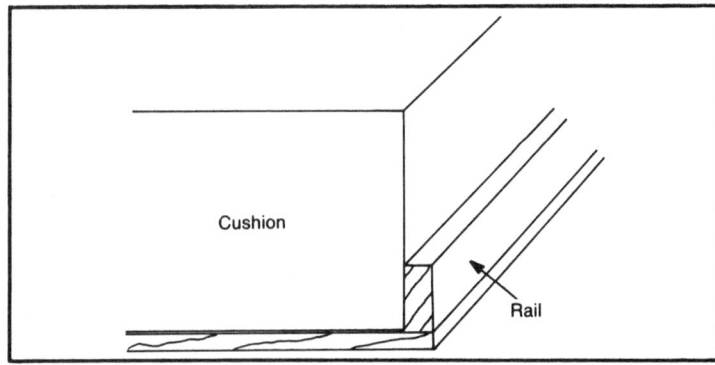

Fig. 14-1. Rail used to hold cushion in place.

placed on this. A fabric cover is fitted over the foam and brought around over the edges of the plywood to the back side, and the fabric is attached to this with staples, tacks, or other means.

Cushions can be constructed for indoor or outdoor use, such as for cockpit seating in a boat. Special foam padding that won't soak up water like a sponge should be used for these.

Shaped seats and chairs are used in boats and recreational vehicles. You may want to make new covers for these. These seats and chairs usually have some type of framework that holds the padding and springs, if used, in place. There is often a means for connecting the fabric covers to the frames. Driver and passenger seats in recreational vehicles and cockpit pilot chairs and fishing chairs in boats are often of this type.

MATERIALS

The difficulty of constructing cushions and seat covers varies greatly, depending on the particular job and how it is accomplished. Even beginners, however, can usually do a satisfactory job provided that they first learn and practice the necessary skills and take the time necessary to do the job right. This section includes descriptions of the materials you will need to achieve professional results.

Fabrics

A great many upholstery fabrics are suitable for cushion and seat covers. Some fabrics allow water to pass through; others don't or are highly resistant to this. Some fabrics allow air to pass through. These are called breathing fabrics. Other fabrics are of a nonbreathing-type. Although the nonbreathing waterproof type won't allow water to pass through, any water that does get inside won't have a way to get out. Trapped air can also be a problem unless small grommets or other openings are installed so that air can escape.

Vinyl fabrics with cotton, nylon, or polyester backing are widely used for cushions and seat covers on boats and recreational vehicles. Naugahyde is a popular brand, but other brands will also work well. Look for thick and pliable vinyl and a closely woven backing, preferably of synthetic materials. Avoid those without backing or thin cheesecloth-type backings.

Quality vinyl upholstery fabrics wear well and are easy to clean with a damp cloth or sponge, but hot matches and cigarettes will cause them to melt, a problem also shared by most other upholstery fabrics. Perhaps the main disadvantages of using vinyl are the difficulties involved in working with and sewing this fabric and the fact that it is a nonporous plastic, which means that it is cold and stiff in cold weather and sticky in hot conditions. Vinyl upholstery fabrics are available in a variety of colors, however.

Many people prefer woven fabrics without vinyl or other plastic coatings. These are generally more comfortable and attractive, although they may be more difficult to clean than vinyl and may not last as long.

Woven polyester fabrics, like Herculon, are popular for use in both boats and recreational vehicles. These often have latex backings. Woven polyester fabrics are available in a variety of colors and pattern designs.

The same types of acrylic fabrics that are popular for exterior covers and tops, such as Acrylan®, are also suitable for cushion and seat covers. This material seems to work well on boats, and it gives a yachty appearance. It also works well in covers for cockpit and other cushions that will be used outdoors.

Other possible fabrics are detailed in Chapter 2. Actually, a wide variety of fabrics can and have been used for cushions and seat covers. Unless you have a special reason for doing otherwise, however, I suggest that you use one of the proven fabrics detailed above. In general, boat and recreational vehicle cushions and seat covers must stand up to rougher use and harsher environmental conditions than, say, living room furniture. Select fabrics accordingly.

Thread

Polyester thread is generally recommended for use with all common upholstery fabrics. A #24 thread size can usually be used with a #18 sewing machine needle, the largest size needle that can be used with many home sewing machines. For commercial upholstery sewing machines and other machines that will take a #21 or #22 needle, #16 thread can be used.

Piping

Piping is available with a covering already in place over cording, or you can make your own by sewing cording inside strips of fabric. Nylon or polyester cord about 1/8-inch in diameter is frequently used.

Zippers

Zipper openings are frequently used in cushion covers so that padding can be removed when cleaning covers. Plastic, heavy-duty zippers are recommended, because metal ones tend to corrode and break. Either separating or nonseparating zippers can be used, because the ends can be fixed together to form the required closed system so that the zipper slide cannot come off at either end.

Velcro®, Snaps, and Other Fasteners

Velcro® is sometimes used as a fastener for cushions. Velcro® is available in widths from about 5/8 inch to 2 inches.

Snaps are often used to hold cushion backs in place and for other related functions. Although snaps are most often used for these purposes because they don't stick out very far, Lift-the-Dot and Common Sense fasteners can be used in some cases.

Buttons

Buttons are sometimes used on cushions to help keep padding in place and for appearance's sake. A variety of suitable buttons are available. You can purchase buttons that are already covered with fabric, or you can cover your own, as detailed later in this chapter.

FOAM PADDING

Standard latex and polyether foams are commonly used in block or sheet form for padding in cushions and seats for boats and recreational vehicles, even though these will usually absorb moisture and water to a certain extent. Special closed cell foams are also available. They will not absorb water, making them ideal for use on boats, especially as cockpit cushions. An added advantage is that closed cell foam also serves as a flotation material. In fact, it's the same material that is used in flotation vests and other similar devices. The extremely high cost as compared to standard latex and polyether foams is a disadvantage.

Foam padding for individual seats and cushions is usually made in one piece. Bolster cushions and pillows are sometimes padded with chopped up foam.

The latex foam padding is often called *foam rubber*. This term is also applied to other types of foam used for padding.

Firm, high density foam padding is recommended for most boat and recreational vehicle cushions and seats. A foam requiring a 30- to 36-pound load for 75 percent compression per square foot is about right for most seating and sleeping cushions. This foam weighs about 1.5 to 1.65 pounds per cubic foot.

For comfortable seating and sleeping, the cushions should not only be of firm, high density foam, but also thick, usually from 4 to 6 inches. A common modification is add thickness to existing foam padding or to replace existing padding with thicker foam. There are limits, however. It usually doesn't take long sitting on furniture padded with a couple of feet of foam to realize that you can get too much of a good thing.

Standard foam is available in sheets, in thicknesses from about 1/4 inch up to 6 inches or more, and in blocks of a variety of shapes and sizes. The closed cell foam is presently only available in 1-, 1 1/2-, and 2-inch thicknesses. Separate sheets can be joined together with special adhesives, as detailed later in this chapter, to build up greater thicknesses. The special adhesives are available in liquid and spray can form. Use the kind that is formulated especially for foam padding.

Patterning and Cutting Foam

Most foam padding deteriorates in time, and it may be desirable to replace existing foam. If the old foam still fits properly, it can be used as a pattern to shape new foam. In many cases, the old foam is still in satisfactory condition, but more thickness is desired. New foam can be joined to the old foam to give the added thickness.

In some cases, the old foam will be in such poor condition or fit so poorly that it is essentially useless as a pattern. In this case, the pattern for the foam can be taken from the area where it will fit and transferred to the new foam. You might want to shape foam to original cushions, as when designing interiors for boats and recreational vehicles.

When recovering cushions, first decide if the old foam can be used. If it has crumbled, lost its firmness, or stinks, replacement is probably in order. Although separate pieces of foam can be joined together with adhesive, it's better to purchase pieces of foam that are large enough without having to join separate pieces together.

The foam should be of the desired thinness as well. It's impractical to attempt to reduce the thickness of large areas of foam by cutting it without special industrial equipment. You can, however, increase thickness by joining sheets of foam together.

Foam is commonly available in popular sizes, such as 24 inches by 74 inches, 30 inches by 74 inches, and so on. Some suppliers will cut the foam to the desired rectangular size and sometimes even to odd shaped patterns. In many cases, however, if they don't have the exact rectangular size that you need, you will have to purchase a larger size and cut it to fit. If the cushion is some shape other than rectangular, you will need to purchase a piece of foam that is large enough so that you can cut it to desired size. Keep in mind, however, that the cutting will be through the thickness and not to reduce the thickness, at least not large areas of it.

To use old foam with a rectangular shape and straight sides as a pattern for new foam, place old foam on new foam. Line up one side and one end of old foam with one side and one end of new foam. Mark pattern line following edges of old foam on new foam. You can mark on foam with a felt tip pen. Remove old foam and check lines with a long straightedge and large square. It's also a good idea to mark identical pattern lines on the opposite side of the foam. This will serve as a guide for making straight cuts.

Odd shaped patterns with straight or box sides, such as shown in Fig. 14-2A, can be patterned similarly. When placing old foam on new foam, position it to take advantage of the precut straight edges on the new foam whenever possible. If the old foam is round, you won't be able to do this. In this case, position old foam on new foam in such a way that waste is kept to a minimum. In general, you will want to keep the cut-away pieces of foam as small as possible, yet have the main part of the extra foam in as large a piece as possible.

Odd shaped patterns with one or more angled sides, such as a boat's typical forward berth cushion, shown in Fig. 14-2B, are more difficult to pattern. Place largest side of old foam face down on new foam. Trace pattern onto new foam. The foam is usually cut to square or box sides to this pattern (cutting is detailed below

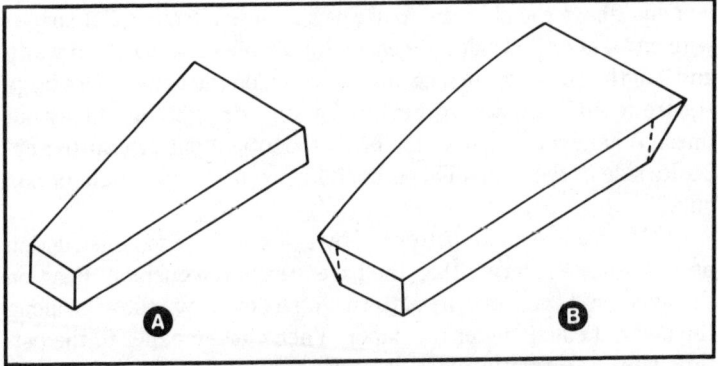

Fig. 14-2. Odd shaped foam with straight or box sides (A) and odd shaped pattern with two angled sides (B).

in this chapter). Pattern for smaller side is then laid out on this same side by measurements. The angled sides are then cut.

An alternate method is to trace large and small sides of old foam on construction paper. Cut the paper patterns out. Place pattern of large side on correct side of new foam. Trace pattern line from paper pattern onto foam. Then position pattern of small side on other side of new foam and carefully line it up in relation to pattern lines on other side of foam.

To pattern foam for adding thickness to existing foam, decide whether new foam is to be added to top or bottom of old foam. Then place new foam face to face with this side. If old foam is rectangular and has straight or box sides, line up one side and one end of old foam with one side and one end of new foam. Trace pattern lines from old foam onto new foam for remaining two sides of new foam. Remove old foam and check lines with long straightedge and large square. It's also a good idea to mark identical pattern lines on the opposite side of the new foam to serve as a guide for making straight or box cuts. Odd shapes with straight or box sides can be patterned similarly, except that you may not be able to take advantage of straight sides on new foam.

Odd shaped patterns with one or more angled sides are more difficult to pattern. First, pattern the sides that go together on the old and new foam. Then determine areas where the opposite side of new foam needs to be larger or smaller. Measure and mark this pattern on the other side of the new foam.

An alternate method is to join the two pieces of foam with adhesive and then do the cutting, following the sides and angles of old foam for cutting the new.

In some cases, it will be necessary to shape foam to fit when you don't have the old foam to use as a pattern. Rectangular shapes with straight or box sides are easy. Simply measure required width and length and lay these measurements out on the foam. Use a large square to make square corners and a long straightedge to lay out lines. Whenever possible, lay out an identical pattern on the opposite side of the foam. This is useful when making straight or box cuts.

Odd shapes can be patterned by using a piece of construction paper somewhat larger than the base area of the cushion. Position the paper and trace out the pattern with a pencil by following along the desired edges under the paper. Then cut the paper to the pattern line. Try this in place to make sure that it fits. Make any necessary changes. If the paper is too short, glue or tape additional paper in place.

Once you have the required paper pattern, transfer this to one side of the foam. Then position the opposite side of the paper pattern on the opposite side of the foam. Line the two patterns up. Then mark pattern on foam.

If one or more edges are angled, make the base pattern as detailed above. Then make a matching pattern on opposite side. Next, determine how much larger or smaller foam needs to be. Note any variations in the thickness of the foam on the base paper pattern. Transfer these measurements to the required side of the foam.

Special saws are made for cutting foam padding, but these are expensive. A less expensive alternative is an electric kitchen knife. These work well, and even many professional upholstery shops use them. When cutting foam, make certain that the electric knife is held at the correct angle. This is the reason for marking the pattern on both sides of the foam, even when straight cuts are made. For angled cuts, it's even more important.

Fine tooth hacksaw blades and serrated steak knives will also work if enough care is taken. It usually works best to saw or cut only while pulling the saw blade or knife towards you. It's important to keep the cutting blade at the correct angle.

Practice the cutting method on scrap pieces of foam before trying them on foam pieces to be used, then cut foam to be used to the patterns marked. Try the foam in position where it is to be used. Mark any required corrections. Hopefully, these will require cutting more foam away rather than adding to it, but it's possible to add additional foam by using an adhesive, then trimming this as necessary after the adhesive has set.

Gluing Foam

Use only the special adhesive intended to glue foam padding or foam rubber. Many types of adhesives won't stick, will dissolve the foam, or will leave a hard area. The two layers of foam should be smooth and flat where the joint is to be made. For joining sheets of foam on top of each other, this usually isn't a problem, but it can be when making end to end or side to side connections.

Follow manufacturer's directions for using adhesives, and observe health and safety precautions. The liquid-type applied with a brush is generally safer to use than that in spray cans. In either case, use in well ventilated areas and avoid breathing the fumes.

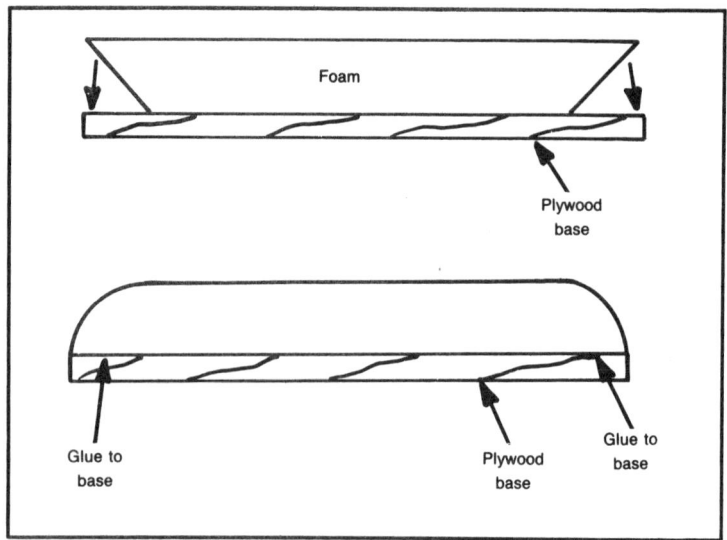

Fig. 14-3. Method for forming rounded corners.

Foam padding can also be glued to wood using the same adhesive. This method is often used when plywood backed cushions are constructed. This will prevent the foam from sliding around under the fabric covering.

It's also possible to form rounded corners for cushions and seats by cutting the foam at an angle, as shown in Fig. 14-3, and then gluing these edges to the plywood base.

FABRIC COVERS FOR CUSHIONS WITH WOOD BASES

This type of cushion (Fig. 14-4) consists of a wood base, usually plywood; foam padding placed over one side of the wood; and a fabric covering placed over the foam and brought down around the wood base. The cover is attached to the back side of the wood by staples, tacks, or glue, or some combination of these. The foam padding is sometimes glued to the wood base to keep it in position.

This type of construction is sometimes found in manufactured boats and recreational vehicles. It is often used in amateur constructions, perhaps because it can be done without sewing, provided that tucked corners are satisfactory. By sewing, these cushions can be given a shape and appearance similar to independent cushions. The wood base cushions tend to be more cumbersome; to present difficult cleaning problems, because the covers cannot be easily removed for laundering or dry cleaning; and the fabric covering tends to wear through in areas where contact with the wood base is made unless special precautions are taken to prevent this.

Construction begins by cutting the plywood base to size. If you have an old cushion with a plywood base, you might be able to use it again if it is still in good condition. Even if it needs to be replaced, you might be able to use it as a pattern for the new plywood. Once you have the base, try it in the boat or recreational vehicle to make sure that it fits properly and that there will be room for fabric if the cushion must slip into tight space.

The wood base can be used as a pattern for cutting the foam. The edges of the wood should be slightly rounded and sanded smooth to reduce friction with fabric cover. Fabric can be glued, tacked, or stapled over the edges of the wood to help protect the fabric cover, or cloth tape can be applied similarly. The foam padding can be left free on the wood surface or glued to it, as desired.

The simplest, though not the best, method for adding fabric covering is to place fabric over foam and fold it around over the sides to wood backing, where overlapping fabric edges are stapled, tacked, or glued to the wood backing. Unless the fabric has a lot of stretch, tucks or folds will be necessary to make the fabric corners. This, of course, tends to give the job an amateurish appearance, which is the main drawback of this method.

The appearance can be improved by folding box corners and slip or blind stitching seams in these by hand, as detailed in Chapter 4. Similar corners can be machine sewn. To pattern, place fabric in position over foam. Fold dart for box corner and mark pattern. Do this for each corner. Remove fabric from foam. Fold darts to wrong side and make plain seam. Cut off excess fabric, leaving

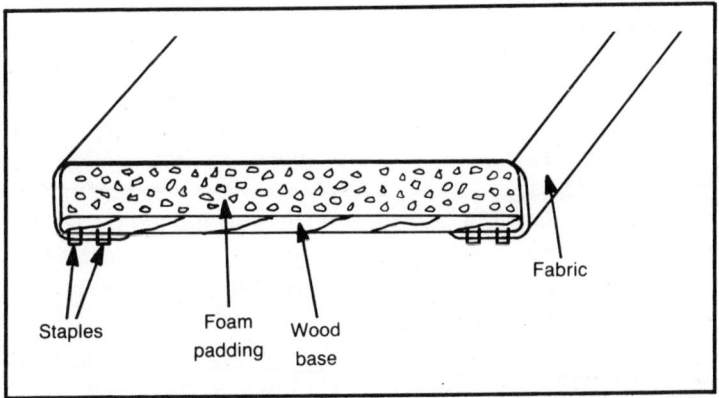

Fig. 14-4. Cushion with wood base.

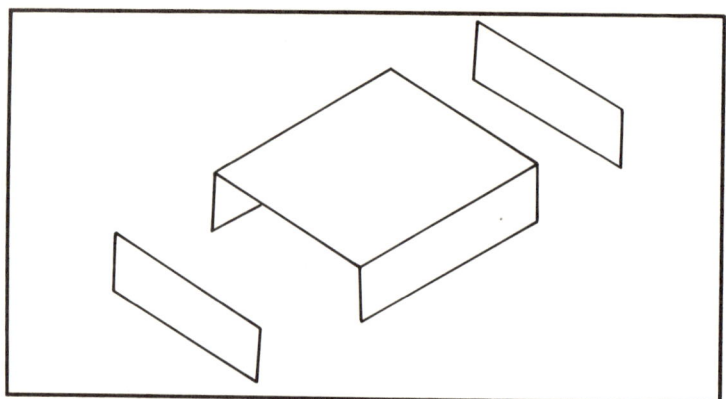

Fig. 14-5. Pattern for cover.

1/2-inch flaps. Fold both of these to one side and fold 1/4 inch under, and sew through this to form flat-felled seam.

A number of other sewn patterns are possible. One method is to sew on end pieces, as shown in Fig. 14-5. Make patterns, allowing 1/2 inch for seam allowances and 3 inches on edges for going around backing plywood. Sew end pieces to main fabric with plain seams. If desired, these can then be flat-felled for added strength.

Piping can be used to improve appearance and help protect seam. Piping can be made up by sewing cord inside strips of fabric, as detailed in Chapter 5, or you can purchase piping that is already made up. The piping is first sewn to end fabric. A zipper or piping foot is used on sewing machine so that stitching can be made close to cord in piping. If a square corner is desired, a single dart is cut in piping fabric. If a slightly rounded corner is desired, three or more darts are usually required. Piping is sewn to the right side of the fabric.

The main fabric is then sewn to the end fabric with the piping in between. The main fabric and end fabric are placed right side to right side, just as with a regular plain seam. The seam should be made close to the piping cord. At the same time, the edges of the fabric should be lined up. The plain seam will usually suffice, but the seam flaps can be folded to one side and sewn to one of the layers of fabric to strengthen the seam if desired. After both end pieces have been sewn in place, turn the cover right side out. It is now ready for installation.

Figures 14-6 and 14-7 show other possible patterns. These can be with or without piping, as desired. First, pattern fabric, allowing necessary seam allowances and ample fabric to go around to

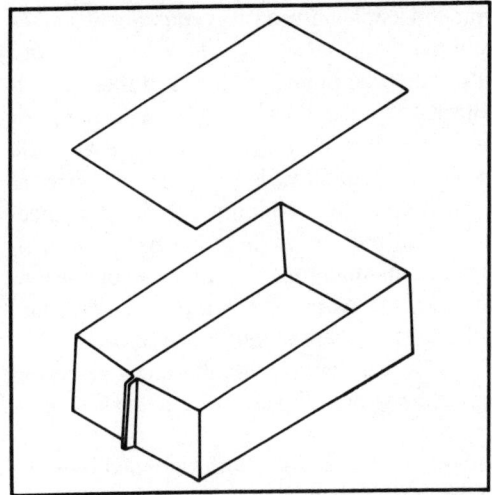

Fig. 14-6. Pattern for cover.

plywood backing. Overlap this about 3 inches or more.

Next, cut fabric to pattern. If piping is to be used, you can make up your own piping by sewing cord inside strips of fabric, as detailed in Chapter 5, or you can purchase piping that is already made up. If piping isn't used, sew fabric pieces together with plain seams. These can be flat-felled for greater strength. If piping is used, first sew piping to the fabric that will be flat on finished cushion. Then sew the fabric pieces that go around corners to this. When sewing is completed, turn cover right side out. It is now ready for installation.

Regardless of method used for cover fabric, the next step is to place it over the foam padding and fasten the edges of the cover to the plywood backing. Although staples, tacks, or fabric adhesives

Fig. 14-7. Pattern for cover.

can all be used, I recommend staples. I use rust proof monel staples and a heavy-duty staple gun.

All sides of the fabric must be pulled evenly, and if sewn patterns are used for the fabric covering, these must be in proper position so that the finished cushion will be symmetrical. The fabric should be pulled so that the foam padding is compressed about 1/2 inch at the sides. This will give the cushion a good appearance.

You might want to install buttons to keep covering and padding in position and to break up monotony. Buttons can be uncomfortable, though, unless they are sunk far down into the cushion. Decide on the number and arrangement of buttons to be used. Also, select buttons. These can be purchased with the fabric covering already in place, or you can add your own covering to cushion-type buttons.

Mark desired locations for buttons on both plywood backing and fabric sides. Drill 1/16- to 3/32-inch holes (use smallest size that twine and needle will fit through) 1/4 inch apart at each button location through the plywood backing. Use a long straight upholstery needle and heavy polyester twine. Thread needle. Pass threaded needle through one of the holes in plywood, then on through foam padding and fabric covering. Pass needle through button hole and pull thread through. Then pass needle through cover fabric and foam padding and second hole in backing plywood. Tie slip knot, as shown in Fig. 14-8. Pull knot up until button is sunk desired

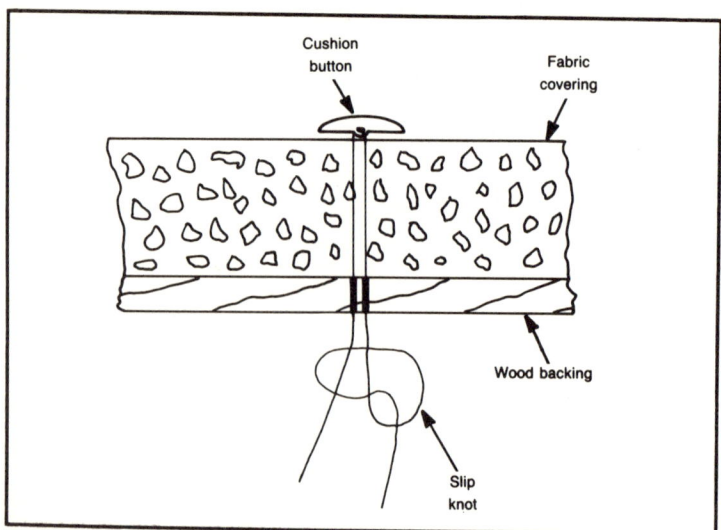

Fig. 14-8. Method for installing cushion button.

amount in cushion. Then tie off with a reef knot to keep slip knot from loosening. Repeat procedure for each button.

This completes construction of cushion with wood base, foam padding, and fabric cover. This type of construction can be adapted to fit a variety of special requirements.

INDEPENDENT CUSHIONS WITH FOAM PADDING AND FABRIC COVERS

This type of cushion is extremely popular for use in boats and recreational vehicles. Although almost anyone can make some sort of fabric covers to go over foam padding, it takes skill and practice to do a professional looking job.

A good starting point is the following two practice projects. These will teach the skills and techniques that will enable you to do a good job on actual boat and recreational vehicle cushions.

First Practice Project

The first project is to make the pillow shown in Fig. 14-9 that

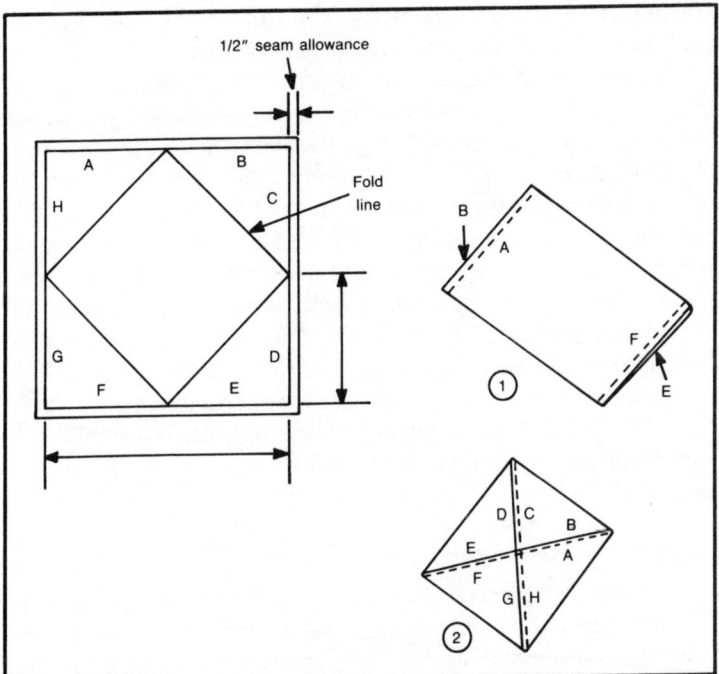

Fig. 14-9. Pattern for pillow padded with chopped foam.

is padded with chopped foam. The basic pattern for the fabric is shown. A 19 × 19-inch square piece of fabric is required. Pattern this on the wrong side of the fabric with an 18 × 18-inch square with 1/2-inch seam allowance all the way around, as shown. Mark midpoints of each side of 18-inch square. Join these points with lines to form a 12 × 12-inch square inside the 18-inch square, as shown. Mark lines outward from each corner of the 12-inch square to outside edge of seam allowance and at right angle to sides of 18-inch square. Label the sides from A to H, as shown.

Fold fabric in half, right side to right side, so that A and B are together and F and E are together, as shown. Line up edges and sew plain seams to join A and B together and F and E together.

Next, position fabric so that edges D and C are together and edges G and H are together. Sew plain seam along this to join D and C together. Continue seam to join G and H together, except leave about 3 inches of seam open for turning pillow fabric right side out. Turn pillow fabric right side out through open area left in seam.

Add chopped foam through open area in seam until pillow is padded desired amount. Then hand sew opening, using slip or blind stitching, as detailed in Chapter 4. You will need two cushion buttons. Cover these with matching or contrasting fabric.

Thread a long straight upholstery needle with polyester twine. Pass needle and thread through hole in one button and pull all but about 4 inches of the twine through the button hole. Then pass needle through center pillow side where fabric pieces are joined, through chopped foam padding, and out the middle of opposite side of pillow. Pull all thread through except for the 4 inches extending from the button. Pass needle and thread through hole in second button. Then pass needle back through pillow to starting side. Pull thread through and up tight. Tie slip knot, as shown in Fig. 14-10. Pull this up until buttons are a desired depth in cushion. Then tie off with reef knot to keep slip knot from loosening.

This completes the first practice project. This pillow is something that you can probably use aboard a boat or on a recreational vehicle.

Second Practice Project

The second practice project is to make a cover for 12 × 12 × 4-inch piece of foam padding using the same type of construction that is commonly used for larger cushions, as shown in Fig. 14-11.

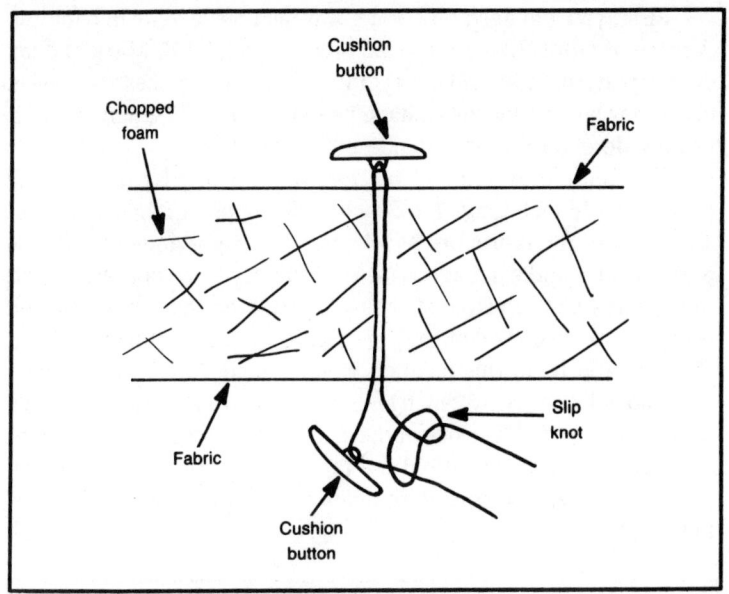

Fig. 14-10. Method for installing cushion buttons.

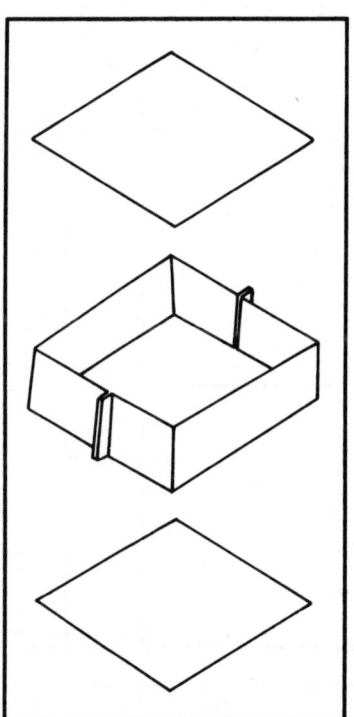

Fig. 14-11. Fabric cover for cushion.

First, you will need a 12 × 12 × 4-inch piece of foam padding. A piece of fabric 28 inches by 26 inches is required. Mark and lay out the patterns as shown in Fig. 14-12. The cutting lines are shown; necessary seam allowances have been included. The patterning is usually done on the wrong side of the fabric.

Cut fabric into required pieces. Make piping by first sewing two of the 26-inch long, 1 1/2-inch wide strips of fabric together. The ends of the fabric are overlapped at a right angle, right side to right side. Make a diagonal seam from corner to corner. Cut off fabric flaps 1/4 inch from stitching. Straighten out fabric. Place it right side down on bed of sewing machine. Fold seam flaps out flat. They should be in this position when the cord is sewn in place.

You will need two 52-inch long pieces of 1/8-inch diameter nylon or polyester cord. Place one of these in the center of the fabric strips that are sewn together. Fold the fabric in half over the cord, and sew a seam close to cord. Use a zipper or piping foot on the sewing machine.

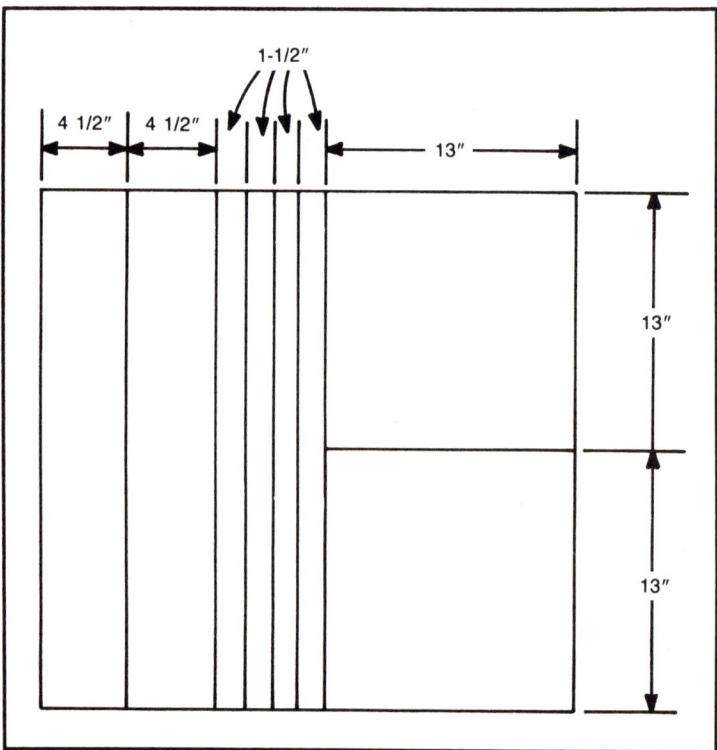

Fig. 14-12. Pattern for cover fabric.

Repeat same procedure with other two 1 1/2-inch strips of fabric and other piece of cord. When finished, you should have two pieces of piping, each 52 inches long. Mark and cut flaps off 1/2 inch from stitching.

Next, take one of the 13 × 13-inch pieces of fabric and place it wrong side down on bed of sewing machine. Position piping end at center of one side and start stitching about 3 inches from end of piping. This section will be used to join the ends of the piping.

Make seam close to cording. Keep edges of piping cover fabric lined up with edge of main fabric. Stitching line should be 1/2 inch from edge of fabric.

Stop stitching 1/2 inch from corner. Cut a notch in piping cover fabric. Stop short of the piping stitching, however, so the cut will not show through on the right side of the finished cushion. With sewing machine needle in down position, raise presser foot and turn fabric to new sewing direction. Lower presser foot and start sewing again. Sew to next corner and repeat turning procedure. Continue until piping is sewn to approximately 3 inches from starting point.

Open piping cover seams about 3 inches on each end, from point where stitching stops, to join piping to main fabric. Cut cording so that it forms the correct length when ends are placed end to end.

Determine amount of fabric required for joining ends of piping covering fabric so that it will be the correct length for the diagonal seam. Place fabric ends right side to right side, at right angles to each other, and make diagonal seam. Cut off excess fabric 1/4 inch from stitching. With flaps folded back, fold piping covering around piping cord. Complete stitching by sewing through piping fabric and main fabric to complete seam all the way around the main fabric.

Repeat same procedure with other piece of 13 × 13-inch fabric, again sewing the piping all the way around to the right side of the main fabric.

Next, join the two pieces of 4 1/2-inch wide fabric to form one piece. Place the pieces of fabric right side to right side, and make a plain seam 1/2 inch from end of fabric pieces. Flaps will each be folded back when sewn to main fabric pieces. This method reduces the number of fabric layers in any one area to keep lumps from forming in cushion cover.

Next, sew the 4 1/2-inch side piece to one of the main fabric pieces. Start about one third the way along the side of the main piece of fabric. The main idea is not to have more than one seam allowance flap in any one spot.

Position main piece of fabric wrong side down on bed of sewing machine. Place side piece of fabric right side down on top of this. Start stitching a couple of inches from end of side piece to allow room for joining ends later. A zipper or piping foot is used on sewing machine. Sew close to piping cord. Keep edges of fabrics lined up and maintain an even 1/2-inch seam allowance all the way along. Stop stitching 1/2 inch from end of main fabric. With sewing machine needle in lowest position, raise presser foot. Turn main fabric to new sewing direction. Lower presser foot. Continue seam around edge of main fabric, repeating turning procedure at each corner. Stop stitching a couple of inches short of start of seam. Mark end-to-end length for joining ends of side fabric. Add 1/2-inch seam allowance to each end. Cut off excess fabric. Place fabric ends right side to right side, and join them with a plain seam 1/2 inch from end. Turn each flap back and continue original seam, joining side piece to main piece.

Place other main piece of fabric wrong side down on bed of sewing machine. Fold box corner in other part, which should still be wrong side out. Line up corner fold on side piece with main piece of fabric, which is wrong side down on bed of sewing machine. The purpose of this is to make sure that the corners of the two main pieces of fabric are lined up in relation to each other. Lower presser foot. Lower needle by turning hand wheel. Needle should be at exact corner point, with 1/2-inch seam allowance.

Make seam around main piece of fabric, maintaining 1/2-inch seam allowance and making square corners as was done when sewing the side piece to other main piece of fabric. Sew around three sides, leaving one side open.

Turn cover right side out through opening. Install foam padding through opening, then hand sew opening closed with slip or blind stitching, as detailed in Chapter 4.

This completes construction of second practice project. If done properly, the cushion should have box corners, and the cover fabric should fit snugly over the foam padding. If your first cushion doesn't turn out very well, repeat the practice exercise. It's much better to make mistakes on practice work than actual cushions for a boat or recreational vehicle.

MAKING COVERS

After you have the foam padding cut to shape, the next step is to make fabric cover to fit. We will first consider a rectangularly

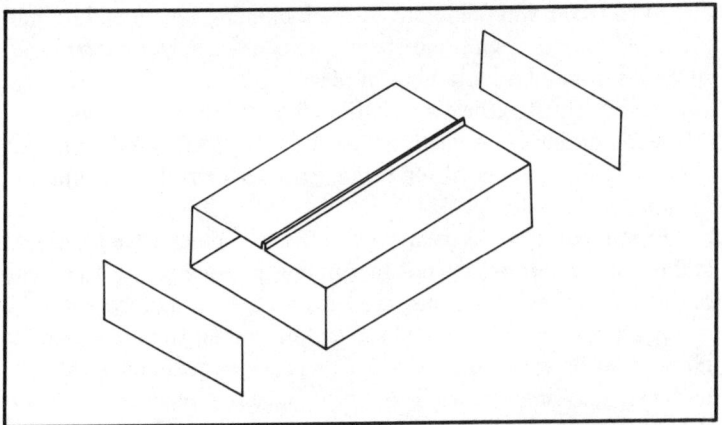

Fig. 14-13. Pattern for cushion cover with separate end pieces.

shaped cushion with straight or box sides. The basic pattern is shown in Fig. 14-13. To give a tight fit, all side pieces are patterned 1/2 inch less than the thickness of the foam padding to be covered. A 1/2-inch seam allowance is added all the way around all three pieces of fabric.

Rectangular Cushion With Box Sides

Take pattern from foam padding. Transfer pattern to fabric, then cut fabric into three required pieces.

Fold main piece of fabric, right side to right side, and make plain seam to join ends 1/2 inch from fabric edges. This seam will go in the center of the back side of the finished cushion. Place one of the end pieces wrong side down on the bed of the sewing machine. Leave the main piece of fabric wrong side out. Position one end of the seam in the main piece of fabric in the center of one end of the end piece. It's important to get this as exact as possible. Seam flaps should be turned outward. Start stitching in center, and sew outward. Stop stitching 1/2 inch from edge of end piece. With sewing machine needle through fabric, raise presser foot and turn end piece of fabric to new sewing direction. Lower presser foot. Sew seam to next corner and repeat turning procedure. Continue same pattern all the way around end piece back to start of stitching. Overlap start of stitching an inch or so to fix stitching. The flaps from the plain seam in the main piece of fabric should be folded back flat. Next, sew main fabric to other end piece using same method, except only sew half way around from center of one end of end piece to center of other end of end piece.

Turn cover right side out through opening left in end. Install foam padding through same opening. Then close opening by hand, sewing slip or blind stitching in place.

This completes the construction. The center three quarters of the seam joining the ends of the main piece of fabric could be left open instead, to be used for turning the cover right side out and installing the padding.

Piping can also be used around the end pieces. Construction is the same as above, except that piping is sewn to the right side of the end pieces before they are sewn to the main piece of fabric.

A zipper can be installed instead of joining the ends of main piece of fabric with a plain seam. The previous seam lines will now be fabric fold lines. Sew the zipper tape to the main fabric. Alternate methods for installing zippers are detailed in Chapter 7. The ends of the zipper are often sewn together with whip stitching. Fabric flaps are often sewn in place at zipper ends.

Box Cushion With Separate Top and Bottom

Another method for making a cover for a rectangularly shaped cushion with straight or box sides is to use separate pieces of fabric for the top and bottom, as shown in Fig. 14-14. Separate pieces

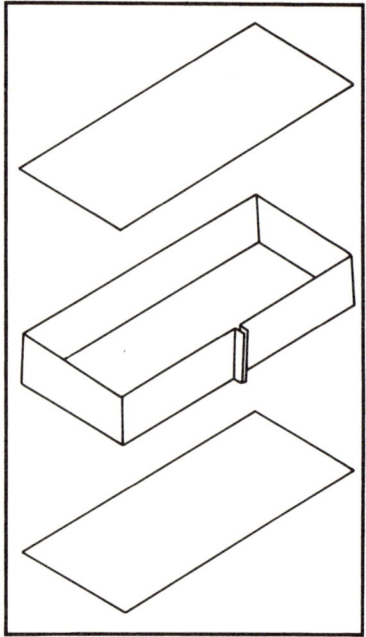

Fig. 14-14. Patterning method with separate pieces of fabric for top and bottom.

of fabric can be used for each end and the front and back sides, or one long piece of fabric in one piece or sewn together from two or more pieces can be used, as in the second practice project detailed above. The first method produces seams at each corner of side pieces; the second method usually places the seams elsewhere around the cushion. This is the method most commonly used to make cushions for boats and recreational vehicles. Manufactured cushions are usually made this way.

We will first consider a cushion of this type with plain seams without piping. The seam lines for the top and bottom pieces should be patterned to the same size as the foam padding. A 1/2-inch seam allowance is added to this all the way around to mark the cutting line pattern.

The height of the side pieces should be patterned 1/2 inch less than the thickness of the foam padding. This will compress the foam padding somewhat and give a good appearance to the finished cushion. Add 1/2-inch seam allowances to each edge of fabric for side pieces, and to each end of separate pieces.

If there are to be four separate pieces of fabric for the sides, with a seam at each corner, these must be patterned carefully. If you use one long piece, or if the length is made from more than one piece with seams placed at random around the cushion, the total length should be at least long enough to go around the top and bottom pieces, plus a 1/2 inch at each end for seam allowance. If the piece is a little longer than this, excess can be trimmed off later. Pattern and cut fabric.

If four separate pieces of fabric are used for sides, with seam at each corner, join the pieces of fabric with plain seams. Place the pieces right side to right side. A 1/2-inch seam allowance is used.

If one long piece will go all the way around the cushion, do not join the ends to form a loop at this time. This will be done later. If more than one piece of fabric is required to make this length, join the pieces together with plain seams to form one long strip, but do not join ends to form loop at this time.

Next, place either top or bottom piece wrong side down on end of sewing machine. If side pieces have a seam for each corner, start seam at one corner. Side piece should be wrong side out.

Start sewing seam. Keep fabric edges lined up and maintain an even 1/2-inch seam allowance all the way along. Stop seam 1/2 inch from edge of fabric at next corner with sewing machine needle in lowest position through fabric. Raise presser foot. Turn main fabric to new sewing direction. Lower presser foot. Sew to next corner and repeat turning procedure. Continue seam until you are back to starting point. Then overlap stitching an inch or so to fix seam.

Place second main piece of fabric wrong side down on bed of sewing machine. Sew opposite edge of side piece to this, starting in one corner, as on first side. This is important for lining up the top and bottom fabric pieces in relation to each other.

Sew seam the same as before, except this time leave one end open for turning the cover right side out and installing foam padding. After seam has been completed around the three sides, turn cover right side out through opening. Install foam padding through opening. Close opening by hand, slip or blind stitching in place, as detailed in Chapter 4.

If a long strip is used for sides rather than one with seams at each corner, construction is basically the same. Start seam a couple of inches from end of side fabric strip so that ends can be joined later. Make seam all the way around, up to a couple of inches from starting point. Mark stitching lines for joining ends of side piece fabric. Add a 1/2-inch seam allowance on the end of each piece. Cut off excess fabric. Position fabric ends, right side to right side, and join them with a plain seam. Go back to seam joining side piece to main piece of fabric and finish seam.

When sewing second main piece of fabric to side pieces, it's important to box and mark exact corners. Start seam at one of the corners. The remainder of the construction is the same as described above for cushion with seam at each corner of side piece.

If desired, a zipper can be inserted along the center of the back side piece using one of the methods detailed in Chapter 7 for zipper installation.

The strength and appearance of this type of cushion can generally be improved by sewing piping in seams around bottom and top pieces of fabric. Construction is basically the same as without piping, except that piping is made up by covering cord with strips of fabric as detailed in Chapter 5 or preformed piping is sewn to right sides of top and bottom fabrics. (Refer to the second practice project above.) A zipper foot is used on the sewing machine.

Odd Shaped Cushion With Box Sides

The same general patterning method is used for cushions with odd shapes with straight or box sides. Basically, you need bottom and top pieces patterned to the shape of the foam padding, plus 1/2-inch seaming allowance all the way around. Top and bottom pieces will be wrong side to wrong side or right side to right side copies of each other.

The height or width of the side pieces should be patterned 1/2 inch less than the thickness of the foam padding. This will compress the foam padding somewhat and give a good appearance to the finished cushion. Add a 1/2-inch seam allowance to each edge of fabric for side pieces, and to each end of separate pieces.

If there are to be separate pieces of fabric for each side piece, with seams at angle turns, these must be patterned carefully. If you use one long piece, or if the length is made from more than one piece with randomly placed seams around the cushion, the total length should be at least long enough to go around the top and bottom pieces, plus a 1/2 inch at each end for seam allowance. If the piece is a little longer than this, excess can be trimmed off later.

Pattern and cut fabric for the particular cushion. If separate pieces of fabric are used for sides with seams at turns, join the pieces of fabric with plain seams. The fabric pieces are placed right side to right side, and a 1/2-inch seam allowance is used.

If one long strip will go all the way around the cushion, join separate pieces if this requires more than one piece of fabric, but do not join ends to form loop at this time. This will be done later.

Next, place either top or bottom piece wrong side down on bed of sewing machine. If side pieces have a seam for each turn, start at a corner. Side piece should be wrong side out and a corresponding seam placed at this point.

Start sewing seam. Keep fabric edges lined up and maintain an even 1/2-inch seam allowance all the way along. Stop seam 1/2 inch from edge of fabric at next turn, with sewing machine needle at lowest position through fabric. Raise presser foot. Turn fabric to new sewing direction. Lower presser foot. Sew to next corner and repeat turning procedure. Continue seam until you are back to starting point. Then overlap stitching an inch or so to fix seam.

Place second main piece of fabric wrong side down on bed of sewing machine. Sew opposite edge of side piece to this, starting at a corner, as on first side. This is important for lining up the top and bottom fabric pieces in relation to each other. Sew seam the same as before, except this time leave a section open for turning cover right side out and for inserting foam padding.

After seam has been sewn to this point, turn cover right side, then install foam padding through opening. Close opening by slip or blind stitching in place, as detailed in Chapter 4.

If a long strip of fabric is used for sides rather than one with seams at corners, construction is basically the same. Start seam a couple of inches from one end of the strip so that ends can be joined later. Make seam all the way around to a couple of inches from starting point. Mark stitching lines for joining ends of side piece fabric. Add a 1/2-inch seam allowance on the end of each piece. Cut off excess fabric. Position fabric ends right side to right side, and join them with a plain seam. Go back to seam, joining side piece to main piece of fabric, and finish seam.

When sewing second main piece of fabric to side fabric, it's important to match the positions of the top and bottom pieces. Box and mark exact corners on side piece. Then start seam at one of these corners. The remainder of the construction is the same as above.

If desired, a zipper can be applied along the center of the back side piece using one of the methods detailed in Chapter 7 for zipper installation. One method is to first install zipper between two pieces of fabric. This is cut to same width as remainder of side pieces and is sewn to other side pieces and top and bottom fabric pieces in same manner as regular side pieces. When this is done, seams can be completed all the way around and cover can be turned right side out. Foam padding can be installed through zipper opening.

The strength and appearance of this type of cushion can generally be improved by using piping in the seams around bottom and top pieces of fabric. Construction is basically the same as for construction without piping, except that piping is sewn to right sides of top and bottom fabrics. To make your own piping, piece 1 1/2-inch wide strips of fabric together until you have the necessary length to go around cushion. To make the seams, ends of fabric are overlapped at right angles, right side to right side. Make a diagonal seam from corner to corner. Cut off fabric flaps 1/4 inch from stitching. Straighten fabric out. Place it right side down on bed of sewing machine. Fold seam flaps out flat. They should be in this position when the cord is sewn in place.

Place 1/8-inch diameter nylon or polyester cord in center of fabric strips that are sewn together. Fold the fabric in half over the cord and, using a zipper or piping foot on the sewing machine, sew seam close to cord. Follow same procedure for making second piece of piping the same length as the first one.

Next, mark and cut flaps off 1/2 inch from stitching. Regardless of whether you use piping that you made up or preformed piping, place either the top or bottom piece of fabric wrong side down on the bed of the sewing machine. Position piping and start stitching about 3 inches from end of piping. This section will be used to join the ends of the piping together later.

Make seam using zipper foot close to cording. Keep edges of piping cover fabric lined up with edge of main fabric. Stitching should be an even 1/2 inch from edge of fabric all the way along.

Stop stitching 1/2 inch from first corner. Cut a notch in piping cover fabric. Stop short of the piping stitching, however, so the cut will not show through on the right side of the finished cushion. With sewing machine needle in lowest position through the fabric, raise presser foot and turn fabric to next sewing direction. Lower presser foot and start sewing again. Sew to next corner and repeat turning procedure. Continue until piping is sewn to approximately 3 inches from starting point.

Open piping cover seams about 3 inches on each end from point where stitching stops for joining piping to main fabric. A seam ripper can be used. Cut cording so that it forms and end-to-end butt joint.

Determine the amount of fabric required to join ends of piping covering fabric so that it will be the correct length to form the diagonal seam. Place fabric ends right side to right side, at right angles to each other, and make diagonal seam. Cut off excess fabric 1/4 inch from stitching. With flaps folded back, fold piping covering around cord. Complete stitching by sewing through piping fabric and main fabric, to complete seam all the way around main fabric. Repeat same procedure for sewing piping around edge of other main pieces of fabric. Assemble the pieces of the cover, following directions given above for a cushion cover without piping.

Cushions With Angled Edges

The same general patterning method is used for cushions of rectangular or odd shapes with one or more angled edges, as shown in Fig. 14-15, except that the angled side pieces must be taken into account. The bottom and top pieces of fabric can be patterned to the top and bottom of the foam padding. Be sure when marking pattern. Add a 1/2-inch seam allowance all the way around. Mark which is top and which is bottom fabric, because they will not be the same size.

You will need separate side pieces for each angled or slanted side. Straight or box side pieces can be separate pieces with a seam for each corner, or you can use one continuous strip, or two or more pieces with randomly placed seams.

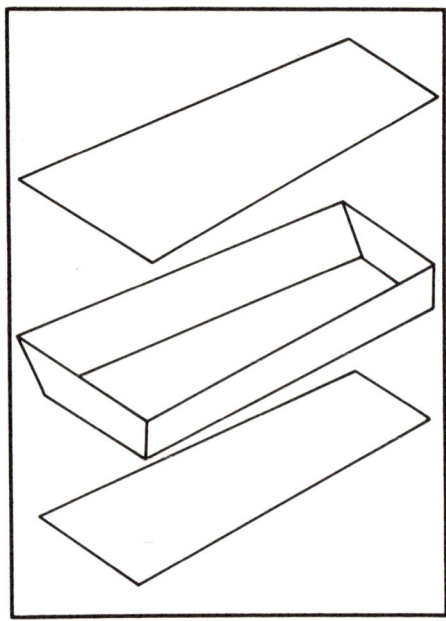

Fig. 14-15. Pattern for cushion cover with an angled side.

The height of the box or straight side pieces should be patterned 1/2 inch less than the thickness of the foam padding. The angled or slanted sections should be patterned as though the foam padding were 1/2 inch less in thickness perpendicular to the top and bottom surfaces of the foam. This will compress the foam padding inside the coverings somewhat and give a good appearance to the finished cushion. Add a 1/2-inch seam allowance to each edge of fabric for side pieces, and to each end of separate pieces. When joining straight side piece to angled piece, cut the straight side piece at the angle, as shown in Fig. 14-15.

Pattern and cut fabric for side pieces. Join pieces of fabric together with plain seams, with the fabric pieces placed right side to right side. A 1/2-inch seam allowance is used.

Next, place either top or bottom piece wrong side down on bed of sewing machine. If side pieces have seam at corner of straight side pieces, start at corner. If not, start at an angled corner. Side pieces should be wrong side out. Make sure that you have the edge of side fabric that corresponds to the main piece of fabric you are sewing it to.

Start sewing seam. Keep fabric edges lined up and maintain an even 1/2-inch seam allowance all the way along. Stop seam 1/2 inch from edge of fabric at next turn, with sewing machine needle at lowest position through fabric. Raise the presser foot. Turn fabric to new sewing direction. Lower presser foot. Sew to next corner and repeat turning procedure. Continue this sewing pattern until you are back to starting point, then overlap stitching an inch or so to fix seam.

Place second main piece of fabric wrong side down on bed of sewing machine. Sew opposite edge of side piece to this, starting at a corner, as on first side. This is important for lining up the top and bottom fabric pieces in relation to each other.

Sew seam the same as before, except this time leave one section open for turning cover right side out and installing foam padding. After seam has been sewn to this point, turn cover right side out through opening. Insert foam padding. Close opening by hand, sewing slip or blind stitching in place.

If desired, a zipper can be installed along the center of the back side piece using method described previously in this chapter or one of the methods detailed in Chapter 7 for zipper installation.

The strength and appearance of this type of cushion can generally be improved by using piping in the seams around bottom and top pieces of fabric. Construction is basically the same as for construction without piping, except that piping is sewn to right sides of top and bottom fabrics.

To make your own piping, piece 1 1/2-inch wide strips of fabric together. To make seams, ends of fabric are overlapped at right angles, right side to right side. Make a diagonal seam from corner to corner. Cut off fabric flaps 1/4 inch from stitching. Straighten fabric out. Place it right side down on bed of sewing machine. Fold seam flaps out flat. They should be in this position when the cord is sewn in place.

Place 1/8-inch diameter nylon or polyester cord in center of fabric strips that are sewn together. Fold the fabric in half over the cord and, using a zipper or piping foot on the sewing machine, sew seam close to cord.

You will need two pieces of piping: one long enough to go around seam line for top main piece of fabric and one long enough to go around bottom piece. Because this type of cushion is not reversible, the piping on the bottom seam is optional.

Mark and cut flaps off piping fabric, 1/2 inch from stitching. Regardless of whether you use piping that you made up or preformed piping, place top piece of fabric wrong side down on end of sewing machine. Position piping and start stitching about 3 inches from end of piping. This section will be used to join the ends of the piping together later.

Make seam, using zipper foot to sew close to cording. Keep edges of piping cover fabric lined up with edge of main fabric. Stitching should be an even 1/2 inch from edge of fabric all the way along.

Stop stitching 1/2 inch from first corner. Cut a notch in piping cover fabric. Stop short of the piping stitching, however, so the cut will not show through on the right side of the finished cushion. With sewing machine needle in lowest position through the fabric, raise presser foot and turn fabric to next sewing direction. Lower presser foot and start sewing again. Sew to next corner and repeat turning procedure. Continue until piping is sewn up to approximately 3 inches from starting point.

Open piping cover seams about 3 inches on each end from point where stitching stops to join piping to main fabric. A seam ripper can be used. Cut cording so that it forms an end-to-end butt joint.

Determine the amount of fabric required to join ends of piping covering fabric so that it will be the correct length for forming a diagonal joining seam. Place fabric ends right side to right side, at right angles to each other, and make diagonal seam. Cut off excess fabric 1/4 inch from stitching. With flaps folded back, fold piping covering around cord. Complete stitching by sewing through piping fabric and main fabric. Complete seam all the way around main fabric. If piping is to also be sewn to bottom fabric, sew this in place as described above for top. Complete construction of cover, following the directions given above for a cover without piping.

Cushions With Old Covers

If you have cushions with old covers already on them, you may want to leave these in place and put new covers over these, as detailed above. If the old covers have piping, however, this will probably show through on the new covers.

If you have old covers that fit properly, they can be used as patterns for new covers. Before removing foam padding from old cover, first check fit and mark any required modifications on the old cover fabric.

Remove cover. Mark assembly of separate pieces of the fabric. Open seams. A seam ripper can be used for this.

Transfer patterns to new fabric, including cutting, stitching, and folding lines. Tracing paper and a tracing wheel can be used for this on many fabrics. Cut fabric.

Sew fabric pieces together, using same seams as were used on old cover. Add zipper or other fasteners. Install foam padding.

Installing Buttons

Buttons can be installed to keep cushion covers from slipping, and to break up monotony. They must be sunk sufficiently deep into the cushion so that they will not be uncomfortable to sit on.

Decide on pattern and arrangement for buttons. If cushions are reversible, buttons are usually placed on both sides of the cushion. If cushions are not reversible, buttons are usually placed on top side only.

You can purchase cushion buttons that are already covered with fabric, or you can cover your own with matching or contrasting fabric.

Buttons On Both Sides. To install, thread a long straight upholstery needle with polyester twine. Pass needle and thread through hole in one button and pull all but about 4 inches of the twine through the button hole. Then pass needle through fabric on one side of cushion in desired location for button, through foam padding, and out through fabric on other side of cushion. Pull all thread through except for the 4 inches extending from the button. Pass needle through hole in second button. Then pass needle back through cushion to starting side. Pull thread up tight. Tie slip knot, as shown in Fig. 14-10. Pull this up until buttons are desired depth in cushion. Then tie off with reef knot to keep knot from loosening.

Buttons On One Side. To install, thread a long straight upholstery needle with polyester twine. Place tuft of fabric on back side of cushion in desired location for button twine. Pass needle and thread through tuft material, cover fabric, foam padding, and out top layer of cover fabric. Pull all thread through except for about 4 inches, which should be left extending from the tuft. Pass needle and thread through hole or eye in button. Then pass needle and thread back through cushion and tuft fabric to starting side. Pull thread up tight. Tie a slip knot. Pull this up until button is desired depth in cushion. Then tie off with reef knot to keep slip knot from loosening.

Snap and Velcro® Fasteners

Snaps are frequently used to hold cushion backs in place, yet allow their easy removal for use as cushions for berths. The stud part of the snaps are attached to the boat or recreational vehicle.

The socket or button parts are attached to a piece of fabric sewn to the back of the cushion, as shown in Fig. 14-16.

A similar arrangement is to use Velcro®. One part of the tape is attached to the boat or recreational vehicle by adhesive, staples, or other means. The other part of the tape is sewn to the back of the cushion fabric, as shown in Fig. 14-17. This method can also be used to hold a variety of other cushions in position.

SEAT COVERS

Framed seats are often used in boats and recreational vehicles. Although construction of these from scratch is generally quite complicated, making new covers for existing seats, using the old covers as patterns, should be possible for many do-it-yourselfers.

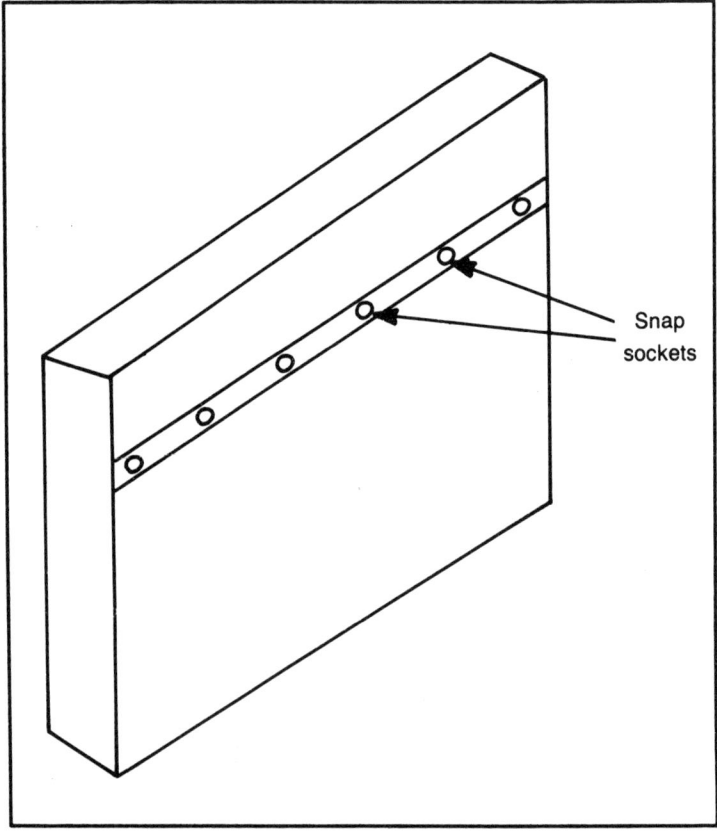

Fig. 14-16. Socket parts of snaps are attached to a piece of fabric sewn to back of cushion.

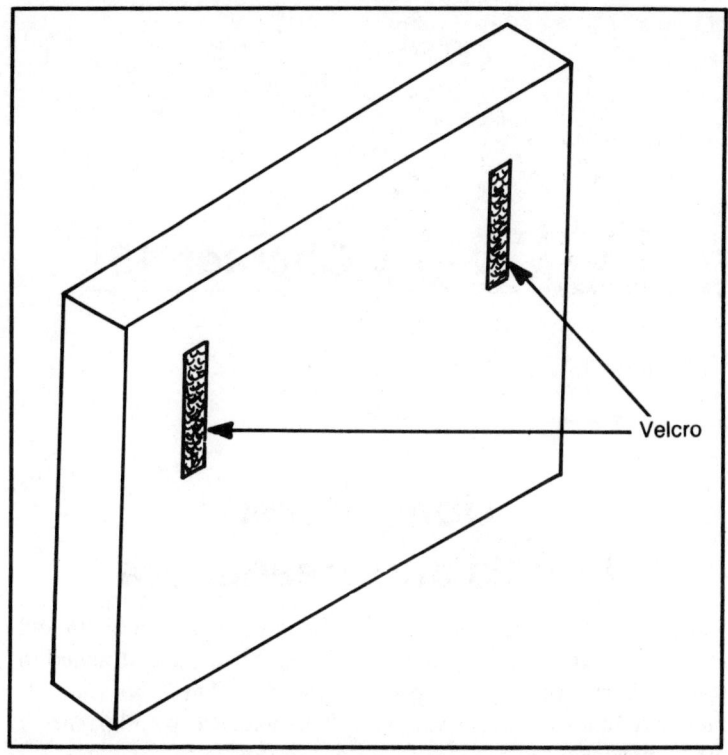

Fig. 14-17. One part of Velcro® tape is sewn to cushion fabric.

Before removing old cover from seat, first check fit and mark any required modifications on old cover fabric. Remove cover from seat. The method for doing this depends on particular seat.

Mark assembly of separate pieces on fabric. Then open seams. A seam ripper can be used for this. Transfer patterns to new fabric, including cutting, stitching, and folding lines. Tracing paper and a tracing wheel can be used for this on many fabrics. Cut fabric.

Sew fabric pieces together using same seams as were used on old cover. Install new cover on seat.

An alternate method is to leave old cover in place on seat and construct a new cover that is placed over the old one.

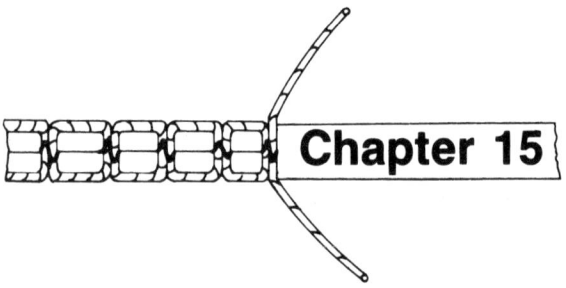

Chapter 15

Upholstered Panels and Headliners

Various upholstered panels and headliners are used in boats and recreational vehicles. The upholstery fabric is usually attached to wood, fiberboard, or other backing material. These are then attached to the boat or recreational vehicle with screws, clips, or by other means.

REPLACING FABRIC ON UPHOLSTERED PANELS AND HEADLINERS

When the fabric fades, wears, or otherwise becomes damaged, or when you feel it's time for a change of color, you might want to replace the fabric portion of existing upholstered panels and/or headliners. This job can range from quite easy to difficult, depending on the way the panels are attached and other factors.

First step is usually to remove old panels or headliners from boat or recreational vehicle. Attachment may be by screws (Fig. 15-1), clips (like those shown in Fig. 15-2), or other means. Be careful when removing fasteners so that you do not damage them. You may have to remove trim strips before upholstered panel can be removed.

The upholstery fabric usually extends around to the backing and is attached by adhesive, clips, staples, or other means. The fabric may also be glued to the front side of the backing material.

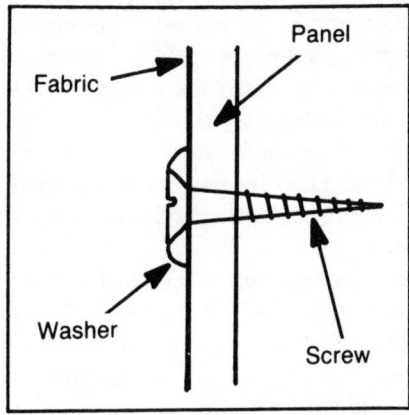

Fig. 15-1. Screw attachment of panel.

In some cases, foam or other padding is placed between the panel and the fabric.

New fabric can be placed over the old fabric, or the old fabric can be removed from the panel backing and replaced with new fabric. A decision should be made on which is the best method.

If the old fabric is to be removed, do this carefully, so that the old fabric can serve as a pattern for the new. If old fabric is attached with staples, remove these carefully. If the old fabric is held by clips, release the fabric by carefully straightening the metal tabs. If fabric is held by adhesive, carefully peel it back.

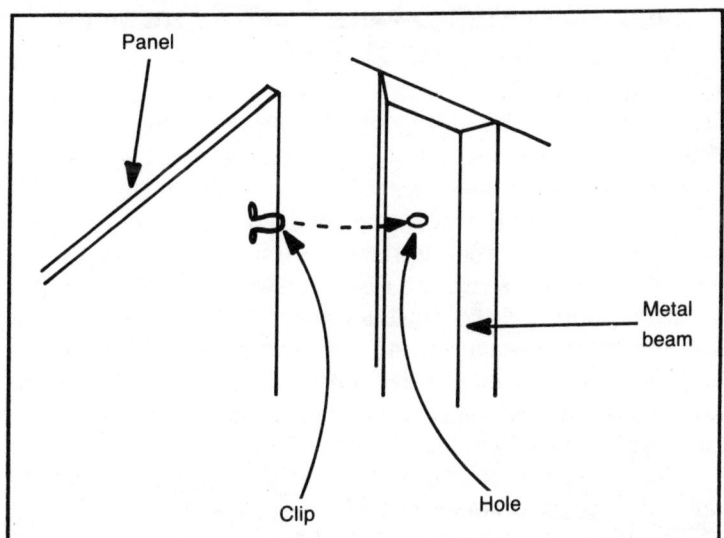

Fig. 15-2. Clip attachment of panel.

Regardless of whether old fabric is left in place or removed, make a pattern for the new fabric. You may want to use the same kind of fabric as was used previously, or change to some other kind. Vinyl upholstery fabric with a cloth backing is frequently used. This wears well and is easy to clean. Vinyl upholstery fabric is also available with a thin foam backing. This type sometimes has small holes through the vinyl to reduce condensation underneath when the vinyl is attached to a panel.

Cut fabric as required. Then position fabric over panel. Smooth fabric out and fold edges around to the back of the panel. Attach fabric to backing, using same method as was used for attaching old fabric. If old fabric was left in place, attachment may have to be further inward than that of old fabric. If clips were used to attach old fabric, there might be room on the clips for the new fabric, too. If not, new fabric can be attached with fabric adhesive or by other means. Fabric should be pulled evenly on all sides so that there will not be wrinkles on the forward side of the panel. The panel is then reinstalled back on boat or recreational vehicle.

Upholstery fabric is sometimes glued directly to fiberglass on interiors of boats and recreational vehicles to form headliners and other upholstered areas. To install new fabric, remove old fabric and use it for a pattern for the new. Cut new fabric as required, then glue in place.

ADDING UPHOLSTERED PANELS AND HEADLINERS

You may want to add upholstered panels and/or a headliner to a boat or recreational vehicle. A backing panel of wood, fiberboard, or other material is usually first fitted. A means must be found for attaching this to the boat or recreational vehicle. Screws can usually be used in wood and metal, but attachment to fiberglass can be more difficult. One method of doing this is to first attach blocks or strips of wood to the fiberglass, using epoxy glue or fiberglass bonding strips and resin. Screws can then be installed in the wood to hold the panel in place.

The backing panel is then covered with fabric. Mark outline of panel on fabric, using panel as pattern. Allow extra fabric for overlapping the backing panel. This usually requires 2 to 3 inches all the way around.

Next, install fabric on panel backing. Various methods are used for attaching the fabric, such as staples, adhesives, and so on.

It may be desirable to glue the fabric to the forward side of the backing panel also. This is especially important for headliners and other areas where the fabric might sag if it isn't fastened in place. Use fabric adhesive, and test it first on a scrap piece of the fabric to make sure that it will not soak through. After backing panel has been covered with fabric, install panel in boat or recreational vehicle.

FRAME-SUSPENDED HEADLINERS IN RECREATIONAL VEHICLES

Vans and other types of recreational vehicles sometimes have headliners suspended by frames, similar to the headliners found in many automobiles. Replacing fabric on these can be difficult and should only be attempted by an experienced do-it-yourselfer.

Remove old headliner from the vehicle. Mark all frames and other parts so that you will be able to get everything back together again. Mark assembly of parts of old fabric headliner. Then open seams. A seam ripper can be used for this.

Use old fabric parts to pattern the new fabric. Tracing paper and a tracing wheel can be used to transfer patterns on many fabrics. Cut fabric.

Sew fabric pieces together, using the same seams as were used on old headliner. Install headliner in recreational vehicle.

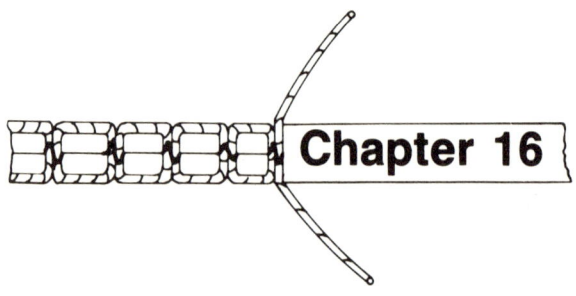

Chapter 16

Curtains

The curtains used on boats and recreational vehicles should be both functional and attractive. Curtains can generally be opened and closed. For privacy, they should completely cover windows and stay in position despite drafts from an open door or hatch or the rocking of a boat. They should be easy to open and close, and finally, they should be attractive in style, color, and design.

Curtains are generally fairly simple sewing projects as compared to most other boat and recreational vehicle canvas and upholstery work. In fact, sewing curtains is more like regular home sewing than most canvas and upholstery work.

CURTAIN SUSPENSION SYSTEMS

Numerous tracks and rods are used to hang and suspend curtains. Various fasteners and hardware are used to attach these to the boats and recreational vehicles, and many methods are used to attach the curtains to the rods.

Many curtain systems in boats and recreational vehicles have suspension systems that are inadequate in one or more ways, and a frequent modification is to improve or change these.

A simple system uses a curtain rod. Casings sewn to the curtain fabric fit over it, as shown in Fig. 16-1. The main problem that I have found with this system is that it is difficult to open and close the curtains. This is especially a problem when there are curtain rods and casings at both top and bottom, as shown in Fig. 16-2.

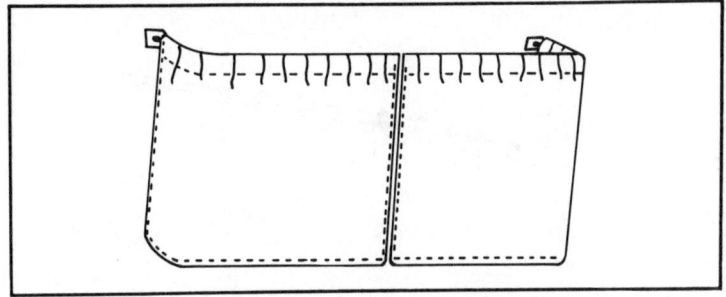

Fig. 16-1. Curtains suspended by casings over curtain rod.

The system is generally improved by using curtain rings, which are attached to the curtains. The rings fit over the rods, as shown in Fig. 16-3.

A generally more satisfactory system is to use a track with slides. The curtain is attached to the slides. Typical tracks and slides are shown in Fig. 16-4. These are available from marine and recreational vehicle suppliers. Stick to tracks, slides, and mounting hardware that won't rust, such as those made from aluminum, brass, stainless steel, and plastics. This is especially important for boats, where rust can quickly become a problem by staining curtain fabrics.

You can use several methods of mounting curtain rods and tracks to boats and recreational vehicles. Brackets and mountings for curtain rods are commonly attached with screws or bolts, but when fastening to fiberglass, this may not be practical. One solution is to first attach wood blocks or strips to the fiberglass. Use epoxy, or bond the wood in place with fiberglass and resin bonding strips. Screw fasteners can then be attached to the wood.

Curtain tracks are frequently mounted by means of screws or bolts attached directly to the mounting surface, or by mounting brackets, which are in turn used to hold the track. Some tracks

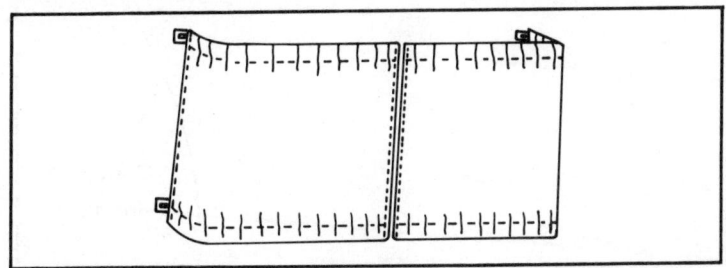

Fig. 16-2. Curtain mounted by casings over rods at both top and bottom.

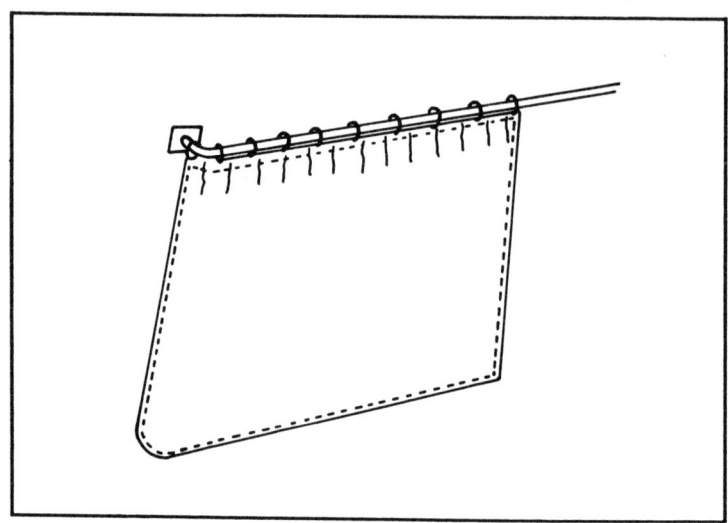

Fig. 16-3. Curtain suspended by rings over curtain rod.

have a pressure sensitive adhesive backing for mounting, but I have not had much luck with this method. Those that I have tried to attach in this manner have not held.

The tracking and rod systems can use either a single system

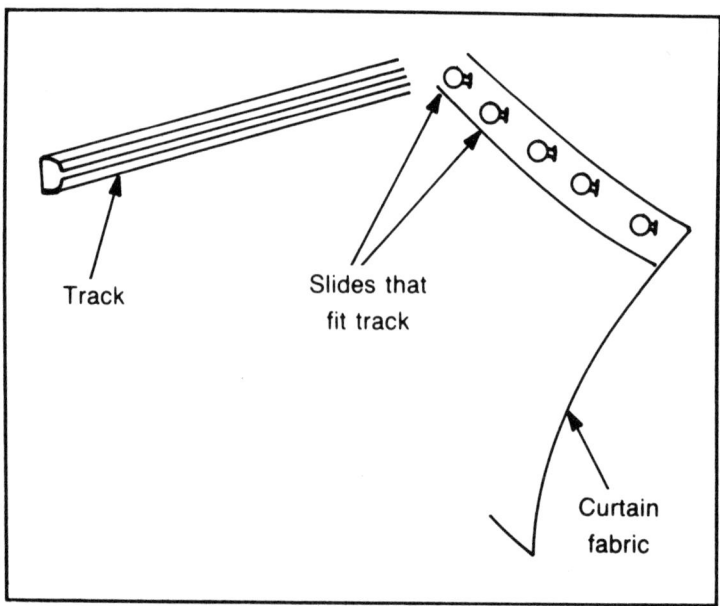

Fig. 16-4. Track and slide mounting system.

at the top of the window, or parallel rods at top and bottom. The dual tracking system is especially important for windshields, angled windows, and in boats, where changing angles can swing single track curtains away from window.

Solidly mounting the curtain hardware to boats and recreational vehicles is extremely important, because much more strain is generally placed on curtain rods and tracks than is commonly imagined. A frequent failure of many is that the fasteners pull out or break.

A variety of slides is used. These slide in a track and allow attachment to curtain fabric. One type has snap stud carriers. A snap socket tape is sewn to the curtain fabric.

Another type of slide has an eye, which is sewn to curtain fabric. These are usually sewn to the fabric by hand, which can be a long job. Some home sewing machines have special features that will allow you to machine sew these.

Still another type of slide has a sew-on tab, as shown in Fig. 16-5. These can be easily machine sewn to the curtain fabric. Simply position the tab on the fabric and sew across it.

Still another suspension system uses Velcro®. A long strip of the hook half is attached to the boat or recreational vehicle by adhesive or other means. Round "coins" of the loop half are sewn to the curtain fabric. This method can be used as a complete suspension system, or in combination with rod and tracking systems to secure edges of curtains.

In general, curtains should overlap windows sufficiently so that open spaces will not be a problem around the curtain when it is closed. This must be taken into account when mounting curtain rods, tracks, and other fasteners.

The rods and tracks should be positioned so that the curtains can be opened and closed easily without catching in the window frame and so on. This sometimes means mounting the track outward to give enough clearance.

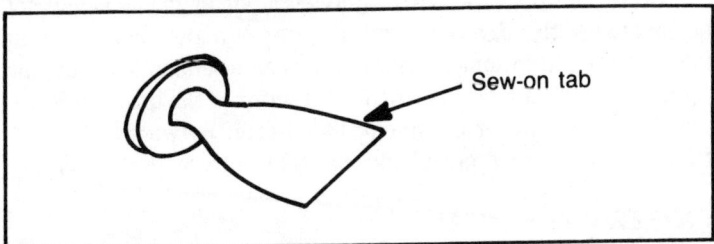

Fig. 16-5. Slide with sew-on tab.

When a dual tracking system is used at the top and bottom of a window, the tracks must parallel each other, even if the top and bottom sills of the window don't parallel each other. In general, the curtain tracks should be horizontal when the boat or recreational vehicle is in a normal, level position.

Still another important consideration is appearance. The tracking and suspension systems should be located so that they present a neat appearance, while at the same time keeping the above practical considerations in mind.

The mounting and suspension system for curtains is extremely important. Without a good setup, the total system will probably be unsatisfactory, regardless of how well the fabric curtains are made up. The mounting and suspension system can be considered the foundation.

If there is an existing system already in the boat or recreational vehicle, a decision should be made on whether or not it is adequate. If not, decide if it can be modified. In some cases, it will be necessary to go to a new system.

CURTAIN FABRICS

Although cotton and other natural fabrics are sometimes used for boat and recreational vehicle curtains, synthetic fabrics such as nylon, polyester, and acrylic are generally more suitable.

Fabrics used should not fade in sunlight. They should also be washable, unless you want to go to the trouble of having them dry cleaned.

Unless you are highly experienced at sewing, select a pattern that does not have to be matched. Also, it helps to use a fabric that is finished on both sides so that a liner will not be necessary.

Colors and patterns can be selected to enhance interior space. In general, light colors tend to enlarge interior space; dark colors tend to make it appear smaller. You will also need to take into consideration the colors used elsewhere in the interior.

Fabrics used can be fairly lightweight, as long as you will not be able to see through them and they do not allow too much light to pass through. In some cases, a lining can be added. Usually, the right side of main fabric faces to the interior of the boat or recreational vehicle. The wrong side or lining faces outward and shows from outside the boat or recreational vehicle through the window.

PATTERNING CURTAINS

Curtains are patterned to fit the suspension or supporting

devices rather than the window opening. A first measurement to take is finished length. Measure from where top edge of finished curtain will be down to bottom edge.

To the desired length, add necessary allowances for hems, casings, and headings at top and bottom of curtain. Sketch these out on paper and mark dimensions. Do not trust them to memory.

Figure 16-6 shows a pattern for a casing to fit over a curtain rod. Size of opening will depend on size of curtain rod used, but should be large enough to allow the curtain to slide on the rod. Figure 16-7 shows a typical method for installing heading.

The width of the hem at bottom can vary. About 2 inches is typical for boat and recreational vehicle curtains, although hems as narrow as 1/2 inch will usually suffice.

Next, determine finished width for each section of curtain, including any overlap where curtain sections meet at center. The finished width is the straight line distance. To give adequate fullness for an attractive curtain, the fabric for a casing hung curtain should be one and a half times the finished width; track and ring suspended curtains should be twice the finished width; and pleated curtains are usually calculated at three times the finished width. Add to this a hemming allowance on each side of each section of curtain. Take measurements and make sketches on paper of curtains with dimensions.

Next, determine the amount of fabric required for all curtains to be made. If fabric designs are to be matched, take this into consideration, because you will probably need extra fabric for this. If

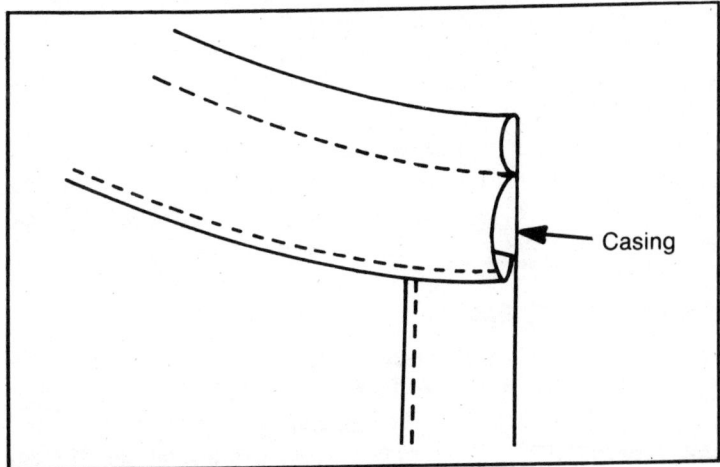

Fig. 16-6. Pattern for casing.

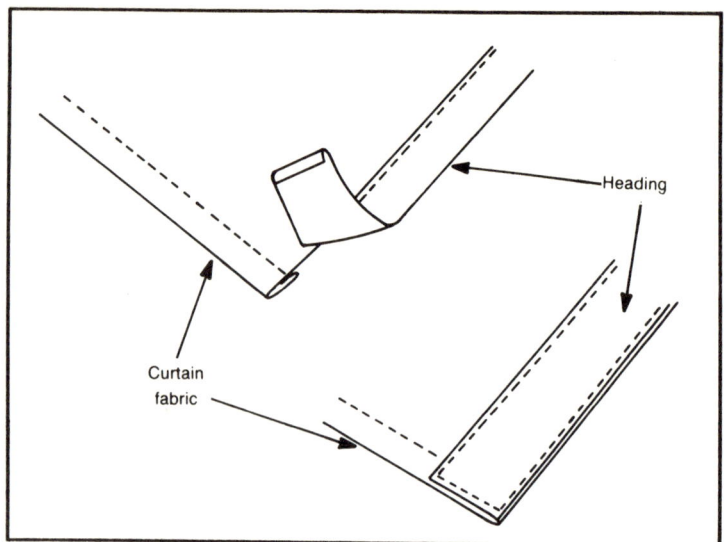

Fig. 16-7. Method for installing heading.

lining is to be used, you will need approximately the same amount of lining fabric as curtain fabric.

If heading stiffeners are to be used, you will need a length equal to the finished width of each curtain section. Double this length if stiffeners are also to be added at the bottom for dual track suspension. Heading fabric is available with guide markings for pleating.

When laying out patterns on curtain fabric, it's important to follow the grain of the fabric. One method for determining this is to cut and pull a thread out of the fabric.

Lay fabric out on table or other flat surface and smooth out wrinkles. It may be necessary to use an iron on some fabrics. Then mark patterns on fabric.

It's also helpful to press in with a steam iron all folds for hems, seams, and casings. This will make stitching much easier. If linings are to be used, also pattern fabric for these. Next, cut fabric as required.

SEWING CURTAINS

If a lining is used, the usual method is to first hem lining fabric, then sew this to curtain fabric, wrong side to wrong side.

The order of remaining sewing steps for curtains without linings is to sew side hems first, heading or casing next, and bottom hem last.

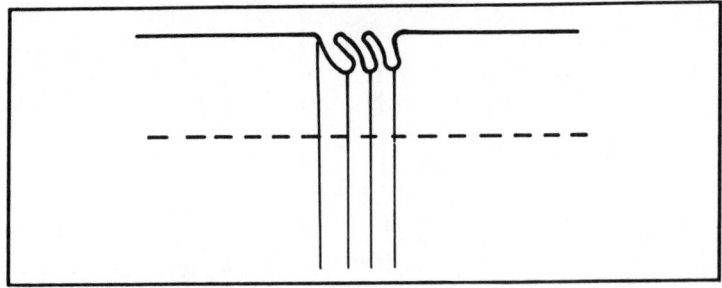

Fig. 16-8. Pinch pleats.

Figure 16-7 shows a typical straight-stitched side hem. When sewing, take care to keep grainlines of hem and curtain aligned.

A method for sewing a heading to an unpleated curtain is shown in Fig. 16-7. If pleats are used, these should be sewn in the curtain fabric. These can be *pinch* (Fig. 16-8), *box* (Fig. 16-9), or other. Markings on heading can be used to evenly space these throughout width of curtain. On curtains with casings, sew casing seams.

The bottom hem is then sewn is place. This can be a single hem with 1/2 inch edge turned under or double with turn-under equal to hem depth.

Slides, rings, and other fasteners are then attached to curtain. This completes the basic sewing. Curtains can now be installed on rods or tracks.

There are also many other patterns and methods for making curtains. If you are using old curtains for patterns, the same seaming and hemming techniques can be used on the new curtain.

CURTAIN TIE-BACKS

Tie-backs (Fig. 16-10) are useful for holding curtains back out

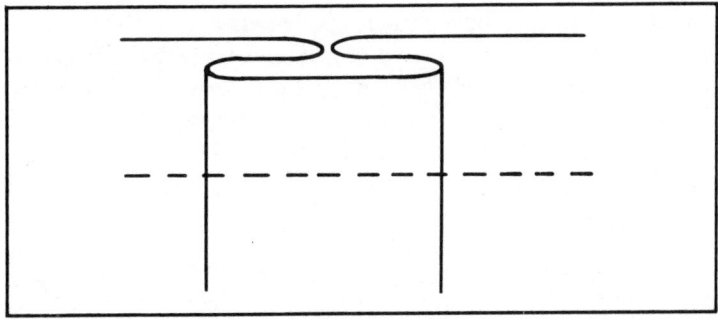

Fig. 16-9. Box pleat.

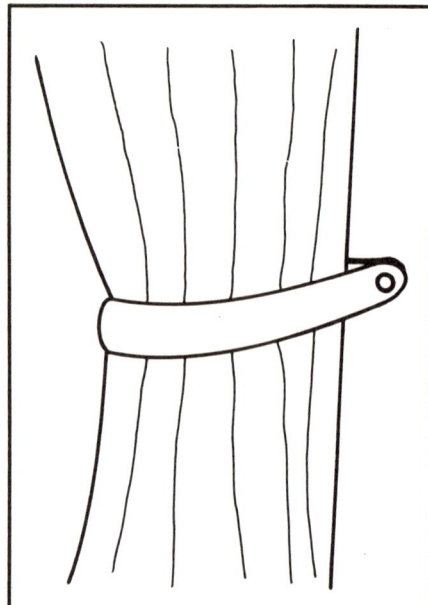

Fig. 16-10. Curtain tie-back.

of the way. These can be made out of same fabric as the curtains. Cut a strip of fabric 2 inches wide and 1 inch longer than the desired finished tie-back. Fold in half, wrong side to wrong side, and sew seams along edge. Use a dowel to force fabric through itself to turn right side out. Then hem ends closed. A snap stud is usually fastened through one end of tie-back to boat or recreational vehicle. Snap socket is installed in fabric at other end of tie-back.

PARTITION CURTAINS

Partition or privacy curtains are sometimes used to separate one section of a boat or recreational vehicle from another. These are often suspended by curtain rings that slide over a rod or bar. It also helps to have weighted bottom hems. Individual and chain-type weights are available from drapery suppliers for this purpose. The remainder of the construction is generally similar to that of regular curtains, except that heavier fabric is commonly used for the partition curtains.

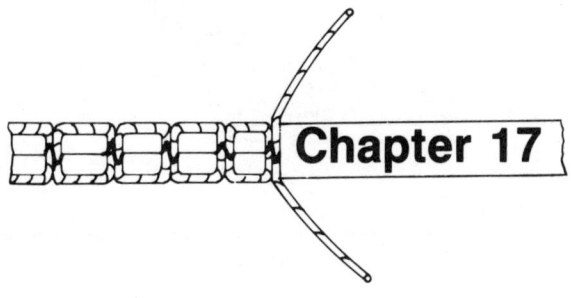

Chapter 17

Carpets

Carpeting, especially indoor-outdoor, is frequently used for covering floors and sometimes for upholstering walls and ceilings on boats and recreational vehicles. Because there are different installation techniques for boats and recreational vehicles, these are treated separately below.

RECREATIONAL VEHICLE CARPETING

Vans, campers, and trailer houses frequently have wood floors or subfloors. Carpet can be glued, tacked, attached to tack strips (the same type is used for home carpets) that are nailed to the edges of the wood floor, or held in place with double-backed carpet tape. Metal trim strips can be used to protect edges at doorways and other vulnerable areas.

If carpeting is permanently attached to wood floors, however, water must not be allowed to get underneath the carpet or else dry rot is likely to result.

Sometimes a carpet pad or foam padding is placed under the carpet to give a softer surface. This method is often used when customizing vans.

Another possibility is removable carpeting. The carpet is cut to shape and laid in place. Slipping will not usually be much of a problem as long as the carpet has a rubber backing. The edge of the carpet can be trimmed with a vinyl hem, as shown in Fig. 17-1. A heavy-duty sewing machine, however, is required to sew this in

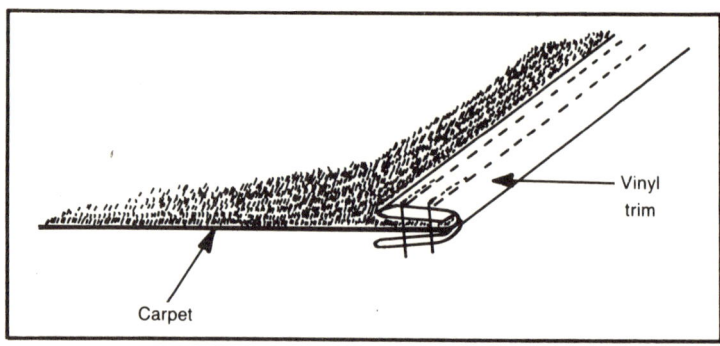

Fig. 17-1. Vinyl hem sewn to edge of carpet.

place to most carpet fabrics. A variety of carpeting can be used for recreational vehicles, including shag and plush types.

Mark cutting pattern on carpet. Then cut carpet with a sharp knife or razor blade.

Carpeting is sometimes also used as upholstery fabric for walls and ceilings. A main problem is attachment. Although adhesives will sometimes suffice for holding carpeting to wall panels, this is usually inadequate for ceilings. Screws, trim strips, and other types of mechanical fastening are often used. Whenever possible, the raw edges should fit against something or go under something.

When carpeting is replaced in a trailer house or motor home, you will probably want to install it in same manner as the original. The old carpeting can be removed and used as a pattern for the new carpet.

A word of warning about the use of carpeting in bathrooms, kitchen areas, and other locations where water is likely to get on the carpet. This water is likely to get underneath the carpet and cause dry rot in wood and rusting in metal. Over molded fiberglass, it should be okay, but is best avoided over wood and metal surfaces.

BOAT CARPETING

Opinions vary on the use of carpeting in boats. For one boat owner, the installation of carpeting is a pride and joy; then the next owner of the boat rips out all that stinky carpeting. And so on.

I personally don't think permanently attached carpeting has much place in boats. If it's glued or tacked down to wood, dry rot underneath is almost a sure thing. If glued down to molded fiberglass, dry rot won't be a problem in the fiberglass, but the carpeting may rot, and it certainly can stink. But, you say, I won't let the carpet get wet. Well, maybe, but then you are talking about some type of boat use with which I'm not familiar. Condensation alone will usually take its toll.

If you want to permanently install floor carpeting, use a quality grade indoor-outdoor carpet. Mark pattern and cut the carpet with knife, razor blade, or shears. Check fit, then attach to floor with adhesive or by other means. Whenever possible, raw edges should fit against something or go under something. In some cases, aluminum, stainless steel, wood, or plastic trim strips can be used to hold down carpet edges.

A removable carpet is generally a better idea. The carpet can be removed from time to time, to shake it out and dry and allow the sole or floor area to dry out.

If the carpet has a rubber backing, slipping should not be much of a problem. The edge of the carpet can be trimmed with a vinyl tape, as shown in Fig. 17-1. A heavy duty sewing machine is required for sewing this to most carpet fabrics, however.

Measure area to be covered with carpeting and purchase carpeting. Measure and mark pattern on carpet. Cut slits and holes to go over table legs, as shown in Fig. 17-2. Use a sharp knife, ra-

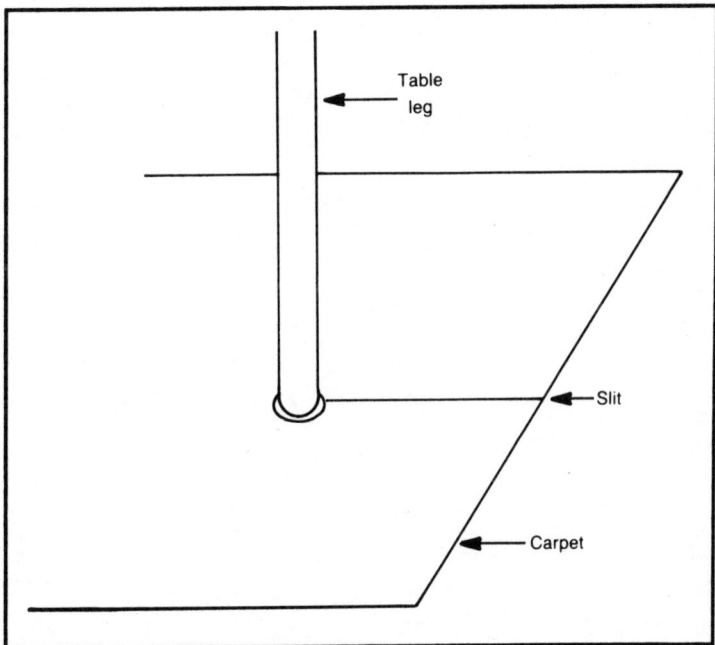

Fig. 17-2. Slit and hole cut in carpet for fitting over table leg.

zor blade, or shears to cut the carpet to shape. If vinyl trim is to be added, sew this around the edges of the carpet material.

Carpeting can also be used as upholstery on sides and tops on boat interiors. This can be glued to fiberglass surfaces. It will provide some insulation and help to cut down condensation, but it generally isn't recommended for use over wood, because dry rot is likely to result in the wood underneath.

Measure areas to be covered, then purchase necessary carpet material. Measure and mark pattern on carpet. Use a sharp knife, razor blade, or shears to cut the carpet.

Carpeting is commonly attached to fiberglass with adhesive. This can be satisfactory for side panels, but whenever possible, supplement this by mechanical fasteners and trim strips placed over edges of carpet material.

For headliners and other overhead areas, attachment can be much more difficult. Adhesive alone is usually inadequate. Some type of mechanical fastening is usually used to supplement the glue. Finally, I should point out that I have seen many attempts at using carpeting for headliners, and I don't know of any that were very successful.

Suppliers

Astrup Company
2937 W. 25th Street
Cleveland, OH 44113

Complete boat top frames, clear vinyl window material, convertible top fabric, hardware.

Cook Marine Products
P.O. Box 1133
Stamford, CT 06904

Reads Sail Maker sewing machine.

Cut & Stitch Sailkits
Rt. 1, Box 525
Summer, WA 98390

Sail kits

Defender Industries, Inc.
255 Main Street
New Rochelle, NY 10801

Complete line of canvas fabrics, fasteners, top fittings, sewing awls and palms, flexible window plastic, marine supplies and equipment at discount prices. 168-page catalog: $1

Du Pont Company
Textile Fibers Department
Centre Road Building
Wilmington, DE 19898

Dacron synthetic polyester fabric.

Flexible Foam Products
P.O. Box 5527
Great S.W. Station
Arlington, TX 76011

Foam padding for cushions.

Howe and Bainbridge, Inc.
220 Commercial Street
Boston, MA 02109

Upholstery fabrics.

Recmar Marine Corp.
17875 Skypark North
Suite B
Irvine, CA 92714

Curtain track systems.

Sailrite Enterprises
Route 1
Columbia City, IN 46725

Sailrite Sailmaker sewing machine; kits for sails, sail covers, awnings, dodgers, and boat covers; canvas fabrics and supplies.

Segil Carpet Mills, Inc.
P.O. Box 3034
Dalton, GA 30721

Complete line of marine carpeting.

TRW Dot Division
P.O. Box 710
Waterbury, CT 06720

Pull-the-Dot (snap), Lift-the-Dot, and Common Sense fasteners.

United Textile and Supply
795-61 North Spring Street
Los Angeles, CA 90012

Upholstery fabric.

Velcro® USA, Inc.
521 Fifth Avenue
New York, NY 10175

Velcro® fasteners.

Weblon Inc.
Yellowstone Avenue
White Plains, NY 10607

Weblon fabric.

Index

A
acrylic, 15
adhesives and fasteners, 120
adhesives and sealers, 21
attachments
  tie down and snap, 267
awl
  sewing, 32
  using a sewing, 54
awnings
  enclosures, and weather cloths, 211

B
bags and carrying cases, 147
bags with drawstring closures, 157
bags with handles, 147
  zipper closed, 162
basting, 38
beeswax, 17
Bimini tops, 254
boat carpeting, 318
boat covers
  canvas, 206
bobbin, 81
bobbin thread breaks, 88
bobbin winding, 69
buttons, 275

C
canvas curtains
  suspension systems for, 308
canvas, 2
  appearance of, 4
  boat covers, 206
  cleaning, 4
  durability of, 3
  maintaining, 4
  natural fiber cotton, 13
  repair, replacement, and modification of, 5
  synthetic, 14
canvas cover
  drop, 182
  fitted, 183
canvas covers, 168
  binnacle and wheel, 181
  boat, 175
  boom sail, 192
  box hatch, 187
  companionway hatch, 190
  drop, 191
  hatch, 187
  outboard motor, 185
  pickup bed, 173
  tiller, 178
  winch, 175
canvas curtain tie-backs, 315
canvas curtains
  partition, 316
  patterning, 312
  sewing, 314
  side and stern, 261
  stern and side, 221

canvas fasteners, 20
canvas frame support systems, 138
canvas pattern, 107
canvas projects
   design and construction of, 6
canvas top attached to fixed windshield, 233
canvas tops, 221
   extension, 257
canvas tops, Bimini, 254
canvas work
   classes in, 9
   do-it-yourself, 10
   how to learn, 9
   scope of, 5
carpeting, 21
   boat, 318
carpets, 317
cement
   fabric, 21
cloth, 12
cording, 98
core material, 15
cotton, 13
cover hooks, 138
covers
   recreational vehicle, 169
   seat, 302
   spare tire, 169
   top luggage rack, 172
cushions, 280
   angled-edged, 297
   box, 292
   buttons on, 301
   independent, 285
   odd-shaped, 294
   rectangular, 291
cushions and seat covers, 271
cutting and patterns, 106

D

D-rings, 136
Dacron, 14
darn
   sailmaker's, 46
darning, 44
dodgers, 245
draw strings and ropes, 137
drop feed, 61

E

elastic and cord, 137
equipment
   tools, and work areas, 23
equipment and tools, 8

F

fabric, 144
   cords and ropes sewn to, 135
   replacing, 224, 304
   sewability of, 103
fabric covers, 280, 285
fabric mosquito screens, 264
fabrics, 12, 16, 143, 273
   curtain, 312
   hand sewing heavy, 47
fabrics and hardware curtain, 21
fasteners
   common sense, 131
   hook and eye, 133
   Lift-the-Dot, 129
   snap, 127
   take-apart and opening, 122
fasteners and adhesives, 120
fastenings
   mechanical, 122
   permanent, 120
fasteners
   canvas, 20
feed
   drop, 26, 61
   walking foot, 27, 62
feed dog, 61
feed dogs and presser foots, 82
flat seam, 39, 47
flat seaming stitch
   diagonal, 39
foam
   closed cell, 18
   gluing, 279
   latex, 18
   patterning and cutting, 276
   polyester, 18
foam adhesives, 18
foam padding, 275, 285
frames and fittings
   top, 21

G

gluing foam, 279
grommets, 134

H

hand sewing, 36
   basic, 37
hems and tablings, 95
herringbone stitch, 51
hot knife, 33

K

kits, 119
   canvas project, 6

upholstery project, 6

L
laminated convertible top material, 15
lock stitch, 24
looper, 58

M
machine
  threading the, 68
materials, 143, 144, 265, 273
  cost of, 4
materials and supplies, 12
  where to purchase, 21

N
Naugahyde, 16
needle breaks, 88
needle thread breaks, 87
needles
  bayonet, 31
  hand sewing, 31
  machine, 66
  sewing machine, 30
  slipping, 31
  triangular shank, 31
nylon, 14
nylon monofilament, 17
nylon mosquito netting, 18

P
padding
  foam, 275, 285
palm
  sailmaker's, 31
  seaming, 31
panels
  upholstered, 304
paper
  tracing, 20
patch
  adding a, 53
pattern
  measurements for a, 111
  using a, 109
pattern markings
  making and transferring, 106
patterning, 114
patterning and cutting work
  organizing, 118
patterns
  cutting, 117
  fitting, 119
  laying out, 116
patterns and cutting, 106
piping, 19, 98, 274

polyester, 14, 17
polyester foam, 18
pullers
  top-driven, 27

R
recreational vehicle carpeting, 317

S
sail covers, 192
  jib bag, 201
  jib boom, 201
  mainsail and mizzen, 194
sailmaker's palm, 31
scissors, 32
sealers and adhesives, 21
seam
  flat, 39, 47
  flat-felled, 43, 97
  plain, 93
  round, 42, 49
seam ripper, 33
seaming palm, 31
seams
  basic, 102
  sewing basic, 93
seat covers, 302
seat covers and cushions, 271
sewing, 74
  basic hand, 37
  hand, 36
  preparation for, 65
  twine and wax for, 16
sewing awl, 32
  using a, 54
sewing canvas curtains, 314
sewing machine, 57
  cleaning and oiling a, 85
  timing a, 86
  troubleshooting a, 86
sewing machine adjustments, 79
sewing machine drop feed, 26
sewing machine needles, 30
sewing machine troubleshooting, 79
sewing machines, 24
  simple repairs of, 79
staples and tacks, 121
stitch
  blind, 46
  herringbone, 51
  lock, 24
  round, 42
  slip, 46, 52
  straight, 25
  zigzag, 25
stitch machine

chain-, 57
lock-, 58
stitches
  basic hand sewing, 37
  loose, 90
  skipped, 89
  uneven, 89
supplies and materials, 12
  where to purchase, 21

T

tablings and hems, 95
tacks and staples, 121
tape
  binding, 19
thread, 274
thread tensions
  upper and lower, 80
threading
  lower or bobbin, 72
  upper, 70
tools, 85
  equipment, and work areas, 23
  making, 34
  measuring, 33
tools and equipment, 8
top frames and fittings, 227
tube benders, 34
twine, 16

U

upholstered panels and headliners, 304
upholstery
  appearance of, 4
  cleaning, 4
  do-it-yourself, 1, 6, 8
  durability of, 3
  functional aspects of, 2
  repair, replacement, and modification of, 5
upholstery fabrics, 16
upholstery pattern, 107
upholstery projects
  design and construction of, 6
upholstery work
  classes in, 9
  do-it-yourself, 10
  how to learn, 9
  scope of, 5

V

Velcro®, 19, 126, 275, 301
Velcro® attachments, 266
vinyl
  transparent flexible, 17
vinyl and other coatings, 15

W

wax for hand sewing, 16
weather cloths
  awnings, and enclosures, 211
webbing, 135
work areas, 35
  tools, and equipment, 23

Z

zippers, 19, 123, 274

Other Bestsellers From TAB

☐ **ROOFING THE RIGHT WAY—A STEP-BY-STEP GUIDE FOR THE HOMEOWNER—Bolt**

If you're faced with having to replace your roof because of hidden leaks, torn or missing shingles, or simply worn roofing that makes your whole house look shabby and run down . . . don't assume that you'll have to take out another mortgage to pay for the project. The fact is, *almost anyone can install a new or replacement roof easily and at amazingly low cost compared with professional contractor prices*! All the professional techniques and step-by-step guidance you'll need is here in this complete new roofing manual written by an experienced roofing contractor. 192 pp., 217 illus. 7" × 10".

**Paper $11.95   Hard $19.95
Book No. 2667**

☐ **66 FAMILY HANDYMAN® WOOD PROJECTS**

Here are 66 practical, imaginative, and decorative projects . . . literally something for every home and every woodworking skill level from novice to advanced cabinetmaker: room dividers, a free-standing corner bench, china/book cabinet, coffee table, desk and storage units, a built-in sewing center, even your own Shaker furniture reproductions! 210 pp., 306 illus. 7" × 10".

**Paper $14.95   Hard $21.95
Book No. 2632**

☐ **TILE FLOORS— INSTALLING, MAINTAINING AND REPAIRING—Ramsey**

Now you can easily install resilient or traditional hard tiles on both walls and floors. Find out how to buy quality resilient floor products at reasonable cost . . . and discover the types and sizes of hard tiles available. Get step-by-step instructions for laying out the floor, selecting needed tools and adhesives, cutting tiles, applying adhesives, and more. 192 pp., 200 illus. 4 pages in full color. 7" × 10".

Paper $12.95   Book No. 1998

☐ **111 YARD AND GARDEN PROJECTS—FROM BOXES AND BINS TO TABLES AND TOOLS— Blandford**

Expert woodworker and metalcrafter Percy Blandford gives you step-by-step building guidance that's based on years of experience as a teacher and author of bestselling project guides. Plus, he provides a wealth of basic know-how on how to choose and work with wood and metal. He gives invaluable tips on constructing tool handles. And he shows how to custom design exactly the outdoor tools, accessories, and gardening aids that are right for your own particular needs!

**Paper $16.95   Hard $25.95
Book No. 2644**

☐ **UPHOLSTERY TECHNIQUES ILLUSTRATED—Gheen**

Here's an easy-to-follow, step-by-step guide to modern upholstery techniques that covers everything from stripping off old covers and padding to restoring and installing new foundations, stuffing, cushions, and covers. All the most up-to-date pro techniques are included along with lots of time- and money-saving "tricks-of-the-trade" not usually shared by professional upholsterers. 352 pp., 549 illus. 7" × 10".

**Paper $16.95   Hard $27.95
Book No. 2602**

☐ **CABINETS AND VANITIES—A BUILDER'S HANDBOOK—Godley**

Here in easy-to-follow, step-by-step detail is everything you need to know to design, build, and install your own customized kitchen cabinets and bathroom vanities and cabinets for a fraction of the price charged by professional cabinetmakers or kitchen remodelers . . . and for less than a third of what you'd spend for the most cheaply made ready-made cabinets and vanities! 142 pp., 126 illus. 7" × 10".

**Paper $12.95   Hard $19.95
Book No. 1982**

Other Bestsellers From TAB

☐ **HARDWOOD FLOORS—INSTALLING, MAINTAINING AND REPAIRING—Ramsey**

Do-it-yourself expert Dan Ramsey gives you all the guidance you need to install, restore, maintain, or repair all types of hardwood flooring at costs far below those charged by professional builders and maintenance services. From details on how to select the type of wood floors best suited to your home, to time- and money-saving ways to keep your floors in tip-top condition . . . nothing has been left out. 160 pp., 230 illus. 4 pages in full color. 7" × 10".
**Paper $10.95   Hard $18.95
Book No. 1928**

☐ **PRACTICAL LANDSCAPING AND LAWN CARE—Webb**

Make your lawn the envy of the entire neighborhood . . . *without* spending a fortune or putting in never-ending hours of maintenance time! Here's absolutely everything you need to successfully plan, plant, and maintain lawn grasses and groundcovers, vines, and flowering ornamentals . . . annual, biennial, and perennial flowers . . . shade trees, lawn trees . . . even decorative (and delicious) fruits and berries. It doesn't matter whether your climate is cold and damp or hot and dry . . . whether your soil is sandy, rocky, or gummy clay, *everything* you need is here! 240 pp., 84 illus. 7" × 10".
**Paper $13.95   Hard $21.95
Book No. 1818**

☐ **DO-IT-YOURSELF DESIGNER WINDOWS**

If the cost of custom-made draperies puts you in a state of shock . . . if you've had trouble finding window coverings of any kind for cathedral or other problem windows . . . or if you're unsure of what type of window decor would look right in your home . . . here's all the advice and information you've been searching for. It's a complete, hands-on guide to selecting, measuring, making, and installing just about any type of window treatment imaginable. You'll even get an expert's insight into selection and installation of decorative storm windows and thermal windows, stained glass windows, woven or wooden blinds. 272 pp., 414 illus. 7" × 10".
**Paper $14.95   Hard $21.95
Book No. 1922**

☐ **TROUBLE-FREE SWIMMING POOLS**

Here is the ideal sourcebook for anyone thinking of installing a swimming pool—in ground or above ground from wading pool size to large indoor public pool. It shows how to plan, excavate, construct, and safely maintain all types and sizes of pools. You'll find out how to have your own pool for as little as $1,000 . . . or how to get more pool for the money no matter how much you're able to spend! 176 pp., 306 illus. 7" × 10".
**Paper $11.95   Hard $18.95
Book No. 1808**

*Prices subject to change without notice.

Look for these and other TAB books at your local bookstore.

TAB BOOKS Inc.
P.O. Box 40
Blue Ridge Summit, PA 17214

Send for FREE TAB catalog describing over 1200 current titles in print.